HANDBOOK OF SELLING

Second Edition

HANDBOOK OF SELLING

Psychological, Managerial, and Marketing Dynamics

Second Edition

GARY M. GRIKSCHEIT
David Eccles School of Business
University of Utah

HAROLD C. CASH
Personnel Development Associates

CLIFFORD E. YOUNG
Graduate School of Business Administration
University of Colorado at Denver

JOHN WILEY & SONS, INC.
New York • Chichester • Brisbane • Toronto • Singapore

Library of Congress Cataloging-in-Publication Data

Grikscheit, Gary M.
    Handbook of selling : psychological, managerial, and marketing dynamics / Gary M. Grikscheit, Harold C. Cash, Clifford E. Young.
      p. cm. — (Wiley series on marketing management, ISSN 0275-875X)
    Includes bibliographical references and index.
    ISBN 0-471-60085-7 (cloth)
    1. Selling. I. Cash, Harold C. II. Young, Clifford E.
    III. Title. IV. Series.
HF5438.25.G74 1993
658.8'5—dc20   92-32439

Printed in the United States of America

10 9 8 7 6 5 4 3 2 1

To Penny with love

Contents

° The numbers in parentheses beneath the titles of the appendixes refer to pages in the text.

Preface

No one in business should need to be reminded of the importance of personal selling. The very survival and viability of enterprise depends on it. Whether you are selling products, services, ideas, or yourself, effective personal selling is necessary. Despite its patent importance, however, the practice of professional selling is one of the "dark corners" in marketing. More often than not, successful practitioners are "unconscious competents" who have acquired their knowledge and skills through trial and error. Books and articles about selling either attempt to capture the experiences of the star salesperson or contain exhortations that, allegedly, will aid your rise from mediocrity to greatness. We claim no such "seven secrets of sales success," nor do we think they exist. In contrast, this book will provide you with a comprehensive treatment of the significant knowledge about selling and will fully acquaint you with the basic objectives, concepts, and tools that you need to be an effective salesperson. In addition, we have operationalized each of the major ideas in an appendix, which is cross-referenced with the text for easy use. The graduates of our programs for business, professional, and academic audiences routinely become the sales leaders in their areas.

The title of this book—*Handbook of Selling: Psychological, Managerial, and Marketing Dynamics*—provides an overview of the major topics. Psychology is concerned with human behavior and how it may be influenced. This volume develops the basic principles of psychology required in selling, providing the foundation for understanding both the communication and managerial dimensions of selling. To be an effective salesperson, you must be a proficient manager as well as an adept communicator. No matter how convincing you are as a communicator, you cannot achieve full success unless you are also astute in concentrating on the prospects and customers with the greatest potential. In practice, you must be an effective strategist and tactician. The unique power of modern selling rests on your strategic ability to plan personalized presentations based on the known as well as on your tactical competence in adjusting to the unknown. This book fully develops both the strategic and tactical dimensions of selling. Finally, in most organizations, selling is practiced within the marketing concept. To enhance your productivity, you must understand how computer data bases and programs, advertising, telemarketing, and other marketing tools are related to creating and retaining satisfied customers.

You can master the fundamentals of selling through careful study and application of the contents of this book. The subject matter is broken down into separate knowledge and skill sets, which you can acquire individually and merge at the point of sale. This is analogous to teaching golf by separating the techniques of driving, putting, and so on, as opposed to playing 18 holes as though each stroke were the same.

To facilitate your mastery of selling, we have taken great care to use examples from many fields. Principles and methods are illustrated and are applicable to all types of sales situations. Major topics are liberally cross-referenced throughout the book. In addition, we have made a genuine attempt to write the book in a compact style.

To stimulate inquiry and mastery, topics for thought and discussion follow each chapter, and the appendixes provide the tools for applying the principles to actual selling situations. The Bibliography, organized by chapters, enables you to do additional reading and exploration of the basic ideas.

Many books on selling are written by academicians with no practical experience or by businesspeople who have had little academic training. We have both academic and business experience and have engaged in sales training with a large number and variety of companies. This book, which we wrote after acquiring substantial experience, is based on the following assumptions:

1. Selling is both an art and a science. Much of what you do as an effective salesperson is intuitive and stems from your unique personality. On the other hand, an accumulating body of knowledge about selling is adding to the mass of proven principles and techniques.
2. Both the content and methods of psychology can be applied to the science of selling. Psychological methods are scientific and provide for the collection and analysis of information about human beings.
3. Sales training encompasses both "people" and "thing" knowledge. Too frequently, training is restricted to the latter—the products or services available for sale. Psychology can contribute markedly to knowledge about people and ultimately to a deeper understanding of the selling-buying process.
4. The most fruitful way to view selling is to see it as a process that you cause in buyers. To be effective, you must master both the managerial and communication dimensions of selling.
5. The crux of sales training is your education and individual development. Besides knowing how to sell, you must comprehend the underlying proven principles and techniques. This gives you greater insight into the selling-buying process and more self-confidence in utilizing what you know. Thus, education should replace the inspiration and exhortation often used in sales training.

You may be interested to know how this volume came to be written. In part, it is a thorough revision of the *Handbook of Selling: Psychological, Managerial, and Marketing Bases*, but it is also based on nearly a decade of research, consulting, and laboratory experience since the earlier book. The ideas presented here have been refined, extended, and updated, reflecting our primary motive to provide a comprehensive treatment of all aspects of selling in one volume. The biggest single change is the integration of computers in selling.

If you critically evaluate the materials currently available on selling and wish to go beyond these in the practice of your profession, you will want to master and apply the insights in this book. They will provide you with a basic understanding of the objectives, concepts, and tools required to sell professionally.

No project of this magnitude is solely the work of the authors. A number of people have been instrumental in bringing this book out: Barbara Campbell, Sonja Dodenbier, Penny Grikscheit, Neal Maillet, Dee Metcalf, Jennifer Sadler, and Debbie Scammon. Numerous colleagues, clients, and students offered advice, examples, ideas, and helpful reviews of parts of the manuscript. The support of the David Eccles School of Business and the Garff Associates Program greatly contributed to the timely completion of this manuscript as well.

If you have comments for the improvement of this book, examples of successful practice based on the principles herein, or questions about how to implement the Need Satisfaction Method, please write, fax, or call:

> Dr. Gary M. Grikscheit, Chairman
> Department of Marketing
> David Eccles School of Business
> The University of Utah
> Salt Lake City, Utah 84112

Telephone: 801-581-7733
Fax: 801-581-7214

GARY M. GRIKSCHEIT
HAROLD C. CASH
CLIFFORD E. YOUNG

Salt Lake City, Utah
Garden City, New York
Denver, Colorado
January 1993

ONE

High-Performance Selling for the 1990s

The secret of success is constancy to purpose.

BENJAMIN DISRAELI

In this chapter:

1. THE CARDINAL OBJECTIVES FOR PROFESSIONALS

What is critical in creating and recreating customers? If you think about this question, you will realize that *knowledge, skill,* and *motivation* determine performance. Most other factors are beyond your immediate control. The starting point, then, is to ask: "What am I trying to achieve?" To begin answering this question, consider the following definitions for the terms labeling the axes in Figure 1.1.

Strategic objectives guide your future efforts to attain your goals. Planning and analysis to determine strategic objectives must precede any interaction with prospects or customers. Inputs include prospects' purchasing habits, the people involved in each account, the competitive situation, and your current relationship with each prospect. While strategic planning is vital to success, interaction with customers seldom goes exactly as planned. The prospect may be in an unanticipated mood, the inventory situation may differ from your estimate, you may not be able to see the person you had planned to meet, or the competition may have injected a new element into the equation. Because so many unpredictable factors can impair your success, good tactics are indispensable. *Tactical* objectives focus on the present and on the control of your actions to implement your plans in real time.

Managerial objectives are related to the allocation of time and effort. Who are you going to call on? Who are you going to omit? No matter how polished your communication skills, your ultimate effectiveness depends on concentrating on prospects and customers with the greatest potential. Remember, since your key customers are prime targets for your competition, you need a strong defense.

	MANAGERIAL	COMMUNICATION
S T R A T E G I C	To create profitable differential competitive advantage TIP-IT!	To accord uniqueness
T A C T I C A L	To manage a set of selling-buying relationships for mutual profit	To control the interview without seeming to do so

Figure 1.1   Cardinal objectives for professional salespeople.

Conversely, your competitors' select accounts are an important potential source of additional profit for you so you also need a strong offense. An important component of selling is managing the process for maximum impact and productivity.

A salesperson may be a topflight manager but fail to communicate adequately with buyers. *Communication* objectives refer to what you want to achieve through interaction with clients. When face-to-face or on the phone with a prospect, what are you going to do? What are you going to say? How are you going to say it? The following subsections develop each of the four cardinal objectives.

The Strategic Managerial Objectives

To Create a Profitable Differential Competitive Advantage

As you think through what you are trying to accomplish, you must begin where each prospect or customer is psychologically. The prospect or customer is "buying" oriented: A customer seeks value. The buyer will select the offering perceived to be *different* and *better;* therefore, your strategic managerial objective in the sales process is *to create a differential competitive advantage* in the buyer's mind.

There can be no buying without selling or selling without buying. On the one hand, customers and prospects seek to satisfy their needs and wants by searching out sources for products and services that satisfy their requirements most efficiently. On the other hand, salespeople strive to ferret out those buyers who have the greatest potential for purchasing their offering on a mutually profitable basis. All of this takes place in an increasingly competitive environment.

If salespeople and buyers possessed all pertinent information about each other—*if* salespeople knew all the needs and wants of their buyers, and *if* buyers had total knowledge of available offerings—the problems encountered in buying and selling would be reduced to questions of logic. This is, however, clearly not the situation buyers and sellers face. Their dual search behavior operates on imperfect information, which is unevenly dispersed. The underlying rationale for personal selling is that each of the participants possesses unique information of particular capabilities, requirements, and needs or wants. When the selling–buying process functions effectively, the participants bridge innumerable informational "gaps." For example, a prospect might learn of a timesaving production process thanks to a salesperson's expertise. Or, a salesperson, in visiting an account, might learn of a new product application from the plant manager.

For any particular pair of sellers and buyers, the exchange process breaks down if prospects and customers find the sales offering neither better than nor different from that currently in use or available from competitors. Some basis of favorable differentiation is imperative.

You must determine how customers or prospects view your offering relative to those available from competitors. In short, how do customers and prospects perceive, think, and feel about each of the alternative products and services on the market? Some salespeople will argue that their product or service "has no competition." The truth of the matter is that there is *always* a competitor—the option of the customer to not buy at all!

A competitive relationship has five dimensions: To make a sale, you must show that your offering is advantageous on some combination of Tangible, Intangible, Price, Image, and Team factors (TIP-IT). Figure 1.2 illustrates this concept by summarizing how a customer might evaluate your company and the competition on each of the five factors. An evaluation score of 10 is assumed to be maximum for each factor. Thus, if a buyer considers the Tangible factor, your product superiority alone, your company would enjoy a 2-point edge over Competitor 1 and a 4-point advantage over Competitor 2. However, if the Intangible factor, service superiority, is evaluated in addition to the Tangible, Competitor 1 would have a 1-point superiority over both your company and Competitor 2. (Factor weights are assumed to be equal for illustrative purposes; use appropriate weights for your major accounts.) If the buyer is Price minded as well, Competitor 2 would have a 2-point advantage over your company and a 1-point lead over Competitor 1. Continuing the example, if the buyer is concerned about Image—which sources of supply to do business with—Competitor 1 is preferable to the other vendors. Finally, if the buyer thinks comprehensively and evaluates the Team or human factors, your company enjoys a differential competitive advantage over its competitors as indicated by the cumulative scores of 42, 41, and 40, respectively.

Exhibit 1.1 illustrates specific elements that could make up the five factors of differential competitive advantage. Appendix I provides a work sheet, together with a procedure designed to help you determine your relative differential competitive advantage in a particular account.

	Customer/Prospect's Evaluation of Offerings					
FACTOR	**Your Company**		**Competitor 1**		**Competitor 2**	
	Factor Score	Cumulative Total	Factor Score	Cumulative Score	Factor Score	Cumulative Score
Tangible (1)	10	10*	8	8	6	6
Intangible (1)	6	16	9	17*	10	16
Price (1)	7	23	7	24	9	25*
Image (1)	10	33	10	34*	7	32
Team (1)	9	42*	7	41	8	40

* Highest cumulative total for the row.

Figure 1.2   Differential competitive advantage.

Illustrative Elements
in
The Five Factors of Differential Competitive Advantage

Tangible Superiority
- Appearance. Aesthetic? Clean in use or on display?
- Design. Trouble free? "Idiot-proof?"
- Life expectancy. Wear resistant? Unlikely to become obsolete?
- Packaging. Distinctive? Easy to open? Close? Reuse?
- Adaptability. Special fittings? Unusual applications?

Intangible Superiority
- Customer service. 24-hour availability? Scheduling?
- Delivery. Timeliness? Frequency? Convenience?
- Training. Meetings? How delivered? One-on-one?
- Maintenance. Service contracts? Training?
- Merchandising. Displays? Demonstrations? Deals?

Price Superiority
- Price. As listed? How negotiable?
- Discounts. What percent of list? Discount structure?
- Terms of payment. Dating? Cash?
- Packaged pricing. Quotation by item? Reduction for all items?
- Additional elements. Trade-in allowances? Cancellation-of-order penalty? Services available at no charge? Free installation?

Image Superiority
- Industry standing. "Firsts" scored? Imitation by competition? Prestige accounts? Government contracts?
- Time in business. Old firm with experience? New one that innovates?
- Community image. Good citizen? Prestige place to work?
- Financial soundness. Earnings growth? Balance sheet?
- Policies and practices. Ethical? Equitable? Consistent?

Team Superiority
- Knowledge and skill of personnel. Problem solvers? Idea sources?
- Integrity and character. Confidentiality? Trustworthiness?
- Available for emergencies. Nearby? Any hour?
- Mutual friends. In sports? In industry? In church?
- Cooperation. Willingness to invest time and effort required?

Exhibit 1.1 Dimensions of a competitive relationship.

The concept of differential competitive advantage is a basic diagnostic tool for evaluating your relationships with major customers and prospects over time. After making or losing a sale, ask yourself: "How did my offering stack up against the competition in the customer's eyes?" A thoughtful answer to this question provides you with an overall analysis of your competitive strengths and weaknesses, pinpointing areas vulnerable to the inroads of competitors, as well as opportunities to enhance rapport with your customers.

Successful seller-buyer relationships depend on more than "price" or "product" alone. All dimensions of differential competitive advantage are essential in varying combinations. Research indicates product factors tend to be more important for the introduction of a new or highly technical product. Over time, these short-term competitive advantages diminish and the offerings of surviving competitors tend to become equivalent. Therefore, the impact of the personal ingredient varies with the product life cycle, tending to become more important as markets mature and as technological differences between competitive products diminish. At any given time, most of a nation's markets are mature and personal selling is, therefore, one of the crucial ingredients in creating an edge in the customer's eyes.

Of course, staying extremely close to your customers is not enough. Your organization must provide support by placing a high priority on responding to customers' needs and on developing sophisticated systems to deliver superior customer service, usually based on state-of-the-art computer technology.

For selling-buying relationships to endure, however, the transactions must be "valuable" to the buyer as well as "profitable" to the seller. In addition to determining customer willingness to purchase your offering, you must decide whether or not customers are likely to be profitable. By definition, profit is the excess of sales revenue over total cost:

$$\text{Profit} = \text{Revenue} - \text{Cost}$$

Understanding what is and is not profitable business for your company is important. Conceptually, you must allocate your selling efforts on a set of customers and prospects, some of whom will be more likely to purchase than others and some of whom will be more profitable. This means an important dimension of professional selling is the management of selling-buying relationships for profit. At any point, your customers and prospects can be segmented according to their relative differential competitive advantage as well as their profit characteristics, as depicted in Figure 1.3.

Despite your best efforts to service current profitable accounts (Cell 1), over a period of time the number of your accounts in this category will decline as your clients' businesses evolve and as competitive salespeople create greater differential competitive advantage for these customers. This is a fact of business life. Consequently, as a professional you must identify potentially profitable prospects (Cell 3), both to replace the ravages of attrition as well as to provide for future growth. Generally speaking, prospect accounts falling into Cell 3 are key customers of the competition. Equally important, you should *not* solicit unprofitable business (Cells 2 and 4). Unprofitable accounts (Cell 2), are a normal part of every business caused by a mismatch within the selling-buying relationship between value and profit economics. It occurs frequently where profitable accounts have changed the manner in which they buy, where a new account has yet to reach its potential, and where the salesperson

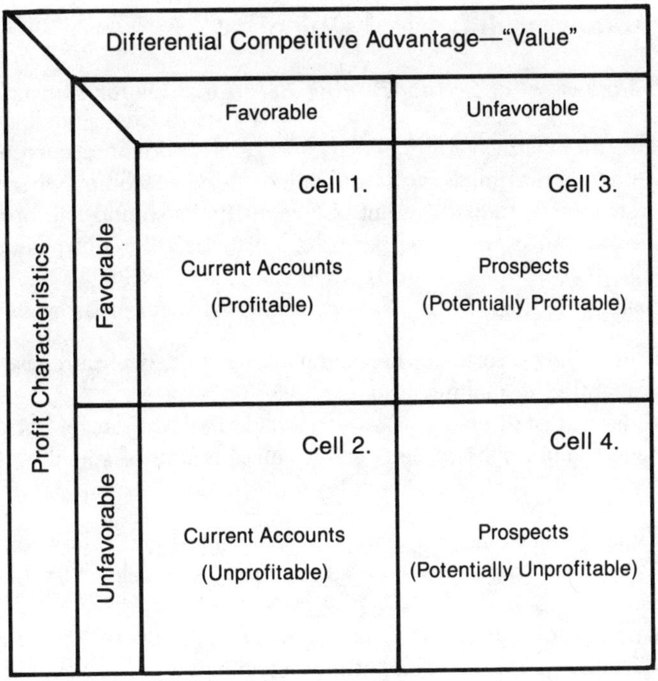

Figure 1.3 Value and profit within the selling-buying relationship.

is calling on the wrong prospects. These are the accounts that make unwarranted service demands relative to the volume they purchase, buy in such small quantities that they sharply increase selling costs, and/or require extended terms of payment. You may be tempted to feel you can do business with everybody; such is not the case. Sound business practice dictates retention quotas to limit unprofitable accounts. Clearly, you should neither solicit nor book business from Cell 4.

Creating value for your customers and prospects is not enough. You must also concentrate your time, talent, energy, and company support services on those customers and prospects with favorable profit characteristics. Consequently, the professional salesperson's strategic managerial objective is to create a *profitable* differential competitive advantage. Achieving this goal marries the two most important ingredients of a successful seller-buyer relationship: profit for the seller and value for the customer. Note that this does not mean that every transaction between a seller and a buyer must be mutually advantageous, only that the overall relationship will be favorable to both parties. For example, a large regional printer customarily places large orders two or three times a week with a paper wholesaler on a mutually beneficial profitable basis but occasionally will order small quantities of required items that are unprofitable for the wholesaler on their own merits. Overall, if the seller earns adequate profits and the buyer receives competitive value, the relationship will be viable.

The Managerial Tactical Objective

To Manage a Set of Selling-Buying Relationships for Mutual Profit

The effective tactician carefully allocates sales efforts among current and potential accounts to maximize profit and value added. Based on what you know about your accounts—their differential competitive advantage and profit characteristics—you can design a selling program to fit the requirements of your company and customer/prospect mix.

Why manage selling-buying relationships? Two cogent reasons exist:

1. Focusing selling efforts on the customers most likely to purchase increases the probability of making a sale.
2. You reduce wasted effort when you avoid the twin dangers of calling on customers impervious to competitive inroads and of spending too much time with "long shot" customers loyal to the competition.

Equally important, understanding this managerial tactical objective guides you away from those prospects who tend to require so much effort that they are ultimately unprofitable.

These points are summarized in Figure 1.4. Accounts are arrayed from highest to lowest differential competitive advantage (e.g., accounts *a* through *e*). You are most vulnerable where you have the least differential competitive advantage. Therefore, you should focus the bulk of your attention on defending your position in accounts between *b* and *c* as well as invading your competitor's weakest positions in customers between *c* and *d*. Investing in accounts like *a* or *e* makes relatively little sense. In the first instance, still greater favorable evalu-

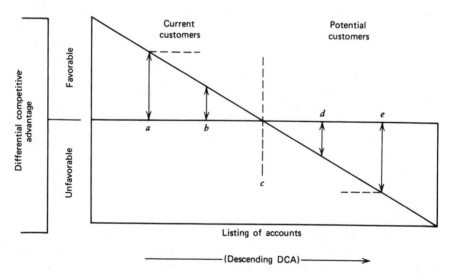

Figure 1.4   Managing conscious awareness.

ation is unwarranted; in the second, it is unlikely that these prospects will become paying customers in the immediate future.

An additional question is: "Why should salespeople manage a set of selling-buying relationships for *mutual* profit?" At least four important reasons exist:

1. All prospective customers think their needs are important, but no firm can afford to be all things to all people. You must avoid unprofitable business and allocate time on the most profitable prospects. Similarly, you should focus on the prospects with the greatest long-term potential. *Note:* This does not bar experimenting with new sales approaches and techniques that could ultimately lead to improved productivity and profitability. Such efforts, however, should not undermine the effectiveness of your present selling system.
2. Unremitting attention to profitable business hones your understanding of profitability. Improving your ability to satisfy customer requirements ultimately leads to a superior edge in the market and to improved margins and profits.
3. Continuous attention to profit also provides you with insights on how to alter your firm's offering to better fit evolving market requirements.
4. By understanding profitability, you are better able to manage customer relationships in the best interests of the buyer and your own company. Ultimately, enduring selling-buying relationships will result based on delivering value to the customer.

Achieving the tactical managerial objective is difficult. One problem is that salespeople frequently fail to deploy their selling efforts in proportion to their profitable market potential, as shown in Figure 1.5. Time management lies at the heart of this objective. First, the nature of selling provides the salesperson with wide latitude in deciding who to call on and when. Second, the larger the potential profit of a customer, generally the greater the competition for the account. In addition, the probability of more professional purchasing is high. Third, the smaller the account, the less the competition and the less formalized the purchasing. Consequently, if congeniality replaces profitability as the actual criterion for determining sales effort, some valuable market potential will not be covered. All these effects undercut profitability as well as the development of lasting selling-buying relationships.

Enduring selling-buying relationships are based on an equitable exchange of value for profit that is planned and controlled. How you can achieve your managerial objectives is covered in Chapters Nine and Ten.

The Strategic Communication Objectives

To Accord Uniqueness

This objective is based on the fundamental idea that each individual is unique. Geneticists calculate a "1 over 10 to the power of 3,000" chance that any two individuals can be clones. Hence, if you assume that the person you are talking

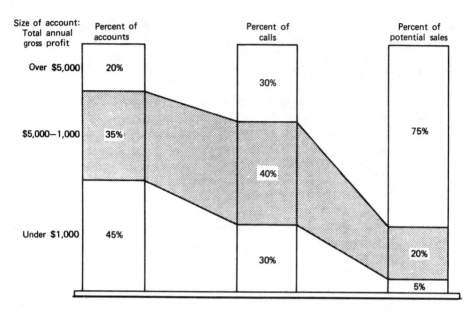

Figure 1.5   Are accounts with little potential receiving too many calls?

to is "just like you," the odds are that you are wrong. Stated differently, "You are the worst estimator of the person you are talking to." Recognizing and according uniqueness to another person is the basis of persuasion in selling.

You can grant uniqueness to prospects and customers by using the need satisfaction method of selling. According to this method, decisions to buy products or services are based on the needs of individuals and/or organizations. Therefore, to market your offering, you must discover the prospect's needs and then show how your products or services will fill them.

According uniqueness to the customer is so important that it will be treated at greater length in Section 2 of this chapter.

The Communication Tactical Objective

To Control the Interview without Seeming to Do So

Effective tacticians pay close attention to the prospect or customer and use what they have heard, seen, and felt to adjust their own behavior to favorably influence the buyer. Prospects and customers respond to persuasiveness, not coercion. Therefore, you cannot control the interview effectively by talking louder and faster than the buyer. Rather, tacticians attend *from themselves* and *to the other person*. The acid test is the extent to which the technician achieves the tactical communication objective: *To control the interview without seeming to do so.* Why should you want to control the interview? There are several important reasons:

1. It increases the probability of achieving the objectives of each call. Only through control can you capitalize on your advance planning.

2. You are able to profit from experience and apply the lessons learned to each succeeding call on customers, improving your productivity per unit of time invested.
3. You are better able to establish favorable relationships with prospects and customers through mutually beneficial calls.

Why is it desirable to control the interview *without seeming to do so?* Again, important reasons exist:

1. Prospects understandably like to think that they have freedom of choice in purchasing products and services. Therefore, obvious control is most likely regarded as coercive and evokes negative reactions.
2. When you handle the interview so that prospects see the decision to buy from you as their own, buyers are able to both defend the decision and become ego involved in it.
3. Prospects who are relatively more submissive or less self-confident tend to look on such salespeople as helpful advisors and consultants.
4. Communicators who use subtle control, attend more to feedback, and talk less gain insight into how well the buyer understands the offering as well as any blocks in the way of acceptance. Selling is an active process.

When the prospect participates rather than merely listens, you have more control over the interview. When people listen passively, you cannot be sure that they are paying attention to you. Only when they participate in the conversation can you determine whether they have followed the reasoning and have accepted or rejected the ideas presented (Figure 1.6). Prospects must literally persuade themselves to buy. This is the epitome of control in the sales interview.

Such participation tends to bring about a gradual change in the prospect's viewpoint. The alternative, where the salesperson does all the talking, may require an abrupt change of opinion by the prospect if the interview is to be successful. Such an abrupt change is likely to be in conflict with the prospect's ego.

You will be most effective in controlling the interview when you pay attention to what prospects say and do, how they say it and how they do it. When you have observed the reactions, your task is to do or say what will influence the prospect to move toward the interview's objective. This procedure has the additional advantage of making the prospect feel pleased that you are so attentive.

Developing skill in controlling the interview is discussed further in Chapter Three. Practicing the suggestions presented will contribute substantially to your ability to master the technique.

No matter how effective you are in achieving your managerial objectives, your performance will suffer if you fall short in reaching your communication objectives. But, how do you measure performance? The answers lie in the customer's perceptions, thoughts, and feelings at the end of the sales process. These reactions are an operational measure of the degree to which you have achieved your objectives. If the customer feels you dominated the sales interview, the objectives were not met (high pressure); if the customer feels he or she dominated the sales inter-

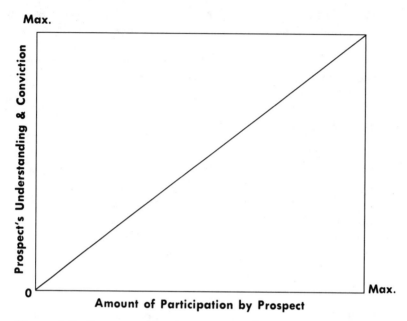

Figure 1.6 Participation by the prospect enhances both control of the interview and attention by the salesperson.

view, your objectives were achieved (low pressure). Two more thoughts are necessary to complete this concept. First, you may actually control the interview, yet leave the customer feeling he or she was in control. Second, at the end of the sales process, the customer may feel there was an even exchange of information and neither party was in control (zero pressure). In sales situations where the buyer expects considerable advice and assistance, zero pressure should prevail.

If you could use essentially the same technique on a series of prospects, some would feel they controlled, and others that you controlled the sales interview. Therefore, the feelings of the buyer, as indicated in Figure 1.7, constitute a criterion for how well you have achieved your communication objectives.

Effective Selling Is Professional

Selling is a professional career opportunity, not a job. In contrast to most occupations with relatively defined duties, responsibilities, and work flows, professional salespeople must create opportunities before they can apply their knowledge and skill. This means establishing and nurturing selling-buying relationships with prospects and customers as a basis for future activity. Few prospective customers come to the salesperson spontaneously. Effective selling requires a high degree of initiative as well as managerial and communication competence, but its foundation is professional responsibility. The ethics of professional life stem from a foundation of competence and a motive of service.

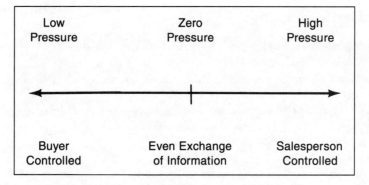

Figure 1.7   Pressure: How does the buyer feel?

This guide clearly has application in personal selling and is consistent with the four cardinal objectives of selling.

2.   NEED SATISFACTION: THEORY AND PRACTICE

Traditional literature on selling stresses that salespeople must master a thorough knowledge of their products, services, accounts, competition, and industry as well as hone their skills in presentation and persuasion. The literature assumes that the salesperson's function is to sell and that success depends on the person alone, independent of the prospect and the situation. A more tenable position, however, is to see selling as a selling-buying process engaged in actively by both salespeople and customers. In addition to the required skills and knowledge, salespeople must also learn to monitor verbal and nonverbal feedback from the customer/prospect and the situation. Acquiring this ability will allow you to assess the needs and wants of an individual decision maker or buying group, to adjust to other people, and to customize your presentations. Your role is not to sell but to induce people to buy. This viewpoint—personal selling as an interpersonal communication process—recognizes that the prospect as well as the salesperson is an active participant.

Three methods of bringing sales points to buyers' attention exist:

1. Stimulus-Response (S-R)
2. Selling Formula (S-F)
3. Need Satisfaction (N-S)

Proponents of each of these methods can be found among salespeople and sales managers. For practical purposes, you can switch from one method to another, but you cannot combine them. Reviewing each of them is beneficial so that you can then guide your selling efforts appropriately.

Stimulus-Response

This is the simplest of the three methods. Its psychological origin is in early experiments with animals. Investigators found that a given stimulus, food, would cause a given response, salivation. Associated with each stimulus is a particular response.

Applying this to selling, you need to have a repertoire of verbal and nonverbal behaviors (stimuli) to bring about buying (response). The implication is that if you say and do the right things, an order will follow.

You select any one of the sales points and tell the buyer all about it. After presenting all the information on one sales point, you ask for the order. If the response is "yes," the sale is completed; if "no," you select another sales point and repeat the procedure.

Eventually a sale will result or one of the parties—buyer or seller—will have had enough, and the interview will be terminated.

The S-R concept says nothing about how you might identify the stimuli to be used or how you would know when to use a specific appeal. Strictly speaking, with this method, information flows primarily from the salesperson to the prospect but not from the prospect to the salesperson. This precludes tactical adjustment during the presentation. The assumption is also implicit that all prospects are identical and will respond similarly to a given stimulus. The prospect is viewed as a closed system or buying machine, and your objective is to push the start button.

The S-R concept is essentially signal sending. Before the interview, you must construct the messages that you use and these are largely distilled from experience.

For a very simple situation, where the unit sale is low and the time that you have is very brief, operating on this basis may be feasible. However, experienced salespeople know that a stimulus that works with one customer does not necessarily work with another. As a result, you will be in the dark when you attempt to analyze the reasons for your success or failure. Salespeople who work on this basis have little likelihood of improving their performance as a result of their experience.

Selling Formula

Two differences exist between the selling formula method and the preceding one:

1. The salesperson decides on the number of, and order of, the sales points to cover before starting the interview.
2. The salesperson delays the request for an order until he or she has covered all intended sales points.

The test of this method is whether the outline of the sales call is predetermined. It lies in the attitude of the salesperson toward the buyer. Did the salesperson plan the whole presentation in advance or not?

By contrast, no planning occurs in the Stimulus-Response method. The sales points are selected haphazardly. This is an important psychological distinction.

When the selling formula is mentioned (sometimes the term "canned" sales talk is used), the acronym AIDA usually comes to mind. These letters stand for Attention, Interest, Desire, and Action. The originators of this method wanted the sales points ordered to attract attention, generate interest, arouse desire, and get action. They also wanted the salesperson to instill conviction and provide satisfaction.

Proponents of this method claim that it ensures the presentation of all important product information to each customer and that using this approach is necessary to make a sale.

According to critics, the method requires analyzing the situation from the salesperson's point of view rather than the customer's and its use tends to make salespeople feel they are technicians following a standard procedure that can persuade customers to buy. Critics also point out that a customer may not experience these states in any given order and that they are not of equal importance. Introduction of the states, however, requires a fundamental change. Because salespeople must detect success at Step 1 before proceeding to Step 2 in the method, they must now begin to analyze feedback from the prospect. Note that feedback is used to determine when to proceed to the next stage, not for the creation and selection of unique messages. In the S-F and the S-R methods, you are assuming that all sales points have equal attraction to the buyer. This does not seem warranted. More likely, some sales points are of more interest to a given buyer than others. Instead of finding and pushing one button, as in the stimulus-response concept, your objective now is to push a *series* of buttons to induce buying.

This method may be valuable when customers have similar or identical needs and you cannot develop a sales approach based on each customer's individual needs. The method also has considerable utility for writers or teachers of sales techniques. It provides a framework for the presentation of most ideas on selling.

This approach runs into difficulty when the customer wants the answer to a specific question. If you fail to perceive this, you may literally talk yourself out of a sale.

Need Satisfaction

Characteristics of the Method

Purchases are made to satisfy needs. To make a sale, therefore, you must discover the prospect's needs and show how your products or services will fill them. The starting point is the prospect's needs. This is a customer-oriented approach in contrast to the two previous methods, which are salesperson-oriented approaches, emphasizing appeals.

This method requires greater skill and maturity on your part because you cannot talk about your product or service until you have discovered the customer's needs. Consequently, your initial emphasis is on monitoring feedback instead of on sending signals. This is in sharp contrast to the selling formula, which encourages you to point out all the important features of your offerings. It also requires that you have sufficient self-confidence to control the sales interview through questioning rather than by dominating the conversation.

A related point is that prospects were considered mechanistic or passive in the previous two methods, but in the need satisfaction method, they are active and may appear to exercise a certain degree of influence over you. The methods discussed previously attempted to explain the *individual* behavior of the salesperson only. The need satisfaction method attempts to explain the *social* behavior of both the salesperson and the prospect. Finally, the need satisfaction method is grounded on the fundamental principle that the sale begins and ends in the buyer's mind.

In the need satisfaction method, your strategic objective is to *accord uniqueness*. The salesperson who achieves this objective exerts influence because of each person's fundamental quest for individuality. You are charged with treating each buyer as a unique individual. This stands in sharp contrast to the button-pushing objectives of the preceding theories. In addition, this approach is analytic, while the others are at best descriptive.

For more serious and complex sales situations, this method is appropriate. In one sense, the need satisfaction process is more time-consuming, but the increased likelihood of making the sale by matching the customer's needs with the appropriate product features and benefits makes this approach more attractive, particularly in situations where the potential margins and/or commissions are great enough to warrant the extra expenditure of time.

The need satisfaction method is definitely preferable as a basis for all selling above the canvassing level. It is especially appropriate where repeat calls are in order. The following explanation of the method is extensive enough so that anyone can adopt it for his or her own use. Figure 1.8 further clarifies the basic premises.

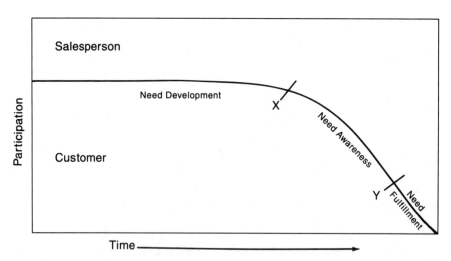

Figure 1.8   The need satisfaction method of selling.

The Three Phases

Figure 1.8 shows the phases of the need satisfaction method of selling. At the beginning of the sales interview, you ask questions to encourage conversation with the prospect. Each reply should trigger the next question. This results in your talking a much smaller percentage of time than the prospect in the opening stage. This is portrayed by assigning the space above the curve to the salesperson and the space below the curve to the potential customer. Your goal is to get prospects to talk about their needs. This is called the "need development" phase of the sales interview and should continue until you have an in-depth understanding of the prospect's needs.

At point X, you have insight into the needs and, as can be seen, start to take over more and more of the conversation because you now know what to discuss. This is seen in the change of the curve. Now that you understand the prospect's needs, your objective is to get him or her to see them. The term applied to this phase is "need awareness." When you get the prospect to see his or her needs clearly, you have reached point Y.

The final phase, "need fulfillment," consists of your showing the prospect how the product/service will meet the demonstrated needs. If you have developed a clear understanding of the prospect's requirements, as well as made him or her aware of them, you are ready to make a personalized presentation. To do this, you necessarily monopolize more of the conversation. As the curve approaches the bottom of the chart, the prospect does less of the talking. While you have assumed the bulk of the talking, the prospect should not feel dominated because you are talking about satisfying his or her needs.

To contrast the three methods on the single variable of salesperson-prospect participation in the sales interview, examine Figures 1.8, 1.9, and 1.10. In the stimulus-response situation, the salesperson makes a point, then allows

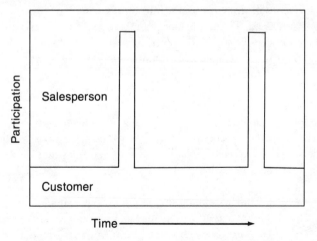

Figure 1.9   The stimulus response method of selling.

Figure 1.10 The selling formula method.

the customer to reply. If the answer is "no," the salesperson again monopolizes the conversation. In the selling formula method, the salesperson dominates the conversation except during the interest and desire stages. Only in need satisfaction selling do buyers have the opportunity to talk about their needs before the salesperson makes a presentation.

Need Development.   Each prospect has individualized needs and specifications for a product or service. You are generally equipped with all the sales points to show how your product or service will meet the needs of any buyer in any situation. The temptation is strong to explain all sales points to each customer. But, in the beginning of the sales interview, you should refrain from telling what your product or service will do and concentrate on determining what your prospects need or think they need. The important point is to use open questions not only to identify needs but also to get an in-depth understanding of each one. You should continue the need development process until you are confident you understand what is in the *mind of the buyer.* Nothing is more important to closing the sale than understanding the buyer's needs. Once you have that understanding, the product features and benefits that will meet those needs constitute the basis of the sales presentation for that particular person. To bring out the needs, you must ask questions that will keep the prospect talking freely. Your questions should be clear, open, and concise. Verbal garbage and poorly worded questions detract from the power of need satisfaction selling (see Exhibit 1.2).

Need-Awareness.   Even though you understand the prospects' needs, they may not fully realize their own needs. You may have to go back over some of the ground covered in the need-development phase to focus them. If you concentrate the conversation on those areas where you detect needs, prospects will

```
Pivotal Points
The Need Satisfaction Model in Practice
```

- Keep the questions clear, open, and concise. Verbal garbage and poorly worded questions detract from the power of the question technique.

- After identifying a need, ask questions to get an in-depth understanding of the need. Avoid making assumptions based on surface information.

- Continue the need development process until you are confident you understand what is in the MIND OF THE BUYER.

Exhibit 1.2   Need development.

eventually see such needs themselves; but you should not start to close until you have reached point Y. At that point, both the salesperson and the prospect have a clear picture of the needs.

In practice, be certain to state the needs you discovered and briefly explain why they are important. This "what/why" summary assures your understanding of the prospect's needs is complete. It also focuses the prospect's attention where you need it to be. In addition, always ask a check question. The check question serves as a safety net for any needs missed during need development.

The best preparation for closing consists of you and the prospect developing needs together. This is the epitome of credibility. The need awareness segment assures that you are not getting ahead of the buyer's mind (see Exhibit 1.3).

Need Fulfillment.   Once both you and the prospect agree on his or her needs, you can identify those features/benefits that will meet them. In other words, you show the prospect how the needs can be filled by purchasing your offering. This is the meaning of need fulfillment.

```
Pivotal Points
The Need Satisfaction Model in Practice
```

- Be certain to state the needs you discovered and briefly explain why they are important. This "what/why" summary assures your understanding of the buyer's needs. It also focuses the buyer's attention where you need it to be.

- Always ask a check question. The check question serves as a safety net for any needs missed during need development.

- The need awareness segment assures the salesperson he/she is not getting ahead of the buyer's mind.

Exhibit 1.3   Need awareness.

You can now customize your presentation based on your analysis of the prospect's needs. Present your sales points using the buyer's words as well as image-evoking language that enables the prospect to visualize how your products or services will meet specific needs.

If the prospect has been participating in the sales process, you can anticipate objections in the need fulfillment phase. The appropriate technique for handling these will be covered in the next section.

Finally, close for the sale. If the sale requires additional involvement, close for the demonstration, trial period, or the next appointment. Never leave a sales call or end a phone conversation without knowing where you stand (see Exhibit 1.4).

The traditional course or book on selling, based on either the stimulus-response or selling formula method, starts with the need fulfillment phase. Need development and need awareness are usually omitted and ignored. When you treat the problem of understanding needs lightly or skip it, you are limited to telling the customer what the product or service will do. This is one-way communication. In addition, traditional approaches seldom recognize the salesperson's strategic communication objective: *to accord uniqueness.* In short, understanding the customer's needs and being sure that the customer understands how you obtained your information is better than any alternative. The following sections review the tools required to implement the need satisfaction method of selling.

Operationalizing the Need Satisfaction Method

Although the need satisfaction method of personal selling was introduced in the middle 1920s (E. K. Strong, 1925), it was largely ignored until the late 1950s

---

Pivotal Points
The Need Satisfaction Model in Practice

- Customize your presentation based on the buyer's needs. Avoid rambling on about every aspect of the company's offerings.

- Present the feature/benefit statements using the words used by the buyer. Image-evoking language will enable the buyer to visualize how the product will meet the needs.

- Be concise but thorough. Be cautious of talking yourself out of the sale.

- Handle objections appropriately.

- Close for the sale. If the sale requires additional involvement, close for the demonstration, trial period, or the next appointment. Never leave a sales call or end a phone conversation without knowing where you stand.

Exhibit 1.4 Need fulfillment.

(Cash and Crissy, 1957–1965) and has only recently been developed to the point where it can be readily applied in any line of professional selling (Cash and Crissy, 1977; Grikscheit, Cash, and Crissy, 1981). The concept required to operationalize the need satisfaction theory is called the Salesperson-Oriented Product Manual (SOPM) or the Salesperson-Oriented Service Manual (SOSM), depending on the nature of your offering. It consists of four tools: a feature-benefit table, need-developing questions, alternate phrasings, and questions designed for handling objections. Properly executed, the manual provides the linkage between product knowledge and sales skill necessary for effective selling.

Perhaps the major reason operationalizing the need satisfaction method has taken so long is that companies often seek to achieve too many purposes with their product/service manuals. Three purposes are frequently attempted: (1) to influence the customer to buy the offering, (2) to assist salespeople in selling the offering, and (3) to guide the effective maintenance of the product in use. Rarely can a single manual achieve these three objectives effectively. If the first purpose is paramount, the manual becomes a promotional piece, and too often salespeople parrot it uncritically instead of personalizing their presentations to the particular needs of the prospects. If the third purpose is emphasized, much of the content does not directly concern either the salesperson or the person making the buying decision.

A second key reason SOPM/SOSMs may not have enjoyed wider acceptance is that many people do not view selling as a profession requiring dedication and preparation. Mastering knowledge and skill, which is normally associated with other personal service professions, tends to be played down.

Consequently, relatively few companies have custom-built manuals oriented to the salesperson's needs and used in daily practice. We suggest viewing selling as a professional practice and advocate a SOPM or SOSM as an important sales tool that all serious salespeople should master. Although client requirements vary, the manual basically has a three-part structure:

Part	Content
1.	Feature-benefit table
2.	Sales points, including:
	a. Need-developing questions
	b. Alternate phrasings
3.	Handling objections

Using this book—*Handbook of Selling*—as an example, Appendix II provides a salesperson-oriented product manual. Although this example is abbreviated because of space limitations, it does reflect the basic structure and content of an SOPM. In practice, the manuals tend to be developed in greater depth, reflecting the complexity of many modern products and services. Following is a detailed explanation of the three parts of the manual together with a suggested procedure for implementation.

Feature-Benefit Table

When completed, Part 1 should provide an accurate answer to the question: "What do I sell?" The first step is to list all conceivable sales points. Brainstorming may facilitate generating a comprehensive set of sales points (see Appendix III). Sales points are the reasons to buy that you could give customers and prospects to help them decide to place an order with you. Next, examine each point to see whether it is a feature or benefit. The test is simple. If the sales point refers to or is based on the product or service *itself*, it is a feature. If it derives from the product or service in *use*, it is a benefit. You must have complete and clear knowledge of all possible sales points to match your product or service with the needs of each unique buyer.

A caution is in order, however. Many writers and speakers use a variety of terms such as features, benefits, advantages, needs, and wants. Some feel only benefits should be verbalized to buyers; others prefer needs; still others, wants. Nevertheless, classification beyond a feature-benefit table is unwarranted. The reason for this is that what is a *want* for one buyer is a *need* for another. Thus, there is no stability to the classification and, hence, no value to you.

When all sales points have been classified, they should be arranged in two columns—the features on the left, the benefits on the right. Appendix IV provides a work sheet for developing a feature-benefit table.

Examining the two columns will show many repetitions or varied wordings. These alternate phrasings will be useful later, but for now they should be combined or dropped so that a mutually exclusive and exhaustive list of features and benefits remains. Note that the features are identified by numbers and benefits by letters.

The features and benefits can now be cross-referenced. Start with Feature 1. Compare it with each benefit. If there is a positive relationship, place the number of the feature after the benefit and the letter of the benefit after the feature. Do this for each feature and, as a cross-check, repeat for each benefit. If any feature does not lead to a benefit, consider dropping that feature.

Any given feature may provide more than one benefit, and any given benefit may derive from more than one feature. Assuming a one-to-one relationship between features and benefits is erroneous. For example, power brakes are a feature on many automobiles. Some benefits are ease of braking and faster stopping, improving safety. Safety is a benefit that derives not only from power brakes but also from the steel supports used in the construction of the body.

When you have completed the feature-benefit table, you will have a clear picture of your offering and can match sales points against buyer needs. You can communicate a clear picture to the buyer. Without such clarity, salespeople have a fuzzy impression of their product or service. *You cannot communicate a clearer picture to the buyer than you possess yourself.* In addition, the buyer who lacks a clear understanding of a product will feel no impulse to buy.

Sales Points

After formulating a feature-benefit table, the next step is to develop sales points, as well as need-developing questions and alternate phrasings (Appendix II).

In the sales process, your first real objective is to identify the three or four sales points in the list of available points that most clearly fit the needs of a particular buyer. To do this, you must ask questions. The questions must meet the criteria detailed in Chapter Three, Section 1. They must also relate to your sales points. If you develop needs that your product or service cannot fill, the buyer-seller relationship will deteriorate. To ensure understanding and clarity, each sales point should be stated briefly and followed by an explanatory paragraph. For products of intermediate complexity, each sales point can be described adequately in about a half page of double-spaced text. If more information is required, appendixes can be cited.

In Appendix II, several model questions follow each sales point. They are not questions intended to be used serially or verbatim. You should, instead, modify the questions to fit your own vocabulary and manner of speaking.

If questions do not flow freely, a buyer will feel he or she is facing an inquisitor. The objective is to establish and maintain a conversational manner. This is need development (Chapter Two provides thorough coverage of the communication process).

When the questioning has enabled you to tentatively identify the three or four most important needs and you have developed each need in depth, you should review the conversation to see whether the buyer agrees and whether the needs are clear to both parties. You do this by asking a check question. This is the need awareness phase. If you reach agreement on needs, the interview can proceed to need fulfillment. If not, you must revert to the need development phase and seek further clarification.

If you are skillful in asking questions, the buyer may not have noted that you have identified his or her needs. That is why the need awareness phase is important. The buyer's realization that you understand his or her needs is the best possible basis for credibility.

The three or four needs on which you mutually agree are the basis for closing the sale—need fulfillment. Appendix II shows a series of positive statements, referred to as alternate phrasings, that follow the questions. These are literally alternate phrasings of the sales points and should include benefits that derive from the features. Your original list of sales points probably had many leftover items that can now be used to compile these alternate phrasings. Again, these are models that you should adapt to your needs.

Why do you need to identify three or four sales points and prepare alternate phrasings? A sale will seldom result from a single statement of a single sales point. You should expect to make more than one point and state each one more than once. If you repeat a sales point verbatim, you and your prospect will both become bored and your presentation will suffer. With alternate phrasings, you can make the sales points more interesting. A detailed explanation of the rationale for using repetition and summation is available in Chapter Three, Section 2.

Handling Objections

If you follow the principles of need satisfaction selling, you studiously avoid making any positive statements until you reach the need fulfillment phase. As long as you limit yourself to questions to develop needs, you will encounter few objections.

When you enter the need fulfillment phase and offer positive statements with alternate phrasings, you must expect objections. In fact, you should welcome them because they show that:

1. The buyer has been attentive.
2. The buyer has been tempted.

To appreciate the procedures recommended here, you need to consider and adopt two assumptions:

1. When buyers and sellers disagree, buyers are more likely to act on their own verbalizations than on yours.
2. When buyers ask sellers for information, they are more likely to listen than if you supply the information on your own initiative.

Accepting the two assumptions makes it clear how you should respond to an objection. Your first effort should be to get buyers to answer their own objections. Failing this, you should get buyers to ask you for the answer. Appendix II illustrates the method.

When you encounter an objection, *mentally* formulate an answer. Do *not* verbalize it, but phrase a question that encourages the buyer to think through the answer to his or her own objection or ask for the information.

Most objections have more than one answer. Therefore, when compiling the equivalent of Appendix II, work out each answer-and-question series separately. When you encounter an objection, you must use clarifying and probing questions to select the best answer. You can then proceed as described earlier. Chapter Four, Section 2, will be helpful in this regard.

Recommendation

Each sales manager, sales trainer, and salesperson should have a salesperson-oriented product manual or salesperson-oriented service manual to implement the need satisfaction method of selling. However, because the skills required to write manuals and to sell are different ones, it is easier to implement this recommendation when your company takes the responsibility for developing a manual and you can work through the exercises required. If you wish to become a manager, you should master both the development and use of SOPM/SOSMs.

Construction and use of such a manual will provide a thorough understanding of the product or service you are selling, and it will also ensure use of the need satisfaction method of selling. When creating a manual, it may be desirable to review the references to information in other chapters of this volume.

3. IMPROVING YOUR PRODUCTIVITY

The keystone to improving your productivity is the effective management of your sales calls. No matter how well you perform your other duties, you will fail if you are unable to make a favorable impact on customers and prospects.

Your productivity hinges on a number of factors that influence the effectiveness of each call. These are identified and discussed in detail in the following chapters. All of them influence the degree of impact of your calls.

These factors are both *interrelated* and *interactive*. Weakness in one impairs the strength of the others. To develop greater impact during sales calls, you must develop mastery of all these areas:

1. Knowledge of your company's products and services and the uses and applications that can be made of them (Chapter One).
2. Awareness of competitive products and services and their advantages and limitations (Chapter One).
3. Adeptness in call management—setting objectives and formulating a program for achieving them (Chapters Nine and Ten).
4. Ability to communicate understandably, interestingly, believably, and persuasively (Chapter Two).
5. The timing and reinforcing of points within the call (Chapter Three).
6. "People" strategy based as necessary on (1) an accurate assessment of personality and motivational factors in individuals (Chapter Five), and (2) recognizing the role that each person plays in a group presentation (Chapter Six).
7. Communication tactics guided by reactions observed in the other person (Chapter Three).
8. Problem solving and creative thinking ability (Chapter Seven).
9. Strategic handling of sales resistance (Chapter Four).
10. Skill in inducing learning (Chapter Eight).

Knowledge of Your Company's Products and Services

Here your task is twofold. First, you must thoroughly learn all your sales points—the features and/or benefits—for each of your firm's products and services. You then face the second and more difficult task of converting your offering's features and benefits into words your customers and prospects can understand. This is basically a translation process. Product features and characteristics that are not translatable into specific, understandable uses and applications are likely to be ones of little significance to the buyer in the sales presentation. If you know all your sales points as well as how to express them in language the customer can easily understand, you have an enormous advantage over your less-well-prepared competitor.

Awareness of Competitive Products and Services

Knowing your own products and services is not enough: You must also be familiar with those of the competition. Only then can you make a comparative analysis. Appendix V provides a layout for accomplishing this. Needless to say, the number of features will depend on your particular product or service. You should note all the features and covert each one into benefits and uses. Further, you should pay particular attention to the features of your company's products that do not exist in competitive offerings. Similarly, you should pay particular heed to the features of each competitive offering that do not exist in your own line. Obviously, the foundation of effective strategy is to stress the unique characteristics of your firm's offering and to arm yourself with offsetting advantages for the unique characteristics of the competitive products and services.

Once you have completed the task outlined in Appendix V, you can then prioritize the elements for each sales presentation, taking first the points where your product or service has the greatest advantage. For any given call, however, you must meet an additional criterion; namely, the discovered needs of the particular customer or prospect and the priority of those needs from the customer's or prospect's point of view.

On any given call, you are likely to use a very small portion of your available knowledge. In fact, salespeople often mute call impact because they make too many points and unwittingly furnish customers or prospects with so many ideas that they cannot reach a buying decision. This is particularly true in selling services because the buyer cannot evaluate something physical. The choice of words to describe a service is critical if the buyer is to understand it.

As a practical matter, you often face situations where a customer or a prospect brings up a competitive product's or service's superior points. The best course of action is to reduce the advantage with additional benefits that accrue from your product. This is another reason for having a large repertoire of uses and applications on tap.

Call Management

Call management encompasses the many matters you must attend to before you are face-to-face with prospects, the effective execution of each call plan once you have formulated it, and the critical analysis and evaluation of what you have achieved.

Effectiveness of call planning hinges on the amount and relevance of the information that you have available for consideration. In addition to knowledge of your own and competitors' products, you must know the firm you are calling on: its organizational structure, the nature of its business, its products and services, and the markets it serves. Knowledge about the specific competition that you will meet in the account provides an additional input for effective call planning: who the competitors are, what relationships they have with the customer or prospect, and the strategy and tactics that they are using to command a share of the business. Because of the relatively large number of uncontrolled variables, sound call management requires you to have alternative courses of action in mind to cope with the unforeseen and unexpected. Fortunately, you can maintain much of the data required for effective call management in your computer system.

The two key factors in call execution are *flexibility* and *adjustability*. Once you are face-to-face or on the phone, you must deal with customers or prospects as you find them. You must be prepared to cover what is paramount with the other person. Further, as the call progresses, you may have to discuss points or problems that you did not anticipate in your plan.

Effective call management also includes analysis or evaluation after the face-to-face or on the phone portion of the sale. You identify "lessons learned" for use with this and other accounts. In reality, this phase of call management becomes the first input for planning the next call. You should store pertinent information in your computer for ready use.

Ability to Communicate

The content of the sales message and the manner in which you deliver it markedly influence call input. If the call is to be effective, you must be receiver oriented and, in most instances, must ensure two-way communication. A frequent deterrent is the "sin of the obvious." Because you are so well schooled in your product or service information, you may gloss over details, assuming the customer or prospect has more background for the presentation than in fact he or she does. Similarly, the customer or prospect has made many items of information "second nature" and may assume these are known to you. A related impediment in customer-prospect behavior is a reluctance to admit ignorance. Often prospects will not only fail to signal when they do not understand something but also may even try to cover up their ignorance by affirmative statements or by nodding their heads.

Mere awareness of these two impediments—the sin of the obvious and reluctance to admit ignorance—is likely to help you achieve understandable communication. In addition, however, if your calls are to have impact, you must use language, examples, and illustrations within the background of your experience and the level of sophistication of the customer or prospect. Understandability, however, is not enough. You must achieve interest by relating your presentation to the needs, desires, and interests of the prospect or customer.

You must build a personal stake in the sales message for the person hearing it. In addition, you must achieve believability, possibly by testimony as well as by research findings. Commendatory statements of a pleased customer have tremendous impact. With many customers, there is no substitute for "third party selling." You must, of course, gauge the personality of the customer or prospect before using such testimonials. When the prospect displays traits such as suggestibility, submissiveness, or uncertainty, this approach may be necessary. In contrast, the same strategy may backfire if used with a self-sufficient, highly confident person.

Even though prospects understand your message, and find it interesting and believable, you still need to be persuasive by using both suggestion and reasoning. You must be perceptive enough to know when to use each.

When you have established full attention and interest, reasoning may be the best way to induce a favorable decision. In contrast, if the prospect is under time duress and is paying only limited attention, suggestion may be more effective. The use of each also depends on the trait analysis you have made of the prospect (see Chapter Five, Sections 1 and 2).

Timing and Reinforcing Points

This is primarily a matter of being aware of the customer's perceptual process. If the call is to have impact, your pace of presentation must enable the customer or prospect to understand your points as you make them. Paradoxically, the better prepared you are, the more likely you are to set too fast a pace for the other person's comprehension. You must make points repeatedly until you have some indication that they have been understood. To be effective, you must realize that what counts is not so much what you say or show, but what the customer or prospect hears or sees. Thus, you must reinforce points either by repeating them in many different ways or by presenting them through several senses simultaneously. If your visual aids are so well organized that you can select what you need without losing eye contact with the customer or prospect, you have a powerful way of reinforcing the impact of your call.

People Strategy

The better you understand your prospects, the more likely you will be able to influence them favorably. You have a continuing task of *according uniqueness* to each customer or prospect. The inputs you need for doing this are careful assessments of the traits, motives, and background of the other person. In fact, with each call you make, you should set an objective to know the person called on better after that call. Your conscious awareness of this goal will tend to direct your attention to the unique aspects of the person. In contrast, if you type buyers or are influenced markedly by first impressions, you will, by projection, make erroneous assumptions about the motives of the customer or prospect and are unlikely to make calls with as favorable an impact.

In Chapter Five, we propose a five-step method for coping with personality factors:

1. Identify outstanding traits.
2. Ensure the accuracy of the traits with relevant evidence.
3. Decide what to do or not do for each trait.
4. Note the behavior patterns reflected in trait combinations.
5. Formulate strategy based on Steps 3 and 4.

For handling motivational factors, Chapter Five suggests three steps:

1. Observe the aspects of the physical and social environment that have incentive value for the individual.
2. Infer his or her motives from this observation.
3. Build appropriate incentives into the presentation.

The trait analysis reveals the *manner* you should adopt, and the motivation analysis highlights topics of interest to the buyer—the *matter* of the interview.

Communication Tactics

You have to adjust your strategy to the other person's behavioral consistencies. However, you must be flexible enough to adjust tactically to his or her reactions as you encounter them during face-to-face meetings or telephone conversations. To be a good tactician, you must first be a good strategist. However, the latter does not guarantee the former. As noted earlier, flexibility and adjustability are of critical importance in selling. On every call, your tactical objective is to *be in control without seeming to do so.* You can only accomplish this objective by being sensitive to the nuances of the reactions you observe in the customer or prospect. You must then relate your own adjustive responses (tactics) to those reactions. The keys to tactical control are involuntary reactions (see Chapter Three). If you observe and adjust to these reactions appropriately, you, in effect, lead the customer or prospect without his or her awareness. Adeptness with *negative-involuntary reactions* prevents the occurrence of the more-difficult-to-handle *negative-voluntary reactions.* Similarly, taking advantage of each *positive-involuntary reaction* and reinforcing the point that elicited it make closing the sale come naturally.

Perhaps the single largest block to effective selling tactics is inadequate preparation on the part of salespeople. This prevents them from directing sufficient attention to the customer/prospect to catch each reaction as it occurs. The second important factor in tactical adjustment is the need for salespeople to think tactically. If you do this, you then put the burden on yourself to adjust to the other person rather than taking negative reactions (such as objections) as personal affronts. Specifically, you have to think: "If I handled this differently, then this negative reaction would not have happened. However, now that it has, what is the best way for me to influence this person to react positively?"

Problem Solving and Creative Thinking

The extent to which you can solve problems and provide worthwhile ideas will differentiate your presentation from those made by competing salespeople. To capitalize on these factors, you must be an attentive observer and a discerning questioner. By observation and thorough questioning, you determine what the opportunities are in a particular account and where new ideas are needed. If the customer or prospect perceives potential suppliers and their offerings as equal or nearly so, your solutions and ideas become the value added that sets your proposition apart from the others.

Managing Sales Resistance

Strategic handling of sales resistance hinges on your ability to diagnose the basis for resistance and to react appropriately. The most recurrent form of resistance is a customer's or prospect's objection. Hence, if you are to give your calls maximum impact, you must be adept at handling objections. Chapter Four, Section 2, provides a procedure for handling objections consistent with the need satisfaction method of selling.

Covert resistance most often stems from the other person's reaction to proposed change. Many people fear the new. To cope with this unverbalized resistance, you must understand people's possible reactions to change. The relatively insecure customer or prospect views change as a threat. You must arrange your presentation to minimize the new. In contrast, the more self-confident person views change as a challenge and as a chance to cope with the situation. You challenge this person by stressing the new.

Skill in Inducing Learning

This requires a blend of attitude, knowledge, and skill on your part. If you take the approach that your task is to induce the customer's action, then you must teach him or her the desired response. To accomplish this, you must be a knowledgeable and skillful teacher. You must know how people learn and why they do. Then you must review each call plan from the learning perspective, because in a sense, each call is a lesson to be taught. Customers or prospects remember ideas from those calls in which they learn something worthwhile. Learning principles as they apply to selling are treated in detail in Chapter Eight.

Other Considerations

The 10 factors that have been discussed in this section will improve the productivity of your sales calls. However, there are several other considerations of varying importance, depending on your particular knowledge, skills, and motivation;

the prospect; and the nature of the buying-selling situation. For example, if you are making a call on an account whose volume does not warrant more than one call every three months, you must devise special ways of sustaining the impact of your call until the next visit. You may augment the occasional personal visit with telemarketing or letters, or leave reminder materials with the customer. In this era of fierce cost containment, you must manage your selling system to provide a service level consistent with the commercial worth of the account.

A second situation that often exists is where you know that the prospect is not in a position to buy the product or service at the present time. If you are aware of the nature of forgetting, you realize that the longer the time lapse between your presentation and the decision to purchase, the more you need to reinforce your message and to build in some form of follow-up reminder.

Third, the prospect may be a professional purchasing agent, who listens to presentations during much of his or her working hours. In this case, it is imperative to incorporate into your presentation distinctive sales points that differentiate it from hundreds of others. You must also assume that the prospect is not going to remember everything. Thus, again you need to use some kind of follow-up reminders. For example, recapitulating the essential points of a sales presentation in a follow-up communication is often effective.

The fourth circumstance where problems exist in gaining impact is where the prospect is not the buyer but an influencer of buying decisions. Examples are a building-supplies salesperson making a presentation to an architect or a textbook salesperson detailing a college professor. In these instances, the impact must be such that the individual called on learns and remembers enough to influence someone else to make the actual purchase.

SUMMARY

The selling-buying process operates in an environment of imperfect information. Your starting point, therefore, is to ask: "What makes my products/services valuable to my customers?" As a professional, your strategic managerial objective is to *create profitable differential competitive advantage*—to have customers perceive your offering as different and better. A practical method for determining how customers value your offerings is provided. Your tactical managerial objective is *to manage a set of selling-buying relationships for mutual profit*. Achieving these objectives requires allocating effort both within and among buyers. In addition, selling effort must be allocated defensively where competitive inroads are most likely and offensively where the competition is most vulnerable.

Your strategic communication objective—*to accord uniqueness*—is based on the fundamental idea that each individual responds to the personal touch and abhors being treated as one more number in a queue. In addition to being a strategist, you must be a master tactician.

Prospects and customers respond to persuasion, not coercion. You will most likely achieve the tactical communication objective, *to control the interview without seeming to do so,* if you:

- Prepare carefully for every call.
- Focus attention on the prospect or customer.
- Encourage the prospect to participate actively in the interview.
- Achieve control through persuasion rather than authority.

The foundation of effective selling is professional responsibility based on the achievement of the four cardinal objectives.

Three methods of selling are described. The need satisfaction method is the most valuable for higher level selling and is necessary to achieve your communication objectives. Accordingly, the need satisfaction method is elaborated to the point where you can apply it. Implementation is facilitated by use of the Salesperson-Oriented Product Manual (SOPM) and/or Salesperson-Oriented Service Manual (SOSM) linking the need satisfaction method of selling with in-depth knowledge of your particular products and/or services.

Ten factors can markedly improve your productivity: knowledge of the company's products and services, awareness of the advantages and limitations of competitive products and services, adeptness in call management, ability to communicate effectively, timing and reinforcing of sales points, formulation of people strategy, skill in face-to-face tactics, problem solving and creative thinking ability, strategic handling of sales resistance, and skill in inducing learning. Special considerations were noted depending on the particular salesperson, the prospect, and the nature of the selling-buying situation.

Satisfied customers are your most valuable asset.

TOPICS FOR THOUGHT AND DISCUSSION

1. Review the four cardinal objectives, schedule a meeting with your manager, and make a brief presentation entitled "What the Cardinal Objectives Mean to Me."
2. Choose a client you (or a colleague) are working on and analyze your competitive position. Use Exhibit 1.1 to evaluate Tangible, Intangible, Price, Image, and Team factors. What can you do to improve your position?
3. What differences do you perceive between a Lexus and a Miata? Why do these differences exist?
4. What do buyers consider when deciding whether or not to buy from you?
5. Why should salespeople manage selling-buying relationships?
6. Why is it important to accord uniqueness?
7. What does it mean to be in control without seeming to be?

8. Compare and contrast the roles you would play in the exchange process, operating with both perfect and imperfect information.
9. Why is it important for you to fully understand what is and is not profitable business for your company?
10. Discuss the differences implied in a salesperson-oriented approach compared with a customer-oriented approach.
11. Consider the statement that most sales training is concentrated on the "need fulfillment" phase. Do you agree or disagree? Why?
12. How do you feel about going directly to the close if you, the salesperson, already know the customer's needs?
13. What steps are required to operationalize the need satisfaction method of selling?
14. What factors that impact your productivity would you add to the 10 listed?
15. What value-added ideas have you provided on a recent customer call? Prospect call?
16. How do you sustain impact in accounts that do not justify frequent calls?
17. What are some overall strengths (weaknesses) you have noticed in salespeople you know?
18. What specific steps can you take to improve your productivity?

TWO

The Communication Process in Selling

To say the right thing at the right time,
keep still most of the time.

JOHN W. ROPER

In this chapter:

- **The Nature of Communication**
  — The sales call is a complex two-way communication process that is fundamentally driven by the state of the buyer's mind.
- **Analysis of Human Processes in Communication**
  — You are naive or egotistical to assume that each of your customers perceives, thinks, and feels about your propositions just the way you do.
- **Developing Real-Time Skills**
  — The effective salesperson must be an able conversationalist.
- **Summary**
  — Your firm's entire marketing effort hinges on your ability to communicate in a manner that induces purchase.
- **Topics for Thought and Discussion**
- **Application Exercises**
  — Appendix VI   Factors Influencing Communication
  — Appendix XVI Motivation Analysis—Work Sheet and Checklist

1.   THE NATURE OF COMMUNICATION

You have a critically important role as a communicator for your company in a competitive marketplace. In its total promotional program, your firm employs a customized mix of personal selling, advertising, merchandising, and sales promotion to achieve its strategic objectives. Yet the success of your company's entire marketing effort hinges on your ability to persuade people to buy.

34

Selling: The Critical Communication Assignment

Why is your position so critical to the success of your firm? If marketing is viewed as having three phases—*pretransactional, transactional,* and *posttransactional*—your role as a communicator is important in all three. First, your task is to assist in the cultivation of demand. You bring all the market-cultivating forces to bear in a customized presentation for each customer and prospect. While the strategic objective for the total promotional effort is to create a perception of uniqueness for your firm's products and services as well as its people, your strategic objective is to accord uniqueness to each account and each person in the account. To accomplish your objectives in the pretransactional phase, you must reinforce your persuasive efforts with in-depth knowledge of your firm's advertising, sales promotion, merchandising, and other demand-cultivating forces.

Second, you handle the transactional phase. You induce the purchase. More than anyone else, you are the marketing tactician. You deal with events "now," adjusting to the unforeseen and unexpected. To do this, you must know the extent of the commitment you can make in terms of price, delivery, and service. You may lead a team or coordinate the efforts of other personnel to assist in this phase, but you are responsible for obtaining the order.

Third, in the posttransactional phase, you might also play an important communication role by following through to see that each customer derives satisfaction from purchasing your offering. Part of your job may be to provide certain services, for example, assisting with the start-up of the equipment, helping display merchandise, guiding the promotional effort of the wholesaler or retailer with respect to your product line, or instructing customers' personnel in the use of the product. If other company personnel are designated to provide such posttransactional service, you still must see that they handle the services to each customer's satisfaction. Even when everything is in order, this follow-through is bound to increase the customer's satisfaction. Only when you assume such responsibility can you sustain a selling-buying relationship.

Your success in each of the three transactional phases rests squarely on your competence as a professional communicator. You must be able to personalize and

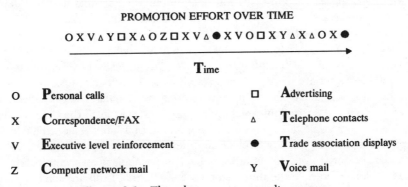

Figure 2.1 The salesperson as a media manager.

dramatize the benefits of your offering to the individual customer. You must be able to make effective presentations to groups such as buying committees or the field forces of resellers. In communicating effectively, you are really a media manager. You have to select the mix of media most appropriate for your purposes. The challenge is to combine personal calls, telephone calls, voice mail messages, computer network mail, fax, correspondence, executive level reinforcement, advertising, and trade show displays to achieve maximum impact on your buyer's conscious awareness (Figure 2.1). Finally, as a professional communicator, you integrate your activities with the other elements in the firm's promotional program to ensure maximum productivity of the total marketing effort.

Communication Objectives

Every salesperson—industrial, consumer, wholesale, retail, and service—shares with every other salesperson two cardinal communication objectives. The strategic objective is to *accord uniqueness*. Because each prospect has different needs, problems, and perceptions, as a successful salesperson you must vary your presentation from one call to the next. Each prospect and customer seeks individuality. Therefore, if you customize the benefits of your offering to the needs of the individual customer, you exert influence. The tactical objective is *to be in control without seeming to do so;* you must be able to size up buyers and be willing to adjust to them. Adoption of the cardinal objectives has important implications for you as a professional communicator.

To be most effective, you must exercise considerable control over your communication behavior. Normal or instinctive communication behavior frequently results in poor strategy and tactics.

The natural inclination for a person with an audience is to talk. This is dangerous for you. The outcome of the interview is in large part determined by your ability to get the buyer to see the proposition in a favorable light. This means that you must discover and point out a relationship between the sales points of your product or service and the buyer's needs. This, in turn, calls for skillful questioning to learn enough about the buyer's knowledge and attitudes to establish this relationship. You can acquire this information only by listening, not by talking.

Most people assume that other people's values are similar, if not identical, to their own. The psychological term for this is *projection;* it can be fatal to your success. You should tease out the buyer's values so that your recommendations will make sense and instill confidence. A buyer will have scant confidence in recommendations that are not based on an analysis of his or her needs.

You must note and evaluate the buyer's every word and action so that you not only bring out the desired information but also note cues as to the times of closing. Many salespeople talk themselves into and out of a sale because they do not stop when the buyer is ready to place an order.

To be effective, you do not talk at a pace or vocabulary level comfortable to yourself alone. You note the impression (or lack thereof) you are achieving and adjust your vocabulary and rate of speech to the buyer. In this way, you can avoid either talking down to or over the head of your listener.

If you are to achieve your firm's cardinal objectives, you must be sufficiently mature and self-controlled to put the buyer's interest ahead of your own. This is the principle of indirectness. To achieve your own objectives, you must satisfy the buyer's needs first. If you attempt to satisfy your own needs first—to make a sale—you will fail.

Failure to pursue and achieve the cardinal communication objectives results in your ignoring the different perceptions and problems of each prospect and customer. If you cannot or will not vary your presentation from one call to the next, you are in effect an animated advertising medium rather than an effective salesperson. The cost of keeping you on the job is too high to warrant your use as a substitute for advertising. Moreover, your company loses the capability to adjust and individualize its offering to each buyer.

Most of the firm's promotional forces—advertising, merchandising, sales promotion—are *mass* and *one-way* communication. Effective selling, however, is *individual* and *two-way*. Hence, you have a unique opportunity to determine the effectiveness of your communication as you proceed with the interview, and to adjust your presentation accordingly.

The interpersonal communication net is complex but provides a framework for understanding seller-buyer communication as well as for improving your effectiveness as a professional communicator, as shown in Figure 2.2. You, the salesperson, represent the sender; and the buyer is the receiver. You have two major activities to perform: *signal sending*, the transmitting of messages to your buyer, and *monitoring*, analyzing and deciding how to act on feedback from the buyer and the situation. Similarly, the buyer is *monitoring* signals from you and *sending feedback*, that is, returning information to you. Each participant, as long as the interaction lasts, is sending as well as monitoring. Indeed, inputs serve to prompt the next transmission.

Monitoring consists of two important activities: *understanding* and *selecting*. Understanding is a measure of the quantity and quality of the information you (or the buyer) have available for decision making. By asking yourself "What do I see, hear, and feel?" you identify what you consciously know about the buyer. The next step, *selecting*, is to choose an appropriate response by answering the question "What will I do and say next?"

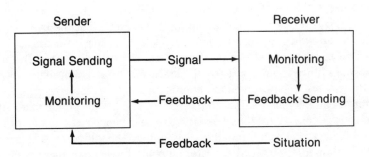

Figure 2.2 Salesperson-buyer communication.

Sending is your (or the buyer's) transmission of a signal (or feedback) to express a meaning. Sending the signals you wish to emit requires attention to both the verbal and nonverbal components of the message. While most people are generally more concerned with *what* they say rather than with *how* they say it, recent research suggests you should do just the opposite. According to several studies by Dr. Albert Mehrabian, of the University of California at Los Angeles, only 7 percent of the feeling communicated in a spoken message is conveyed by the words alone. Thirty-eight percent comes from *how* we speak, and the remaining 55 percent is conveyed nonverbally. Tempo, poise, appearance, diction, and mannerisms may be more important in creating an effective signal than the words you select. When you use the telephone, you do not have the luxury of using nonverbal signals; therefore, you must rely on *how* you speak. To achieve your communication objectives, you must be in control of both what you verbalize and how you transmit the message. All your communication behavior should serve the purpose of contributing to your objective, or you should not use it.

Feedback encompasses the content and the manner of the buyer's responses and also includes the information inherent in the setting in which the responses are made. In conveying meaning, manner cues may be as important as or more important than the actual content of the message. Consider, for example, the significance of hesitation, spontaneity, and intensity as characteristics of an incoming signal.

Noise is technically the discrepancy between the signal transmitted and the message received. Obviously, as your communication with the buyer proceeds, discrepancies will occur between what one person means to convey and what the other person understands. Noise typically clears up as a result of continued interpersonal interchange, especially through questions and answers.

Situation is the environment in which communication occurs and can be an important source of feedback for you for several reasons. First, the circumstances in which the buyer is willing to meet you might reflect the importance the buyer attaches to the communication. The buyer who desires to meet in a conference room or away from the regular interruptions of the office environment may be indicating greater interest than the buyer who prefers to meet in the office, where he or she can take incoming calls. The work environment might also furnish you with insights helpful in sizing up the buyer.

This conceptualization of seller-buyer communication underscores two key points. First, to be an effective communicator, you must be more than an accomplished signal sender. Second, you must recognize that the more adept you become at attending to incoming feedback and basing your subsequent responses on it, the more effective you will be as a communicator. In fact, it is your responsibility to interpret the feedback you receive and make any necessary adjustments to ensure you are communicating successfully.

Our research found that the more effective salespeople obtain more information or cues per encounter than less effective salespeople. The number of *verbal* cues received per encounter failed to differentiate the salespeople. However, the effective salespeople obtained a greater number of *nonverbal* cues per encounter than did the less effective salespeople.

What do these findings signify? First, your effectiveness in the face-to-face encounter hinges on placing full attention on the prospect. You can do this only if you are well prepared. Second, the prospect or customer's nuances might convey more than their actual spoken words. Seasoned salespeople focus on the total situation while their less sophisticated counterparts attend selectively to the verbal aspect of the situation and ignore the manner cues.

These findings seem to validate the proposition that the cues that allow you to maintain subtle control in the interview are the ones the prospect is unaware of providing. Most nonverbal cues or reactions fall into this category.

Also, as the sale progresses, more effective salespeople accumulate more cues than do less effective salespeople. This provides empirical confirmation of the frequently given advice to focus on the prospect. The more effective salespeople appear to be better able to do this than their less effective counterparts.

Finally and significantly, the more effective salespeople tend to build a consistent account strategy on the basis of the trends they observe in the cues they have received. In contrast, less effective salespeople tend to treat each incident in isolation and thus do not evolve a plan of attack. Or put in another way, the more effective salespeople appear to be both strategists and tacticians. They plan their moves, refine their plans, and adjust their strategy on a continuing basis as a result of the cues they obtain. Less effective salespeople adjust on a tactical cue-to-cue basis and do not form an overall strategy.

For effective need satisfaction selling, you must master the Seller-Buyer Model of Communication. One of its most important uses is as a diagnostic tool for improving your sales results. As a professional salesperson, you should be continuously asking the following questions:

1. How well do I *monitor* feedback?
2. How can I *understand* more of the feedback I am given?
3. How can I *develop* my skill in decoding nonverbal feedback?
4. How well am I *selecting* my responses?
5. What can I do to polish my *signal sending*?

If you are a professional salesperson, you undoubtedly would like to develop yourself. To do this, you must analyze your communication behavior in terms of each component of the model and plan an improvement program. Perhaps that is why you are reading this book.

One-way communication, illustrated by the stimulus-response and selling formula methods of selling, is salesperson oriented. Two-way communication, associated with the need satisfaction theory of selling, is customer oriented. The essence of the difference between one-way and two-way communication is that one-way is sender oriented and does not require or depend on feedback from the receiver. By contrast, two-way communication provides the necessary feedback to customize presentations. Use two-way communication to gain a considerable advantage in most instances. Need satisfaction and two-way communication are practically synonymous.

Advantages of Two-Way Communication

Perhaps the most important advantage of two-way communication is its *receiver-oriented feedback*. Without such feedback, you may make an infinite number of claims without knowing what effect you are having on the prospect. Not only do you waste time and energy, you may also irritate the prospect. While you are congratulating yourself on your verbal facility and thinking how superior you are to the prospect, you could be actually causing that person to dislike you.

Feedback also increases the *accuracy* of communication. You can achieve accuracy by varying the content, detail, and style of your message based on the prospect's reactions. Ideally, the discussion of a particular point continues until the message transmitted and the message received coincide. With strictly one-way communication, the sender never knows when or if this has occurred.

In two-way communication, prospects are stimulated to talk at length and are encouraged to state opinions on a variety of topics related to their needs and experiences. Through the salesperson's adroit questioning, prospects might relate his or her proposition to their own situations. Under some conditions, prospects may be encouraged to talk about their personal interests to establish better rapport before making the presentation.

An important psychological principle is at work here. Conviction and belief are, for the most part, self-induced. Through participation, prospects convince themselves of the value of your proposition. Figure 2.3 depicts this process.

You can safely assume that most prospects would rather talk about their own needs than listen to you talk about your offering. Hence, the participation of prospects in the discussion tends to inflate their egos. This, in turn, makes them favorably disposed as well as inclined to listen to you.

In one-way communication, you make one sales point after another and, at some stage of the presentation, ask for an order. Implicit in the approach is a very dangerous assumption that the prospect will grasp the sales points after hearing them a single time. Having learned your presentation thoroughly over a period of time, you might forget that the prospect could be hearing it for the first time. If you recall your early experiences with the product or service, you will realize the difficulties facing the customer in attempting to follow the presentation. A much

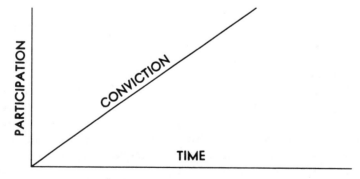

Figure 2.3   Prospect's conviction is based on participation and time.

safer assumption is that the prospect will need to have each point repeated several times before the achievement of communication (understanding). This calls for *repetition*, which you can accomplish through two different methods when using two-way communication.

You achieve repetition if you and the prospect make the same point. You make the point and then ask appropriate questions to induce feedback from the prospect. When the prospect shows an understanding of the point, you can safely move to the next one.

Often, however, when you make a point, you receive feedback indicating a difference in the prospect's understanding. When this happens, you must repeat your original position with a slight change either to move closer to the position of the prospect or to bridge the difference. You should take the first alternative if it does not weaken your basic position. The second approach is useful to lessen the discrepancy between the message sent and the message received. Several exchanges might be necessary to bring the two points of view into agreement, and in the process, you will repeat the basic point over and over. Repetition is important in obtaining agreement and ensuring retention of the ideas.

Looking ahead, in Chapter Eight we will view the exchange between the seller and the buyer as a learning process. Repetition is fundamental to basic learning. Hence, if a prospect is going to learn to buy your products or services, repetition is essential.

The mechanism of projection is the tendency to substitute your own ideas of the prospect's needs for that envisioned by the prospect. This is a serious tactical error. Two-way communication automatically *lessens the tendency toward projection* by focusing your attention on developing the customer's needs.

Timing is the rate at which the prospect can understand sales points. The basic objective is to *avoid going on to the second point until the prospect has fully grasped the first point*. The feedback in two-way communication reveals very clearly the pace to set and the point at which you can safely introduce a new reason for buying.

Two-way communication *provides intervals during which you can devote your full attention to observing and listening*. This enables you to catch cues and nuances of meaning you might miss if you were talking. These signals are vitally important in sizing up buyers.

We have long advocated the use of low pressure in selling. You achieve it, in large part, when you *cause the prospect to voice the desired action*. Two-way communication is far more likely to accomplish this objective than is one-way communication. In one-way communication, the prospect remains relatively passive; in two-way communication, the prospect has an opportunity to actively participate. When both prospect and salesperson participate significantly, the interview often becomes a joint problem-solving process to fulfill the customer's needs.

Dangers in Two-Way Communication

As a communicator you must be aware of certain dangers to avoid dissipating the many advantages of two-way communication. The interchange with the prospect may become so interesting that you invest an undue amount of time, preventing you from making your other calls. Also, you can easily be diverted from the business at hand and spend an excessive amount of time on irrelevant matters. Generally speaking, the prospect who is eager to converse endlessly about extraneous topics is unlikely to have much commercial potential. You may be talking to the wrong person. However, assuming the person does have the authority to buy, the prospect who talks endlessly or on irrelevant topics presents a technical challenge that you must overcome before you can discover needs. If you cannot "control" the interview, however, the prospect's potential profitability goes down as the time consumed goes up. At the other extreme, you must avoid being so businesslike and hurried that rapport is lost. Often the prospect sets time restrictions for the call, and you must gauge progress to ensure that you have sufficient time to successfully close the call. This can prove difficult when the prospect is very interested and participates fully. You can determine the amount of irrelevant discussion that is warranted by an analysis of personality traits (see Chapter Five) and the commercial value of the prospect.

When to Use One-Way Communication

Although the advantages of two-way communication are persuasive, there are occasional opportunities to use one-way communication without reducing sales effectiveness. One-way communication may be appropriate in two instances.

First, one-way communication is feasible when the message you are communicating is brief and simple, and the prospect is highly interested and therefore motivated to attend carefully. Under these conditions, you need not belabor the point by repeating it. Also, eliminating repetition and direct participation by the prospect saves time. To be effective, however, this approach requires the receiver's simulated participation. You can achieve this by using rhetorical questions and inserting such phrases as "in your business," "as you know," and so on. Although one-way communication might be quicker than two-way communication, remember that substituting speed for accuracy seldom represents good judgment.

The second instance where one-way communication might occur is when salespeople are not fully knowledgeable about their products and/or lack the capacity to deal with the give and take of a real analysis of the prospect's situation. (We are not recommending one-way communication as a substitute for competence. However, this kind of situation sometimes exists as a psychological reality, and the cause of good selling cannot be advanced by ignoring the facts.) Salespeople who monopolize the conversation may think they are less likely to reveal weaknesses and errors in their understanding of the relationship between the benefits of their products or services and the prospect's needs. However, salespeople should realize that monopolizing a conversation is a sign of weakness rather than of strength. In addition to revealing inadequacy to a competent prospect, such salespeople appear egotistical, overbearing, and generally unpleasant. Master the details of a product or service and develop the skill necessary to have prospects sell themselves by communicating their knowledge and feelings.

Difficulties in Communication

To list all the possible difficulties that a salesperson might encounter in trying to communicate is not feasible. The following, however, are some of the more common difficulties, together with suggestions for minimizing them.

- *Low Interest Level by Prospects.* The best assumption to make about prospects' interest is that they are satisfied with things as they are. Their needs are in a state of homeostasis. Chapter Three, Section 1, provides an in-depth analysis of this problem. If this situation exists, you will encounter passive resistance. Prospects will refuse to consider your proposition seriously and will give evasive answers to questions designed to reveal their needs. Under such conditions, true communication is not likely to occur. You will necessarily have to disturb the prospects' complacency by designing questions to develop a realization that the status quo is not necessarily the best solution to the problem.

  Actually, the interest level of some prospects might be so low that they do not listen to you. While you are talking, they remain quiet but think of what they will say when you stop long enough to give them an opportunity. Salespeople who are naive and egotistical enough to feel that such prospects are listening to them will be shocked to discover that they have wasted most of their efforts. This will be revealed by the irrelevance of the prospect's next statement. Drawing such prospects into the conversation is a good way to maintain interest.

- *Poor Attention by Prospects.* Even though prospects appear interested in discussing a proposition, they might not attend carefully enough to catch the intended meaning in your statements. Poor attention may be due to the prospects' poor habits or to distracting elements in the environment. Still another factor is attention focused on a task left incomplete when you began the interview. Whatever the cause, you should frequently ask questions or make statements that will reveal whether your meaning is being received. If the prospect does not understand your meaning, you should restate the gist of your message. In an extreme case you might choose to call again at a more opportune time.

- *Poor Memory Shown by Prospects.* Prospects may attend closely to each sales point as you make it but not assimilate the complete presentation. This suggests poor memory and might be due to low intelligence. This situation calls for frequent reviews and summaries of the main points in the presentation. Such action is necessary to ensure that prospects acquire enough of your presentation to be comfortable buying your product or service.

- *Limited Knowledge of the Proposition by Prospects.* Superficially, this would not appear to be a problem because all that seems to be required is that you give more details and more background knowledge than usual. However, when prospects are loath to betray their ignorance, they attempt to conceal their lack of understanding and so fail to grasp what you are saying. The way to overcome this difficulty is much the same as for poor attention: You must ask frequent questions. From the answers you receive, you can gauge the extent of understanding of the information you have presented. When you notice that the limited knowledge of prospects is retarding communication, you can then supply the necessary information.

- *Low Verbal Facility.* This difficulty has two facets. One is limited vocabulary, which may be general or peculiar to the technical body of knowledge related to the product or service. The other is semantic—an individual interpretation of word meaning. People tend to develop private meanings for words and to assume these meanings in their conversation. When two parties attach different meanings to words, difficulty in understanding arises. You should suspect that the difficulty lies in a definition of terms whenever you sense misunderstanding by a prospect on a sales point where logic indicates there should be complete agreement. You should ask the prospect to define the term and then accept the prospect's definition for purposes of the discussion. You cannot ask the prospect to accept your definitions, even though they might be the commonly accepted ones. Where the difficulty is a limited vocabulary, rather than misunderstanding, you should state your message in the simplest possible terms and thereby save the prospect from embarrassment that might otherwise occur. Here alternative media—demonstrations, site visits, and visual aids (including samples)—might prove invaluable.

- *Different Goals.* Assuming that prospects are striving to evaluate all products and/or services objectively and to purchase the ones that best meet their needs would be heartening. But, the more tenable assumption is that a discrepancy might exist between the prospect's goals and your own. Your task is to so communicate that the purchase of your products or services will meet the prospect's goals. You may find it profitable to remind yourself that your goals include learning enough about the prospect's needs to enable you to match the sales points of your proposal with those needs. When you have done this, the customer will find it difficult to resist entering into a discussion.

  The psychological mechanism of projection may also enter into this situation: You may try to present the benefits that would fill your own needs if you were the prospect rather than describe the benefits that suit the prospect's needs (Section 2 explores this topic more fully).

- *Physical Obstacles.* Effective communication faces many physical barriers: factory noise, poor seating facilities, other persons present, and other factors in the environment. As these are physical causes, the obvious remedy is to change the environment or to seek a more appropriate place for the interview. Conducting sales interviews over lunch or elsewhere to eliminate these problems may be necessary.

  Good communication does not come naturally. It must be planned. The natural reaction to other people is to tell them something if they are not talking or, if they are talking, to think what you will say as soon as they stop. On the other hand, effective communication requires that you find a way to cause prospects to generate interest and to attend closely. You must give up your private ideas, preferences, and word meanings, and concentrate on presenting your message within the prospect's frame of reference. This requires a high degree of emotional maturity and considerable practice.

2. ANALYSIS OF HUMAN PROCESSES IN COMMUNICATION

Buyers, during their waking hours, are engaged in three interactive human processes: *perceiving, thinking,* and *feeling* (Figure 2.4). To communicate effectively, you must understand the characteristics of each of these processes. You aspire to have your offering *perceived, thought,* and *felt to be different and better* from the *buyer's standpoint.* To gain this competitive advantage you must appreciate how your individual prospects and customers react to you, your company, and your products or services as well as to your competitors' offerings. You can then use these insights to customize the communication of your offering to fit your buyer's basic human processes. You should not consider the three processes singly. Human beings react as total organisms. However, separate treatment facilitates understanding of each process and its key characteristics, which must be considered to achieve high fidelity communication and favorable purchase decisions (see Appendix VI).

Psychology of Perceiving

Every general psychology textbook devotes one or more chapters to sensation and perception. Sensation designates the awareness of a stimulus object;

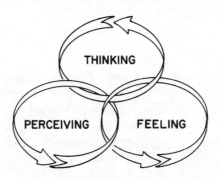

Figure 2.4 Three basic interactive human processes.

perception, the interpretation of the sensation. The sensation actually consists of nerve impulses carried from the receptor organs to the central nervous system. A person notes an object through the visual sense because light waves from that object have set up nerve impulses that travel over the optic nerve and reach the brain. Other senses work in a similar manner.

Perception is the process of attaching meanings to stimuli received through the various senses. To appreciate the complexity of communication, you must be aware of four characteristics of the perceptual process. First, perception is *subjective*. No two persons perceive the same event, object, signal, or other person in the same way. Thus, you, as the signal sender, may have one meaning in mind when you say, "a high-quality product." The buyer, as receiver, might attach another quite different meaning. Perhaps you had in mind the long life of the product even under repeated use in adverse circumstances. The prospect, on the other hand, might convert the incoming signal to a message implying high price. The reason for the subjectivity derives from the differences in background and experience of the two individuals. Truly, how an individual perceives a present event depends greatly on the past events in his or her life.

Salespeople commonly assume that a prospect will buy their products or services for the same reasons they would purchase if they were the prospect. As pointed out previously, this tendency is called *projection* because you may project your own perception onto the buyer. This can be a fatal step. As a result of projection, you open the sales presentation with sales points you find interesting yourself instead of using the opening to discover the prospect's needs. If you do not discover the sales points that interest your prospect in the early stages of the interview, he or she is unlikely to pay serious attention to the presentation. Even though the prospect permits you to make your presentation, if you do not bring out those critical sales points, your chances of making a sale are very slim.

Rather than assuming that your initial perception of the customer's or prospect's needs is accurate, you should take the time and trouble to determine how prospects perceive their own needs so that your sales communication can stress points relating to the buyer's perceptual background and psychological adjustment. Second, even if you make appropriate sales points, perception is *selective*. Of the many signals impinging on the senses, relatively few are converted into messages reaching the buyer's conscious awareness. In addition, an individual buyer's comprehension will vary with the complexity of the sales points or ideas presented.

In most cases, you know significantly more about your product than does the buyer; therefore, the danger is that you will ignore the buyer's selective capacity and present more ideas or more complex ideas per unit of time than the buyer can assimilate. You should choose only a fraction of your total product knowledge for use in any particular presentation. This has several benefits. The buyer will be more receptive to your message because he or she can better understand your signals sent at a comfortable rate. At the extreme, it is psychologically painful to be inundated with signals received at a rate too fast for comprehension. Also, you will be a more effective communicator because you will have to use feedback to determine what the prospect has selectively perceived before you decide which sales points you will send to relate your product or service to the buyer's needs and background. You must remember that just because you stated a particular sales point, you cannot be sure that the prospect received and understood it in the way you intended. This is why you must be alert to feedback.

Third, perception is *summative*. Reception of your message often depends on the cumulative effect of repeating the signal. A person might not receive your signal the first time you send it. Almost everyone has had the experience of being alone at home and suddenly becoming aware that the telephone has rung three times. What happened to the first two rings? Initially the ringing was sensed, but only after several rings was it perceived. Further, when you transmit the message to two or more of the receiver's senses, it enhances the likelihood that the customer will receive your message. That is why you use visual aids, samples, demonstrations, and mock-ups to reinforce your oral presentation. Chapter Three, Section 2, covers this topic in depth.

Fourth, perception is influenced by *present needs and experience*. For example, assume an object is round, red, and about three inches in diameter. Different people could receive the same sensations, but they would not necessarily react in the same way. The interpretation of the sensations governing their reactions is their perception. Perception is the result of combining sensations with experience and current needs. To the extent that customers' experience and needs differ, they will differ in their perceptions of your product or service, even though they are basing those perceptions on identical sensations.

Returning to the round, red object, a 10-year-old might perceive it as a ball and think about starting a game with friends. The child's mother sees the ball as one more object to pick up because if someone should step on it, a serious injury might result. Her need is to keep the home free from hazards. The youngster's father, seeing the round, red object, might fear that he would have to pay for replacing a broken window. His need is to conserve cash. Thus, different needs bring about different perceptions of the same object.

Experience has a similar effect on perception. Visualize a building site on which a sign announces a new Wal-Mart opening in six months. Shoppers might welcome a new retail source, engineers would observe the type of construction, and the police would think about future traffic congestion. Thus, experience, as well as needs, can alter the interpretation of identical sensations.

When you reflect on the preceding principles, you will realize that making presentations to customers is a complex matter. Although you can treat it as a simple process by assuming that customers perceive your presentation the same way you do, such an approach is outmoded.

A person's perceptions are highly subjective and are influenced by experience and needs. The focus here is on the effect of needs, both immediate and long range. Therefore, the first step in making a sales presentation is to discover the customer's needs. When you know them, you can present your product or service in terms of filling those needs.

Experience, an important factor in perception, does not require extensive treatment. The way to understand the effect of experience on perception is to learn as much as possible about your customers' background. Normally, you will accumulate a large amount of such information directly from customers and prospects as well as indirectly from nonbusiness contacts. For example, common occupations are widely understood, so when you know that a person has been a carpenter, a basketball player, or a salesperson, you may know how that person would likely perceive a situation.

Whenever customers have specialized experience that allows them to appreciate certain product features, you should cover those points thoroughly.

Psychology of Thinking

Thinking is a process influencing the interpretation of a message. A thought combines elements from the past with elements in the present. The elements from the past emerge into consciousness from *memory*; those in the present come mainly from *perception*. As a communicator, you can have far more control over the prospect's present than past. Yet the more you know about the prospect's experiences or background, the better able you will be to send relevant signals. This is why effective salespeople learn as much as they can about the background of each buyer they must influence. To achieve effective communication, you must understand four characteristics of the thought process.

First, *memory*, like perception, is subjective and selective. Every buyer has countless experiences stored in memory, yet only a few of these ever emerge into consciousness. Further, when people recall ideas or experiences, they tend to be simplified compared with the original inputs. Also, in retrospect, pleasant happenings become more pleasant. Most of the unpleasant ones are, fortunately, forgotten. A common example is our inability to remember the name of someone distasteful at a previous meeting. For you, as a communicator, these dimensions of memory have several important implications.

- If you are to send relevant signals to your buyers, you must determine what knowledge the buyers have available for use. You must be aware that the recollection of previously perceived knowledge might be incomplete or distorted.
- If your message is to remain in the buyer's conscious awareness at the time he or she makes a purchase decision, it must be designed to overcome the ravages of forgetting. For example, to achieve a competitive edge in introducing a new product, you might remind your customers of the exciting and profitable experience associated with previous successful innovations.
- When you plan your next call on a customer, you must also gauge how much of the information transmitted during the previous call will be retained and available in the next interview.

Second, thinking involves *logical reasoning*. In logical thinking, the mind often takes one of two paths. Either the present thought in conjunction with other similar past thoughts leads to a generalization (*induction*), or the present thought is interpreted in terms of a previous generalization (*deduction*).

Inductive reasoning, then, requires systematically considering all aspects of the situation before drawing a general conclusion from the specific facts. You might, for example, investigate a large number of important issues before deciding on the best general solution to your buyer's problem. Hence, by observing a series of specific instances, you may be able to find a relevant statement or common denominator that solves a problem. However, the jump to a generalization might be based on too few particular instances. The person who says, "All Indians walk in single file, especially the one I saw" illustrates this pitfall. You need to keep an open mind to revise concepts as new evidence occurs.

Deductive reasoning, on the other hand, depends on previous generalizations. You can use such generalizations, developed through inductive reasoning, to solve other problems of a similar nature. In using deductive reasoning, you relate a present problem to generalizations based on experience. If human beings were unable to reason deductively, they would be unable to follow rules and principles (see Figure 2.5).

Sometimes in deductive reasoning, a person applies an inappropriate generalization to a particular incident. A recurrent example of this occurs in selling when the salesperson takes a customer's objection literally, missing the manner cues that would have indicated the prospect was stalling.

Mastery of logical reasoning is important to you in several ways. First, buyers vary in the degree to which they employ deductive and inductive reasoning as well as in their ability to reason about things and people. While some buyers are "thing" centered, others are "people" oriented. Similarly, one buyer might reason inductively most of the time, while another reasons deductively. As a professional communicator, you are vitally concerned about the quality of the message the buyer receives. One way to reduce the noise in the transmission is to determine how the buyer thinks and to structure the message to fit the buyer's reasoning. You may unwittingly reduce the effectiveness of your communication if you assume, "the buyer thinks the way I do." Second, any particular buyer may combine deductive and inductive thinking. Therefore, you should be alert to the situations in which the buyer uses a particular method of reasoning so that you can adjust the content of your presentations to fit the buyer's thought processes.

Third, thinking has an important property called *reification*. This term, from the Latin words *res* and *facio*, which mean "thing" and "make," literally means "to make things out of." The mind abhors abstractions. It operates much like a camcorder, translating each incoming abstract word into a concrete image, usually from previous experience. For example, the word *purity* might be converted into soap, virgin, white, water, and so on. If you use the expression "quality product," one buyer might think you mean "high priced"; another, "well designed"; and still another, "overengineered for the application." This is

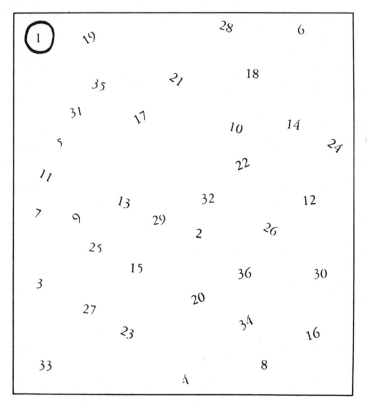

Figure 2.5 Reasoning experiment. *Instructions:* Start at the circled number 1 in the upper left corner and draw a line connecting it to the number 2; continue joining the consecutive numbers until all 36 numbers have been linked. As you start, be sure to note the time. Also record the time when you finish, and compute the time required to complete the task.

Start: ___ Finish: ___ Elapsed Time: ___. Now turn to Figure 2.6 on page 52.

why you should avoid abstract terms in the sales interview and use concrete, image-provoking language. Examples and comparisons abound in an effective presentation. When you cannot avoid an abstract term, you might want to define or illustrate it to avoid misunderstanding. The task is to paint the intended thought or idea on the mind of the buyer.

How Perceiving and Thinking Interact to Form Concepts

To further understand the nature of thoughts and ideas, consider how the mind accumulates information. Some research evidence shows that even before a child's birth, the surrounding environment impinges on the senses. At birth and thereafter, the infinitely more complex and varied environment imposes thousands of stimuli that each person senses every moment of life. Relatively few of these reach conscious awareness and have meaning attached. When this meaning does take place, *perception* has been added to *sensation*. As the person perceives similar stimuli, a generalization occurs and a *concept* is formed. Memory can be thought of as a computer—the concept being visualized is one of the files; the perceptions, past and present, are inputs to that file. However, memory is not fixed or static. Through a combination of inductive and deductive thought processes, the concepts are continually being refined and changed, and new concepts are being formed.

The more varied and diverse a person's experiences, the broader his or her perception is likely to be. The more experiences recur, the more refined and accurate concepts are likely to be. These two statements suggest several strategies for salespeople who wish to become effective communicators and to develop skill in solving problems and thinking creatively.

First, be attentive to and observant of not only prospects and customers but also the surrounding environment. Thoughtful answers to questions such as "What do I see, hear, and feel?" as well as "What should I do and say next?" provide you with the direction you need to send a buyer meaningful messages. In addition, questions such as "What does this mean to me?" "How can I use that?" "What principle applies?" should be in your mind on and off the job.

Second, periodically review your selling efforts with particular buyers and seek to identify what is effective and what is not. For example, your review of rejoinders to an objection will lead to useful generalizations that you can then follow when you next encounter the objection.

Third, refine your salesperson-oriented product/service manual from time to time (explained in depth in Chapter One, Section 2). On the one hand, the buyer's needs change over time for a variety of reasons. On the other hand, acquire a clearer picture of your product or service as you work with it and apply it to an increasing number of customer requirements.

Thinking is a complex process, and it is not always orderly, logical, or direct. Perception, which furnishes one of the inputs, is subjective and selective. What is seen or heard may be misperceived. Our thoughts might not include the whole picture. Omission of inputs can occur. The feeling state or mood of a person can markedly influence his or her thinking and perception.

Psychology of Feeling

The feeling or emotional state of individuals is a manifestation of their temperament, stemming from genetic makeup or body chemistry as well as the environment. Feelings influence markedly how individuals perceive and think. Salespeople, by the manner in which they conduct themselves, become important determiners of customers' feeling states. In the first few seconds of the interview, you must gauge the mood of the other person and adjust your own behavior accordingly. Four characteristics of feelings are especially important in achieving effective communication.

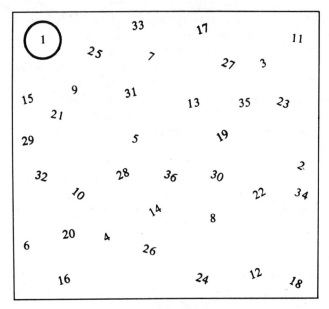

Figure 2.6 Reasoning experiment continued. After completing Figure 2.5 you will probably have noted that all the odd numbers are on the left and all the even numbers are on the right. This generalized conclusion, drawn from the specific facts, may be considered an example of *inductive* reasoning, which can be applied to the solution of Figure 2.6. Although the numbers in Figure 2.6 are arranged alternately on upper and lower areas of the page, the experience with Figure 2.5 will soon come into play— an example of *deductive* reasoning. Normally, Figure 2.6 will be solved more quickly than Figure 2.5 as a result of the previous experience. Repeat the experiment you have just completed, joining the consecutive numbers, starting with number 1, and keep a check on the time it takes you to complete this experiment.

Start: ___ Finish: ___ Elapsed Time: ___

First, feelings have an *inertial* effect. A feeling response, once aroused, lasts a long time. You often confront either favorable or unfavorable feelings toward you, your company, or your products and/or services—feelings that can date back to long before you began calling on the particular customer or prospect. When customers have an unpleasant experience with a product, they forget the prior pleasant experiences but remember the unfortunate one and often vow never to buy the product again. Often individuals are upset even though they can no longer remember what originally upset them. Every parent has observed this in the young child who continues to cry long after he or she has forgotten what caused the crying in the first place. In physics, we learn that a physical body continues in its state of uniform motion until it encounters opposing forces. A similar statement appears to be true for emotional and feeling responses.

Second, feeling responses *expand* and *radiate* to aspects of the environment other than the stimuli that elicited them; they become displaced. Often a prospect's feelings toward a salesperson or the salesperson's products bear no causal relationship. The upset could have been initiated by a competitor or even a family argument. For example, a purchasing executive who has just had an unpleasant altercation might take out upset feelings on the next salesperson who enters the office. Similarly, when something makes a person happy, the happiness extends to other people without regard to causal relationships. This combination of *inertia* and *expansion* is referred to as a person's *mood* or feeling state. A mood is a pervasive, sustained feeling state. Often you will direct a significant part of your promotional effort toward creating a favorable mood in your prospects and customers. Favorable feelings bias perception in a positive direction.

The importance of mood in industrial purchasing decisions is confirmed by recent research indicating the single most important reason for selecting a supplier is that the buyer has used the source before. Japanese manufacturers are famous or infamous (depending on whether or not you are on the approved list of suppliers), for building long-term relationships with suppliers. Similarly, in service industries, leaders typically experience repurchase rates ranging from 75 to 85 percent. When commercial relationships are mutually rewarding and constantly improving, little incentive to change exists. In contrast, upset feelings can cause negative perceptions, which block and distort the thought process.

Third, feelings are subject to *catharsis* and *reinforcement*. Catharsis refers to the fact that the *intensity* of negative feeling responses *shrinks* in the telling. It is wise to allow upset people ample opportunity to describe their disturbances. Salespeople who apply this principle are far more tolerant of the explosive complaints they encounter when their products or services do not measure up to the buyer's expectations. Let upset individuals verbalize what is bothering them. Salespeople should also expeditiously handle complaints received. Feelings become more intense when there are no opportunities to vent them. Remember, "Every big problem was little once!"

Verbalization of positive feelings *reinforces* them. This also has implications for you. When pleased customers spread the word about you and your offering, their own feelings become more favorable in the telling.

Fourth, words and phrases often have *emotional* significance beyond their normal meaning. For example, you might elicit an emotional reaction with the word "homemade" strong enough to block out the intended meaning. In one case, it might suggest nostalgic memories of homemade pies; in another, a makeshift contraption of questionable value.

To be an effective communicator, you must sense the feeling state or mood of the prospect during the first few minutes of the sales call. When encountering an ugly mood, the best tactic might be to listen attentively until the buyer "has gotten it out of his system," and then reschedule the call. When buyers are in a happy mood, you may achieve more than was planned. You must be alert to affective or feeling reactions from what the buyer says and does. In general, people reveal feelings in the style of response rather than in what they say or do.

If you are to be an effective communicator, you must take into account the three interactive human processes just described. Clearly, buyers' feelings and emotional states markedly influence their perceptions of you as well as of your products and services. Persons who are disturbed have biased views of whoever or whatever comes in contact with them. Also, feeling reactions influence the clarity and orderliness of the thought process. Similarly, what customers think about a business proposal will influence their feelings as well as their perceptions. Finally, buyers' perceptions color both their thinking and feelings toward your offering (Figure 2.7). You must be vitally concerned with understanding the buyer's total reaction to your offering if you are to achieve your communication and managerial objectives. However, you must consider two additional groups of factors before you can achieve high-fidelity communication.

Role Relationships and Status

The way two parties perceive one another will influence communication between them. If one party is perceived as having higher status and both accept each other on this basis, no real problem exists. The one with the lower status shows enough deference to the other to facilitate conversation and communication.

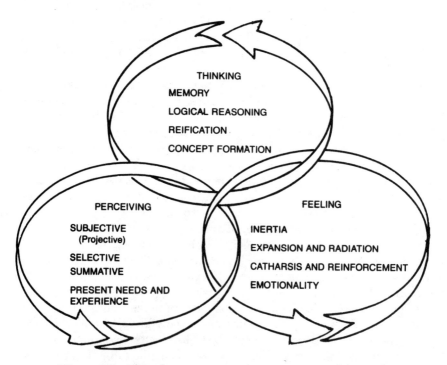

Figure 2.7   Three basic interactive human processes elaborated.

In contrast, if one of the parties feels entitled to special consideration because of his or her status and the other party does not acquiesce, a barrier to communication exists and must be resolved. Examples of status are executive level in a company, social standing, and prominence in a trade or professional association. Because your objective is to influence the other person, you should recognize the status feelings of your prospects and make sufficient adjustments to facilitate the interview. You should be interested in making the sale, not in raising or maintaining your ego at the expense of your prospect.

Background Factors, Personality Traits, and Motives

Your prospects' outstanding characteristics and idiosyncrasies influence the way they send and receive information. You must know as much as you can about the background, personality, and motivational makeup of your prospects and use this information in communicating with them. Chapter Five presents a method for sizing up the other person's unique characteristics as well as creating an appropriate sales strategy.

3.   DEVELOPING REAL-TIME SKILLS

We are not privileged to judge our own conversational skill. Those with whom we converse make that judgment. The common denominator of those who are judged to be good conversationalists is that the other party enjoys their company. What better feeling can you generate than one where prospects enjoy your visit and would welcome you again? Serious thought and effort should go into developing the conversational skill that will give you an advantage over salespeople handling competing lines. It is well known that, when products or services are competitive in all respects, the salesperson's manner and personality are the determining factors in the customer's decision where to place the order.

Elements of a Good Conversation

In a social situation, a good conversation results in both parties feeling that the discussion was enjoyable. If it were otherwise, we could safely predict that social contact would eventually terminate. In the sales process, while the prospect can refuse to see you, you are not free to terminate the relationship. Rather you must attempt to reach all the customers and prospects in your area of responsibility. Rarely can you limit your calls to those whom you like to visit.

First of all, then, it is important to make yourself personally acceptable to prospects and customers so that you can enjoy repeat business. Two major techniques exist for making yourself acceptable. One is to recognize other persons as unique individuals and to adjust to their idiosyncrasies or outstanding qualities. Chapter Five spells out the general procedures for this technique.

The other technique is to develop the communication and conversational skills outlined in this section.

A second important element of good conversation is mutual understanding. When good friends finish a conversation, they know each other's perceptions, thoughts, and feelings. Agreement does not automatically follow understanding, but even more importantly, agreement can seldom occur without understanding. If a person has insight into how a friend perceives, thinks, and feels as well as the information on which he or she bases reactions, the two are more likely to find agreement than if the person hears only the friend's opinions.

A third element in a conversation is tolerance of the other party's viewpoint. Because you do not agree with the opinions of your friends does not necessarily mean you attempt to keep them from expressing their views. Actually, the best way to change people's opinions might be to get them to express their ideas fully. If an idea is unsound, the speaker will detect weakness more quickly in the process of explaining it orally than by being told it is wrong before fully expressing the opinion. If the speaker's idea appears sound, you may adopt it; if not, you are certainly in a better position to attack it after you fully understand it. If you are to attack the idea, the first step is to try to bring out the information and opinions behind it. Many times you can show that the idea, while having some plausibility, is based on an unsound concept. If the foundation of an opinion is destroyed, the opinion itself is very likely to collapse.

Part of being tolerant is to show the necessary interest and attention to grasp and retain the ideas presented. This is simply a matter of courtesy.

Comparison of a Sales Interview with a Social Discussion

Applying the preceding thesis to some actual situations will demonstrate the importance of the elements. If two friends are discussing the merits of a new-model automobile, they will normally conclude the conversation with complete knowledge and understanding of each other's position. They have achieved this by expressing their ideas fully (and repeating them if they are complex) and listening carefully to each other. Generally you hear people ask not only for the opinion of the person they are talking to but also for the opinions of several other friends. We tend to take it for granted that people know the opinions of their friends as well as they know their own.

Reflection on these points will show that all the elements of a conversation were present before the final stage was reached. The discussion was enjoyable or it would never have been pursued to the point of achieving mutual understanding. Tolerance is obvious. Courtesy can also be assumed if the friendship is to continue.

Applying the same elements to a sales interview, you can see that all the considerations in a social discussion are necessary. One real difference is that a sales interview starts out with the objective of getting the prospect to adopt a particular viewpoint. The proper way to accomplish this is, first, to find out the prospect's present point of view. If the present perspective fits in with your plans, no persuasion is necessary. If the present viewpoint is not acceptable to you, at least you have a clear idea of what you must do to change it to meet your needs. Without knowing the present viewpoint, you cannot intelligently attempt to change a person's opinion.

The sales interview, then, goes one step beyond the ordinary conversation. After exchanging points of view, you might try to change the prospect's opinion.

Another difference between the sales interview and the social discussion is that generally the outcome is more important to you than to the prospect; in a social situation the two parties are likely to have approximately the same interest in the outcome. The significance of this difference is that you must assume the responsibility for the outcome and, hence, work much harder at being a good conversationalist and therefore a good communicator.

The Importance of Listening

Analysis of people's reports on what makes a conversation enjoyable reveals that a prime factor is the feeling that they had an opportunity to express themselves fully. Very seldom does a person state that the information received was the highlight of the conversation. Thus, the effective conversationalist—the individual people like to talk to—is, above all, an effective listener. Listening does not come naturally. The natural thing to do in a conversation is to talk. If listening is important and you are to assume the responsibility for the prospect's enjoyment of the interview, then you must develop the art of listening.

Mastery of the art of listening rests squarely on recognizing and overcoming two barriers. First, effective listening is an unnatural act. Physiologically, the human brain processes information at a rate two to four times the average rate of speech. This means listeners think at a rate several times the rate at which they hear. Problems can arise when you misuse your excess listening capacity. In this case, you take a "mental holiday" and think about things that interest you rather than the feedback from the buyer. Of course, you can check in with the speaker from time to time, but research shows you will miss significant parts of his or her message.

Alternatively, the effective listener deploys unused thinking capacity toward understanding the feedback from the speaker. Specifically, the high-fidelity listener (1) thinks about the conclusions the speaker is building toward, (2) evaluates the evidence the speaker provides and looks for errors of omission as well as of commission, (3) does not attempt to retain all the facts introduced but selects key points in each major segment of the conversation, and (4) recognizes that not all meaning is carried in the verbal band and monitors the nonverbal elements in the speaker's message. You can utilize nonverbal behavior in a number of ways to modify verbal messages. For example, it might explain a pause in the conversation or provide information related to the content of the spoken message. The effective listener understands how the verbal and nonverbal components of a message interact.

Second, although the wisdom of developing effective listening skills has long been recognized, actual training has been scanty, for the most part consisting of admonitions such as "Listen!" or "Pay attention." The formal development and refinement of listening skill as a vital selling tool has yet to become widespread. This discrepancy is probably the result of a bias in conventional communication training to focus on speaking or output behavior rather than on the analysis of incoming messages or input behavior. Whatever the causes, recent research by Communispond, Inc., indicates that only 28 percent of buyers are favorably impressed by salespeople's *listening skills*. This implies buyers are unimpressed by 72 percent of the salespeople calling on them. On the one hand, this performance gap represents an enormous opportunity for those who will discipline themselves to learn how to listen effectively. On the other hand, it is a tragedy that many salespeople are perceived as not having mastered a skill that is so basic to success in a highly competitive field. Listening is one of the major avenues through which we acquire information. Every professional salesperson should be a Black Belt in listening!

The Art of Listening

Listening can be active or passive. A passive listener is one who merely listens to what is said. If the other party to the conversation is aggressive, talkative, and resourceful, passive listening might be adequate. However, as a salesperson, you can seldom, if ever, afford to be a passive listener. When prospects are not highly motivated to talk and you want a clear picture of how they feel and also want them to enjoy the conversation, then you must use active listening.

Active listening means that you take the initiative in drawing out the content of the conversation. The most obvious way to get information is to ask a question or to make a statement that calls for an answer. (Chapter Three outlines tactics to use if answers are not forthcoming.)

The following list describes three specific approaches to being a good listener. Combining these approaches with appropriate questions and tactics should help you develop considerable communication skill as well as enhance your sales productivity.

1. *A Friendly Manner.* Questions may be designated as the *matter* of the stimulus to conversation and the attitude of the listener as *manner*. A friendly manner makes the other person feel like revealing information. This manner encompasses, among other things, a smile, a pleasant voice, and a sincere interest in what the person says. To show a critical, hostile reaction is unfriendly, and hence is likely to shut off the flow of information. It is axiomatic in interviewing, as well as in general conversation, to avoid controversial topics until you have established rapport. In the early part of the interview, therefore, you should appear to accept whatever is said at face value. You should defer any necessary probing and clarification until the conversation has reached a point where loss of rapport is unlikely.

2. *The Use of Gestures.* Another characteristic of an active listening manner is nodding your head to show acceptance and implied agreement with whatever is said. You can accompany this gesture by saying "very interesting," "tell me more," "I see," along with eye contact. Such actions tend to maintain the flow of conversation. Moving the entire body toward the speaker also tends to symbolize interest as well as confidence and, hence, to maintain the conversation as desired.

3. *Emotional Capacity.* The next approach to good listening is to develop the emotional maturity and self-confidence necessary to allow and, in fact, encourage other persons to express their views fully, even though that viewpoint is contradictory to the one desired. The instinctive reaction to an opposing position is to interrupt and rebut. Good conversation and effective sales technique call for the opposite. Specifically, you should draw out the full opinion of the prospect and continue to seek the basis on which the opinion was developed. Only then can you make a meaningful and intelligent attack on the unfavorable opinion.

The essence of maturity is a person's capacity to delay responses. The immature conversationalist blurts out whatever comes to mind, but in a sales interview, you must get the other person's complete viewpoint. Any interruption will have two adverse effects. First, the speaker will be more determined than ever to maintain his or her opinion. Depending on the nature of the interruption, the speaker might insist on expressing his or her views or simply "clam up." In the latter case, you have cut off the feedback you need to personalize your presentation. Second, if you do not fully understand the opinion and its basis, you will have great difficulty providing the necessary information to bring about a change.

Self-confidence is similar to maturity in this instance because it underlies the ability to tolerate the development of an opposing point of view without being disturbed. The confident person realizes that the more the prospect expresses a viewpoint, the easier it will be to supply the kind and amount of information necessary to modify the position to one consistent with the call objectives. Thus, the ability to tolerate an apparently opposing point of view and the capacity to delay responses are essential to being a good conversationalist—and hence an effective salesperson.

The Results of Prejudice

The final approach to being a good conversationalist is to recognize and to discount your own prejudices. Prejudice literally means to prejudge an issue. It is the opposite of openness of mind or the desire to rationally analyze a situation. Prejudice is evident in any refusal to listen to and to consider opposing ideas. This obviously interferes with good conversation. Self-analysis would reveal many ideas, acquired from parents and other sources of authority, that you have accepted uncritically. Possibly, some of these ideas are wrong or at least are in conflict with changes in culture and technology. Whether the prejudices are right or wrong, they interfere with good conversation because they reduce the willingness to listen to a conflicting point of view. It would be Utopian to expect all people to give up all their prejudices, but it is not too much to expect you, as a salesperson, to reflect on some of your attitudes and to try to understand why you feel the way you do.

If individuals do not admit to holding any prejudices or being opinionated on any subject, they need only ask a friend or acquaintance to point out some of the areas in which they are adamant. Only when individuals recognize their own prejudices can they learn to control them and tolerate the opinions of others. As we pointed out earlier, you must assume the responsibility for the outcome of the conversation or the sales interview. It is not good business sense to let prejudices interfere with earning a living. It is also not fair to an employer for you to use your job to propagate your own opinions. The sensible thing to do is to learn your prejudices and to control them by keeping them out of business discussions. Self-analysis or analysis with the help of a friend or co-worker should bring out the prejudices that tend to interfere with effective sales performance. Understanding is the first step toward the self-control that is essential to good listening.

The Zigzag Effect in Conversation

The preceding material has dealt with general criteria for good conversation. One common specific practice that violates good conversational technique warrants special treatment. This practice can be designated the *zigzag* effect.

In the ideal conversation, one party introduces a topic and gives the other party an opportunity to state a position, which the second party then does. Through a series of interchanges, the parties fully state their points of view and learn each other's position.

More often than is pleasant to contemplate, however, one of the parties introduces a new topic before the old one has been fully explored. Thus, a situation is set up where neither party is attentive to what the other is trying to communicate. Instead of the conversation proceeding in a straight line toward a goal of mutual understanding, it zigzags—creating an unsatisfactory experience for both persons.

In sales work, several situations can lead to zigzag conversations unless you take precautions. The most common situation arises when the prospect raises an objection that the salesperson does not wish to answer. The salesperson who ignores the objection has set up conditions for the zigzag effect.

Techniques for Meeting Objections

There are several techniques you can try before acceding to the prospect's objection. One possibility is to concede the objection but try to present it as such a minor issue that it is not an obstacle to the sale. Another possibility is to suggest that the objection can be better handled later in the interview. If these techniques do not work, you must decide whether to keep the prospect discussing the topic you originally selected, and thus risk the zigzag effect, or to follow the topic introduced by the prospect and thus dilute the impact of your presentation. Either solution leaves you in trouble.

When you reach such an impasse, you should first analyze the events leading to it and see whether you created some part of the difficulty. If so, you can make the necessary adjustments and continue the presentation. A difficulty caused by the prospect's conversational manner requires a more intensive analysis (see Chapter Four, Section 2, for further details).

Barriers to Good Conversation

Barriers to good conversation can be either active or passive. Active barriers are caused by the action of one of the parties. Passive barriers are caused by the failure of one of the parties to carry an appropriate share of the conversational load. The common active causes of poor conversation are monopolizing the conversation and frequently changing the subject (zigzag). The passive causes are failure to respond when the other party asks for an opinion and failure to attend to the other party.

Thus, you should be able to determine which party is primarily responsible for the breakdown in the conversation and whether the causes are active or passive. You must exercise the necessary self-control to correct the situation if you are at fault. If the prospect is at fault, properly classifying the nature of the difficulty will suggest the correct action.

Remedial Steps

If the prospect's active interference with the conversation causes the difficulty, you can assume that he or she is quite aggressive or disinterested, so an adequate presentation will require strong and positive steps. If the difficulty has a passive cause, you might need to draw out the prospect and break the presentation into small, easily understood sections, whereas when a person monopolizes the conversation, you might need to interrupt to bring the subject to one you want to discuss. This situation is still different from one where the prospect keeps changing the subject.

The person who monopolizes the conversation is probably willing to take up any topic so long as he or she can do most of the talking. You need only to introduce the preferred subject. With the person who changes the subject, you must keep coming back to the basic topic. This requires tact and a supply of questions such as "Did we finish our discussion about . . . ?" or "Could we finish talking about . . . before we take up . . . ?" While these tactics are not conducive to the ideal conversation, persons who actively interfere with good conversations are relatively callous persons and are probably used to being interrupted; hence, they do not take offense readily.

In the case of passive prospects, an analysis of why they do not talk freely will be helpful. For the inattentive prospect, more participation is key. Use of questions and frequent review is appropriate.

When prospects are so lacking in conversational skill that you cannot make an adequate presentation, you will need to do a complete analysis of their background, personality, and motivation (see Chapter Five).

Topics of Outside Conversation

The normal topics of conversation in a sales interview are the needs of the prospect and the features and benefits of the product or service that will fill these needs.

Still, on many occasions, you must engage in general conversation. Sometimes, the prospect is not ready to plunge into the heart of the presentation, and "small talk" is necessary. Often you are left with a receptionist, secretary, or other person while waiting to see the prospect. This might call for conversation.

Formal sales training is designed to prepare you to make presentations. No ready training is available for making social or nonbusiness conversation. The following ideas are for those who would like to develop topics of conversation outside of the actual sales presentation. (Appendix XVI provides a checklist to help you determine *what* to talk about.)

To be a good conversationalist, you introduce topics you know are of interest to the other party. If you are meeting a person for the first time, this might not be possible. If the setting is in an office or at a desk, you may see clues in the form of pictures or trophies. Some persons display "conversation pieces" for this purpose. The alert salesperson will note them and use them accordingly.

A proper introduction includes something about the person such as "Mr. Jones heads up our _____" or "Ms. Brown is responsible for _____." Again, the alert salesperson will attend to the introduction for possible clues to conversational topics.

Sometimes an obvious method of discovering a topic of conversation does not exist. In such instances, you must fall back on your own resourcefulness. Have a ready list of timely topics for such occasions. One accepted way to ensure readiness for conversation is to use a mnemonic device to help remember suitable topics.

A common device is to choose a word and use its letters as clues to the first letters of the words you want to remember. Because the objective here is to think of suitable topics of conversation, we will use the word *conversation* as an example of this technique:

C   Competition within the industry and from competing industries
O   Occupations
N   News in general
V   Vacations
E   Entertainment—TV, Broadway plays, movies, etc.
R   Research in industry; reading done recently; recreation
S   Sports

A   Arts and culture (music, dance, etc.)

T   Travel

I   Investments (stocks, bonds, etc.)

O   Obituaries of prominent persons

N   Novels

The preceding are not necessarily the best or only topics suitable for general conversations. They merely illustrate the possibilities of using a mnemonic device to recall suitable topics. Every salesperson can and should prepare his or her own list. There is no particular virtue in the word "conversation." Any other word will do as well. If you have compiled and learned the list, it will help you over what might otherwise be embarrassing situations.

SUMMARY

Your communication responsibilities are—*to accord uniqueness* and *to be in control without seeming to do so*. As a professional, you recognize that effective communication is *receiver* oriented, not *sender* oriented. The sales call is a complex two-way communication process, fundamentally driven by the state of the buyer's mind. Based on continuous feedback from the buyer, you have a challenge to individualize your communication. From the customer's perspective, this form of communication is more pleasant, results in greater conviction, and generates a sense of freedom. From your standpoint, it requires adjustment to the buyer, active participation, flexibility, subtle control, and a high level of communication skill.

You would be naive or egotistical to assume that each of your customers perceives, thinks, and feels about your propositions just the way you do. To communicate effectively, you must take into account the characteristics of the three basic human processes as well as the other person's needs. Your task is to recognize the individuality of each buyer and to customize your presentation to accommodate the buyer's unique requirements. Customers and prospects are entitled to receive messages that are relevant and that they can understand. The result you seek is to have your offering perceived, thought of, and felt to be different and better from the buyer's standpoint. This is essential for survival in today's competitive marketplace and requires superior communication skills.

The effective salesperson must be an able conversationalist. You must be aware of the three elements of good conversation: acceptability as a person, mutual understanding, and tolerance. You must also recognize that the responsibilities of professional sales communication are higher than those of social conversation. Conversational ability and skill hinge in part on the ability to listen actively. You must cultivate the art of listening. Finally, you must build a repertoire of suitable topics of conversation.

Your firm's entire marketing effort hinges on your ability to communicate in a manner that induces purchase.

TOPICS FOR THOUGHT AND DISCUSSION

1. Why is it unlikely that a person will instinctively be an effective communicator?

2. Compare and contrast mass and interpersonal communication.

3. How would the statement "people are more likely to believe the things they say themselves than the things they hear" relate to one-way and two-way selling?

4. To what extent can you accept the point of view that lack of product/service knowledge might lead a salesperson to use one-way rather than two-way communication?

5. Relate the seven enumerated difficulties in communication to some recent sales calls where you failed to make a sale. Were any of these difficulties present in the calls? How can you overcome them on future calls?

6. How can knowledge of perceiving, thinking, and feeling contribute to improving communication effectiveness?

7. What personality characteristics would probably be associated with salespeople who assume customers' needs to be the same as their own? With salespeople who naturally consider the prospects' needs?

8. What cues might indicate to a sales supervisor that a salesperson is losing sales because of a tendency to project? What can be done to reduce this tendency?

9. Distinguish between "summation" as used here and "summarization" as used in many books about selling.

10. Expand on the statements (a) The more varied and diverse a person's experiences, the broader his or her perception is likely to be; and (b) The more recurrent his or her experiences, the more refined and accurate the concepts are likely to be.

11. Describe a recent situation where you applied inductive thinking to one of your accounts.

12. What are some ways you can gauge the feeling state or mood of the prospect?

13. How do you feel about the proposition in the book that conversational skill must be judged by others, not by oneself? What factors might prevent a person from making an objective assessment of his or her conversational skill?

14. Select 10 of your closest friends and acquaintances, and list one or more prejudices that creep into their conversations. Check your own conversation to see whether you have the same or similar prejudice on any of the topics.

15. Review the active and passive causes of poor conversation, and decide which areas are most responsible for poor conversation in people in general and in yourself.

THREE

Strategy and Tactics for Conducting the Sales Call

It is a luxury to be understood.

RALPH WALDO EMERSON

In this chapter:

- **Sales Strategy for Control of the Interview**
  - Questions are general tools for controlling the interview and, specifically, are a means for triggering participation and information.
- **Filling Needs**
  - Not only must you use more than one sales point, you must also state each sales point more than once.
- **The Importance of Timing**
  - The timing of sales points within the sale, and of follow-up calls where multiple calls are necessary to effect a sale, should be a matter of planning rather than impulse.
- **Prospects' Reactions and Sales Tactics**
  - Close observation of the prospect's reactions to your statements provides cues to the prospect's attitude.
- **Summary**
  - To achieve your strategic and tactical objectives, you must be adept in applying the need satisfaction method.
- **Topics for Thought and Discussion**
- **Application Exercises**
  - Appendix II   Salesperson-Oriented Product Manual
  - Appendix IV   Work Sheets for SOPM
  - Appendix VII   Work Sheet for Compiling Examples of Prospect Reactions
  - Appendix VIII Sample Sales Interview: Observing the Prospect's Reactions
  - Appendix XIV Common Trait Terms with Definitions and Strategies

1. SALES STRATEGY FOR CONTROL OF THE INTERVIEW

Control of the sales interview can be examined from two different perspectives. The first involves the technique the salesperson uses in exercising positive control of the interview to arrive at a successful conclusion. The second deals with fitting this technique into various practical situations that you will face in dealing with both friendly and disinterested prospects.

In this section, the discussion will center on the basic technique for interview control as well as on the use of the technique under a variety of conditions.

Alternate Forms of Control

You can control the interview by two methods. You can talk louder and faster than the prospect and thus ensure a full presentation. Alternatively, you can introduce topics of your choosing in such a way that the prospect participates in the discussion, usually by answering your questions.

We have suggested that the tactical objective is to control the interview without seeming to do so, so the first method is not consistent with this precept. Initially, using questions may seem to be less effective. Yet more thorough examination will demonstrate the greater degree of control that you can achieve through the question technique.

A demonstration far removed from selling will illustrate the difference. A parent whose child has done something wrong can deliver a lecture devoted to the child's misdeed or can ask the child a few pointed questions. Suppose the child stayed out beyond his or her curfew. The parent can "read the riot act" or, on the other hand, ask questions such as "Where were you?" "Whom were you with?" or "What hours have we established for your return home?" While the latter approach requires more self-discipline on the part of the parent, it is likely to have a more lasting effect, and if the child answers satisfactorily, the parent has certainly controlled the interview. If punishment is forthcoming, it will be more effective since the child will have measured his or her behavior against agreed-on standards.

In the sales interview, you have two objectives: (1) making a complete presentation and (2) changing the mind of the prospect. Since, in the minds of many salespeople, the first objective leads to the second, they tend to monopolize the conversation. Yet, as has been pointed out earlier, the first step in getting prospects to change their minds should be to find out their current opinions. This, obviously, calls for the question approach.

Personality Differences as a Factor in Control

Personality differences in salespeople are likely to account for an instinctive preference for one or the other method of control. One category of salespeople may wish to monopolize the interview because of egotism: "They like to hear themselves talk." They think that what they have to say is important and that others will want to hear about it. Again, they may be lacking in self-confidence. Implausible as it may seem, people's behavior is often the opposite of what you might expect. This is called "compensatory" behavior. For example, Theodore Roosevelt was a weak and sickly boy. Yet, instead of conserving his energy, he engaged in a strenuous program of athletics and outdoor activities—he "compensated" for his weaknesses.

Similarly, salespeople who are unsure of themselves may talk incessantly instead of giving the prospect a chance. By talking about familiar subjects, they perceive themselves to be knowledgeable and, furthermore, prevent the introduction of topics on which they feel inadequate.

On the other hand, salespeople who choose the question technique of control exhibit resourcefulness and confidence. Thorough advance planning and close attention to the prospect's reactions are essential to ensure that what salespersons say and do will create an awareness of value of the proposition in the prospect's mind. This form of control takes considerable self-confidence. You must be willing to allow the prospect to talk at length, even on irrelevant topics, yet keep the interview under control by introducing pertinent questions when the opportunity arises.

Self-control is closely related to self-confidence. You can always interrupt the prospect to make a statement more to the point. Yet, to be effective with the question technique, you must not appear to be concerned about the course of the conversation. Rather, you must wait for the opportunity to raise another question that will get the conversation back on the track you planned.

Another personality characteristic a salesperson needs for the question technique is maturity—the ability to work for long-range objectives in an account. The salesperson who wants to do a thorough job of "selling" a prospect by developing a climate that will gain a competitive edge will have to forgo the temptation to accept a small or token order and wait until conditions are right to press for a proper order.

Monopolizing the Conversation

The effect of monopolizing the conversation may be more readily appreciated by noting the effects of this behavior in other situations. A cliché in our culture is the tendency of people to fall asleep in church. Assuming that the objective of the clergy is to give parishioners a clearer perception of their relationship to God, a sleeping audience is unlikely to achieve this objective. The church sermon is a clear example of monopolizing the conversation. If the clergy were to ask questions of the audience or, better still, have the parishioners ask questions of them, it is readily apparent that they would increase control over the audience.

The field of education also provides examples of the authoritarian and question techniques. At the college level, much classroom instruction is provided in the lecture format. The instructor delivers a prepared address, and the students take notes. Any college graduate will recall the considerable degree of inattention in a typical class. However, when the instructor asks questions, the attention level rises. Also worthy of note is that when the instructor spends too much time with a single student, the balance of the group tends to lose interest. Some control over the group is lost.

In the field of education, the practice of tutoring provides further evidence of the value of participation as a means of control. A student who has done poorly in the classroom often makes good progress under the leadership of a tutor. The difference is not only undivided attention but also the degree of participation that the tutoring process requires of the student.

Companies vary greatly in the degree of adherence required to the basic sales presentation. At one extreme is the fully structured, scripted, or "canned" sales talk. At the other is the individualized question approach to selling.

Each has its place, depending on the nature of the proposition, the sophistication of the prospects, the size of the sale, and the legal implications of what is said. The more structured the sales talk, however, the greater the tendency of the better salesperson to avoid appearing to monopolize the conversation during the presentation. A powerful way to inject seeming participation into the interview, even in a fully structured presentation, is to use *rhetorical questions,* which the salesperson then answers. If the presentation is organized in question-and-answer fashion, it is more likely that the prospect will pay attention.

In more sophisticated situations where the question technique is more useful, the salesperson may limit direct statements to the small bits of information needed by the prospect to understand the proposition more fully.

Control by the Question Technique

The question technique requires considerably more skill than mastering a "canned" sales talk. In fact, the first attempts to use the question technique may be discouraging. The novice may get unsatisfactory answers to the questions asked and blame the technique. Actually, the wording of the questions may be too poor to elicit a suitable answer, or the delivery may lack confidence or conviction.

You cannot usually develop good questions merely by starting to ask questions at the interview. You need to budget time outside selling hours to write out questions designed to reveal specific information. If, after trial, they do not work, they should be revised. Over a period of time you will develop a "library of questions" that will enable you to control sales interviews. Initially, you should review the list of questions before each call so that you can open the interview with suitable questions.

Actually, the best questions occur as a result of listening to the prospect's remarks. If, however, you have no questions to open the interview, the prospect may never make any remarks that are worth exploring through further questioning. The prepared questions may be likened to training wheels on a child's bicycle. Almost as soon as the child can ride with training wheels attached, they can be removed. The conclusion might be that the wheels were unnecessary, yet they provided the confidence and minimal support required. The same is true with the salesperson. The prepared questions permit a good, confident start. To the best of our knowledge, you can not fully master the question technique by limiting your efforts to the actual sales interview. Those who have been effective technicians have invested hours in developing the method outside the interview environment. In addition, frequent practice is necessary to keep the skill at a high level. This is a good example where the cultural attitude toward selling as an "easy-to-enter" occupation differs from the truth. Selling is a professional calling and like any other profession requires diligent study to master the basic principles.

Criteria for Good Questions

An effective question elicits a significant amount of information on a topic of the asker's choosing. The five criteria for a good question are listed in Table 3.1 and are discussed in the following text.

Questions Should Elicit Information from the Buyer beyond "Yes," "No," or Very Short Responses. "Yes" or "No" responses usually require a follow-up question. For example, with the question "Have you heard about our services?" a "No" response will require a follow-up question as to "why"; a "Yes" response will necessitate an inquiry into what the prospect heard. This is an important criterion. When the prospect can answer a question adequately with a single word, you have gained little or no information and you are faced with the task of formulating another question. You may miss cues because you are busy thinking about what to say and/or do next. The effective communicator attends to the other person. A

Table 3.1   Criteria for Effective Questions

Rule	Poor Question	Effective Question
1. Questions should elicit information from the buyer beyond "Yes," "No," or very short responses.	Have you heard about our services?	What have you heard about our services?
2. Questions should be open.	Why does the engineering department like this product?	How would engineering evaluate this product?
3. Questions should be indirect.	Why do you use that product?	What considerations were made before adopting the product?
4. Questions should be short.	With so many complicated products to choose from, do you spend a lot of time studying manufacturers' claims?	What kind of pictures will you take?
5. Questions should be one part.	Do you spend a lot of time studying manufacturers' claims and making cost estimates?	How much time is spent studying manufacturers' claims? Making cost estimates?

little preparation would have resulted in a question phrased to get the job done. The question "What have you heard about our services?" would probably elicit useful information and with one question rather than two or more.

Not only does the "Yes" or "No" question put an additional burden on you by requiring two questions rather than one, it also creates the atmosphere of an inquisition rather than a conversation. The inquisition atmosphere makes you appear as a less pleasant personality and thus reduces your potential for gaining the order in highly competitive situations.

Keep in mind that in the need satisfaction method of selling the goal is to have the buyer talk freely during the need development phase of the interview. "Yes" or "No" questions are counterproductive because they (1) yield too little information, (2) leave a negative impression of you in the mind of the buyer, and (3) require too much time to gain required information.

Questions Should Be Open.   Questions should not be leading or imply an answer. By definition, leading questions make one answer more likely than another. In effect, they "put words" in buyers' mouths. They do not reveal the prospects' own ideas; they rubber-stamp your ideas. For example, the question "Why does the engineering department like this product?" tends to exclude any negative response. This type of question is common and, perhaps, useful in a legal interrogation of a witness where the lawyer wants to control the response. In a sales situation, where objective information provides the basis for serving the customer, answers to such questions tend to mislead. In short, leading questions increase the noise in the feedback from the buyers. If the salesperson uses unbiased questions to develop a common understanding, prospects will feel that they have made the decision to buy, and they will have a clear idea of *why* they bought. In this instance, the salesperson might have asked, "How would engineering evaluate this product?"

The real danger in using leading questions is in the need development phase because the buyer may pay lip service to an idea rather than consider and adopt it. When you present the idea again in the need fulfillment phase, the buyer may reject it and thus cause you to retreat and return to the need development phase. This is time consuming and unnecessary, not to mention unprofessional.

Questions Should Be Indirect.   In selling, indirect questions are preferable. "Indirect" means that you phrase questions so they do not reveal your objectives. If buyers know your plan, they can give answers that please you or answers that interfere with the plan. When buyers do not know the plan, their answers can be considered to be more valid.

In selling, indirect questions have great value. Many buyers are reluctant to commit themselves. You can overcome this by phrasing questions that do not require buyers to give their own opinions, but to explain how other people feel. Actually, they will reveal their own views under the guise of saying what some other person or persons think. "What considerations were made before adopting the product?" and "How does engineering decide which product to use?" illustrate indirect questions. Neither question suggests the asker's opinion or objectives. The one answering does not need to express his or her views. Yet all evidence indicates that the answer will be approximately the same as if the question had been direct. The safety factor is that, if necessary, buyers can change their position by denying that they stated their own position. Direct questions can put individuals on the spot unnecessarily; indirect questions are less threatening. Most importantly, you should use indirect questions with buyers who are reluctant to reveal their needs. Indirect questions give them more freedom in phrasing their answers.

You can determine relatively easily whether a question is leading, while indirect questions fall on a gradient rather than into distinct categories. Any two questions can be ranked in order of directness; they cannot be absolutely judged as direct or indirect. The following questions range from indirect to direct.

1. What considerations were made before adopting the product?
2. What discussions have you had with people in your line of work about the product?
3. How did you decide which product to use?
4. What about the product appeals to you?
5. Why do you use that product?

The first two questions are very loosely structured. Almost any answer could result. Questions 3, 4, and 5 are more structured and increasingly reveal what the questioner is seeking.

Proceeding from indirect to direct questions is very important. An indirect question is by nature ambiguous. The listener cannot tell what the questioner wants to learn; hence answers cannot be manipulated. You can miss the point the questioner is seeking, and herein lies one of the virtues of indirect questions. *The respondent may provide information much more important than was sought.* If so, you can follow up. If the answers are useless, you can rephrase the question to make it more direct.

Another advantage of indirect over direct questions is that by proceeding from indirect to direct questions, you will have asked a series of questions rather than a single one. This introduces repetition into the conversation, allowing you to spend more time on the subject and to stress key points. Thus, when the interview is over, the prospect is likely to have a clearer understanding of the topic discussed.

A final advantage of the indirect question is that prospects will feel they are providing information of their own selection rather than answering the demands of the salesperson. Therefore, when the salesperson presents reasons for buying based on this information, prospects will feel they made the decision to buy rather than that they were "sold" by the salesperson.

While questions can always be made more direct, practically speaking, you cannot go from direct to indirect questions. Once you have revealed your objectives with a direct question, you cannot turn back and conceal your plans.

Thus, four important reasons for using indirect questions are:

1. By concealing objectives, you obtain more valid answers.
2. More important information than was sought may turn up.
3. Respondents do not have to commit themselves and, hence, do not feel pressured.
4. You can always make indirect questions more direct if necessary.

Questions Should Be Short.   When questions are longer than the receivers' memory spans, they cannot remember the questions hence they cannot answer them. This calls for restatement, which could be embarrassing to both parties. A question such as "With so many complicated products to choose from, do you spend a lot of time studying manufacturers' claims and making cost estimates?" is far too long. "How long does it take to evaluate a product?" will probably trigger off the same or better information. If the respondents need clarification, they will ask for it. A series of short exchanges leads to more accurate communication than a long statement or question by one party.

Questions Should Be One Part.   When questions have two parts, respondents will not know which part to respond to nor will the salesperson know which part was answered. In fact, if a "Yes" or "No" answer is possible, it will create even more confusion. "Do you spend a lot of time studying manufacturers' claims and making cost estimates?" A "Yes" or "No" answer is possible to either part of the question and would be meaningless. The questioner wants to know, how much time is spent in studying manufacturers' claims, in making cost estimates, or the percentage of time spent in each area. You should ask the question properly the first time.

Uses of Questions

In addition to providing general control of the selling process, questions have specific uses within the interview.

One use of questions is to determine the nature and amount of information the prospect has about your proposition as well as competitive offerings. When you know the areas of adequate and inadequate knowledge, you can concentrate on information gaps and points of disagreement.

Another closely related use of questions is to determine the prospect's needs for more information on a particular point. When you sense that a prospect is uninformed or misinformed in a specific area, you can, through questioning, get the prospect to see the need for the necessary information and ask for it.

Yet another use of questions is to upset a prospect's complacency with things as they are. Prospects with a complacent attitude will usually be unwilling to participate in an interview because they see no need to devote time and energy to evaluating a new product or service.

Perhaps the most *basic use of questions* is to bring out the prospect's needs and values regarding a proposition. This is essential in selecting suitable features and benefits to use for closing sales. Any well-informed salesperson has discovered an infinite number of reasons why various prospects will buy a product.

Accordingly, you should explore the prospect's needs and values, and select appropriate features and benefits as your basis for closing the sale. When a sale is closed on features and benefits that prospects agree are pertinent to their uses of the offering, they are more likely to be satisfied with their buying decisions.

The following sections amplify the use of questions in developing needs, need awareness, and disturbing complacency.

Developing Needs

The material in Chapters One and Three can now be related and put to work. In Chapter One, we established the rationale for itemizing the sales points of your product, services, and/or company as well as probing the prospect's needs. The preceding section presented the criteria for effective questions. To identify the buyer's needs, you must ask questions (that meet the criteria for effective questions) *oriented around the sales points* (Appendix II).

This insight—that questions should be related to the sales points—is very important. Without this caution, you might develop needs that you cannot fill. This could be disastrous. At best, it will take you longer to achieve your objective if buyers' minds are focused on something irrelevant to the sale. At worst, you will fail to make the sale and will have squandered your time.

All need development questions should be based on one of the sales points and should meet the five criteria listed in Table 3.1.

Before you can phrase a question properly, the purpose in asking the question should be clear. Specifically, because you are trying to identify the two or three sales points that are most likely to produce a buying response, the objective is to determine whether to earmark a sales point for use in the need fulfillment phase or drop it from further consideration in the present interview.

Equally important is to define what the question is *not* supposed to do. The natural thing for you to do is use a leading question to establish a sales point. In discussing brick, one sales point is "Wide range of colors available." The question "Having a wide range of colors to choose from is important, is it not?" illustrates a leading question. The contractor being solicited will probably say "Yes." But the contractor would have no inclination to buy because the sales point has not been related to his or her needs. Moreover, you have not gained a clearer picture of the prospect's needs.

One function of the question is to determine *whether* the sales point is related to a need; hence, "What is the role of color in achieving your objectives?" or "How does color affect the design?" is more likely to discover information bearing on the buyer's needs. If the architect says, "It is really not an issue for me," the point on color can safely be dropped from further consideration. If the response is, "My primary interest is to design a building that can be built very quickly," this sales point will not likely intrigue the buyer. Another function of the question is to establish *how important* a need is to the buyer.

On the other hand, the answer "A quality image is my chief concern" is one that may set the stage for stressing color, not speed of construction, as part of the closing-Need Fulfillment phase. The recommendation here is to make an honest inquiry to see *whether* a sales point is relevant. Upon discovering that a sales point is relevant, the natural inclination is to ask for the order. Nonetheless, you should resist that impulse and *identify two or three sales points before attempting a close.*

Thus, when you discover that the opportunity to select color, not speed of construction, is relevant, you should ask questions oriented around other sales points until you have identified two or three significant points. However, even when you have pinned down two or three major points, it is not yet time to ask for the order.

Need Awareness

Frequently, an effective salesperson will recognize buyers' needs before the buyers do so themselves. Hence, between the time you sense the needs and start to close, you must obtain agreement from the buyer to the needs (See Chapter One, Figure 1.8).

When you are satisfied you have identified and can fill buyers' needs, you should summarize the interview(s) to date and ask whether you are correct in your understanding of the situation. This is called *asking a check question.* For example, it might be as basic as asking, "What have we missed?" If you and the buyer agree on the needs, the buyer is *aware* of his/her own needs, and you can undertake the need fulfillment phase. If you have not achieved agreement (awareness), you must return to the need development phase and resume questioning.

We are frequently asked, "Should questions used in need awareness and need fulfillment also meet the five criteria?" When you start the interview (need development), you have little or no knowledge of the buyer's situation. You must take every possible precaution to obtain valid data. The five criteria are the best guide for this purpose. By contrast, when you reach the need awareness phase and the need fulfillment phase, you have a reasonably clear understanding of the situation. You are no longer primarily concerned with collecting information. You want to provide information. In the need awareness phase, you want buyers to know that you understand their needs. In the need fulfillment phase, you want to show that your product will *fill* the needs. Thus, after completing the need development phase, you can risk using leading questions and revealing your plans (direct questions).

Having said this, however, we must consider the consequences. How do buyers feel when you try to put words in their mouths (leading questions)? Would buyers prefer to state their own opinions or rubber-stamp yours? Obviously they prefer the *freedom* of open questions rather than the *coercion* of leading questions. Therefore, we recommend observing the five criteria for questions at all times. It may be wiser to meet the criteria all the time rather than attempt to turn them on and off. As a practical matter, many sales can be made with or without polished sales technique, but this misses the point. You should always be practicing so that when the sale depends on your skills, your skills are ready to meet the challenge. Although the criteria may not be necessary at times, your presentation will never be impaired through their use.

The preceding discussion is based on the assumption that buyers will allow you to engage them in meaningful conversation. This is not always the case. Frequently, you hear buyers say: "I don't need any," "I'm satisfied with my present sources of supply," or "I have all I need right now." Unless you can find some way to disturb this complacency, you will not be able to obtain an order.

Disturbing Homeostasis

Before prospects will buy they must experience a sense of dissatisfaction with their present "need satisfiers," the products or services they are currently using. To be effective, you must disturb prospects before you can use the need satisfaction model and ultimately show how your product or service will relieve the dissatisfaction. Satisfaction with the status quo is a good example of a psychological phenomenon called *homeostasis.*

For many years, scientists have recognized that an equilibrium exists in each organism. Not only does the organism resist change, but when it does take place, a tendency to revert to the original state exists. Walter B. Cannon, an eminent physiologist at Harvard University, coined the word *homeostasis* to describe this principle. It means that every organism has a tendency to stay the way it is. The implication of this for selling is the warranted assumption that buyers are satisfied with their present state and that before any sale is likely to take place, you need to disturb their sense of well-being.

Examples of Homeostasis

You can easily see applications of this principle in the field of physiology. Take the case of body temperature. It stays at approximately 98.6 degrees. As soon as this temperature rises for any reason, the pores open, the body perspires, and the blood comes to the surface in large quantities. The cumulative effect is to give off heat and hence restore the normal body temperature. The opposite action takes place just as readily. If the body temperature drops, the pores close, the blood flows to the interior of the body, shivering sets in, and body heat is conserved so that the temperature tends to rise.

The same principle operates in the psychological functioning of the organism. When you try unsuccessfully to remember the name of a person or place, a state of tension or restlessness persists until you recall the name. James Thurber wrote an essay about the night he spent awake trying to recall the name of a place in New Jersey. A more concrete, everyday example might be the tension that arises when you are waiting for an important phone call. When the call comes, a feeling of satisfaction or well-being sets in that more than compensates for the long wait and discomfort experienced.

The point is that restless states are invariably followed by a state of well-being. Each person knows this and, therefore, when experiencing a state of tension, the person looks forward to relief.

Implications of Homeostasis for Salespeople

The lesson for salespeople is that you should approach potential customers with the assumption that they are satisfied with the status quo and are likely to resist change, even when it has the potential for significant improvement. The first task, then, is to explore the prospect's needs and ascertain which ones you can meet with the products and services for sale. This involves drawing out prospects on their problems and what they currently use to solve them. When you know their needs and problems, the points on which your offering can *better* meet the needs becomes evident. Showing prospects how to obtain more satisfaction is equivalent to making prospects dissatisfied with their present solution or disturbing homeostasis. When the prospects feel this dissatisfaction, they will willingly listen to your presentation. The next step is to show how the new product or service can relieve the dissatisfaction. When the prospect anticipates the end of the tension, you increase the likelihood of a sale.

The salesperson should develop special questions for disturbing buyers' homeostasis when necessary. A complete *Salesperson-Oriented Product Manual* (Chapter One, Section 2, and Appendix II) would include a section on "Questions for Disturbing Homeostasis." For example, a salesperson for a food manufacturer calling on a food retailer might develop the question, "How would you like to increase your profit 10 percent on the frozen foods you sell?" to obtain the buyer's attention. An office equipment salesperson calling on a purchasing agent might use "How would your management view a 25 percent reduction in clerical payroll?" The following experiences of a software salesperson illustrate the use of questions to disturb homeostasis.

The salesperson discovered that a number of fuel oil companies were using an obsolete program of computing degree-days and delivery dates. (Degree-days are a measure to calculate fuel consumption and determine the date of the next delivery.) The use of new software would reduce inventory in the system and improve margins. The salesperson's statement that the new program could save money evoked no interest at all. Then the salesperson developed a question, "How long has it been since you revised your program for computing fuel delivery dates?" This made the prospects realize that newer and better programs might be available, and the salesperson had no difficulty in getting them to explore the possibility of using the new software.

Organization of Questions

To make the most effective use of the question technique, you need to develop a set of written questions in advance and organize them for ready use. While the specific outline will vary from company to company, the most profitable approach recognizes that success in selling depends on selling the full line to the full marketplace. This suggests a twofold basis for organizing the questions you formulate—by product or product group (service or service group) and by prospect category. The discussion that follows will use the word "product" to identify what you sell. The word "service" would be equally appropriate. The justification is that the word "product" seems to be used most often in business to describe what is sold.

By Product or Product Group

For each product or product group, you should prepare questions to achieve three basic objectives:

1. First and foremost, questions should disturb prospects' complacency and should raise doubts in their minds regarding how they now satisfy their needs as well as how they should satisfy their needs in the future.
2. Additional questions should ascertain the amount of information prospects now have about the product. You may include questions to reveal prospects' general sophistication regarding the product as well as their specific knowledge of your offerings.
3. Questions should also determine prospects' needs for the product or product group. Questions in this category are likely to center around the current and contemplated uses they make of such products.

These criteria are of obvious value when the product is a specialty that does not have a regular repeat sale. They are also valuable when you have a line of products and only a few customers who buy the whole line. Building bigger sales volume by converting partial-line users to total-line users is logical here. Questions to determine needs (Objective 3) are particularly useful in deciding which additional products a customer should be buying.

The procedure is to list each product or product category on a separate sheet of paper and prepare questions relevant to each of the three objectives. In theory, distinct differences among the three types of questions should be evident, but in practice the particular situation will indicate which questions are desirable. The basic principle is that *a good question produces a significant amount of relevant information.* Practice will soon develop your skills in using the questions efficiently.

By Prospect Category

Sometimes a salesperson calls on distinctly different types of accounts. For example, a salesperson for a drug manufacturer may call on physicians, retail druggists, wholesale druggists, and hospitals. On the other hand, a salesperson may have to call on people in the same account who have radically different interests and roles in purchasing decisions. For example, in industrial tools and equipment, salespeople may have to see the purchasing agent, the director of research, the production manager, the toolroom supervisor, and the controller in the same account. When you must interview different categories of accounts or people within an account, arrange your questions in terms of the categories called on. This is important for two fundamental reasons: first, different buying motives are involved; second, the amount and kinds of product information will differ.

To illustrate, the drug salesperson will probably find the physician interested in the possibility of a product's side effects; the retail druggist, only in the likely rate of turnover and profitability of stocking the item; the wholesaler, in the competency of the sales force to sell the product; and the hospital, in whether its board of doctors will approve the drug. In the case of tools and equipment, the purchasing agent's main concern may be whether the product meets the company's specifications; the director of research may want to hear the results of the operational tests performed on the product; and the production manager, whose goal is trouble-free production, may be looking for uniformity of quality. The toolroom supervisor may focus on the ease of inventory control, while the controller's interest may be the profitability of the product to company operations. (For a more detailed treatment of this topic, see Chapter Ten, Section 4. It includes an example—Figure 10.4—of how one company handled this problem.)

There are certainly alternative ways of classifying questions other than by product or prospect. These, however, must be developed in conjunction with the specific sales position and the needs of particular prospects and customers.

Other Kinds of Questions

Thus far, questions have been discussed as general tools for controlling the interview and, specifically, for triggering participation and information. In addition to these primary functions of questions, there are some finer distinctions in classification that are also helpful in thinking about questions as tactical devices.

Preliminary Questions

Preliminary questions are designed to precede the actual sales interview. They can cover topics such as the weather, conditions of highways, sports, or changes in the organization of the company. They provide time to adjust to the tempo of the prospect. One principle applies at this stage: You should use questions of fact, not opinion. The reason is that most people are reluctant to state their opinions until they have some rapport with the person asking the question and some idea why their opinion is desired.

Clarifying Questions

Many times customers reveal information in bits and pieces. In such an event, ask a question or make a statement that will bring system out of apparent disorganization. A question might go something like this: "How does your comment a moment ago with regard to 'computer pricing' relate to your last remark?"

Reverting Questions

Closely related to the need for putting the bits and pieces together is the need to return to a topic that was inadequately discussed. When this is necessary, wait for a lull in the conversation and say something along the lines of "Could we go back to the subject of . . . ?" or "I was wondering . . . ?"

Completing Questions

Many times, you may need a small bit of information to complete a topic or supply missing details. You can handle this problem with a preface question such as "You have given me the broad picture, but I need some small details. What can you tell me about . . . ?" This type of question might be considered a probing question. In the sense of this section, you should avoid probing questions except in areas where the prospect is perfectly willing to supply the information but has inadvertently omitted some necessary detail. (When a prospect is reluctant to talk, more than a simple question is necessary. Strategy for such cases is covered in Chapter Five, Section 2, and Appendix XIV.)

Credibility

One of the real problems in selling is credibility. The buyer does not always believe the salesperson. Picture yourself as a buyer. A salesperson (using either the stimulus-response or selling-formula approach) calls on you, proceeds to describe a product, and urges you to buy it. If, instead, the sales approach (using need satisfaction selling) were to bring out in your own words how the product would work for you, the product would be more attractive and the presentation would be more believable. It would have credibility. This may very well be the greatest single advantage to you in using the customer-oriented rather than one of the seller-oriented methods.

Consider a buyer wanting to add "surroundsound" to a stereo system with new speakers. As she enters the store, a salesperson immediately offers to help. Finding that the buyer wants to update a stereo system, he says, "We have just the one for you" and proceeds to show and tell about a new stereo system that is on sale.

Had the salesperson used the need satisfaction method, he would have inquired into all or some of the following topics:

1. What do you mean by "update?"
2. How is your current stereo system configured?
3. What do you want to change?
4. How satisfied are you with your components?
5. How many additional speakers can your receiver support?

Thus, while the salesperson is thinking what a wonderful job he is doing, he has not done a good job at all!

In contrast, if he had used need development, the salesperson might have sold the same stereo system, but the buyer would know that the purchase fit her needs. She would have confidence in the system, the salesperson, and the store. Credibility would be high.

2. FILLING NEEDS

When you have identified two or three needs (need development) and obtained agreement from the buyer that the needs are pertinent through the use of a *check question* (need awareness), you are ready to start closing the sale (need fulfillment).

In theory, all you need to do is to state the pertinent sales points—features or benefits—you have already itemized. In practice, closing is more complex. Not only must you use more than one sales point, you must also state each sales point more than once.

Why Repetition Is Used in Selling— The Principle of Summation Revisited

Briefly, *summation* means that a stimulus that is not strong enough to elicit a response on a single presentation may, if repeated at appropriate intervals, elicit a response even though the intensity of the individual stimulus does not increase.

For an example of this in everyday life, consider a dripping faucet. Who has not suddenly realized that the faucet has been dripping for some time? Yet up to the moment of realization, you were not aware of the condition. Another example is the sensation that the alarm, as it awakens you in the morning, has been ringing for some time.

Psychologists explain this phenomenon as follows. Nerve fibers do not actually touch each other. They end in a spreading of small fibers that overlap in a longitudinal sense but do not actually touch. The point where this occurs is called a synapse. When the nerve impulse travels along a fiber, it meets resistance at the synapse; that is, it takes a stronger impulse to jump the gap between nerves than merely to travel along a nerve fiber. When a nerve impulse is not strong enough to cross a synapse, it dies there, but it does cause a temporary change in the nerve called a *local excitatory state*. In time, this state will entirely disappear. However, if another impulse of the same strength comes along before the first one dies out, it will add its effect to the original impulse (*summate*), and collectively, they may have the strength to cross the synapse and elicit a response.

Salespeople who appreciate this principle have at their disposal a tool that will increase their effectiveness. All you have to do is realize that a single sales point, while it may not produce a sale, may very well affect the customer in such a way that subsequent sales points will add to the initial effect and, collectively, produce a greater impact than if the points were considered separately. You should also recognize that when you make a sale, you cannot necessarily attribute it to any particular sales point.

Before you can put this principle to effective use, you must distinguish two kinds of summation, *temporal* and *spatial*. In the technical sense, if the same spot on a person were stimulated repeatedly, the person would eventually respond. The stimulus has been repeated at time intervals. This is an illustration of *temporal summation*. If, instead of applying the stimulus to one place at time intervals, the stimulus had been applied at first to one place, then another, or applied at different locations at the same time, the effect would be *spatial summation*. This concept is broad enough to include stimuli received through different sense channels, such as vision, hearing, and touch.

How You Can Use Summation

In selling, there is an analogy to both temporal summation and spatial summation. Several sales points exist for any given product or service. Any particular sales point can be expressed in many ways through various phrasings or *alternate phrasings*. If you were to repeat the same sales point over and over, merely varying the wording, you would be applying the principle of temporal summation. If you were to reinforce your statement of a sales point with a picture, sample, demonstration, or testimonial, you would be using spatial summation. Also, were you to use a repertoire of appeals, you would be illustrating the principle of spatial summation.

Taking an automobile as the product to be sold, here are some possible sales points with alternate phrasings:

1. This car is the ultimate in appearance and style:
   a. It has a classic look.
   b. It comes in a wide choice of your favorite colors.
   c. You can select a customized interior that fits your personal tastes and needs.
   d. It is designed by a famous high-fashion designer in conjunction with a team of automotive engineers.
   e. Its new style instrument panel provides excellent visibility of digital readouts.
   f. It offers a selection of color-coordinated interiors and exteriors.
   g. It is designed for the future; it has understated elegance.
2. This car has advanced engineering features:
   a. Efficient—four cams/four valves per cylinder—design.
   b. Computer-controlled fuel injection.
   c. Speed-sensitive rack and pinion steering.
   d. Excellent EPA gas mileage estimates.
   e. Air suspension and ride control.
   f. Traction control system.
3. This car has all the latest safety features:
   a. 4-Wheel antilock braking system.
   b. Airbag supplemental restraint system.
   c. Redesigned door locks to keep you in the vehicle, should an accident occur.
   d. Seat belts with emergency tension retractors and buckle-up chime.
   e. Specially designed crushable dashboard.
   f. Collapsible steering column.
   g. Rear spare tire that provides additional energy absorption.
   h. First-aid kit.

4. This car has all the features to ensure your comfort:
   a. AM/FM radio, CD, and cassette audio system.
   b. Cellular telephone system in steering wheel.
   c. Remote door lock/unlock system.
   d. Automatic temperature control for air conditioning and heating.
   e. Sophisticated antitheft system.
   f. Automatic speed control.
   g. Power seats with setting memory.
   h. Center console.

The numbered items are different sales points or appeals, while the lettered items are alternate ways of repeating the same sales point. If you use one numbered item, then another, you are applying spatial summation; if you stick to the lettered items within a given number, you are using temporal summation.

Both kinds of summation are theoretically effective and you can use them interchangeably, but practical considerations point to a logical way to use the two systematically and in combination.

When prospects indicate their interest in your proposition and are, therefore, ready to listen to a presentation, you should quickly run through your sales points (via questions) and note which appeals appear to interest the prospect. These are the points that, in your opinion, will lead to a sale if the prospect accepts them singly and collectively.

Taking a single point, you make an overall claim (one of the numbered items) that reinforces the major point. When the prospect accepts that point, you can go on to the next with the same technique. While individual points are made through temporal summation, the sale itself is likely to be the result of spatial summation.

Agreement with the concept of summation and acceptance of the point of view expressed here introduces a new principle for salespeople. You should write down all the major sales points or appeals related to your product or service, and then list as many alternate phrasings as you can. This outline should be practically memorized. When, in the sales interview, it becomes apparent which point or points you must make to accomplish a sale, you can go through your presentation effortlessly. You already know approximately what you are going to say, which will give you a more natural and convincing manner. At the same time, you free yourself to concentrate on other aspects of the sale, including closer observation of your prospect for signs that a close is in order (see Appendix IV for work sheet).

Additional Applications of the Principle

You can also see the principle of summation in the sequence of calls you make on your prospects. Even though a sale does not follow from a single presentation, a series of calls at appropriate intervals will likely result in a sale because of the cumulative effect or summation of the individual visits.

The location of retail outlets for consumer goods is another example of summation. Three or more retail stores for the same general category of merchandise are usually located nearby. The likelihood that buyers will purchase merchandise increases as they see similar or comparable goods the second or third time. As a consequence, in major shopping malls several specialty stores are always in apparent direct competition; yet if one was discontinued, those remaining would probably do less, rather than more, business.

3. THE IMPORTANCE OF TIMING

Many times salespeople believe calling at the "right time" accounts for a sale. They express this belief as though it were a matter of luck rather than good planning. That may be the case, but timing can be a matter of planning. When current books on selling mention *timing*, they usually have in mind the best time of day to call.

While calling at the right time of day is important, other and more important considerations exist. These are timing the delivery of individual sales points within the interview and timing follow-up calls. Timing the sales points within the sales process can be explained directly in terms of nerve function. Timing follow-up calls requires reasoning by analogy from the same principle. The psychological principle that explains the basis of timing is known as the *refractory phase*.

Refractory Phase

The concept of *refractory phase* will appear in any study of the nervous system. It means that, because of the nature of nerve structure and function, an impulse traveling along a nerve fiber affects it in such a way that the fiber cannot carry another impulse until it recovers from the passage of the previous one. This very brief time is referred to as the *absolute refractory phase*. In this period, no impulse can pass over the nerve fiber. If another stimulus is applied during this period, it will have the effect of prolonging the period of nonconductivity.

As the nerve recovers, it passes through *relative refractory phases*. During these phases, it will first respond only to a stimulus that is stronger than normally required to elicit a response; then it passes through a period when the nerve will respond to a stimulus that is weaker than normally required to activate an impulse. This concept can explain timing within the interview as well as timing between calls.

Timing within the Interview

The principle of refractory phases suggests that a salesperson may speak to prospects and not be heard because the prospects have their minds on other topics or are still contemplating previous remarks. This means that you may make your entire presentation without customers grasping what you are saying. Small wonder, then, that at the end of some interviews customers do not feel any desire to purchase. They may need and want to purchase the product but may not realize what the product presented will do for them.

You might argue that no prospect would allow you to talk indefinitely if you did not know what you were talking about. This is merely an attempt to put the responsibility for understanding on the prospect. You are responsible for the prospect's understanding, especially since you are the one who stands to gain or lose according to the degree of understanding the prospect achieves. You should make sure the prospect is following the presentation.

How can you be sure that you are not going too fast? Very simply, pause after each point and ask a question to reveal whether the prospect understands what you have said. The answers to these questions will tell you whether the customer has grasped your ideas.

Another technique is to encourage prospects to contribute additional information to the sale points that you offer. It may be advisable to avoid making a point completely at one time. Leaving out material that the prospect can add or that will provide a good reason for returning to the point is one way to find out whether the prospect has registered the point. If the point has not been understood, you can supply additional information. (This technique is often recommended in books on selling. While it is treated here as a minor point, the concept of *refractory phase* provides a rationale for the technique.)

Timing between Interviews

Many sales cannot be made in a single interview. In such cases, the salesperson must plan to return on another occasion. Often you cannot conclude the sale because the prospect must consult with other persons before making a decision. The next interview should follow soon after these consultations have occurred.

In other instances where the buyer can and will be the sole decision maker but desires more time to think it over, another interview, or at least a follow-up phone call, is indicated. (No distinction is made here between personal calls, phone calls, and other rich interactive media.) If the timing of the follow-up comes before the prospect has finished considering the proposition, it will prolong the period of indecision (refractory phase). When you encounter such a situation, you should change the nature of the call to an offer to review the presentation or supply additional information rather than attempt a close.

If the prospect has finished evaluating the proposition, then you can attempt a close. If you do not achieve a close, additional calls will be necessary. That additional calls may result in success is a reasonable expectation, based on the principle of summation. The cumulative effect of the calls is greater than the simple effect of a single effort, providing you make the calls often enough so that the prospect still remembers the previous ones.

As suggested, you should space the calls so that the prospect has more time to consider and dispose of the proposition. If you space them too far apart, however, the impact of the previous call will be lost and you must handle the presentation the same as a first call. The exact timing of calls will vary with the nature of the product, the impact made on the original call, and the intellectual and memory level of the prospect. Reducing the problem to time intervals is not possible in this discussion, but, in a general sense, you can see that calling on a customer every day may be too often to let the impression realize its full effect. On the other hand, if you were to allow 5 years to elapse, it would be necessary to start at the beginning as though you had never made the initial call. Finding the right time, then, will be a matter of observing the results obtained with follow-up calls at varying periods of time until you establish a guide for the purpose.

Planning Follow-Up Calls

The best time to decide when to make a follow-up call is as soon as possible after you become aware that another call is necessary. The prospect may indicate how long a period he or she will need to consider the proposal. If this falls within the time limits of being long enough to allow time for the issue to crystallize and short enough so that the memory of the proposal will not be lost, you can set a date for the follow-up call as the final part of the interview. If the time suggested by the prospect does not seem feasible, you can make a slight effort to adjust it. Certainly no issue should arise over the timing of the next call. Rather, as soon as an opportunity arises, decide when the optimum time will be and make a note to call on that date. When that date arrives, you can move it ahead if necessary. You can also make the call sooner if you learn that the prospect is ready to give the proposal further consideration.

Plan the next call carefully. You should think out a follow-up as part of the regular sales process, not leave it to impulse. Combing prospect lists in spare moments or when you badly need extra sales is not a satisfactory method of scheduling follow-up calls. The point is you are the manager of a selling system. We will develop this topic in Chapters Nine and Ten.

Absolute versus Relative Refractory Phase

The concept of the refractory phase suggests that sometimes customers will buy on the basis of less than usual sales effort, and other times they will buy for sufficient reason, but only after more sales effort than usual. The analogy here is to the relative refractory phase.

When buyers have just received shipments and their warehouses are full, they are in absolute refractory phase. Any inducement to buy might be ineffective. With the passage of time and consumption of some of the supplies, buyers' attitudes change; a time will come when, although they do not really need to reorder, they will do so if there are appealing incentives. More favorable discounts, partial shipments, and other special considerations may clinch orders that would not otherwise be forthcoming.

If buyers are approached when their stock is nearly exhausted and they face possible embarrassment by running out, they may place an order with less persuasion than is normally required.

The warehouse example has a physical basis. The same reasoning is applicable in situations with a psychological basis. Consider automobile owners. Usually, buyers with new cars will not consider another purchase for at least a year, until a new model is available. They are in absolute refractory phase. Even though a salesperson might call in this period, an order is unlikely. When the new models come out, the prospect reaches a relative refractory phase. At times, a salesperson can sell a new car with little effort. For example, the need for an expensive repair job or even a flat tire at an embarrassing moment may make the idea of a new car seem attractive and set the stage so that less sales pressure than normal will result in a sale. On the other hand, right after making a repair, the owner probably resolves to make the car last for another substantial period of time. When the owner is feeling this way, you will need stronger inducements than normal to obtain an order.

The principles described in this section provide a guide as to how much pressure to put on a buyer. Keep in mind that, on some occasions, no amount of sales effort will be successful, while other occasions call for varying degrees of pressure.

In deciding how much pressure to use, you should remember you want to make customers, as well as sales, and you have responsibilities to both your employer and your customers. You should not use so much pressure that you become offensive to the buyer, prejudicing future calls, or give so many considerations that the sale is unprofitable to your employer. Neither should you be unfair to yourself by wasting time or the time of prospects who are just not ready to buy. You should make a note on your calendar for a follow-up call and come back when there is greater likelihood of success.

4. PROSPECTS' REACTIONS AND SALES TACTICS

One of the most fundamental aspects of tactical control is to avoid the attempt to induce prospects to make decisions before they are ready to do so. Certainly, the sale should be closed whenever possible but not before you have convinced the prospect that the decision is the right one. Effective tacticians attempt to close only after they have set the stage.

When a closing attempt fails, two things happen. You may feel discouraged by the lack of success. Also, the prospect finds it easier to say *no* to other attempts in the same or future interviews. Consequently, recognizing when to close and when not to close is vitally important.

The key to success, then, depends on knowing when the prospect is sufficiently impressed with the proposition to warrant closing. By controlling the topics discussed and by inducing prospects to participate (and thus reveal their feelings), you provide yourself with insights into closing opportunities. The Method presented in this section will enhance these insights. By studying the method and practicing it, you can achieve greater effectiveness in closing sales.

Interaction: The Basis for Sales Tactics

In Chapter One, we described the sales process as an interactive interview. In psychological terms, this means that each observed reaction is a stimulus for another reaction. Further, any adjustive reaction by the salesperson in response to a reaction observed in the prospect is a *sales tactic*.

Since your task is to observe, understand, and adjust to prospects' reactions, you need a method of classifying these reactions to provide an organized basis for becoming a successful sales tactician.

Classifying Reactions

Two dimensions of reactions are extremely important to effective sales tactics: The first may be defined as *positive* or *negative;* the second, as *voluntary* or *involuntary.*

Considering the first category, any reaction is positive if it suggests that the prospect is moving closer to a successful close. In other words, any reaction favorable to the call objective may be considered to be positive. Conversely, you would classify an unfavorable reaction as negative. Thus, if you are highly attentive to your prospect, you will be able to determine, after each response, whether you are "closer to" or "further away from" a successful close.

In addition to verbal messages, positive reactions may include nodding the head affirmatively, asking about delivery, or calling in associates to hear the proposition. Negative reactions may include frowning, shaking the head negatively, looking with disbelief, stating objections, squirming, or looking out the window.

The same alertness will enable you to judge, after each reaction of the prospect, whether it is voluntary or involuntary; that is, whether it is consciously or unconsciously made. You can decide whether or not prospects intend to reveal their feelings and opinions. If prospects are deliberately revealing their feelings, the reaction is voluntary and vice versa. For example, voluntary reactions include thoughtful comments, questions, objections, and deliberate actions. Involuntary reactions include a smile, a frown, head-nodding or -shaking, spontaneous irrelevant comments, or doodling on a scratch pad.

Figure 3.1 shows this classification of buyer reactions. The numbered squares are as follows:

1. *Positive-Voluntary Reactions.* Any consciously made reaction by the prospect that tells you that you are closer to a sale and the prospect wants you to know it.
2. *Positive-Involuntary Reactions.* Any reaction by the prospect that indicates that you are closer to a sale, but the prospect is not deliberately telling you so.
3. *Negative-Involuntary Reactions.* Any response or gesture by the prospect that indicates that you are further from a sale even though the prospect did not intend to indicate it.

	Positive	Negative
Voluntary	1. Positive-Voluntary Reactions	4. Negative-Voluntary Reactions
Involuntary	2. Positive-Involuntary Reactions	3. Negative-Involuntary Reactions

Figure 3.1   Classification of buyer reactions.

4. *Negative-Voluntary Reactions.* Any prospect reaction that suggests to you that you are further from a sale and that the prospect wants you to know it.

This classification provides you with a method for interpreting the prospect's reactions. It also assists you in selecting suitable tactics to handle the situation.

Sales Tactics

Because a sales tactic is adjustive behavior by the salesperson to bring the prospect nearer to a close, a suitable response to fit the reaction of the prospect is necessary.

Tactics for Positive-Voluntary Reactions

These reactions are unmistakable signals for closing or, if that is not appropriate, for moving to the next point in the presentation. Do not stay with the point that has won this reaction; rather, capitalize on it by asking for the order or moving along. You should avoid the danger of talking yourself out of the sale by dwelling on an accepted point. If the points made up to that time are sufficient, a close is indicated.

Sometimes you are so encouraged by positive-voluntary reactions that you talk on and on, perhaps raising issues the prospect would not have thought of if you had been more observant of the closing signal. If the prospect asks, "When can I get delivery on this new item?" you should not carry the presentation beyond the point of a suitable answer. For example: "I can have a partial shipment here at nine tomorrow morning and round out your full order in 10 days. I know you are very busy, so if you will give me a purchase order number, I will help your secretary write up the order for a quantity suitable to your needs."

Tactics for Positive-Involuntary Reactions

Prospects who react positive-involuntarily are moving toward your objective even though they may be unaware of it. Here, the tactics you used have proven successful so far, so do not shift. At the same time, closing may be premature. Rather, reinforce the point that developed the positive response. In other words, get full acceptance of the sales point before moving to the next one. This may be a desirable time to utilize sales aids, such as visuals, demonstrations, samples, or mock-ups.

In selling a piece of office equipment, for instance, assume that you observe a smile at the mention of a full-year guarantee, including free maintenance. You can stay with this point by saying, "I see, Mr. Jones, that you realize our guarantee period is longer than any in the industry. Let me tell you why. Our equipment is so well built that we are confident it will outlast any competitive equipment and require far less service. But we value the goodwill of our customers, so we make our own personnel responsible for maintenance."

As another example, assume the sale of a consumer line to a retailer. Noticing a positive "ummm" at the mention of the success attained by the company's national advertising, you might continue, "Ms. Retailer, you know very well that it isn't the mark-up that puts money in your pocket at the end of the year; it's how fast your goods turn over on your shelves. This line gives you $12\frac{1}{2}$ turns a year, just about $30,000 in your pocket."

In handling a positive-involuntary reaction, it is important to avoid the technical hazard of moving too quickly toward the close. Stay with the point that developed the reaction until you attain a positive-voluntary reaction. Don't mistake a smile or a nod for complete understanding or agreement.

Tactics for Negative-Involuntary Reactions

Negative-involuntary reactions indicate that you are losing ground, but the prospect is not openly expressing disapproval or disinterest. You must recognize and adjust to the important subtle signs because continuing the present tactics will lead to a negative-voluntary reaction. Negative-involuntary reactions include fidgeting, doodling, and looking out the window. Comments by prospects that show they are not attending to the conversation also fall in this category.

The proper tactic is to change to another sales point. Suppose you are trying to demonstrate the quality of your product. The prospect who does not consider quality to be a major problem will show it by a negative-involuntary response. If you change the topic, say to price or delivery date, you may find real interest and get a positive response. If, on the other hand, you persist in talking quality, the prospect's reaction may change to open disapproval—a negative-voluntary response.

Keep in mind that the distinction between a negative-involuntary and a negative-voluntary reaction is a matter of degree rather than a clear-cut difference. The important principle is that you must be alert for the subtle signs of disapproval and change your tactics to avoid open disapproval.

Tactics for Negative-Voluntary Reactions

Open disinterest, disapproval, or disagreement by the prospect are examples of a negative-voluntary reaction. Obviously, open disapproval calls for different and greater changes in tactics than is the case in negative-involuntary reactions.

To select the appropriate tactics, you must estimate the cause of the negative-voluntary reactions. Some common reasons are misjudgment of the personality of the prospect, size of the account, the policy of the company, or even emotional resistance by the prospect. Any of these factors will call for a greater adjustment than merely changing the sales point. It may even be necessary to terminate the interview and arrange for a later meeting. The actual steps you take will depend on the estimated cause of the reaction and the situation.

A common reason is misjudgment of personality. In judging personality, you might take an assertive and perhaps blustery manner as evidence of high self-confidence. Generally, you should provide a self-confident person with the essential facts so that he or she can arrive at a decision. If this procedure proves ineffective, reappraisal may show that the behavior is compensatory rather than real. The buyer's self-confident posture simply conceals a lack of competence. The proper approach to a person who is low in self-confidence is to offer evidence that the proposition has proven successful for other persons. Facts are of no help to such persons because they are considering the consequences of a poor decision and need reassurance that they will not find themselves in trouble if they go along with you. Changing the basic approach in this rather radical manner is typical of what the salesperson must do when the prospect makes a negative-voluntary reaction. In Exhibit 3.1, Pat Richards, Senior Vice President of First Security Bank of Utah, N.A., shares a success story with us, illustrating the proper handling of a negative-voluntary reaction.

To note the negative-involuntary signals and make the relatively minor adjustments called for under such conditions is a much better sales technique than to allow a negative-voluntary reaction to occur.

A synopsis of suitable tactics to use for each of the four reactions is shown in Figure 3.2. Obviously, you must assess prospects' reactions and apply the proper stimulus to move them toward Square 1. This brings us to the true value of the classification of reactions. One of its important advantages is that it forces you to pay close attention to the prospect. When followed, it will ensure that each stimulus you apply will be appropriate and will help move the interview to a successful close.

The Bank acted as custodian of the assets of about 50 small self-directed accounts that were part of the pension program of a major medical clinic. The clinic had chosen us as custodian of these accounts for the convenience of their employees. The major part of their assets, amounting to over $2 million in securities, were held in custody at a New York bank.

The relationship was rocky almost from the start. The employees objected to the transactions fees that we charged. We lost money on the accounts in spite of the fees. Eventually, the doctor who chaired their pension committee called me to request my presence at a committee meeting at which they intended to fire the Bank. In preparing for the unpleasant appointment, I was reminded of the sales matrix that was presented in your marketing course. I was clearly in the upper-right quadrant: the box in which they are saying "NO" and acting "NO," and you have lost the sale. I remembered the strategy for that position was to do something unexpected or change something dramatically to try and knock the prospect out of that box and into one of the boxes that represents more ambivalence on the part of the customer. From those boxes, supposedly, the client could be moved toward affirmative agreement.

Because I had nothing more to lose, I decided to try the outrageous. I arrived at the committee meeting at which the doctors sat smugly around the table. I told the doctors that if their intent was to leave only the self-directed accounts with us, we would be quite willing to resign from the relationship. However, I proposed an alternative that I felt would be better for both parties. That alternative was for the clinic to move their multimillion dollar pension fund from New York to us. By so doing, I explained, they would enable us to make a fair profit on the type of business which we did best, and that profit would enable us to continue to handle the individual accounts at a reduced fee. The clinic would be better off because it would receive at least as good service on its large pension plan, better service on the individual accounts, and the added convenience of dealing with only one custodian.

The doctors were stunned. The chairman, who had summoned me to be fired, said, "Let me see if I understand this. We called you here to fire you from this account, and you are asking us to give you all of our business?" "Yes," I replied. "That's exactly it."

Two hours later they called and said the Bank had their business.

Exhibit 3.1   A change in the basic approach—A success story.

Special Considerations in Application

The Salesperson's Characteristics

Consideration of this method of reaction analysis will reveal that it is subjective. It depends on the perspective and judgment of the salesperson. If you and your supervisor were to make a joint call and were to review your respective judgments of the prospect's reactions, you would probably have some differences in the classifications. This subjective character of the method, however, does not limit its usefulness. Rather, it is the basis of its power.

	Positive	Negative
Voluntary	**1.** Positive-Voluntary Reactions Close the Sale	**4.** Negative-Voluntary Reactions Change Approach
Involuntary	**2.** Positive-Involuntary Reactions Provide More Information	**3.** Negative-Involuntary Reactions Change Sales Point

Figure 3.2 The relationship between the classification of buyer reactions and salesperson responses.

Your personal characteristics will influence the classification you make of a prospect's reactions. In general, more aggressive salespeople tend to classify observed reactions as positive. Conversely, less aggressive ones will tend to lean toward a negative interpretation. Consequently, you must *assess your own personality* and make the necessary adjustment in your evaluation of reactions.

Another personality characteristic that may cause difficulty in classifying reactions is the social sensitivity of salespeople. The more socially sensitive salespeople are, the more likely they are to catch cues in the prospect's behavior. For example, if a prospect makes a relatively minor telephone call during the interview, the socially sensitive salesperson would sense that the prospect was bored with the interview and would change the approach. In contrast, the less-sensitive salesperson would not catch the significance of the act and would continue as though nothing had happened. An important aid in developing social sensitivity is to keep attention where it belongs during the call—on the prospect.

Being able to distinguish between voluntary and involuntary reactions is perhaps the most important factor in effective tactics. Consider the category *negative-involuntary reactions.* The tactical principle recommended is to make a subtle shift. A shift to a point of more interest to the prospect is likely to develop a *positive-involuntary* reaction. If you miss the cue or ignore it and continue to supply more information on the point that elicited the negative-involuntary reaction, the reaction probably will move to *negative-voluntary.*

Faced with a negative-involuntary reaction, the natural thing for salespeople to do is to bring up new and more powerful arguments to overcome the objection that they feel to be imminent. While this appears to be a logical step, *psychological analysis of the situation in terms of tactics indicates that you are wiser to avoid a discussion on a point of no interest to the prospect.* Sound tactics dictate moving to an area of mutual interest.

Salespeople may be tempted to argue a point because they fail to distinguish between prospects' objections to a point in the presentation and their objection to buying at all. The method presented in this section is designed to apply to the interview as a whole and the attainment of the call objectives. Prospects may, in the course of the interview, object to one or more individual points; yet they may place an order. Arguing a sales point that is not critical to the sale may be likened to "winning the battle but losing the war."

Refer to Appendixes VII and VIII to see how the technique works in practice. Appendix VIII is a sample sales interview. In the left margin you can indicate the appropriate classification for both your and your prospect's reactions.

Appendix VII enables you to organize and classify the kinds of reactions you encounter in your regular calls. By listing prospects' reactions in the appropriate boxes, you can then prepare suitable responses to move the interview toward a successful close.

Relation to the "Psychological Moment"

Many sales authorities, when giving advice on closing the sale, recommend: "Watch for the psychological moment." This term refers to an intuitive process that you may use to determine when to ask for the order. This concept is not wrong, as far as it goes, except that it is intuitive and, therefore, cannot be communicated to others. Unless the user has instructions to help identify the moment, the advice is as meaningless as the formula for becoming a millionaire: "Pick a job where you can make a lot of money."

Another problem surfaces as well. If the term is limited to the moment when you should ask for the order, it bypasses the positive-involuntary stage, a more significant moment in the majority of interviews. At some points in the interview, you will get agreement on enough sales points to feel you have a sale in the offing. Yet you may not be able to close then because you must supply additional information. In consequence, if the term "psychological moment" is to have real significance, it should apply to that point where you sense the sale is likely but not necessarily the point when you should ask for the order.

SUMMARY

The question technique is more likely to be effective in controlling the interview than is an attempt to outtalk the prospect. In fact, the type of salesperson who monopolizes the conversation is likely to be viewed as less able and pleasant than one who encourages the prospect's participation.

A good question elicits a significant amount of information. There are five principles for phrasing questions: (1) In general, questions should elicit information from the buyer beyond "Yes," "No," or very short responses; (2) questions should be open; (3) questions should be indirect; (4) questions should be short; and (5) questions should be one part.

You may use questions to develop initial interest, reveal the extent of product/service knowledge, and determine the prospect's needs. You may also use questions to initiate the interview, and to clarify and complete the information you need.

Good questions are so valuable that it is wise to develop and practice the phrasing of questions outside of interview time. You can develop skill in phrasing questions only through this extra effort. Mastering the question technique is, by analogy, mastering one of the tools of your trade. Finally, effective use of the question technique provides a foundation for building credibility.

Selling is not so simple that mentioning a suitable appeal always results in an immediate sale. It is usually necessary to use several sales points and state them in a number of different ways. Summation is a psychologically sound principle for organizing your sales points. When understood, it will give you the strength to persevere in the number of calls and in the presentation of sales points within a call. You know that you are making progress by small steps and that summation will give your efforts a greater effect than the simple addition of the individual elements of the sales process.

Proper timing in using sales points is crucial to successful selling. Timing within the sale and of follow-up calls where multiple calls are necessary to effect a sale should be a matter of planning rather than impulse. The concept *refractory phase* provides a basis for such timing. Guidelines to follow in timing are developed.

To maintain control and close the sale, you need to attend *to* the words and actions of the prospect and *from* yourself.

In selling, you are wiser to find areas of agreement and expand on them than to win useless debates. Do not try to induce a decision before the prospect is ready. Close observation of the prospect's reactions to your statements provides cues to the prospect's attitude. If it is negative-voluntary, it indicates you should make a change in approach. If it is negative-involuntary, a subtle shift to a better sales point is in order. A positive-involuntary reaction calls for you to supply more information, while a positive-voluntary reaction calls for an immediate close.

To achieve your strategic and tactical objectives, you must be adept in applying the need satisfaction method.

TOPICS FOR THOUGHT AND DISCUSSION

1. What is the common denominator of personality traits associated with salespeople who use the question approach as compared with those who monopolize the conversation?
2. What exceptions to the question approach can you think of? Define the circumstances in terms of personality traits of the customers.

3. What attitudes do most salespeople have to change before they can adopt the question approach wholeheartedly?
4. What are the benefits of adhering to the five criteria for questions?
5. Discuss "Most people do not, on the basis of the phrasing of their questions, deserve the information they obtain."
6. Analyze your job so that you can prepare a list of situations in which questions will be helpful to you. You can then prepare sample questions for each category.
7. In which of the three phases of the need satisfaction selling—need development, need awareness, need fulfillment—would the salesperson run the highest/lowest risks in violating the five question criteria? Why?
8. Credibility is arguably one of the real problems in selling. The buyer does not always believe the salesperson. What factors are important in establishing credibility? What specific steps can you take to make your presentations more credible?
9. Give examples of the operation of the principle of homeostasis in both physiological and psychological situations.
10. What sales positions call for inducing dissatisfaction in a prospect as compared with canvassing to find prospects already dissatisfied?
11. How does the principle of homeostasis compare with the principle of summation in terms of importance to salespeople?
12. What is the relationship between homeostasis and low-pressure selling?
13. Take a product such as a man's or a woman's suit and develop a sales presentation using the principles of spatial and temporal summation.
14. What are some possible conditions that might negate the operation of the summation principle in selling?
15. Analyze the number of outlets for various products in a nearby shopping center. How do they fit the concept of summation?
16. Why should you work out and master sales points and alternate phrasings ahead of time?
17. Should you ever leave a customer without really trying for a close?
18. How does the advice to check on the understanding of each sales point relate to use of the selling formula or "canned" sales talk?
19. Who should assume responsibility for the customer's understanding—the customer or the salesperson? Why?
20. How does the idea of "feedback" relate to the concept of refractory phase?
21. What steps could you take to increase your social sensitivity and thus improve your ability to correctly classify customer reactions?
22. Why should you distinguish between resistance to some specific aspect of the product and resistance to the product in general?
23. Why is the negative-involuntary category of customer response the most critical as far as you are concerned?
24. How would failure of two different salespeople to agree on the classification of a particular customer reaction affect the value of the overall system presented here?

FOUR

Managing Sales Resistance

Had we but world enough, and time,
this coyness, lady, were no crime.

ANDREW MARVELL

In this chapter:

- **The Nature of Sales Resistance**
  - Sales resistance is a signal that the prospect feels conflict between buying and not buying.
- **Handling Objections**
  - When buyers and sellers disagree, buyers are more likely to act on their own verbalizations than on yours.
  - When buyers ask sellers for information, they are more likely to listen than if you supply the information on your own initiative.
- **Summary**
  - The major kinds of sales resistance—psychological and logical—are defined and illustrated. A psychologically sound process for handling objections is provided.
- **Topics for Thought and Discussion**
- **Application Exercises**
  - Appendix II Salesperson-Oriented Product Manual
  - Appendix IV Work Sheets for SOPM

1. THE NATURE OF SALES RESISTANCE

Sales resistance may be defined as any behavior, verbal and/or nonverbal, by a customer or prospect that appears to or actually does interfere with the likelihood of a sale.

Unless the person being solicited obviously cannot be considered a prospect for the product or service, sales resistance is a signal that he or she feels a conflict between buying and not buying. The pessimist feels discouraged by the resistance. The optimist welcomes sales resistance, realizing that it at least indicates some desire to buy. In most instances, some sales resistance is normal and desirable because prospects have to evaluate the proposal and try to relate it to their situations.

While a person may buy without showing sales resistance, one of the most diabolical forms of sales resistance is where the prospect is overly agreeable to the salesperson. The prospect who never offers an objection or asks a question deprives you of an opportunity to describe the product or service in detail. At the end of the interview, the prospect usually does not understand or appreciate the proposition and seldom feels a need for it.

Sales resistance may derive from either of two principal sources—logical or psychological. In addition, deliberate resistance is sometimes encountered. Psychological resistance refers to an unwillingness to buy based on attitude, emotion, or prejudice. Such resistance is highly subjective and varies from one person to another. Logical resistance encompasses an unwillingness to buy based on tangible considerations such as price, delivery date, or product specifications. Deliberate sales resistance is voluntary customer behavior obstructing the sales process.

Psychological Sales Resistance

Some of the reasons for sales resistance offered by psychologists are:

1. Resistance to interference.
2. Preference for established habits.
3. Budget consciousness.
4. Tendency to resist domination.
5. Predetermined ideas about products or services.
6. Dislike of decision making.
7. Neurotic attitude toward money.

An analysis of each type of resistance follows, together with suggestions for avoiding or overcoming that particular problem.

Resistance to Interference

Unless the prospect has initiated the contact, a visit from a salesperson constitutes interference. Prospects have to stop what they are doing and listen to the salesperson. When no interview has been granted, an even stronger feeling of interference exists. Prospects who are not interested in the line the salesperson represents may be annoyed to think that they were approached at all. Even if they are really interested in listening, they may be engaged in another task so that they consider the visit or telephone call an interruption.

Several suggestions for reducing resistance of this kind are: Be attentive to your physical appearance and personal manner so that you are likable on sight. In addition, a voice that is "interesting to listen to" may intrigue the prospect enough to let you proceed. You may want to tape your voice and analyze it. Consider your rate of speech, enthusiasm, pitch, and diction. A number of courses are available for improving speaking ability. Another suggestion is to set up interviews in advance. There is a wide variety of media for this purpose: telephone, fax, E-mail, and so on. Psychological resistance cannot be eliminated but can be held to a minimum by a little forethought and planning.

Some evidence from psychological research can help you decide whether to press for an interview when you discover a customer is engaged in a task. The nearer the task is to completion, the less likely customers will put it aside to give you their undivided attention. The principle involved is "goal gradient." The nearer people are to completing a task or reaching a goal, the less you can interrupt them. For example, assume a printer is in the process of setting up a press to run an annual report. If he has just begun, is still a long way from completion, and knows he will have to stop for lunch or continue the next day, he will probably give you his attention without question. If, on the other hand, he has been working for 2 hours and expects to be finished in another 15 minutes, you will most likely have to wait until the printer completes the task before you can obtain his undivided attention. You should try to find out the degree of completion of the task before making an effort to begin an interview. You can often discover this from secretaries and subordinate personnel without disturbing the person you wish to see. Unless a return call or a short wait is completely out of the question, make your presentation to a person who is fully attentive rather than to one whose mind is still on a nearly completed task. Section 2 of this chapter covers this point in more detail.

Preference for Established Habits

Habits are a stabilizing influence on society and on the individual. Without habits, behavior would be less predictable, but they are a paradox to the salesperson. When you can learn prospects' habits, you feel you have a better chance of selling them, yet the very nature of selling is such that a sale invariably calls for a habit change. More specifically, you need to get buyers to agree in advance to change their habits before you can make a sale. Obviously, then, anticipated change is a potent source of sales resistance.

Knowing how your prospect will use your products and services is essential. Part of your job is to show how the offering fits into buyers' life styles. When a change in habits will bring about an increased satisfaction in life, your product or service is more attractive.

Another way of reducing the resistance to changing habits is to reduce the apparent difference between the old and new habit. You can do this by talking in language and terms familiar to customers, making reference to people they know, and in general minimizing the novel aspects of using the new product or service.

Remember, the resistance is as likely to be focused on a dislike of giving up old ideas as on a dislike of adopting any new ones. Do not make the mistake of repeatedly stressing the product benefits when the customer has already accepted them. Rather, you should concentrate on minimizing the change in habits resulting from using the new product or service.

Budget Consciousness

Human society is based on needs that outstrip resources. Most customers, therefore, must resist propositions for which they feel little need. Hence, you need to develop a greater need for the product than the existing desire not to spend.

Communicating product information and customer benefits convincingly is the first step in overcoming this resistance. On some propositions, this will suffice to make a sale. When this approach does not generate interest, a deeper resistance is evident and you must define and treat it in accordance with the principle of *homeostasis*, discussed in Chapter Three, Section 1, of this book.

Tendency to Resist Domination

The nature of the sales process is that the salesperson must largely control or dominate it. Most people have a tendency to resist any sort of domination. As soon as customers feel pressure, they tend to resist. In fact, they may anticipate domination and show resistance from the beginning of the sales process. Even though they want the product or service, they may be inhibited from purchasing until they have found a face-saving mechanism that makes it appear to others that they bought the product or service rather than that it was sold to them.

You should recognize your customers' need to feel they, rather than you, controlled the interview. Your satisfaction should be derived from getting an order. If you look for opportunities to make customers feel important and superior, you will eliminate this source of resistance.

Predetermined Ideas about Products or Services

Customers many times have preconceived ideas regarding a product or service. Such ideas and feelings, even though not warranted, might close a buyer's mind to a purchase. If you ridicule prospects' beliefs or try to change their minds with logic, the prejudice will probably intensify.

The first step in dealing with prejudice is to accept that prospects hold the belief as firmly as though it were based on reality. You should show that you can appreciate their point of view. The prejudice, however, is undoubtedly inconsistent with other beliefs. If you can discover an inconsistent belief, you can use it by relating the purchase to this alternate idea rather than by meeting the prejudice head-on. Making people aware they are holding inconsistent ideas is risky, however. In any event, you should not try to dispose of the prejudice on the basis of logic.

When you expose an inconsistency, the prospect might offer another equally inconsistent reason for not purchasing. Recognize that the problem is deep-seated and involves emotional resistance. Such problems may be beyond your responsibility. You might need to ignore the prejudice and try to make the sale on some other basis.

Dislike of Decision Making

Making decisions is a painful process for some people. They fear the consequences of their actions and dread disturbing the status quo. Yet, before you can obtain an order, the customer must make a decision to buy. Many sales are carried to the point of signing the order, but the salesperson is unable to overcome the resistance of the customer to the final act.

Things are not as bad as they seem, however. A strong tendency to buy exists, otherwise you would not be at this point of conflict. The barrier may be lack of self-confidence on the customer's part. A good technique for dealing with this situation is to refer to satisfied customers. The greater the prestige of such references, the more effective they will be for this purpose.

Sometimes the sale bogs down at this point because you have failed to press for a close. Any textbook on selling will provide a number of standard closing techniques that might be helpful once you reach this point. You should also see the specific techniques in Section 2 of this chapter. The important point to remember is that a strong motive to buy exists, and the problem is not to sell the product or service but to think about your customers and search for ways to reduce their apprehension about making a purchasing decision.

Neurotic Attitude toward Money

If money matters were unemotional, your life would be much easier. With the exception of some professional buyers and purchasing agents, most buyers are emotional in making a purchase.

When emotion becomes strong enough to be classed as irrational, ordinary sales methods become inadequate to handle the situation. Whether you can ever deal effectively with such deep-seated problems is doubtful, but you should learn to recognize prospects who fall in this category. If you recognize what you are facing, you will learn to abandon some sales attempts and invest your time more profitably with prospects who are less emotional.

Whenever you recognize that the prospect's excitement over spending money is out of proportion to the amount of money involved, you might suspect the customer has a neurotic attitude toward money. If so, you may be wise to withdraw from the situation and seek other prospects.

Logical Sales Resistance

Logical sales resistance normally originates with an attribute of the product or service in contrast to psychological resistance, which originates in the psychology of the buyer. The causes of logical resistance, of course, will vary from one buyer to another, but some of the principal ones are price, delivery schedule, and specifications.

Price

Price is deceptive as a concept and is interrelated with quality, service, image, and other factors in the minds of both the buyer and the seller. Before you discuss price, you must determine the prospect's perception of the value expected. For example, the qualities you seek in a paper carton that will contain goods in storage will be considerably different from the qualities you expect from a display container in a retail store. In each instance, the prospective purchaser weighs the values expected in relationship to the price asked.

In some industrial situations, chemical additives are used. Where several competitive products are available, the strength as well as the price per pound may vary over the product line. In such an instance, price per pound is deceptive. The true price is the effective use price. Where strength of solution is involved, bulk weight for shipping may be a substantial consideration, and shipping charges on a weak solution may negate apparent savings on a per-pound basis.

To complicate matters still further, you often need to point out many added values that accrue from dealing with your firm. Too frequently, buyers think only of the goods or services in terms of price, quality, and value, neglecting to consider the reliability of the source, the speed of delivery, the flexibility of the formulation, or the ease of dealing with your company's marketing team.

Delivery Schedule

The importance of delivery varies with the production schedule of the buyer. With the development of just-in-time manufacturing systems, however, delivery is becoming significantly more important. When delivery problems are cited as sales resistance, you should attempt to discover the production schedules. With this information, you should be able to determine how well your deliveries are meshing with the customer's actual requirements. You should also clear up delivery problems as part of your customer service.

Specifications

Specifications drawn up by scientists and engineers are frequently provided to purchasing departments for guidance in placing orders. Normally, the purchasing agent follows the specifications very carefully, and this often makes a particular product appear to be unusable.

You should consult with technicians in your company and in the prospect company to discover the flexibility or tolerance in the specifications. Quite possibly when other advantages are available to the purchaser, the specifications will be relaxed to allow you to make a sale.

There are many other logical forms of sales resistance. They can originate in any element of differential competitive advantage: Tangible, Intangible, Price, Image, and/or Team. Sales resistance can be overcome, in many instances, by logical analysis of the situation (see Chapter Seven for an in-depth discussion). You should also talk over such resistance with company personnel who have experience in handling resistance.

Deliberate Sales Resistance

Professor Henry Hepner believes psychologists have as much responsibility to show consumers how to develop deliberate sales resistance as to show salespeople how to overcome it. We present his ideas here so that you may recognize the voluntary sales resistance of customers who deliberately impede your presentation.

A customer can resist the impulse to buy by observing your methods rather than listening to the information. At the end of the interview, the customer will be able to describe your sales techniques but not your product or service. In such a case, little likelihood of a sale exists.

Another way the customer can reduce your effectiveness is to make you angry by belittling you or your products. If you lose your temper, you have lost all possibility of making a sale.

As pointed out earlier, the prospect can also unnerve you by agreeing with you on each point you make. The customer can go even further and compliment you on your skill. When this happens deliberately, the customer is not interested in the presentation.

Sometimes customers use physical techniques to resist your presentation. They may seat you facing a light or a window, which puts you at a disadvantage. Failing to provide a chair or other place to sit is another device of this nature. When you have no place to put your coat, it impairs your ability to make a presentation.

When you encounter deliberate resistance, accept that the customer is not interested at this point and abandon the attempt. On the other hand, if you wish to continue the sales attempt, you can counter the resistance by pointing out the nature of the resistance, with an inquiry as to whether you should continue or whether the customer really has no interest in the proposition.

Overcoming Sales Resistance

There are four basic ways to deal with sales resistance.

1. Try to sidestep or minimize the resistance and obtain an order without going through all the pros and cons of the proposition.
2. Attack the resistance head-on with logic and show that the prospect's reasoning is faulty. (Chapter Seven, Section 2)
3. Get buyers to participate and to answer their own objections. (Section 2 of this chapter)
4. Find the uniqueness in each buyer that distinguishes that person from others, and personalize the sales presentation. (Chapter Five)

Successful salespeople will master all four methods and use them when appropriate.

Some readers may feel that the methods outlined give salespeople an unfair advantage over prospects and customers. While this may be true, withholding relatively well-known principles is not warranted. Our wish and intent is for salespeople to use the methods only to achieve sales that will profit both the buyer and seller. In the next section, attention is focused on handling specific objections, as contrasted with general resistance.

2. HANDLING OBJECTIONS

What is really meant by an objection? One person defines it as anything prospects say or do that inhibits you from attaining your call objectives. Objections are of two types—psychological and logical.

1. Psychological objections are those raised when prospects have no rational basis for not buying but are loathe to make the buying decision.
2. Logical objections are those raised when the prospect seriously and rationally objects to one or more of your sales points.

From a tactical standpoint, a psychological objection is more complex to deal with. You must determine the cause. You can cope with the logical objection directly. Chapter Seven provides problem-solving techniques to handle logical objections.

You can easily determine the seriousness of an objection—ignore it and continue with your presentation. If you can sustain the prospect's interest and attention, you can assume the objection was probably trivial. On the other hand, if you observe waning interest and attention, you must backtrack to cope with the objection.

Psychological Objections

You cannot handle all psychological objections in the same manner. But, if you employ several perspectives effectively, you should increase your success in this phase of selling.

Rationalization

To understand the basis of many psychological objections, you need to understand the significance of *rationalization*. This adjustment mechanism is similar to projection. Basically, the prospect needs to find a socially acceptable reason to justify an act.

When you meet an objection in the sales process, you can never be positive whether you are hearing the real reason or one developed either to protect the prospect's ego or to avoid a more extended discussion. When prospects offer any reason other than the real one, you may consider it a rationalization.

When dealing with a rationalization, you should appear to accept the objection at face value. You cannot insult prospects any more than you can answer the objection directly. You will only breed another equally invalid objection. The recommended procedure is to identify the meaning or social value the objection has for the prospect. When you discover this, you can develop a plan for dealing with the situation.

There is another type of rationalization in selling. Often prospects are tempted to place an order but hold back because they do not see how they can justify their decisions to other people. When you discern that the prospect feels unable to justify a purchase and that this factor, in effect, is the real objection, you should help the prospect find a rationalization or socially acceptable basis for the transaction.

Readiness or Set

If you see an objection as a negative voluntary reaction, you must conclude that what you said to prompt it was inappropriate. You therefore must say or do something next that will elicit a positive response. For example, if the prospect says, "Your price is too high," you might say, "What values are you seeking in your purchase?" or "How are you calculating the cost?"

You might need to continue such a series of statements until you establish a positive rather than a negative set on the part of the prospect.

Status Yield

You also must let prospects know you appreciate their viewpoints. By doing so, you accord status to them. Continuing the preceding example, after you have elicited a series of positive responses, you might continue: "As a professional, I am sure you subject all purchases to intensive value analysis. What value do you place on a nationally advertised brand versus an off-brand product?" This disarms prospects and prepares them further for answers to their objections.

Conviction Based on Participation

You need to consider and adopt two assumptions:

1. When buyers and sellers disagree, buyers are more likely to act on their own verbalizations than yours.
2. When buyers ask sellers for information, they are more likely to listen than if you supply the information on your own initiative.

Your first effort then should be to get buyers to answer their own objections. Failing this, you should get buyers to ask you for the answer. Many authors suggest the salesperson actually answer objections rather than use the question technique to help buyers think through the issues at hand. From a psychological perspective, this amounts to the weakest approach.

The principle can be illustrated by continuing the preceding example. You follow the question on the value of a nationally advertised brand with such questions as: "What dollar value do you place on an item that turns over at least eight times a year?" or "What is merchandising help for your store managers worth?" By eliciting answers from the prospect in terms of dollars, you are leading prospects to answer their own objections. If you *tell* someone something, how much of the message the person actually receives is problematical. Alternatively, if you *ask a question*, a higher probability exists that the other person will consider the issue at hand. A well-crafted question causes another person to think.

Other Considerations

The manner in which you answer an objection can be important. For example, if you are not sure of yourself, your answer will probably not satisfy your prospects, who are likely to come back with more objections. They lose confidence in you. Conversely, if you give a straightforward and satisfactory answer, customers are likely to be satisfied and to have increased confidence in you.

You might face an occasional objection that stumps you. Capitalize on this. You can do so by bolstering the ego of your customers and indicating that you will obtain an answer from the specialists at company headquarters. This is preferable to an inadequate answer, provided it does not happen frequently. Constant use of this method can breed loss of credibility.

Sometimes prospects take delight in harassing a salesperson with a continuing stream of objections.

To show the kinds of comments that may cause prospects to stop objecting, the following list presents three groups of statements ranging from (1) pleasant or complimentary through (2) neutral to (3) disrespectful:

1. Complimentary comments to encourage participation:
   "You have a point there."
   "You have really been giving this some thought."
   "You have a good grasp of the situation."
2. Neutral comments to size up the situation:
   "Why do you ask that?"
   "How would that information help you?"
   "What is the source of that idea?"
3. Discourteous comments to try to reduce objections:
   "You can answer that better than I can."
   "What are you really trying to tell me?"

"Surely you don't believe that."
"You have been misinformed."
"I guess you don't want to talk to me."

While the list provides some helpful phrases, the tone and inflection of the voice are also important. By using cordiality in Group 1 and sarcasm in Group 3, you may be able to control the amount and quality of objections.

Timing in answering an objection is an important consideration. When you answer an objection, you need to consider two factors. If you delay your answer (1) prospects may continue to think about the objection and magnify its importance, and (2) they may pay little attention to your presentation until you answer the objection. You, then, must give special attention to how long you take to ready the prospect for the answer, as well as how much time to use in providing the answer. If you know that you cover the objection in a later point of your presentation, you should get agreement from the prospect to delay the answer. As you proceed, you must be particularly observant to see that the prospect is following you.

Handling Objections: The Four-Step Process

The following process for handling objections reflects their psychological bases and is flexible enough for you to use the most appropriate combination of specific techniques to deal with each objection.

Step 1. *Establish Readiness or Set*

Do or say something that elicits a positive response. If the customer or prospect is in an agreeable frame of mind before considering Step 2, you have a greater probability of handling the objection effectively.

Step 2. *Clarify the Difference of Opinion*

You must understand the exact nature of the buyer's objection. Only with such knowledge will you have a basis for making a response. Clarify the objection for two reasons. First, the problem may be a matter of word meaning rather than a real difference of opinion about your product or service. You can forestall many apparent objections at this stage. Second, most objections have more than one answer. Thus you must probe each objection to the point where you can select the appropriate answer. For example, a buyer might say, "It's too complicated." You cannot intelligently answer the objection as stated. To identify the proper answer, you must use clarifying or probing questions. Here are two examples: (1) "What do you mean by complicated?" and (2) "Who would find it complicated?"

If you assume you know the buyer's objection rather than clarifying it, you lessen the probability of a sale. The buyer will be reluctant to purchase if you fail to address his or her concerns.

Step 3. *Mentally Formulate a Suitable and Effective Answer*

Ask yourself, "What do you know to be true?" This question will help you generate potential answers. List all possible answers to anticipated objections. Do this prior to the interview so that you can be attentive to the buyer during the call. Over time, you will be able to prepare yourself to handle all the objections that frequently arise.

While you should mentally formulate answers to objections, you *do not* respond directly with them. You must now take into account the assumption made earlier that buyers are more likely to act on their own statements than yours. The ideal way to deal with an objection is to have buyers answer it themselves. You do this with a question after you have formulated the desired answer.

Step 4. *Try to Elicit the Answer (Step 3) from the Prospect*

To do this, you must be an adept questioner. Software, for example, comes with training manuals and tutorials as well as help functions and well-staffed 800 numbers. The untrained salesperson does not use the question technique but produces the manual and/or the tutorial diskettes and says, "These will teach you the software in an afternoon." The trained salesperson asks, "How would this manual help you learn the software?" or "How would free customer support help you?" The buyer can see that learning will be relatively simple, answering his or her own objection.

This fourth step in responding to an objection, then, is to ask a question that will cause the buyer either to answer his or her own objection or to ask you for the answer. The dialogue below illustrates this four-step method. The salesperson represents a pharmaceutical firm. In this interview the salesperson is presenting a new proprietary item for inducing sleep.

Step 1.	Prospect:	"I never have any requests for such a product."
	Salesperson:	"You certainly have to consider your customers' needs when ordering anything, don't you?"
	Prospect:	"I sure do."
Step 2:	Salesperson:	"I'm not sure whether the 'lack of requests' you mention means your customers do not use this type of product or do not call for our brand."
	Customer:	"Oh, I sell a lot of sleep aids, but no one ever asks for yours by name."
Step 3:	Salesperson mentally:	(If I show our brand is selling well in other stores, the drug retailer will place an order. The study in *Drug Topics* should be convincing.)

Step 4: Salesperson: "What do you think of *Drug Topics* as a guide in knowing what to stock?"

Customer: "That is a good source of information on leading brands. I am always interested to see what they have to say."

Salesperson: Showing reprint. "How does our brand compare with the competition as shown in this table?"

Customer: "Very well. It looks good in terms of both turnover and markup."

Salesperson: "How would you predict it would perform in your stores if you gave it the same display space you are giving competitive products?"

Customer: "According to this table, it would do better than some of the ones I am carrying."

Salesperson: "As you said, *Drug Topics* is a good source of information. Would you be willing to try our merchandising plan and see for yourself how you can add to your profits?"

Customer: "OK. I'll take the special deal but it had better move."

The salesperson then writes an order and helps the customer decide on the best spot for a display.

See Appendix IV for a work sheet applying this tactical plan to your own profession. An example is provided in Appendix II.

Specific Techniques

Many books treat the subject of objections in great detail and describe numerous techniques for dealing with them; apparently the only limitation on the number is the imagination of the authors. A critical evaluation, however, indicates that some procedures are sounder and more effective than others. Authors frequently present the tactics as though they were of equal value and seldom specify the conditions under which a particular technique is applicable. If you are critical and carefully select techniques appropriate for the problem at hand, you will find them useful and helpful. If you use them blindly, you will find them working on a chance basis, and many times they will work to your disadvantage.

The following techniques are not exhaustive but are representative of those found in sales literature. We make no attempt to detail when each should be used because sales situations are too varied. However, you should be familiar with them and use them when they appear to be warranted in a particular sales call.

Boomerang

Turning an objection into a reason to buy is a standard practice with many sales-people. A typical example is to answer the statement "While the offering seems very desirable, I have no money" with "The reason I brought this to your attention is that it will save you money." Another objection is "Your organization is too small to provide the service we need." You can boomerang this objection by replying, "Our small size is one of our assets; it permits us to give personal service."

Coming to That

Often salespeople wish to avoid answering an objection because they plan to present the information at a later point. This is particularly true in a fully structured or "canned" sales talk. Instead of answering the objection, you say, "I plan to cover that later" and continue your presentation. You can also use this technique when you lack a good answer to objections. By giving yourself time, you may come up with a good answer. It is also possible that the prospect will drop the objection and you may never need to answer it. You must use caution in using this technique as indicated in the discussion of timing (Chapter Three, Section 3).

Yes, But . . .

This is an attempt to show prospects that they can have their cake and eat it too. You appear to concede the objection, but in reality you supply more information to support your point of view.

Closely related to the "yes, but . . ." technique is minimizing the objection and making a minor concession. The basic plan is to play down the importance of the objection and show that it does not constitute a basis for stopping the transaction.

Offsetting

Instead of making a concession, as in the preceding technique, this calls for presenting additional information that contains an advantage equal to or greater than the objection presented.

Comparison or Contrast

This is a special case of offsetting or minimizing an objection. Rather than offering a counter argument or playing down the importance of the objection, you compare or contrast it with something that is quite acceptable. An expensive machine that is designed for many years of service might appear expensive in terms of the list price. By pointing out its daily cost or cost per part produced, the cost can be made to seem small relative to the gain in quality and/or speed of production it will achieve. Such a comparison may neutralize the objection.

Humor

A good laugh may cleanse the atmosphere when you reach a critical point in a sales presentation. Introducing a funny story or anecdote may relieve tension, and the presentation can continue even though you have not fully covered the objection.

Direct Denial

Sometimes customers offer false objections. This could be due to misinformation on their part or might be an attempt to harass you. In either case, a direct denial of their objection together with a statement of the facts may be in order. You should use caution, however, as such an outright contradiction may offend customers.

Questions

Questions can be helpful in handling objections by turning some of the responsibility for the answer back to the customer. Suppose the objection is "Your product is not as good as your competitor's." A simple question "Why?" may bring out the fact that the objection is not well-founded. If a basis for the objection exists, you can either provide a satisfactory answer or request information from your superiors. Obviously, feedback is important to you. The question also helps to clarify the objection in the minds of both the customer and the salesperson.

SUMMARY

During a sales presentation, the customer or prospect may offer general resistance as well as state specific objections.

The major kinds of sales resistance—psychological and logical—are defined and illustrated. Suggestions are offered for avoiding and/or overcoming both. Sometimes, resistance is set up by the buyer who deliberately or voluntarily impedes your presentation. Certain forms of emotional sales resistance cannot be handled efficiently and should be avoided.

It is important to understand the psychological mechanism of rationalization. Getting buyers to participate and to answer their own objections is advantageous. A four-step process for handling objections is provided, followed by an analysis of specific techniques for handling objections.

The major kinds of sales resistance—psychological and logical—are defined and illustrated. A psychologically sound process for handling objections is provided.

TOPICS FOR THOUGHT AND DISCUSSION

1. What do you think of the idea that sales resistance is indicative of conflict in the buyer and hence is a sign of interest in your proposal?
2. Which of the nine kinds of psychological sales resistance are most difficult for you to handle? Why?
3. Which of your own psychological characteristics might influence the relative difficulty you could encounter in handling psychological sales resistance in customers? Why?
4. Which types of voluntary sales resistance have you encountered? How did you deal with the resistance on those occasions? How will you react if you encounter such resistance in the future?
5. Provide examples where rationalization by a prospect prevented you from making a sale. If you were to renew the contact, how would you change your tactics?
6. What are some of the implications of the statement: "People are more likely to believe the things they say themselves than what they hear others say?"
7. How do you feel about using disrespectful comments to reduce the flow of invalid objections?
8. How does the tactical plan recommended in this text compare with the standard techniques for handling objections in other books?

FIVE

Strategy with Individuals

We think in generalities, we live in detail.

ALFRED NORTH WHITEHEAD

In this chapter:

- **Understanding Personality**
  — To sell yourself, and subsequently your offerings, you must develop strategies for each buyer based on his or her uniqueness.
- **Describing an Individual's Personality and Planning Strategy**
  — Properly executed, the trait analysis provides you with clues for approaching the buyer.
- **Understanding Motivation**
  — The two most important facets to examine are: (1) what goes on inside individuals and (2) what they seek in the environment.
- **Analyzing Customers' and Prospects' Motivations and Planning Strategy**
  — A motivational analysis will reveal *what* to talk about to personalize the presentation.
- **Understanding Background and Improving Your Ability to Adjust to Others**
  — Reliance on first impressions is the most frequent error in sizing up an individual prospect or customer.
- **Summary**
  — To personalize your presentation, you must understand the variables—personality, motivation, background, and situation— in the strategic equation.
- **Topics for Thought and Discussion**
- **Application Exercises**

1. UNDERSTANDING PERSONALITY

Modern mass marketing tends to depersonalize the individual. In contrast, selling should accord individuality. Salespeople succeed or fail to the extent that they can understand and adjust to people. To be successful, you must make each prospect feel that he or she is receiving personal attention. You must sell yourself before you can sell your products or services. To sell yourself, and subsequently your offerings, you need to develop strategies for each buyer based on his or her uniqueness. Using the need satisfaction method of selling practically guarantees that you will sell yourself. To implement the strategy, you must adjust to buyers. Understanding their personality is the first step in developing a strategy to personalize the presentation of your offering.

The study of personality, then, is an important part of each salesperson's professional preparation. Salespeople who learn about human personality enjoy these benefits:

1. They increase their knowledge of others.
2. They improve their ability to analyze people.
3. They base their sales strategy and tactics on what they know about each prospect's or customer's personality.
4. They understand themselves better.

Personality is the unique self—the style of a person's behavior—that distinguishes him or her from everyone else in the world. No two personalities are

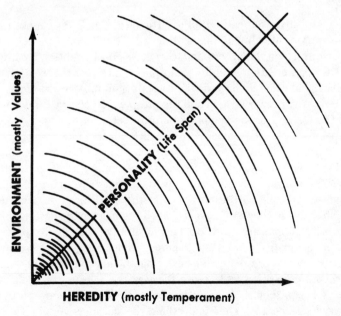

Figure 5.1 Basic ingredients of human personality.

alike, and each is a product of the continuing interaction of *heredity* and *environment* (Figure 5.1). Personality has two principal ingredients: *temperament* and *character*.

Heredity contributes chiefly to the first ingredient—temperament, or body chemistry. Temperament is relatively constant from the time of birth. From the environment come character or life values—the "oughts" and "ought nots"—that provide the basis for behavior choice. Values are established early as a result of learning right from wrong. Home, school, and church contribute considerably to each person's life values or character.

Temperament

People vary greatly in temperamental qualities. One person seems to be devoid of feelings. He or she is calm even in crisis. Others are easily excited, and the slightest disturbance upsets them. The mature individual is able to exercise some control over his or her feelings, but a person's body chemistry is never completely harnessed.

Three manifestations of temperament are of direct interest to you as a salesperson, both in understanding yourself and in getting along with customers and prospects:

1. *Sympathy.* Feeling sorry or happy for the other person.
2. *Empathy.* Sensing how the other person feels.
3. *Recipathy.* The impact of the other person on the observer.

People with little sympathy find it difficult to sell. They cannot readily establish the appropriate climate during the call. The prospect perceives them as lacking warmth. If, on the other hand, they have considerable sympathy in their makeup, they can create a friendly atmosphere and pave the way for making a sale. Similarly, salespeople have difficulty selling an unsympathetic prospect. A wall seems to exist between them and the prospect. In contrast, salespeople can appeal to the feelings of the sympathetic prospect or customer.

Salespeople with little empathy find it difficult to appreciate the feelings of prospects. They are likely to feel the person they call on is an opponent—"the enemy." Only with conscious effort can they temper their presentations to the prospect's feelings. They are also likely to use pressure during the call. On the other hand, salespeople with excessive empathy may find it difficult to control the sales interview so they can make a close. They may be too customer oriented! Successful salespeople are likely to be empathetic enough to appreciate the prospect's or customer's feelings and to close without using undue pressure. Likewise, the customer or prospect who lacks empathy may perceive the salesperson as an intruder. When prospects sense the way the salesperson feels about the product or service, they show empathy. Empathetic persons are pleasantly disposed toward salespeople. They understand the salesperson's point of view for they can place themselves in the other person's shoes.

Recipathy is a less widely used term than either sympathy or empathy and deserves some explanation. You have probably made remarks like these: "I don't know what it is about Jim, but he rubs me the wrong way," or "Tracy is delightful to be with, but I can't tell you why." These are commonplace examples of recipathy. Successful salespeople who seem to say or do just the right thing at the right time are likely to be recipathetic persons. They get many of their cues from the impact of the prospect or customer on their feelings. In contrast, salespeople who have little recipathy find adjusting difficult because they miss these feeling cues. Prospects or customers with considerable recipathy may be easy or difficult to sell depending on the effect the salesperson has on their feelings. If favorable, salespeople have a considerable advantage; but if not, they may have difficulty selling themselves to the prospect.

Character or Life Values

This second major ingredient of personality is relatively unchangeable once adulthood has been reached. The dishonest child will likely become the dishonest adult. Wide individual differences exist in life values just as they do in temperament. What one person does without compunction arouses guilt feelings in another.

Life values come into play only where behavior choice is present. How many times have you said, "I wonder if this is the right thing to do?" or "That would be dishonest." On these occasions, alternatives were available.

You never observe persons' life values directly. Rather, you infer them from people's attitudes, interests, and conduct. Here are some examples: A salesperson may take the attitude that padding an expense account is not dishonest. Others see nothing wrong in giving personal gifts to customers as remuneration for placing an order. Most people feel their word is their bond, yet some see nothing wrong in a broken promise.

Salespeople have the task of understanding and appreciating variation in life values among people. Hoping to change a customer's or prospect's character is unrealistic even though reform would be desirable. Likewise, you cannot function very well if you force yourself to do things that counter your own life values. Successful salespeople have life values that are morally and socially acceptable. In addition to influencing sales, your conduct does much to establish your company's reputation among buyers and in the community.

The Dynamics of Personality

People change continuously. Just as you think you understand a person, his or her behavior seems to change. The reason for this is that our environment is undergoing change and, as pointed out earlier, personality is in large part the product of continuous interaction between the individual and the environment. Therefore, as people meet new situations, change occurs. You, in turn, must change if you are to maintain a successful relationship. Consequently, to manage selling-buying relationships effectively, you must adjust to the buyer, not vice versa. This point requires amplification, however, because you are also part of the environment with which the buyer interacts.

If personality is dynamic—constantly changing—you must continuously try to discover each buyer's uniqueness and develop a sales strategy to modify the buyer's responses to your offering. If you wish to sell accounts that have previously rebuffed you, as well as penetrate existing accounts, you must also vary your approach. An understanding of personality dynamics is critical to your success.

The term commonly used by psychologists to refer to change occurring in persons because of their environment is *adjustment*. In other words, when people meet new situations, they adjust. Generally, there are two ways of adjusting to problems—*positively* and *negatively*. Considering some general ways of adjustment will help us to interpret the behavior we observe both in ourselves and in others.

Positive Adjustment

The most desirable behavior is characterized by a sense of purpose and efficiency. The person pursues certain goals or objectives with a minimum of wasted time or effort: He or she overcomes obstacles as they arise and no distraction occurs. However, no one can claim to adjust this way all of the time.

Sometimes, changing our approach to achieving objectives is more constructive. This is a second method of positive adjustment. As an illustration, suppose you hope to sell certain products to a prospect company by dealing entirely with the purchasing agent. As you progress, you realize he is not the decision maker. You now keep the same goal in mind but you need to make him an internal salesperson, who deals with the plant manager.

A third method of positive adjustment involves resetting our sights and modifying our goals or objectives. Frequently, this means settling for less. For example, on a particular sales call you may have set as your objective the closing of a quantity order. As you proceed, however, you realize a trial order is more realistic.

In positive adjustment, the person sets goals and works toward objectives even though minor setbacks occur. If you realize your goal is unattainable with your present plans, you must develop new methods to reach the goal. All three of these modes of adjustment are worthwhile. Unfortunately, at times we find ourselves behaving in other ways.

Negative Adjustment

When circumstances interfere with purposeful activity, we sometimes adjust negatively to obstacles. A common reaction is directing our attention *to* the interference and *away from* the goals. We attack the person or thing in our path (*direct aggression*) or take out our feelings on someone or something else (*displaced aggression*). An example of direct aggression is a salesperson who loses his or her temper with customers. The salesperson who returns to the office after an unsuccessful day and is abusive to the secretary illustrates displaced aggression.

Sometimes negative adjustment involves *withdrawal*. The person who sulks in the face of problems illustrates this form of adjustment.

In addition to aggression and withdrawal, there is a third method of behaving negatively—*retreat*. Some people, when frustrated, run away from the obstacle and forget the goals. The salesperson who fails to call back after a refusal illustrates adjustment by retreat.

The well-adjusted person makes one of the three positive adjustments most of the time and under most circumstances, only occasionally adjusting negatively. In contrast, the maladjusted individual often adjusts negatively to the environment.

2.   DESCRIBING AN INDIVIDUAL'S PERSONALITY AND PLANNING STRATEGY

As discussed earlier, the successful salesperson, in making calls, treats each prospect or customer as *a unique individual*. Your objective on every call should be to learn more about the customer than you previously knew. To do this, a systematic method of describing each person is required. Two approaches are available.

- Description by type.
- Description by traits.

A type description consists of assigning the person to be described to one of two or more general categories. Many systems exist. The best known classification is that of Carl Jung. He categorized people as introverts or extroverts. This implies that all people fit into one or the other. Another well-known type classification is Sheldon's physical types—endomorph, ectomorph, and mesomorph. By noticing a person's body build, Sheldon could assign any person to one of the categories. Another classification system that has achieved wide notice recently is the Myers-Briggs Type Indicator personality test, which measures four dimensions of personality and classifies people into 16 categories based on how they take in information and make decisions. Many more type theories could be cited, but these will suffice to illustrate the type approach to description. The unflagging popularity of such systems for categorizing people results from the promise to simplify the complexities of real life.

The alternative to using a type description is to describe a person in terms of his or her traits. While there are many formal definitions of traits, the important point to recognize is that a trait is an adjective used to describe some relatively specific and consistent behavioral tendency; for example, *stingy* for the person who never picks up a lunch check or *talkative* for the person who monopolizes conversations. In addition, traits can be expressed quantitatively, in terms of how much of a given trait a buyer possesses in comparison with a standard. Attributing a number of trait terms to a person is another way of describing that individual. The question to decide is which approach—type or trait—is more helpful to the salesperson in planning strategy for each customer.

Description by Type

We have a natural tendency to type people. We observe a characteristic of a person and focus our attention on it as if this single attribute captures the essence of the total person. We miss other aspects of the individual's behavior. We then generalize our description on the basis of the single trait. How often have you heard someone say, "She's intelligent," implying there is nothing else about the person worthy of note.

If salespeople are not cautious, they find themselves doing this same generalizing about prospects and customers. They note outstanding characteristics and put several prospects who possess those characteristics in a group (type) and proceed to deal with each member of the group in the same way. This can be shown diagrammatically.

Assume that the circle in Figure 5.2 contains buyers under consideration. Each symbol inside represents a person. You see quickly three "types" of people. Some are straight lines, some are circles, and others rectangles. (These can be crudely related to Sheldon's body types—ectomorph or linear, endomorph or round, and mesomorph or rectangular.)

Notice that three basic kinds of symbols are shown in the figure, but no two are identical. This is consistent with reality. No two persons are likely to be identical. Deoxyribonucleic acid—DNA—the basic genetic building block, can be arranged in at least 10^{3000} combinations. This even understates the case because it does not reflect mutations and environmental influences. Hence, if you do not vary your presentations, you cannot achieve maximum effectiveness. Any standardized presentation will be more effective with some people than others. For maximum effectiveness, salespeople should study buyers and modify their presentations to suit the buyers' needs and psychological characteristics.

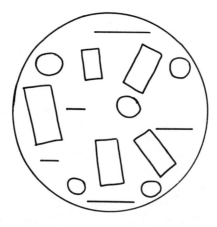

Figure 5.2 Description by type.

Weakness in the Type Approach

There are seven weaknesses or shortcomings in using the type approach to describe a person:

1. Assigning a person to a type may be of some value in making a rough comparison with other people, but it is of little help in planning a persuasive campaign to influence a particular person. It tends to mask, rather than highlight, the individual's behavioral characteristics; hence, it restricts the accumulation of detail really needed to understand a person.

2. The concept of types is not consistent with the latest research on personality. When many people are examined on a particular characteristic, vast individual differences are found. For example, people cannot be categorized as either dominant or submissive; there are gradations of each trait.

3. Type theories combine characteristics not always occurring in a particular person. The introvert type includes persons who are both seclusive and emotionally sensitive. Actually, sensitive persons may be either gregarious or seclusive, and seclusive persons are not necessarily sensitive; again, type theories do not stand up under close examination.

4. A pointed weakness in personality typing is the practice of changing the basis of the classification from one person to another. The same person will describe one acquaintance in terms of physical features, another by mannerisms, still another by attitudes. This results in describing one person as skinny, another as reactionary, another as egotistical. Any system as nebulous as this can hardly be helpful in deriving principles for dealing with various prospects when the objective is the same in all instances; namely, to influence the person to buy.

5. Sometimes typing leads to confusion between cause and effect. Do people withdraw because they are introverts, or are they introverts because they are withdrawn?

6. If the model for a type is unique, using that classification has little value because you will seldom meet a person who can be so classified. If, on the other hand, the model is very common, it will not help in differentiating among people.

7. Type categories are based on common behavioral elements in many different subjects, while traits are derived from behavior observed in a single subject. When you derive common behavioral elements from observing many individuals and use them to influence a single person who may demonstrate only a few of the qualities in the category, the results will be less satisfactory than if you consider only the behavioral characteristics of that particular person.

Types exist in the mind of the observer; traits have reference in the *customer who is being described.* The nature of selling calls for an individual approach to buyers, and a type classification hides rather than spotlights individual differences. Thus, type classifications are inconsistent with good selling.

Common Practice in the Field of Selling

Despite weaknesses in the type approach, books on selling, sales manuals, and magazine articles frequently use this method to describe customers. Not only does each source vary in the number of customer types but also the typing plans have little overlap. This should serve as a further caution in using the type approach.

You are justified in using type descriptions in advertising, where your objective is to influence large numbers of people at one time, or with salesperson-oriented methods of selling, where you cannot use the need satisfaction approach. In customer-oriented personal selling, however, a more precise description—a trait description—is needed to plan an effective sales presentation.

Reasons Salespeople Misjudge Buyers

Before you can understand buyers, you must understand why you have failed to judge their personalities correctly in the past. Experience shows four common problems, which when corrected, result in more accurate judgments and hence better sales performance: (1) Possessing an inadequate vocabulary of trait terms, (2) oversimplifying behavioral cause and effect, (3) trying to justify rather than challenge first impressions, and (4) dealing with one trait at a time.

Possessing an Inadequate Vocabulary of Trait Terms. "Trait" is a word that describes some behavior of a person. A person who always "bargains for the lowest possible price" could be said to have the trait "thrifty."

If salespeople lack the word and an understanding of it in their working vocabulary, they are unlikely to observe that behavior in people. If people watch a baseball game and do not know what "balk" or "fielder's choice" means, they do not appreciate those plays. Other examples are the "blue line" in hockey or a "sound shot" to a hunter.

Every field of endeavor—whether it be the stock market or space travel—has its own peculiar set of terms to express the finer points. Part of your job is to understand and adjust to people. You need a specialized vocabulary for this purpose just as surely as you need a specialized vocabulary for your product, service, and industry.

Oversimplifying Behavioral Cause and Effect. Assuming that all identical behavior takes place for the same reason is normal but wrong. If one person is thrifty and the reason is obvious, the next person who appears to be thrifty will appear to be so for the same reason. This assumption will not stand under close analysis.

Assume the evidence at hand is that the person "always bargains for the lowest price." In addition to "thrifty," here are some other traits that might cause the same behavior:

Childish	Exploiting	Price-minded
Contrary	Jealous	Shrewd
Crude	Malevolent	Stingy
Argumentative	Overbearing	Unscrupulous

You must realize that any given behavior might result from a variety of causes. This leads to the third reason for difficulty in understanding people.

Trying to Justify Rather Than Challenge First Impressions. Once the judgment "thrifty" has been made, you will normally spend effort to find evidence for that trait. You are wiser to challenge the initial judgment by evaluating all other possible causes of the behavior.

Dealing with One Trait at a Time. Often salespeople deal with one trait at a time. They act as though that were the only behavior worth consideration. This approach is similar to a type description that is appropriate for selling-formula or stimulus-response selling. In the need satisfaction method, a trait description is necessary. The procedure will be described fully in the next section.

The reason for this is that traits are interactive. One trait affects the expression of another. While a buyer may be "thrifty," he or she is at the same time alert or sluggish, tactful or awkward, deliberate or impulsive, and so on. Thus, you must consider *all* significant traits before selecting any final strategy.

Description by Traits

The trait description method is a procedure you can use to organize your information about a second person. You can then formulate a strategy to persuade that person to accept a new point of view. A person is a complex organism, so you should keep in mind that developing a meaningful strategy will take considerable thought and planning. The trait approach may first appear to be unnecessarily tedious. However, every application will require less time, and after four or five serious applications of the method, you will be able to do it easily.

In your early attempts to use the method, you may discover that you do not know enough about the person to make a satisfactory trait description. When this is the case, you will find the method helpful to determine the kind of information you need before you can expect to persuade a buyer to accept your point of view.

The salesperson has an objective to understand each customer or prospect as a unique individual. The trait method of describing a person provides a sound basis for achieving this goal. Two proven premises underlie this approach:

- All persons have some amount of each personality trait.
- Each person's uniqueness derives from the combination of traits displayed in extreme amounts.

Let us see what the first statement means. Think about the trait *cooperative*. Every person has some degree or amount of this trait. So it is with all other traits. If you had information on a large group of people with regard to any trait, the individuals in the group would show varying amounts of the trait, as shown in Figure 5.3.

Now, think about the second statement. Each person's uniqueness lies in the combination of traits exhibited in extreme amounts. Relate this to the trait *cooperative*. Unless people are extremely uncooperative or cooperative, the amount of this trait they possess does not set them apart from other people.

How to Use Description by Traits

Every person possesses a trait to some degree. In any particular person, however, most traits are present in an average amount; hence, these particular traits are not helpful in differentiating the person from others.

To ensure that you select the most significant traits, you should use a list of trait terms covering the entire range of personality. If you fail to use such a list, you may consider only the aspects of the person's behavior that you find familiar and/or understandable. A comprehensive list of trait terms will cause observers to note things that they might otherwise overlook. An analogy is a person who has studied music. He or she gets more enjoyment from a concert because of having a vocabulary to describe and communicate the experience. A good list of traits calls attention to behavior that you would otherwise not notice. A list titled *Common Trait Terms to Analyze People* is in Appendix IX.

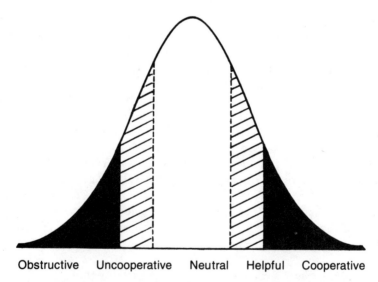

Obstructive   Uncooperative   Neutral   Helpful   Cooperative

Figure 5.3   All persons have some amount of each personality trait.

The list consists of numbered pairs of words. Each member of a pair describes the extreme of the trait. For example, *adaptable-inflexible* represents a trait. Everyone possesses this characteristic in some degree. Only if it tends to be at either extreme, should you consider it significant in describing a particular person.

An important caution is in order. To ensure that you accurately describe people's outstanding traits, base your descriptions on *evidence;* that is, *observations of their behavior.* For example, with the trait *cooperative,* evidence of extreme cooperativeness might include a situation in which the customer: (1) furnished you with information on his or her business; (2) at your request called in a direct marketing specialist to hear your presentation; or (3) was willing to shift an appointment at your request.

Another trait, together with evidence to support it, is *intelligence* perhaps indicated by: (1) a high score on an intelligence test; (2) early graduation from school; (3) standing near the top of the class; or (4) interest in intellectually abstract activities, such as chess.

Another example is *confidence* suggested by: (1) ability to make a decision when given a set of facts; (2) no undue vacillation; (3) a willingness to take reasonable chances; or (4) ability to overlook criticism from others.

You can now use the list of trait terms and the work sheet in Part A of Appendix X to describe one of your important customers. Select a person you know well and use the following procedure:

1. Read each pair of words (in Appendix IX) and consider where your customer is on the scale portrayed by them. If he or she is at *either* end, put an "X" beside that word. If the individual is in between the extremes, skip that pair and proceed to the next pair. Follow this procedure through the 80 pairs. Usually you will have noted 25 to 30 pairs.
2. Copy the words you have marked with an "X" in Column 1 of the work sheet.
3. Summarize the observations on which you based your selection of each trait in Column 2. You may have to delete some words in view of the evidence. Or you may, in light of the evidence, find a better trait term to substitute for the one with which you started. By using only those descriptive terms that you can substantiate, you have ensured the accuracy of your description.

Typically, continuous matching of traits, evidence, and the person being described continues until you establish a stable grouping. This will usually reduce the original list of about 25 traits to 5 or 6. Further, you will have added about 5 new traits, so the final written list will consist of about 10 traits with matching evidence. Experience has shown that if many more than 10 traits are retained, unimportant behavior creeps in. If fewer than 10 traits result, important behavior may be omitted.

After you have described the customer, you are ready to plan a strategy to increase the likelihood of making a sale and decrease the likelihood of offending the buyer.

Planning Strategy

Planning your strategy begins with a review of your trait description of a particular customer.

1. Identify extreme characteristics—traits.
2. Note evidence.
3. Decide *what to do* or *avoid doing* for each trait.
4. Discern patterns; group related traits.
5. Formulate strategic plans.

In Step 1, you selected the trait terms and listed them in Column 1 of the work sheet. Then, in Step 2, in Column 2 you furnished evidence to support your choice of traits. Step 3, utilizing Column 3 of the work sheet, involves thinking through what strategy to use in connection with each trait. For each trait, determine how you must behave to influence the customer most favorably. As you consider each trait, do it as if it were the only information available. A completed work sheet in Appendix XI gives you examples of suitable strategy for the traits present in that particular customer. In planning strategy for a given trait, think how you would handle a person on the opposite extreme of the trait you have selected. The following examples show suggested strategies for persons both high and low in intelligence and self-confidence.

Intelligence

1. *High Intelligence.* Customers who are highly intelligent should not be "talked down to." You should give them just enough information to see the point and should allow them to fill in the details themselves or to ask questions to bring out any additional information they require.
2. *Low Intelligence.* With customers of low intelligence, a more complete and detailed presentation is in order. Leave nothing to chance; the presentation should give not only the facts but also the reasons for them. You may have to repeat important points several times.

Self-Confidence

1. *High Self-Confidence.* Customers who are self-confident want to make their own decisions. All that you need to do is show them the merits of the proposition.
2. *Low Self-Confidence.* With people lacking in self-confidence, you must find a way to bolster their confidence in their own judgment. Testimonials

from other respected clients are often helpful. Presentation of conclusive evidence of the superiority of the product from such sources as laboratory tests is appropriate. After completing the sale, you may wish to supply additional sales points.

See Appendixes XII and XIII for additional practice.

Step 3 in the overall procedure of describing a customer, then, is to plan a strategy for each trait as though that trait were the only information available to you. When you have completed this planning, you are ready for Step 4. In this step, you focus on the customer as a person, as contrasted with Step 3 where you view the customer as a series of independent traits. The way to accomplish this fourth step is to combine the various traits into related groups. The reason for this is twofold. A person is more than the sum of separate traits; certain traits, characteristic of a particular person, are likely to be interactive.

As an oversimplified illustration of how traits interact, take a person who possesses two traits in extreme amounts—intelligence and self-confidence. You have four possible combinations to contend with, each calling for a different strategy (Figure 5.4). The four possibilities are:

1. High intelligence and high self-confidence.
2. High intelligence and low self-confidence.
3. Low intelligence and high self-confidence.
4. Low intelligence and low self-confidence.

In Case 1, you give only the barest information and stick to the facts. Case 2 requires a small amount of information that shows how your proposition has helped other persons. In Case 3 you will need to give a complete presentation and repeat the points, but keep to a factual basis. Case 4 needs the full presentation plus evidence of the merits of the proposition.

Thus you can see that while you first need to consider traits singly, the interrelationship of the traits is even more important. The key to understanding clients lies in considering the individual as a whole rather than by bits and pieces.

To ensure that your strategy takes into account the interrelationship of traits, refer to the first one on your work sheet, then review every other recorded trait in connection with it. If you feel that two or more traits are related, place the number and name of each of these traits in one section of Part B of the work sheet. When you have grouped all the related traits, take the second trait on Part A of the work sheet and compare it with all the others following it. (You have already compared it with the traits preceding it.) Continue this process until you have derived four or five clusters of related traits. You should have used each trait at least once and may have found it desirable to include some traits in more than one cluster. Note the way this has been accomplished in Appendix XI, Part B.

		INTELLIGENCE	
		HIGH	LOW
S E L F C O N F I D E N C E	H I G H	**Case 1** Provide basic information. Stick to the facts.	**Case 3** Give complete presentation and repeat key points. Stick to the facts.
	L O W	**Case 2** Provide basic information. Show how offering has helped others and describe merits of proposition.	**Case 4** Give complete presentation and repeat key points. Show how offering has helped others and describe merits of proposition.

Figure 5.4   Four trait combinations and related strategies.

Step 5 is next. When you have combined the traits into clusters, think through the interaction of the traits in each cluster and develop a principle that will reflect the presence of each trait and serve as a guide to your conduct during the sales interview. You may need to revise some of the trait clusters before you finally complete this step. Again, refer to the example provided.

To facilitate mastery of the trait analysis technique, Appendix XIV provides definitions and strategies for trait terms, enabling you to understand a buyer and rapidly make necessary adjustments in your behavior. You should look at the definitions and strategies as examples and icebreakers. A dictionary, thesaurus, and compilation of synonyms and antonyms are no substitute. Professional selling is based largely on communication skills, and effective communication depends heavily on an adequate vocabulary. Salespeople who start developing their vocabulary early in their professional training will find this practice increases their communications competency and, hence, their overall ability to sell as well as to adjust to buyers.

Some strategies come up so often that rather than repeat them for each appropriate trait, we have assembled them in Appendix XV and have coded them by number.

Continued use of the method will steadily reduce the time you need to analyze people. Eventually, you will be able to understand most buyers adequately and speedily by reviewing the list of trait terms without resorting to a written work sheet.

General Considerations in Applying the Method

Because your goal is to make each customer feel that he or she is receiving individual treatment, the best way to start planning your sales presentation is by describing the customer as a unique person. After you have described the customer, you are ready to plan your strategy so that you will increase the likelihood of making a sale and decrease the likelihood of offending the buyer. Following are some guidelines to keep in mind while describing a buyer and planning your strategy.

1. *Avoid Therapy.* Your function is to develop and fill needs. You should not try to change the buyer except as is necessary to make a sale.
2. *Recognize That Traits Are Dynamic.* They are always changing. Whether or not the change is favorable to the sale depends on the application of appropriate strategy.
3. *Take a Psychological Rather Than a Logical Approach.* You should consider the meaning or value that the observed behavior has for buyers.
4. *Recognize That Behavior May Be Compensatory Rather Than Direct.* You may not be sure of any given trait, but when you evaluate the entire range of behavior in trait terms, you should have no difficulty in distinguishing between bona fide and compensatory behavior.
5. *Personalize the Presentation.* Keep in mind that the essence of the need satisfaction method is to treat buyers as unique individuals, developing and filling their needs. When normal communication is not possible or fails to produce an order, vary your behavior *as long as you are filling bona fide needs.*
6. *Take Situational Factors into Account.* Some traits refer to the buyer's relationship to you and others to the buyer's relationship to other persons not directly involved in the presentation.
7. *Recognize That Buyers Are Influenced by Social Forces.* The strategies were developed with the assumption that the buyer is accountable to other persons. Where the purchase is for the exclusive and personal use of the buyer, a different strategy may be in order.

Experience shows that salespeople who have made trait descriptions of buyers have made many sales where otherwise they would have failed. They have seen the futility of pursuing some accounts and turned their energies to prospects with higher potential. Of even greater importance, they have raised their general level of communication skill for both business and personal use.

3. UNDERSTANDING MOTIVATION

Success in selling depends largely on a knowledge of customers' and prospects' motivations—why they behave the way they do.

Persons are described as *well motivated* when there is a sense of purpose in what they do. Their actions are the result of a plan pointing toward an objective— the achievement of a limited task or a step toward a lifetime goal. Recognizing that either conscious or unconscious purpose may be present is important.

An individual who follows the pattern described in the old navy expression:

> When in trouble, when in doubt
> Run in circles, scream and shout

would not appear to be very well motivated. Here is behavior that seems to lack purpose and choice.

One complication in examining motivation is that seldom, if ever, is our behavior the result of a single isolated motive. Most often many motives underlie behavior. Sometimes motives are mutually enhancing. Often, however, they are in conflict, and the individual, through conscious or unconscious choice, must determine a course of action.

Motivation may be likened to a coin with one side labeled *motives* and the other side *incentives*. Motives exist within the individual; incentives, outside. The latter are aspects of the environment to which individuals attend selectively and after which they strive, in light of their motives. What may have high incentive value for one person may leave the next individual cold. To understand motivation, then, you need to learn about incentives and motives as well as their interrelationships. The two most important facets to examine are (1) what goes on inside individuals and (2) what they seek in the environment.

A Look inside the Individual

To visualize motivation from the standpoint of the individual, imagine four cameras, each focused from a different vantage point but all centered on an individual engaged in purposeful activity.

The first camera sees individuals in terms of their aspirations, hopes, and dreams. Psychologists call this viewpoint the *Level of Aspiration*.

The second camera views the motivation of individuals in terms of their interest in what they are doing. We call the viewpoint of this camera *Interest Pattern*.

The third camera sees the motivation of individuals in terms of the status or standing they are seeking for themselves both in their own eyes and in the eyes of others. This viewpoint is commonly referred to as *Status Striving*.

The fourth camera captures a picture of motivation in terms of individuals' basic character and the moral, social, and personal values they live by. This picture is called *Value Enhancement*.

Ways of Looking at Motivation

Level of Aspiration

Several years ago a popular song contained a line to the effect that *wishes are the dreams we dream when we're awake.* Certainly, everyone has aspirations, hopes, and dreams. Some of these are immediate, some are long-range; some realistic, others fanciful. To varying degrees, however, they are present in most individuals. Most of us want to do what we are doing somewhat better, that is, to improve. Much of what customers or prospects do represents an effort to give themselves a sense of achievement. Consequently, actual performance relative to aspired achievement provides us with a useful framework for assessing individual motivation.

To be purposeful, these aspirations must seem potentially achievable in terms of people's abilities and talents on the one hand and the opportunities afforded by their work and home life on the other. Persons without much purpose are likely to have aspirations that are unrealistic or fleeting and indefinite. They may be aiming too high or too low in terms of their talents and the opportunities provided by their job, or they may not be aiming at all.

Another aspect of aspirations is that many of them are present at any given time. For people to be well motivated, these aspirations must form a cohesive pattern. Career objectives have to be consistent with off-the-job aspirations. Likewise, personal objectives do not conflict with those held by other family members. Poorly motivated individuals have either scattered or conflicting aspirations.

Our look at motivation through this camera also reveals that aspirations must be flexible and adaptable to changing conditions. Well-motivated persons know when to persist as well as when to quit. For example, purposeful salespeople are able to reset their sights when they hear "no" on a call. They immediately start thinking about the callback. Less purposeful salespeople are unlikely to vary their approach and presentation to meet changing situations. Frequently, they rigidly pursue objectives even after they have become inappropriate or obsolete. In fact, they may not even perceive that changes occurred.

A final look through this camera reveals that aspirations must be self-generating. Each hope or goal achieved tends to foster new aspirations. For example, salespeople who are purposeful, having reached their quota, seek to exceed it the next month. Less motivated salespeople lack initiative and depend on their sales manager to set their objectives.

Figure 5.5 portrays the relationship that exists between *actual* performance and *aspired* performance in a well-motivated person. You will observe that while the purposeful individual's actual performance typically shows ups and downs, the trend, both in *amount* and *quality of performance* is upward. Also, at any given time aspired performance is somewhat above actual performance. The poorly motivated person's aspired performance would be either high, "pie in the sky," or below actual performance, "going through the motions."

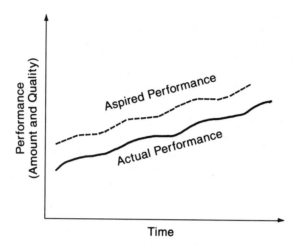

Figure 5.5 Level of aspiration: Relationship between actual and aspired performance.

To profit from the view of motivation that this camera provides, we must remember the importance of four characteristics: realism, pattern and relative absence of conflict, flexibility, and self-generation. We can assess each of these dimensions by answering the following corresponding questions:

1. How realistic are people's aspirations relative to their talents and opportunities?

You will probably help other people raise their sights more frequently than you will assist people in tempering plans and making them more realistic. However, you must be cautious with prospects whose aspirations are unrealistically high. Such persons may want to buy more than they should or buy something they cannot afford. If you encourage inappropriate purchases, you are unlikely to develop or sustain favorable selling-buying relationships.

2. To what extent are aspirations mutually enhancing and conflict free?

You need to learn as much as possible about the other individual as a total human being. To the extent that you can help other persons achieve their aspirations, you are likely to have a favorable impact. When you learn of conflicts in aspirations, you may help that person resolve them. More likely, you can provide your best assistance in such circumstances by warm and attentive listenership. For you to play psychotherapist is dangerous!

3. How flexible are people's aspirations?

This question has many applications in the selling-buying relationship. If you encounter a person without much persistence (for example, in a situation where negotiations are bound to take weeks or even months), you must find ways and means of keeping that person on target. The other extreme is when you encounter the inflexible individual. In this case, you should devote much of your effort to showing such a person the need for changing goals and aspirations to relate to your products and services. Generally speaking, the easiest people to deal with are open-minded persons with flexibility of aspirations.

4. To what extent are their aspirations self-generating?

Here, answers show you how much initiative is needed to influence a customer or prospect. Generally speaking, people with considerable initiative resent being told what to do, while individuals who show little initiative may favor those who can provide direction.

Interest Pattern

On or off the job, we achieve more when we are interested in what we are doing. As we examine motivation through this camera, we find that the best single indicator of interest is what individuals do with their free time. When choice is possible, what duties or activities do individuals turn to on the job? What avocations attract their interest and absorb their time off the job? Two additional questions are pertinent: How much interest do individuals have in a given activity? What kind of interest do they have in it?

Psychologists recognize two kinds of interest—*intrinsic* and *extrinsic*. Intrinsic interest refers to *interest in the activity* in and of itself. It's enjoyable to do. In contrast, extrinsic interest refers to *interest in the activity because of what it leads to*. The person pursues the activity because it is prescribed or must be done, or because of the consequences of not doing it. For example, if you reflect on the kind of interest you have in various aspects of your work, you might find that calling on established accounts has considerable intrinsic interest for you, while you might find only extrinsic interest in completing paperwork. The complication here is that no two people have the same amount of intrinsic and extrinsic interest even for the same activity. You might find another salesperson who would view doing the job-related paperwork as fun.

From this vantage point, well-motivated persons are individuals who have a considerable amount of interest in whatever they may have to do. Most of their interest is of the intrinsic variety. If individuals find little intrinsic interest in their work, they should reexamine their vocational plans. They may not be in the right job. In Figure 5.6, well-motivated individuals are depicted as having more interest in what they are doing, with the bulk of it intrinsic. In contrast, less-motivated persons have less interest and that interest is primarily extrinsic. At one extreme, people who are actively interested in what they are doing grow in their capacity to perform. We say they are *ego involved.* At the other extreme, people engaged in meaningless activity are deprived of a sense of achievement and diminish in capability.

Learning as much as possible about other persons' interests is advantageous for you. You do this through observation and inquiry. You can often enhance

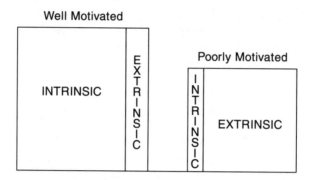

Figure 5.6 Interest patterns: How much? What kind?

your relationships with other people by assisting them with those parts of their jobs in which they have little interest or in which their interest is extrinsic. On the other hand, you may jeopardize favorable relationships if you unwittingly intrude on aspects of people's work in which they have intense interest. For example, an air-conditioning equipment salesperson might determine that the buyer in a construction firm has little or no interest in "board work," that is, in drawing the installation plans for the equipment and ducts. The salesperson might capitalize on this knowledge by having her own firm do the layout and design for the contractor. On the other hand, this course of action would be the wrong one to take if, instead, the person in the construction firm enjoys design and layout and feels expert at it. He would resent the salesperson's offer and might interpret it as a reflection on his expertise as a designer.

Inasmuch as people tend to learn about things in which they have an interest, you can assume that you can expand on and stress aspects of your offering that relate to the interest pattern you have discovered in the prospect or customer.

You may also turn your knowledge of the other person's avocational interests to advantage. Generally speaking, people enjoy talking about their hobbies and pastimes. However, the amount of such conversation should depend on the customer. Such light talk may prove a useful preamble to a sales presentation to help establish rapport for discussing the business. You and your customer might possibly share common pastimes. You must, however, keep in perspective the commercial selling-buying relationship you are seeking to establish. Second, if you give lip service to an activity in which you have only extrinsic interest, your lack of sincerity and competence will betray you. The other person is likely to resent it. Also, if you insist on financing the joint venture, the other individual may resent being obligated.

Status Striving

Motivation from this point of view is a social phenomenon. Purpose is explained in terms of individuals' desires to do more, be more, and seem more in the eyes of other individuals and groups as well as in their own eyes. In fact, people who say, "I don't care what other people think of me," probably are more deeply concerned than those who are more casual about the judgment of others.

When motivation is interpreted in this way, there are as many motivational patterns in individuals' lives as role relationships that have significance for them. In a sense, motivations are unique to every role relationship. Associated with each role relationship is standing or status as individuals perceive, think, and feel it. Status peculiar to each role has two facets: *status being accorded* and the *status individuals think should be accorded*. Well-motivated persons in a given relationship, though they may not admit it too openly, picture the status being accorded them as *greater than* it should be. Because they view it in this way, they then impose on themselves an obligation to measure up to this status. In Figure 5.7(a), the status being accorded outweighs the status the individual thinks should be accorded and therefore the person feels a sense of obligation.

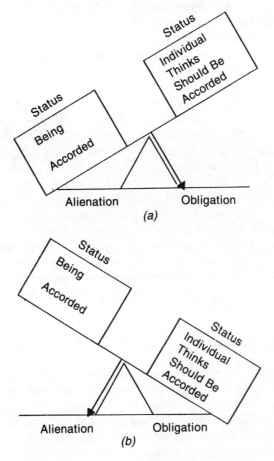

Figure 5.7 Status striving: The status balance.

In contrast, less well-motivated persons often have overexaggerated views of what their status should be and when it is not forthcoming they adjust negatively and feel alienated (Figure 5.7(b)).

The incentive aspect of motivation from this viewpoint is the *status symbol* (an aspect of the physical and social environment individuals associate with status). Purchases having symbolic value include the gamut—from luxury goods to jeans. In the case of a corporation, a private jet or the use of an international consulting firm might be viewed as status symbols.

Our third camera then shows us that well-motivated persons tend to seek the status due them on the basis of their performance of various roles. In turn, they feel the responsibility to maintain performance so as to enhance their reputation. To interpret motivation in this manner, the following questions are useful:

1. With whom do the individuals wish to be associated, or what individuals and groups are important to them?
2. For important role relationships, how certain are the individuals of their responsibilities?
3. What are the individuals' perception of the status being accorded in each of the roles that have significance to them?

With regard to the first pair of questions, sometimes you can develop better client relationships when you share common club memberships and /or when you have mutual friends and acquaintances who are members.

With respect to the second question, if you find that buyers are unsure of certain role obligations, you may be able to assist them in clarifying what is expected. For instance, an industrial salesperson might be able to convince a purchasing agent that she has an obligation to go beyond specifications and requisitions furnished by other departments. Her responsibility as the professional purchasing executive is to recommend new processes to various departments in the firm. She is, in effect, an internal consultant on profitable purchasing.

In answering the third question, you may be able to enhance the status of other people by giving compliments to people who count. Continuing the example of the purchasing agent, you may be in a position to mention to the plant manager what a thorough understanding the purchasing agent has of the problems involved in optimizing inventory.

Value Enhancement

A fundamental part of people's motivation stems from their life values or character. In considering motivation from this viewpoint, you need to distinguish between *behavior* and *conduct*. Behavior includes *all our reactions to the world around us*. Conduct is restricted to *those activities where choice is possible*. An individual's conduct is governed by the moral, social, and personal values by which he or she lives. In other words, well-motivated persons abide by acceptable standards of morality and custom. From this viewpoint, when persons make a purchase, they are reflecting their life values. The purchase is a display of their taste and, in effect, a part of them. Individuals are continually striving to actualize and extend themselves through their possessions, the places they patronize, and the people with whom they choose to do business.

Persons' life values become manifest to others through their *choices* and *attitudes*. Thus, to understand individuals from this motivational viewpoint, you need to observe the decisions they make when choice is possible. The key question to ask is: What attitudes do they hold toward various aspects of their physical and social environments?

For example, you might observe the buyer's values on the job in adherence to company policy, acceptance of proposals on their merits, and/or promptness in keeping appointments. In the buyer's off-the-job conduct, you might detect honesty, personal integrity, civic responsibility, and so on. Clearly, you might also find the opposite of these illustrative behaviors.

Factors in the Environment

Environment includes the conditions, influences, and forces outside ourselves that have an effect on our behavior. When we view motivation from the environmental standpoint, we find considerable variation from one individual to the next. Some people respond better to tangible material rewards and incentives; others find intangible abstract ones more attractive. To some, immediate satisfactions are strongest; to others long-range goals are more meaningful. Differences also exist with regard to the appeal of positive versus negative factors in the environment.

4. ANALYZING CUSTOMERS' AND PROSPECTS' MOTIVATIONS AND PLANNING STRATEGY

Sections 1 and 2 of this chapter covered making a personality analysis of a buyer. Such a step is advisable when normal communication fails to produce a sale and you need to intensify the sales effort by personalizing the next call. Properly executed, the trait analysis provides you with clues as to *how* to approach the buyer.

Section 3 presented various ways of looking at motivation. Now we will apply four of these—level of aspiration, interest pattern, status striving, and value enhancement—to prospects and customers. A motivational analysis will reveal *what* to talk about to personalize the presentation.

Three basic assumptions must be made about the motivation of customers and prospects:

1. No two persons are likely to have identical motives for buying a particular product or service or for dealing with a particular company.
2. The buying behavior of a customer is likely to be triggered by a complex set of motives that vary from one purchase to the next.

3. In most situations, two or more persons must be influenced to buy and their motives for buying or not buying are likely to be different.

If you think about these points, you will recognize the necessity of learning as much as you can about each prospect's or customer's motivation.

Established Customers

Think about your regular accounts and the persons with whom you deal in each of them. What do you know about every person's aspirations *on* and *off* the job? Their interests, especially in that part of their job concerned with seeing salespeople? Their status striving? Their values? Jot down what you know about each one's motivation. You will find some individuals for whom you lack such information. Resolve to get it as a by-product of your future contacts with them. You can do this through conversation, questions, and observation.

Prospective Customers

Before you call, you should not only collect information regarding the potential of a prospective account but also information about the individuals involved including their motivations. How can you obtain the latter kind of knowledge? Many sources are available—people in other departments of your own company, salespeople of noncompetitive lines, your present customers who may know individuals in the prospect company, contacts with the company's personnel at trade shows, industrial/service associations, and community organizations. However, two cautions are in order. First, all this information is secondhand. You must validate it before basing important selling decisions on it. Second, you have to know what information you are seeking.

Obtain the best answers available to the following questions:

General Information

What are the names and titles of the persons who do the purchasing? When is each person most likely to be available? How long has each one been with the company? In the present job? Who really makes the buying decisions? After you decide whom you are likely to deal with, seek more specific knowledge about them.

Level of Aspiration

Are they open-minded and trying to do a better job? Or are they resistant to change and set with regard to suppliers? Are they realistic in what they seek? Or are they after the impossible deal? Do they have a clear idea of what they want? Or are they vague about their needs? Are they likely to follow through once their wants are aroused? Or do they need prodding?

Interest Pattern

Do they see buying as an important and profitable process? Or do they just put up with it as a distasteful assignment? Which of their job duties do they really enjoy? Which ones do they dislike? What are their hobbies and avocations?

Status Striving

Who counts with them? How do they see themselves in the company scheme of things? What is their role in the community? What is their role in professional and trade associations? Are they formal and title-conscious? What about status symbols?

Value Enhancement

Do they live by the golden rule? Or are they "wheelers and dealers"? Is their word their bond? Or should you get it in writing? Are they honest in their buying? Or do they expect you to buy their business? Do they give credit where it is due? Or do they take the credit for goods and services furnished by others? Similarly, in exploring other aspects of motivation, are their goals material or abstract? Immediate or long range? Positive or negative?

Obviously, you may not get complete information for any particular person, especially in advance of the first call. However, if you *consciously* try to build your knowledge, as your contacts increase you will soon have a valuable store of information on tap.

Sales Strategy

Information about customers' motivation is valuable only to the extent that you put it to use. How can you incorporate such knowledge in your sales strategy for each person with whom you deal? The following chart summarizes possible sales strategies for aspects of a buyer's motivation.

Motivation	Examples of Strategies
Level of Aspiration	
Wants to be considered an expert on selling.	Ask his advice on how to sell. Get his criticism of how account is now being handled.
Hopes to move into sales management.	Research and communicate sales and marketing ideas for his company's products, especially those that involve use of products or services being sold to him.

Motivation	*Examples of Strategies*
Lacks aspiration to improve in his present job.	Use the phrase "As you know . . ." when you need to "educate" him.
Wants to exert power and influence over others.	Give sincere praise of his executive ability where justified; let him know when you have followed his suggestions or desires.

Interest Pattern

More interested in selling than in present job.	Indicate his role is that of "internal salesperson," meeting needs of all departments of the company.
Stickler for methodical record keeping.	Double-check all correspondence, shipping details, and so on; keep briefcase, visuals, and other selling aids well organized and neat; point out care own company takes on details.

Status Striving

Self-important with subordinates and fellow executives.	Make all references to him and his colleagues in formal fashion; refer to people generally in same manner; show respect without obsequiousness.
Treasurer of the company's country club.	Show him dollar value in products and attendant services.
Self-proclaimed "knower."	Furnish him technical information that will give him an edge; avoid seeming to know more than he does; let him know own professional activities.

Value Enhancement

Honest to point of being oversensitive about it.	Avoid gifts to him or his associates; (pamphlets, reprints, etc., probably acceptable). Stress strict business policies of own company.

Motivation	*Examples of Strategies*
	Other
Abstract goals—unpretentious in material things.	Give him status-yielding treatment as noted earlier; interest him in problem-solving that company's products have a part in; be conservative in own behavior, especially in money expenditures, such as in selecting a place to eat.
Compensatory about own education.	Avoid reference to own education; stress advantages of experience as best teacher.

You can do similar tactical planning about each of your customers and prospects. The payoff will be increased sales. Appendices XVI and XVII illustrate and provide practice in analyzing customer motivation.

Similarities and Differences in Personality and Motivation Analyses

As discussed earlier, the trait description reveals the *manner* the salesperson should adopt. In contrast, the motivation analysis reveals topics of special interest to the buyer—the *matter* of the interview.

Another difference is that the list of trait terms is a constant for all persons you analyze. The motivational topics can vary with the kind of buyers you call on, the buyer's position in the company and the industry, as well as a host of other factors. Thus, when you understand the method you can easily modify the items on the motivation checklist (Appendix XVI) so they will be more applicable to your clientele.

Like the trait description, the motivation analysis cannot be made without some exposure to the buyer. You need to have some knowledge about the buyer before you can undertake the analysis.

A similarity also exists in the way you make each analysis. Since human beings tend to think typologically and are unduly influenced by first impressions, the critical step in each analysis is to note the *evidence* supporting your judgments about each buyer.

Which Analysis Should Be Made First?

When you know that you should personalize the next call, you need to make a choice between a personality analysis, a motivational analysis, and/or both. As soon as you have mastered both tools, the line separating them will become blurred. The techniques will tend to overlap and merge because there is a strong relationship between the "how" and "why" of behavior. Competent salespeople are prepared with the proper tools and understand their use. You must make the decision which tool to use on the basis of your experience with the buyer. The critical objective is to customize the presentation. Imagine asking a carpenter, "What is the best tool you have in your box?" The carpenter needs to know what the job is before giving an answer.

5.   UNDERSTANDING BACKGROUND AND IMPROVING YOUR ABILITY TO ADJUST TO OTHERS

If you view your selling job as a professional career assignment, you are concerned with continuing self-improvement. How can you increase your skill in analyzing people? Certainly, this is an important part of your work. Success or failure in selling hinges on it. First, two general cautions:

1. *Typological thinking is the most fundamental error in judging people.*
2. *Reliance on first impressions is the most frequent error in sizing up an individual prospect or customer.*

We have discussed Point 1 in Section 2; the pitfalls in Point 2 stem chiefly from salespeople neglecting background factors. In addition, suggestions are provided that allow you to modify strategies to "fit" customers or prospects as you find them.

Pitfalls in First Impressions

Most salespeople have relatively little time with each prospect or customer. Some salespeople, by the nature of their business, have to close or not close in a single call. Others have a continuing series of calls on each person at varying time intervals. Still others conduct the bulk of their business over the telephone, further limiting the data available for decision making. It is imperative, then, that you make the most of the samples of customer behavior that you observe. The tendency for salespeople to jump to conclusions quickly, sometimes too quickly, is natural.

Why do most of us do this? Two personality adjustment mechanisms are at work within us—*projection* and *rationalization*. Projection refers to our tendency to attribute our own self-image to others. Instead of basing our assessment of other persons on samples of their behavior, we color our judgments by projecting our own characteristics. Rationalization is the tendency to conclude first, then justify the conclusion. We observe a small bit of the other person's behavior, conclude he or she is this or that, then use subsequent observations to justify our opinions of that person. In short, our strategy will be based on a biased sample.

As an example of projection, suppose your own personality reflects great amounts of these traits: intelligence, honesty, and friendliness. You are likely to assume, unconsciously, that your prospects and customers have these same characteristics. In making a particular call, you may talk over the head of a prospect who is less intelligent than you are. In another instance you may annoy a less friendly person by your own friendliness. Every salesperson can cite a case where assuming honesty in a dishonest prospect has led to disastrous results.

Attentiveness to the other person's behavior is the best countermeasure for projection. Open-mindedness is the most effective way to offset rationalization.

Here are seven pitfalls in first impressions:

1. *People Do Not Reveal All Their Traits and/or Motives at One Time or under One Circumstance.* The traits that the buyer displays or the motives that you can infer on a first call may not be those in evidence several calls later. Further, the traits or motives a person shows in a buyer-seller relationship may be different from those observed under social conditions.

2. *Antisocial or Asocial Behavior Is Seldom Apparent in the First Interview or Meeting.* People like to make a good impression on others, so they often suppress any behavior that would make them disliked. While they can do this for a brief period, sooner or later their natural mode of dealing with people becomes apparent.

3. *People May Be Nervous in Their First Meeting and Not Appear at Their Best.* Many people cannot relax in the presence of strangers. Once you get to know them they seem to be completely different people.

4. *Many Expressive Movements Are Subject to Voluntary Control and Hence Do Not Reflect True Feelings.* Many times angry people will conceal their anger and force smiles. Until you know them well, you can never be sure that their overt behavior reflects true feelings.

5. *People's Present Behavior Is Markedly Influenced by Their Most Recent Experience.* If you can determine what prospects or customers have done just before your call, you have a clue to their behavior in your presence. Often pent-up feelings are spilled on the first target for displaced aggression.

6. *In Brief Meetings, No Time Exists for Contradictions to Appear.* People may make up their mind only to change it in a few hours or days. If you are with people only a few moments, you may have no opportunity to change their mind. Many orders have been canceled after the call because the salesperson failed to perceive the customer's uncertainty.

7. *First Impressions Are Apt to Depend Too Much on Feelings.* Salespeople who unconsciously let their feelings close out their analytical thought processes may jump to erroneous conclusions not based on behavioral evidence.

How to Improve Evaluation

As a salesperson, you are vitally concerned with accurately judging the uniqueness of each customer or prospect. People vary widely in this ability to analyze others. By conscious effort, however, you can markedly improve your skill. We have considered the two general cautions—*type thinking* and *first impressions or neglect of background factors.* Five important factors influence a person's skill-fulness in understanding the uniqueness of others: (1) attentiveness, (2) friendli-ness, (3) intelligence, (4) background, and (5) vocabulary.

Attentiveness

You perceive your environment, including the people around you, through your sense organs, chiefly your eyes and ears. At any given time, you take in only a very few of the details or stimuli that are there to be seen or heard. Attention is very selective. Further, if you are attending *within* yourself rather than *to* the person on whom you are calling, you take in even fewer stimuli. Obviously, then, the more cues or stimuli you miss, the less able you are to understand customers or prospects and their unique characteristics.

If you consciously attend *to* the customer or prospect instead of to yourself, you will catch many cues that otherwise you would miss. To do this, you must have *overlearned* your presentation. The salesperson who has to search for what to say during a call is unable to keep attention where it belongs—on the other person.

You will increase your attentiveness if you carefully plan *in advance* what you are going to do once the call begins. As part of your preparation, review all you know about the person whom you are going to see.

In attending to a person, you need to distinguish between two categories of details or stimuli—*matter* cues and *manner* cues. Matter cues encompass all the things people say or do; manner cues refer to their style of behavior, the "how" of what they say or do. This distinction suggests that *manner* cues often provide important evidence about an individual's personality and/or motives and that these cues are often missed. Remember, one of your objectives on every call is to get to know individuals better, which means trying to refine and improve your description of them. Sound description is based on observed behavior, *not* on hunch, guess, or prejudice. Effective salespeople are attentive. They miss few cues because they have their attention where it belongs—on the customer.

Friendliness

The friendly person obtains information more easily and in larger quantities than the less friendly person. The more information you have about people, the better basis you have for understanding their uniqueness. As a salesperson, you generate such knowledge firsthand by your observations during personal contact. In some instances you may, of course, complement your own findings with the observa-tions of others who know the individuals. Whether you are learning about a per-son directly or through others, friendliness is essential in obtaining desired information.

The effect of friendliness on judgments of personality and motivation depends on whether the person is a stranger or a friend. You face the former situation more frequently than the latter one; with strangers, friendliness is a must because you need to generate maximum information in a very short time period. Friendliness may be a handicap in understanding close friends and acquaintances. Friendly persons tend to be sympathetic, try to see people in the best possible light, and are prone to overlook faults. People who are less friendly see their acquaintances more objectively—as other people see them.

Another aspect to this tendency is that salespeople often get secondhand information about prospects. In such instances, they must estimate the accuracy of the information. A very close friend who describes a person may present a more favorable picture than is warranted. You have to discount or correct what is said. You must know the informant to evaluate his or her judgments.

Clearly, friendliness is an advantage in understanding other people. How can we improve this quality in ourselves? A ready smile is one physical manifestation. Another is enthusiasm. Still another cue of a friendly person is a warm handshake.

Less superficial evidence of friendliness includes active and attentive listening and readiness to share confidences. Too frequently when another person is talking, listeners do not really listen. Rather, they busy themselves thinking about what they will say next.

Exercise discretion in taking a person into your confidence. But, confidences that can be shared convey an attitude of friendliness. How often have you said to one of your customers, "I want to let you in on something." The buyer reacts favorably to this treatment.

Here are seven adjustment techniques that characterize the friendly person's behavior. Use them as a checklist and guide.

1. Watch other people and cue your behavior to theirs.
2. Note other people's interests and bring them into the conversation.
3. Respond to other people with gestures and facial expressions as well as with words.
4. Ask questions that encourage other people to talk freely.
5. Develop a unique or interesting hobby or avocation—a conversation piece.
6. Assume other people like you.
7. Say complimentary things about other people, especially behind their backs.

When you use these techniques, you will more easily establish a cooperative attitude on the part of the customer. This allows you to obtain more information in a short time. This, in turn, enables you to develop a better basis for judging the customer's personality (which governs your manner of presentation) and motivational needs (which bear on the content or matter of the presentation).

Intelligence

A close relationship exists between intelligence and the ability to analyze people. The process involves deriving generalizations from diverse information.

The person with low intelligence can neither remember many details nor see how they relate. The highly intelligent person, in contrast, is able to observe many items of evidence and arrive quickly at reliable and relevant conclusions. Judging personality and motivation is basically in inductive thought process.

Memory is an ingredient of intelligence and one reason more intelligent people have an advantage judging others. They are able to pull together pieces of evidence from the past and blend them with other information as they become available during each subsequent contact with the person.

We can more effectively size up people if we make a conscious effort to think through the alternative inferences we draw instead of only seeing one or two conclusions. Consider this example: You are making a first call and you discover the prospect is not talking. His secretary is standing in the doorway. You assume that she wants to get his attention, and the reason for his failure to talk is distraction. While you are coming to that conclusion, the secretary tells him an appointment scheduled after yours has just been canceled, leaving him free to spend more time with you. Your original hypothesis is no longer valid. You seek a new reason for the prospect's silence. You decide he lacks information, but in the next instant you hear him deliver a profound statement on it in response to a phone inquiry. You may think a personal hostility is keeping him from talking, yet he dispels this theory by offering you a sample box of the company's products. You experience this kind of mental trial and error whenever you attempt to interpret the behavior of others.

Another sound way to improve the use of your intelligence in relations with people is to avoid judgments under emotional duress. Your emotional reactions block straight thinking. Even though you get valuable cues about others through your feelings, you must guard against allowing these to dominate analytical thought processes.

Background

If you are to capitalize on background as a basis for understanding people, you must broaden yourself. As you discover a customer's interests and activities, learn more about them before the next call. You can also add immeasurably to your background by participating in civic, business, and professional affairs. A third way to improve your background is by regularly reading a wide variety of publications.

A person can better understand another individual's personality when their backgrounds have common elements. There are several reasons for this. First, as stated earlier, personality can only be defined in terms of individuals interacting with their environment.

If you have no knowledge of or experience with the person's background—geographic locale, racial origin, education, socioeconomic level, religious beliefs, and so on—you will find it difficult to interpret what you observe. Second, sharing backgrounds leads to sympathy and empathy. You can more readily put yourself in another person's place and understand that person's feelings if you have had common experiences. Third, because values come from the environment, you are likely to have life values similar to those of the other person if you have a common background.

Many successful salespeople have diversified work experience and varied educational and cultural backgrounds. Consequently, they have elements in common with many prospects or customers. These elements facilitate their understanding of the other person.

Success in using your background to promote sales depends on whether you reflect it with mature behavior. Breadth of background pays off to the extent that you have a basis for *understanding* and *appreciating* the other person. Less mature individuals are prone to impose their backgrounds on others and to evaluate other people's background in terms of their own. When salespeople adjust in this way, their background becomes a liability rather than an asset.

Vocabulary

Words are symbols by which we portray the environment both in our own minds and in our communications with others. Complex thought processes would be impossible without them. Imagine the difficulty of conveying a complicated idea in pantomime!

In general, the larger and more precise your vocabulary, the better able you are to appropriately label the behavior of another person. Another advantage of an appropriate vocabulary is that when you express yourself fluently, you sound more authoritative and enhance your ability to influence your prospect's thinking. If you have a large and varied vocabulary, you are at a considerable advantage in sizing up others because you can communicate more accurately than your competitors.

Before you can fully appreciate the behavior and attitudes of others, you must have a vocabulary that allows you to label or define what you see and hear. To identify the behavior you observe, you need to know words for sorting out and classifying what you perceive. For example, in football, if you cannot distinguish between a forward pass and a lateral pass, the players' actions may confuse you. Similar difficulties arise in describing a person's behavior in a sales situation.

You can improve your vocabulary in several ways. First, use a dictionary to learn the meaning of any new word you encounter. Second, notice the words that describe the behavior of fictitious characters in books or movies. Third, listen to the words spoken by others. People unconsciously develop favorite words and expressions. If you can use these naturally, you gain. People will understand them and will be flattered by your word choice. Fourth, study the list of trait terms in Appendix IX.

Your thought process uses word symbols for observed stimuli to note and immediately label people's behavior. Further, you base your future behavior on the label rather than on the person's actual behavior. If you apply the wrong label, your actions will be inappropriate. Salespeople, then, must translate their observations of customers into an accurate set of labels or descriptions so that in making their sales presentations, they will work within the framework of the customers' uniqueness.

One caution; many people develop private word meanings. The mature salesperson should avoid private word meanings and use language that the buyer is most likely to understand.

Validate Your Judgment

In addition to the preceding methods, there is another important way to improve your ability to analyze people—validate your judgments.

In Section 1, we made two important points: (1) The same person may be perceived differently by different observers and (2) The same person may be perceived differently by another person on different occasions. To improve your ability to describe others, you should use every opportunity to check your observations and descriptions with those of others. After a joint call, compare observations with your colleagues. If other company personnel visit an account, see how their customer descriptions check with yours. Use contacts with other salespeople to compare ideas on prospects and customers. Skillful questioning of other people in the account is another important method for generating information about the individual you seek to sell.

Before each call, take stock of what you know about the individual based on your observations during previous calls. After the call, ask yourself "What revisions must I make in describing the buyer?" "How did I get the wrong impression on previous visits?"

If you validate your judgment with both others' observations and your own experiences, you are bound to improve your ability to analyze others.

Modifications in Strategy

However carefully you plan your strategic handling of a customer, you must be prepared for the unexpected. You must be ready to deal with people *as you find them.* Your task, when the call begins, is to determine the prospect's feelings and state of mind at the moment of contact.

The Customer Is in a Bad Mood and Adjusting Negatively

The best general strategy when confronted with this situation is to be a warm and attentive listener. The prime objective is *catharsis,* to help people verbalize what is bothering them, to allow them to "get it off their mind." Whether you, your company, or its products or services caused the upset is not of great importance. You may be blamed for the upset through the mechanism of *displaced aggression.* If you are in some way to blame (*direct aggression*), you will likely meet exaggeration and distorted facts. Naturally, if you see that you, your company, or its products or services have provoked the upset, you will want to make an adjustment, but do this *after* you have calmed down the customer by listening to his or her complaints. Too frequently, when encountering a complaint, salespeople adjust the "thing side." They replace the goods or arrange for field service help, but they fail to cope with the "people side," cooling down the customer's feelings.

Sometimes, under such circumstances, salespeople erroneously proceed with their planned presentation, hoping the atmosphere will clear as the call progresses. Rarely will this occur. Instead, the customer is likely to become more irritated. The businesslike behavior of the salesperson, which normally a customer admires and respects, now becomes an added thorn in his or her side.

The Customer Is Busy and Bothered by the Interruption

In the first few minutes of the call, you should determine whether you have directed your customer's full attention to the business of the moment. You may have difficulty doing this because he or she was close to finishing something. You have several alternative strategies. *You may offer to wait until the customer has completed the task.* If you choose to do this, you must assure the person you have work you can do. Otherwise, guilt ensues. Or, *You may use the situation to see someone else in the customer account.* Industrial salespeople often find it difficult to get past purchasing agents. Finding them busy may provide a good opportunity to see other people. If you elect this strategy, you must accomplish it with great tact. You may put your request this way, "Mr. _____, I can see you're anxious to finish what you are doing. I know you want Mrs. Jones to evaluate this product anyway. Would you mind if I go out to the plant and visit with her?" *You may offer to come back at another time.* This is the least desirable strategy, yet, under some circumstances you may need to elect it. If so, make a definite appointment for a return visit. The less favorable prospects' attitudes are, the more difficult rescheduling your appointment will be. Therefore, in anticipation of the new appointment, you might fax a confirming letter or telephone the prospect to guard against a recurrence of the previous unsatisfactory call.

The Customer Is with Someone Else

In an earlier section, we pointed out that an individual's personality is definable in terms of the person's interaction with other people. If you have based a trait description on previous occasions when you saw a person alone, you may now expect to see other traits emerge, triggered by the new person's presence. You should first determine the third party's relationship to the customer and how the customer perceives him or her. If the other person is a superior and is viewed as such by the customer, this may provoke submissive and indecisive behavior not previously observed. You can get valuable insights into the degree of dependence by the frequency with which the customer seems to seek approval of the other person. If the individual is a subordinate and is so perceived by the customer, the customer may become domineering and impulsively decisive just to demonstrate authority.

Whoever the third party may be, you must adjust to the new customer behavior and analyze the other person to determine his or her likely influence on the sale (see Chapter Six).

You should not bypass the original customer. On the other hand, if the superior is now the decision maker, you must handle that person, too. You may, by frequent references to your customer's knowledge, enhance your customer's status with the boss. Often, you can shift the presentation to the customer with such statements as, "I'm sure Mr. _____ can explain this benefit to your firm better than I can." If you feel that the superior is not especially interested, you may interject a remark such as, "Perhaps you would like Mr. _____ and me to work out details and see you later when we have the whole proposition ready for your review."

With subordinates present, your strategy may involve enlisting their help by pointing out benefits that will affect them and their work in the company. You may also encourage the customer to display his or her knowledge by recapitulating previously furnished information for the subordinate's benefit. Trying for a quick close so that the customer can display authority to act might be good strategy. A governing factor in your strategy is what you interpret to be the feelings of the customer toward the other person. In any case, however, you must keep your primary focus on the decision maker.

The Customer Is Not In

When this situation occurs, you must rapidly reevaluate your objectives. If the problem you intend to discuss is not critical, you may prefer to go on to your next call after making a new appointment with the customer.

If you cannot put off the matter, you have to request an appointment (in some cases, the absent person may have made arrangements for another contact in the company) with an alternate company spokesperson. Obviously, in such a circumstance, the customer description you prepared will be inappropriate, so your first objective will be to learn as much about the new contact as you can. The secretary or receptionist may be able to tell you the relationship of the person you are interviewing to the one you had intended to visit. You may also be able to open the conversation by inquiring how much the person knows about your company's products or services. In any event, try to put off making the key part of your presentation until you have had an opportunity to size up and mentally prepare a trait description and/or a motivational analysis together with some general strategy for dealing with the new person.

In this kind of situation you are dependent on first impressions, which are notoriously unreliable. Therefore, you should proceed slowly with your presentation until you have picked up clues to the person's motivation, personality, and background. For example, if the buyer is very self-confident, telling him or her about another company's evaluation of your offerings might be disastrous;

while if the person is lacking in self-confidence, he or she might welcome such information.

Although setting aside a carefully prepared presentation is unpleasant, it is better to start with a superficial analysis of a new contact than to try making the same presentation. Remember, after you have used the personality and motivational analyses outlined in this chapter, you will be able to recognize significant facets of behavior and improvise a presentation more effectively than if you had not practiced the technique.

If the new contact represents a permanent assignment and you will be calling on him or her in the future, be wary of your first impressions and avoid getting into the heart of your presentation until you have developed a strategy based on a comprehensive analysis of his or her traits, motives, and background.

SUMMARY

Effective communication in selling means that you understand the buyer's needs and that the buyers understand how your product or service will fill them. Frequently, such understanding will result in a sale. However, understanding and agreement are not the same thing. When this happens, and you still believe the prospect is a logical user of your offering, you must intensify your efforts to personalize your presentation. To do this, you must understand the variables in the strategic equation discussed in this chapter (Figure 5.8).

No two human beings are exactly alike, not even identical twins. They vary on *personality traits, motives,* and *background factors* as well as the *situations* in which the communication takes place.

Personality refers to the style of a person's behavior, the "how," and is reflected in *temperament* and *life values.* Personality is dynamic and can only be described as people continuously interact with their environments. Occasionally, even the well-adjusted person adjusts negatively, though most of the time adjustment is positive.

In describing customers, you are likely to *type* them because your mind works that way. Yet, description by *traits* is the better method because you must deal with each person as a unique individual. Use of the trait method results in accurate descriptions of customers, provides a basis for developing strategies appropriate for each individual, and enables you to adjust more quickly to buyers. Properly executed, the trait analysis provides you with clues for approaching the buyer.

Motivation is concerned with the "why" of human behavior. Success in selling depends on your understanding of motivation, which can be studied in terms

$$\text{Uniqueness} = \frac{f\,(\text{"How," "Why," "What"})}{\text{Situation--1, 2, 3 . . . .}}$$

Figure 5.8   The strategic equation.

of what happens within the individual, or the factors in the environment that trigger an individual's activities. Looking inside the individual, some motives are consciously experienced while others stem from the unconscious.

Your understanding of customers' and prospects' motivation is a powerful tool for developing sales strategy as well as for adjusting your behavior in each interview. A motivational analysis reveals *what* to talk about to personalize your presentation.

Background factors are "what" the buyer has done up to the present. To improve your ability to size up others, you must avoid type thinking and undue dependence on first impressions. In addition, greater attention to manner cues, increased friendliness, more analytical thinking about the customer's behavior, and finding common experiences with each prospect will enhance your results. Validating your judgments also improves your ability to size up people.

In analyzing buyers, you should not neglect situational factors, the "where." Characteristics revealed in one set of circumstances may not be observable in another. Therefore, the more varied and frequent your contacts with buyers, the more observations you will have in your data base for understanding and adjusting to them.

To personalize your presentation, you must understand the variables—personality, motivation, background, and situation— in the strategic equation.

TOPICS FOR THOUGHT AND DISCUSSION

1. Why is an understanding of the dynamics of personality critical to your success in selling?
2. Discuss the influence of heredity and environment on personality. Now, by analogy, apply the same reasoning to a customer, visualizing previous jobs as heredity and the present job as environment.
3. Develop examples of positive and negative adjustment by both salespeople and customers.
4. Consider your responsibility to yourself and to your employer to learn more about personality.
5. Compare advertising and selling in terms of trait versus type descriptions of customers.
6. Develop a trait description of a public figure (e.g., the President of the United States) on the basis of general information from news sources.
7. Why do some books on selling recommend the type approach?
8. Review your experience for examples of acting on the basis of a trait that was not supported by evidence.
9. Review the list of traits and select those you find easiest and most difficult to understand in terms of handling customers. Relate these to your own

traits to see if a relationship exists between yourself and the kind of customers you understand best.

10. Review your experience for instances where you tried unsuccessfully to communicate with a person on the basis of a single trait without considering the interaction of other traits.

11. Review the list of traits and select a few that you feel are as likely to be shown in compensatory as in natural behavior.

12. Discuss the likelihood of two different salespeople arriving at the same strategy for approaching the same prospect.

13. Which camera provides you with the clearest picture of motivation? Why?

14. What relationship do you see between personal productivity and a sense of purpose?

15. Cite examples from your own life of positive motivation. Negative motivation.

16. Often we are unable to identify the reasons for doing what we do (unconscious motivation). What personal examples of this can you cite?

17. "No two people are likely to have identical motives for buying a particular product or service." When would you agree with this statement? Disagree? Why?

18. If you asked three people to describe the motivation of one of your customers, each might have a different idea. How could you use such information?

19. A customer's motivation may be predominantly oriented around work or off-the-job life. Draw up some guidelines to help you in knowing when to emphasize on-the-job or off-the-job factors.

20. Even though you understand a customer's motivation, letting him or her know you have such understanding may not be appropriate. What do you do in such cases?

21. Review the background of your customers. What variety of experience is represented? What can you do to acquire knowledge that will help you understand your customers?

22. What cues do you use to form first impressions? Compare these with the list of "Pitfalls in First Impressions" to see if you can improve your accuracy on first impressions.

23. When a customer forms an erroneous first impression of you, how can you correct the impression?

24. With the seven adjustment techniques of the friendly person in mind, review your relationships with some of your difficult customers to see if you can apply one or more of the techniques and thereby improve your relationship with them.

SIX

Strategy and Tactics with Groups

People are usually more convinced by reasons they discovered themselves than by those found by others.

BLAISE PASCAL

In this chapter:

- **Analyzing Individual Members of Groups and Planning Strategy**
  - You must be as adept at conducting presentations before groups as you are with interviewing individuals if you are to be effective with a broad range of customers.
- **Maximizing Participation by Group Members**
  - You need to get participation from members of a buying group if you are to make an effective presentation.
- **Communicating with Groups**
  - Guidelines are essential for dealing with the problems you face in communicating with groups.
- **Summary**
  - If you are to sell the full line to the full marketplace, you must be adept at selling to groups as well as to individuals.
- **Topics for Thought and Discussion**
- **Application Exercises**
  - Appendix XVIII Description of Roles of Group Members
  - Appendix XIX   Checklist for Summarizing Roles of Group Members
  - Appendix XX   Checklist for Tallying Group Members' Remarks
  - Appendix XXI   Strategies for Use in Group Selling

1. ANALYZING INDIVIDUAL MEMBERS OF GROUPS AND PLANNING STRATEGY

Many organizations place primary responsibility for purchasing on professional buyers, purchasing committees, and/or some combination of individual and group

152

decision makers. This means you must be as adept at conducting presentations before groups as you are with interviewing individuals if you are to be effective with a broad range of customers. The strategic and tactical objectives in selling to groups are the same as in selling to individuals—*to accord uniqueness* and *to be in control without seeming to do so*—because groups, like individual prospects, react adversely to either indifference or coercion.

Selling to Groups versus Individuals

Selling to groups differs importantly from selling to an individual. When selling to an individual, you can identify personality traits as well as infer motives and make appropriate adjustments in the presentation. For example, if you find the prospect to be arrogant and authoritarian, you can show sufficient submissiveness to make the prospect feel comfortable. Or, if the prospect is not sufficiently self-confident to make a decision, you can supply him or her with testimonials and research evidence of the efficacy of the product or service.

In selling to several persons at one time, you cannot concern yourself with the traits and motives of each individual. A dynamic field exists in a group situation that every member, including you, contributes to and affects (Figure 6.1). The term in common use for the behavior seen in groups is *role*. Thus, in selling to groups, the individual's role takes precedence over personality traits and motives. There are several reasons for this.

First, you are concerned with guiding the group to a decision consistent with your objectives. You can do this best by utilizing the resources of the individuals in the group. You should be more concerned with the interaction of group members with each other than with their interaction and/or reaction to you. Your objective is to be as unobtrusive as possible and still control the direction of the discussion without seeming to do so.

Second, you cannot interact with individual group members without considering the impact on the others. For example, if you display deference to a member whom other members hold in low esteem, you weaken your own position.

Third, with the pressure and complications of a group, you cannot note the detail necessary to identify traits and motives accurately. If you depend on previous knowledge of a member's traits and motives, you can be in serious error. The traits and motives apparent in a face-to-face meeting will in all probability be modified by the presence of other group members. A purchasing agent who may act quite self-confident when alone with a salesperson may be significantly inhibited in the company of a senior vice president.

In addition, you must use information provided by other personnel cautiously, if at all. To grasp this fully, imagine the description that any or all of the following sources might furnish about yourself: parents, spouse, children, supervisor, peers, friends, strangers. Descriptions from such diverse sources will, in all probability, be dissimilar.

Fourth, where do you find a group where all the members agree on the objectives and each person will work actively to accomplish them? In practice,

Figure 6.1 Illustrative roles of group members.

some members of the group will have been "sent" to the meeting and show their resentment by heckling the group and the salesperson or chairperson. Some of the members may represent administrative departments; others, technical departments of the company. They may use the meeting to air some of their differences of opinion. Individuals who are sufficiently negativistic to enjoy obstructing the meeting objectives might also be present.

Still another type of person whom you sometimes encounter in a group meeting is the one with a "private agenda." This person wants to achieve an objective unknown to the rest of the group. Until the group leader understands this private agenda the person constitutes an obstacle to progress.

The person who conducts a group meeting must deal with the subject matter as well as the individual behavior of group members. To do this, you must know the roles that you may encounter, be able to identify them, and then apply the proper strategy.

Classifying a Group Member

Researchers in the behavioral sciences have noted that when people assemble in groups, they tend to acquire a role or assume a function in relation to the group. Roles, however, are not simple entities. Any individual might play a variety of roles within a group discussion. The roles will vary with the dynamics of the meeting. For example, a person's role might change as a result of pressures generated by other group members. Without pressure, however, a person's role in any given group is relatively consistent although it may vary from group to group. A person who plays a relatively passive role as part of a company's executive committee may take on an important role in community, church, or school groups. The method of dealing with him or her will depend in part on the group in which the person is participating. Likewise, a person's role may vary with the amount of knowledge possessed relative to other participants as well as other factors, such as interest in the topic of discussion.

The first step in observing group members is to try to classify their remarks. An infinite number of classifications could be used; Appendix XVIII introduces and describes some of the roles played when people assemble in groups. As this is an empirical rather than a research-developed list, you should modify it if by so doing you can make it more useful for your purposes.

The development of role-analysis skill involves three phases. The first is to become familiar with the roles and classifications in Appendix XVIII. You can achieve this by carefully studying the list.

The second phase is to actually observe groups in action and note the roles of the various participants. Appendix XIX provides a checklist for recording observations. (If you change your list of descriptions, you should also change the checklist.) If the group is as small as five people and the discussion is short, you should be able to work up a sheet on each person as soon as the discussion has ended. With large groups and longer discussions, this approach may not be feasible. A checklist such as shown in Appendix XX is likely to be more workable. Here, each of the roles enacted by each participant can be recorded as soon as he or she enacts it. At the end of the meeting, you can use the data to prepare checklists on each participant on an individual form such as found in Appendix XIX. A diagram of the group identifying each member with a number corresponding to the person's location will be helpful in recording roles (Figure 6.2).

Each salesperson who is going to conduct group presentations must develop the ability to observe the roles members play as well as to note their remarks. You can develop this skill only by practice outside bona fide presentations.

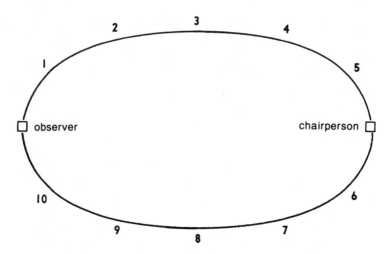

Figure 6.2 A diagram of a group, identifying each member with a number corresponding to location.

Role-playing sessions at sales meetings are the simplest and most efficient way to develop the skill because you can have a discussion suitable for observing roles, followed by a discussion on the accuracy of the observations. At a sales meeting, assign roles to group members to ensure that all possible roles will be represented. Playing various roles will develop empathy, which is a valuable by-product of the training. You can practice the skill of observing roles in any group.

There is no more reason to expect professional performance from a salesperson without practice than there is from a musician. Where are people to be found who can play at a concert level without lessons and practice? Once you have mastered thinking in terms of roles, you will be able to adjust to group members spontaneously.

When you have mastered the problem of classifying and identifying the roles of group members, you can undertake the third phase, which involves the formulation of strategies. These principles are detailed in Appendix XXI and illustrate how to develop strategies for handling persons based on their roles.

Each salesperson needs to develop this line of thinking to suit his or her own needs in group situations.

2. MAXIMIZING PARTICIPATION BY GROUP MEMBERS

Buying is an active process. In two-way conversation you catch the reactions of the other person and adjust to these appropriately. When the prospect participates, you have more control over the interview. Similarly, you need to get participation from members of a buying group if you are to make an effective presentation. However, groups pose special problems. This section details ways to maximize participation by group members.

Before the Meeting

Depending on the importance of the meeting and the time available, you should try to acquire the following background information on the members:

1. Seniority and status in the organization.
2. Nature of interest in content of the meeting.
3. Authority to make decisions.
4. Acceptance by others in the group.
5. State of career progress: growing, stable, declining.

Such background data will help you obtain group participation because you cannot interact with any individual member without considering the impact on the other members.

Triggering Participation by Group Members

When making a presentation to a group, you need to guide the group and, hence, the separate individuals to a decision or feeling consistent with your objective. Utilize the resources of the individual group members. Do not "lecture" to the group. You should be more concerned with their interaction with each other than with their interaction and/or reaction to you. Group participation is essential for an effective presentation. To maximize participation by group members, you should use the following techniques.

Act as Though You Expect Members to Participate

You should make it clear you do not want to make a speech and that your objective is to exchange ideas with members of the group. If time permits, you may provide an opportunity for members of the group to exchange ideas with each other while you are present. Refer to the meeting as a conference, not as a sales presentation. In addition, your actions should reinforce your words. By attending carefully to the reactions of the group members, you can indicate you are sincerely interested in their views.

Do Not Depend on Voluntary Participation

Unless the members of the group are deeply involved in the discussion, you should never address a question to the group hoping someone will answer it. You should direct a question to a specific individual whom you have reason to believe is in a position to comment on the topic. If all in the group are strangers, you can select a person on the edge of the group as a starter, then go to the next person, and so on, until you achieve the desired interaction. Even in fairly large groups, you can attain meaningful participation by selecting participants in different rows, tables, and so on, to provide feedback as you introduce new issues.

Participation is vital in the first part of a meeting. After the "ice is broken" and several persons are interested in the discussion, raising general questions may be safe, but in the warm-up phase or with a new group, raising questions is dangerous.

Develop Interaction between Group Members

When somebody has answered one of your questions, you can ask another member to comment on the answer: "Why do you agree or disagree with the previous answer?" or give an entirely different answer to the question such as, "What other views are defensible?" Once a question has been wholly or partially answered, you will find it easier to get additional comments than to get reactions to a new topic. Consequently, until the group members are participating comfortably, you should introduce new issues carefully. As indicated earlier, when the group is interacting freely with good rapport, you may be freer in introducing new questions.

Avoid Calling on Shy People in the Early Phases of the Meeting

In any group, some people are more at ease than others. Let these people participate until the others seem ready to join in. When a leader calls on a person and receives no reaction because the respondent feels inhibited, it creates an unfortunate situation with several negative consequences. Not only is the person embarrassed, but others in the group feel both sympathetic and resentful. You may have difficulty adjusting to the situation and regaining the previous level of participation.

Open with Questions That Call for Fact Rather Than Opinion

Most people are reluctant to express their opinions to relative strangers. Therefore, asking for opinions before you have established rapport is likely to reduce rather than enhance participation. During the initial phase, it is preferable to ask such questions as "What do you look for when you buy a product/service?" and "What improvements would you like to see?" When some facts are out in the open, you might ask for opinions about the facts presented by others, but direct solicitation of opinions in the early part of the meeting is unnecessarily risky.

Explain That Individuals Will Benefit in Proportion to Their Participation

From the perspective of a group member, the objective should be to exchange information. Participants may receive new information as well as advance their own ideas. In expounding views, group members may receive constructive criticism and clarification that is beneficial. In receiving ideas from other members, a participant can question the contributors of the ideas and learn about their reasoning as well as their conclusions. Also, if their participation is beneficial, participants can raise their status with other group members. The real loser at a group conference is the one who fails to participate.

Use Challenging and/or Controversial Statements

If the group seems passive, members may be stimulated by your stretching a point to which someone will take exception.

Be Tolerant of Poorly Developed Ideas or Opposing Points of View

If you, as a leader, take sharp issue with any member or allow one to severely criticize another, you will discourage others from expressing themselves.

If someone expresses a poorly conceived idea, you can gradually draw out the speaker and expose the fallacy as you would in a private conversation. The participant will either retract the statement, or the group as a whole will see the fallacy. Thus, you can accomplish your objective to demolish the idea without being unpleasant or discouraging others from participating. Be alert and avoid "beating a dead horse."

Present the Meeting as a Means for Members to Demonstrate Their Knowledge

People with enough ego to want to present their views are always available. If you can identify and question these people, they will gladly start the participation. Then you can keep the discussion going.

Restrict People Who Try to Monopolize the Conversation

Nothing is more boring to group members than to have one person do most of the talking. The reaction of the disenchanted listeners is to clam up. Once group members have decided not to participate, they will likely focus on their own private thoughts. Thus, as soon as you sense one member is trying to take over the program, you need to ignore him or her and call on others to avoid losing their attention.

Guiding Participation

You should note two general dimensions of individual behavior in groups as a guide to managing participation. The first can be termed "attitude." Is the group member basically in agreement with or opposed to your objectives? The second is labeled "prestige." Does the group member have high or low prestige in the group? These dimensions are combined in Figure 6.3. If you have acquired background

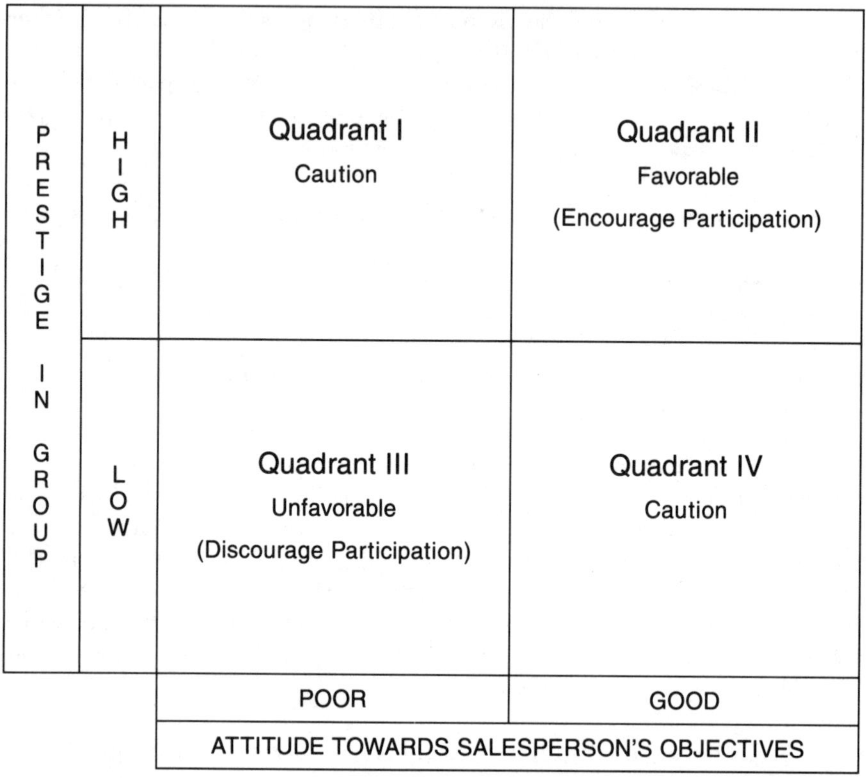

		POOR	GOOD
P R E S T I G E I N G R O U P	H I G H	**Quadrant I** Caution	**Quadrant II** Favorable (Encourage Participation)
	L O W	**Quadrant III** Unfavorable (Discourage Participation)	**Quadrant IV** Caution
		ATTITUDE TOWARDS SALESPERSON'S OBJECTIVES	

Figure 6.3 A guide for managing participation of individuals in groups.

information on group members and have been successful in generating participation among group members during the initial stages of the meeting, you should be able to classify group members.

In general, you will tend to encourage participation by members who are sympathetic to your objectives and have prestige in the group more than those falling on the other side of these dimensions. Allowing a member to talk too much or excluding him or her from participation may cause resentment from others. Thus, you must seek and attain a balance.

To be a successful group leader, you will minimize your comments, other than stating your objectives at the beginning. You will draw favorable comments from the various members, and when you need to refute an idea, seek a group member to state the opposing point of view rather than doing so yourself.

A related consideration is the nature of the group. On some occasions you need to have the group reach a consensus favorable to you. Such a situation is formal approval of the offering. Another frequent situation is an assemblage of a group of peers, such as medical doctors. In this instance, you must attempt to influence each member toward your goal since each person remains free to make an individual decision.

3.   COMMUNICATING WITH GROUPS

Why should you sell to groups as well as to individuals? Three key reasons exist: First, you can deliver your message to more people within the organization in the time you have available. You can generally present a message to a group in the same time you can to a single individual. Therefore, you can multiply awareness of your offering several fold by calling on a group rather than on separate individuals. If you master the principles of promoting to groups, your sales volume should increase.

Second, after you make a number of individual sales presentations, some people reject your message, others are enthusiastic, and still others are neutral. You want to use those individuals who are at either end of the spectrum—either enthusiastic or reluctant to use your products or services—as a stimulus for a group promotion. For the enthusiastic individual, you want to assemble a group so that the buyer can show his or her enthusiasm and help excite others. For the reluctant buyer, whose reasons may be unsound, the social pressure in a group may produce a change in view. You can accomplish this best by including them in a group that is enthusiastic about your offering.

Third, sometimes you will have difficulty identifying the decision makers in an organization by using individual presentations. In a group promotion, you may see the "pecking order" more clearly. If you do not achieve your objectives in the group promotion, you can seek private interviews with the appropriate individuals.

Thus, sound and compelling reasons exist for promoting to groups. Although you use essentially the same techniques to promote to groups as individuals, if you are to be effective, you must understand the special difficulties inherent in group communication.

From the buying organization's standpoint, a group decision may be better than an individual decision. Where several departments share the same supplies and equipment, you will find this particularly true.

Communicating with Groups versus Individuals

To communicate effectively with groups, you must recognize and adjust for three special problems. First, as the number of participants in the communications process increases, the volume of feedback you can monitor from any one individual decreases and the quality of the feedback changes. Because only one person can send verbal feedback at any one time, you must rely heavily on the other participants' nonverbal feedback to gauge their position on any particular sales point. Unfortunately, nonverbal feedback is difficult to interpret accurately, especially when you cannot concentrate on any one individual. Consequently, the quantity and quality of the feedback in a group situation is likely to be less meaningful than that in a one-on-one discussion.

Second, although each group participant is a unique individual, to personalize your presentation is virtually impossible. Rather, you must present your offering differently from and better than the competitive alternatives so that your remarks to the group will address the bulk of their needs and wants. Therefore, your offering might be less well understood at the end of the group presentation than if you had communicated your proposition to each member individually.

Third, as the number of participants increases and the fidelity of the feedback goes down, the potential for unintended communication effects, or noise, increases. As members of the buying group receive your signal, each participant is unlikely to interpret it exactly as you intended. Thus, the receivers add noise—misconceptions, misinformation, and distortion of message. The problem is that, by communicating with limited feedback, you have no clear idea how much noise has been added to your signal. Moreover, minimizing noise in group communication is difficult because of the inherent restrictions on the continued exchange of views required to maximize message impact.

Guidelines are essential for dealing with the problems you face in communicating with groups. The following subsections focus on dealing with groups of three, groups larger than three, and larger group meetings.

Groups of Three

The first situation to analyze is where you find yourself with a two-person buying team (Figure 6.4). If either of the two is clearly senior to the other, the communication would go from the Salesperson (S) to the Senior Prospect (P^1) and from the Senior Prospect to the Junior Prospect (P^2). In such an instance, you can deal with P^1 in nearly the same way as if P^2 were not present. You need only be polite to P^2. Occasionally, you might provide P^2 an opportunity to express his or her opinions, but P^1 will largely decide the degree of participation of P^2.

When the two members of the buying team are approximately equal in rank and interest in the presentation, you must treat each of them as though he or she were the sole prospect. This requires developing a point with one of them, then another point with the other. When both are interested in the same point, you need to get concurrence before going on to the next point. When the two parties are interested in different aspects of the proposition (a Purchasing Agent and a Research Chemist, for example), you may offer to discuss the common points, then see each alone for his or her particular interest. If this is not feasible, then you must risk losing the attention of one while working with the other. Do not ignore one party long enough to allow that person to lose interest or feel neglected. Diagrammatically, the situation is as shown in Figure 6.5.

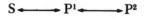

Figure 6.4 Communication in a group of three: One prospect dominant.

Figure 6.5   Communication in a group of three:
Two prospects of approximately equal rank.

In some instances, the prospects may communicate with each other, changing the diagram to the configuration shown in Figure 6.6. When this happens, you must be particularly alert to catch clues that will guide you in choosing the correct topic and manner in making your own presentation.

A situation that starts out as Figure 6.5 may, through the dynamics of Figure 6.6, revert to Figure 6.4 and allow you to concentrate on one of the two people rather than splitting your attention and, thereby, diluting the quality of your presentation.

If the third party is from your own organization, you plan your general strategy in advance.

Groups Larger Than Three

While a large body of research findings is available on discussion groups and group dynamics, very little of it applies to sales situations. The reason is that many of the groups used in research investigations are assembled for that purpose, and precautions are taken to see that there is no leader or objective for the group. In addition, researchers have focused their attention primarily on analyzing individuals in groups rather than on examining the communication relationships between individuals.

In contrast, each person in a sales conference is more or less aware of the objectives and seeks to facilitate or obstruct them, depending on his or her personal needs and relationships with other group members. Another reason that group dynamics research is not too helpful is that the salesperson and others from his or her organization have different roles and objectives from the others in the group.

Either you or the prospect might request that additional persons from either or both organizations sit in on negotiations. When the additional people are from your organization, you can foresee the role each person will play. Ideally, one person should act as spokesperson for all the sales personnel. In the case of additional people from the prospect's organization, you cannot map strategy so precisely.

Figure 6.6   Communication in a group of three:
Interaction between prospects.

Handling the Larger Group Meeting

Several actions can simplify your task and increase the likelihood of success in a larger group meeting.

Starting the Larger Group Meeting.   One thing you can do is to *try to reduce the number of persons you must deal with in the group.* Start the meeting by introducing any people who need an introduction. Next, you can establish the purpose of the meeting and the function of each person in attendance. Some of those present might be there to assist their superiors or merely to learn more about some company problem. At this point, you will become aware that these people are to have a passive role; hence, you can largely leave them out of the conversation without arousing hostility.

In many ways, you must handle larger groups in the same way as a smaller group (three persons). You have to be alert to any dominant person. If the group accepts this person as dominant, he or she may act as a spokesperson, and, hence, you can work with him or her much as though it were a simple sales interview. Until a spokesperson emerges, however, the best strategy for you is to treat each prospect as having equal influence in the group.

Establishing the Agenda.   Another suggestion for working with large groups is to *keep the number of topics to a minimum.* Each active member of the group may wish to discuss some personal problems as well as company ones. This takes time. Members of a group also tend to lose interest when the discussion becomes a sounding board for one individual. You need to restrict the conversation to the essentials of the proposition.

The easiest way to do this is to establish the agenda at the beginning of the meeting. If you use a handout, flip chart, or blackboard to list the specific topics for discussion; you can tactfully cut off diversion into side issues and minor points until the original major items are settled to each person's satisfaction. When individuals raise small points, the chairperson can mention that the plan is to treat the basic agenda first and to add the newer topics at the end if time permits.

Reducing the agenda to a tangible list has another advantage. The group can see the progress being made and predict the length of the meeting. Generally, people are more relaxed and cooperative when they are in a familiar situation than when they are uncertain what will happen.

Achieving Agreement.   When there are several persons in a group, they will represent diverse points of view. A person can sit through a meeting and come out with exactly the same opinion held prior to the meeting. In a simple sales interview, you can get the prospect to restate his or her opinions from time to time and gradually achieve acceptance of your opinion. In the group situation, however, this is not feasible. Therefore, from time to time, *draw specific conclusions from the discussion rather than leave this to each member of the group.*

To accomplish this objective, you need to summarize the discussion on each topic on the agenda and state the conclusion reached so that the group can react to it. If the group does not accept your conclusion, you must decide whether to reopen discussion of the topic or go on to a new point. Whether or not you pursue any specific point under such circumstances, we strongly recommend the technique of frequent summary to ensure that, before the members leave the meeting, you do everything to increase the likelihood that the group will adopt an opinion consistent with your objectives. Keep in mind, however, that members resent the leader making up their minds for them. Therefore, you should try to avoid a decision until the group, as a whole, feels it has dealt thoroughly with the problem.

Taking a few more minutes while the group is convened is better than risking some of the members reversing themselves when it is over. The more members that have affirmed the meeting's conclusions, the greater the likelihood that group members will maintain their positions and that no members will feel left out or ignored.

Handling Objections to the Offering. The three foregoing suggestions offer specific positive steps to take in each group meeting. An additional problem usually exists: *How should you handle weaknesses in your proposition?*

In the two-person interview, this is not a problem because if the prospect raises objections, you can answer them satisfactorily. Also, you have more intimate knowledge of the prospect and can better judge whether to bring out weaknesses or wait for the prospect to do so. In the group, however, you have fewer clues to guide you.

The best advice is to try to estimate the amount of knowledge the group members have about any shortcomings of the proposition and the likelihood of them asking questions or making statements that point out the weaknesses. Also estimate whether competitive salespeople are likely to call and point out any existing weaknesses later. Attempting to conceal weaknesses or deny their existence is unsound. The basic assumption is that no sales proposition is free of weaknesses, but they do not mean that you cannot make a sale. All that is necessary for an ethical salesperson to determine is that his or her proposition is as good as, or superior to, any other proposition available to the prospect.

As a principle, if any of the active participants are likely to bring up the weaknesses, you are in a stronger position to mention and concede them voluntarily than to try to defend yourself after members have produced the weaknesses as reasons not to buy. When conducting a group meeting, you should, therefore, remain alert to this possibility, and if the discussion seems likely to turn to weaknesses, you should minimize their significance by pointing them out before some member of the group does.

Another aspect of this problem is to determine whether the present conference is one of the first or one of the last before a decision is made. If one of the last, you can assume that weaknesses have been considered, and if the group seems satisfied, leave well enough alone. If yours is one of the first presentations, you should assume that weaknesses will emerge before a decision is made, and therefore, you should take them up in a straightforward manner. You should also anticipate the criticism other salespeople will make of your proposition and reduce the impact by pointing out, in a general way, what this group will probably hear from others, along with your rebuttal. You can also alert them to weaknesses in competitive products or services.

When you are sure that other presentations are scheduled, try to arrange for a repeat session that will, as far as possible, give you the last word. In arranging a presentation before a group that plans to listen to several presentations, try to be last. Failing this, being first and asking for an opportunity to come back after the other presentations have been heard is the advantageous strategy. This is analogous to the debater having an opportunity for a rebuttal. Most groups will see the fairness of this and cooperate.

SUMMARY

If you are to sell the full line to the full marketplace, you must be adept at selling to groups as well as to individuals. While the strategic and tactical objectives remain unchanged, the process of selling to groups differs significantly from selling to individuals.

In a group situation, analysis of each participant's personality and/or motivation is not feasible. However, a new unit of analysis—role—is appropriate. Based on observations of the role(s) each participant plays, you can formulate strategy to effectively deal with each member of the group. A method is presented for analyzing reactions of group members together with appropriate strategies.

Participation by the members of a buying group is the basis for formulating your strategy. The problems encountered in obtaining participation as well as techniques for offsetting them are discussed. Finally, the chapter provides a guide for managing the interactions of participants after the "ice is broken."

The ability to promote to groups as well as to individuals is an important sales tool for saving time, identifying decision makers, and gaining support for your offering. If you can reduce the size of the group you must deal with, focus attention on a limited number of agenda items, draw conclusions acceptable to the group, and handle weaknesses in the offering, you will be able to communicate effectively with groups. The effect of these steps is to increase the fidelity of feedback as well as the opportunities to customize the presentation for the group and reduce noise in your communication.

If you are to sell the full line to the full marketplace, you must be adept at selling to groups as well as to individuals.

TOPICS FOR THOUGHT AND DISCUSSION

1. Why is it dangerous to base role strategy on personality traits discovered in individual presentations?

2. What are the differences between salespeople who are effective with groups compared with those whose success is limited to working with individual customers?

3. What opportunities do you have to improve your effectiveness through the analysis of role relationships? What roles are most difficult for you to control? Why?

4. Give examples of group meetings where the private agenda of some members impaired the progress of the meeting.

5. How does a speaker's attitude affect the audience's inclination to participate? Give an example of an attitude that will encourage participation; one that will discourage participation.

6. How does an audience react when the speaker asks a question in general and no one offers an answer? How can you eliminate this risk?

7. What are the pros and cons of a leader commenting on an answer by a group member to one of his or her questions as compared with asking another member of the audience to comment? What are some guidelines as to when the leader should comment and when a member of the audience should be asked to comment?

8. How does the amount of participation relate to the benefits gained in a meeting?

9. Discuss the quantity and quality of feedback the salesperson receives in communicating with groups versus individuals.

10. What are the relative opportunities for two-way communication in group presentations as compared with individual interviews?

11. What are the advantages of establishing an agenda at the beginning of a group meeting?

12. How should you start the large group meeting?

SEVEN

Logic, Creativity, and Suggestion in Selling

There is no darkness—but ignorance.

WILLIAM SHAKESPEARE

In this chapter:

- **Problem Solving**
  - You must be a creative problem solver in your relationships with your customers and prospects as well as within your own firm.
- **Reasoning in Selling**
  - You must be prepared to deal with openly stated conflicting points of view as well as fallacious reasoning.
- **The Creative Approach to Problem Solving**
  - Creative persons characteristically display *curiosity* and *constructive discontent*. They seek a "better way."
- **Applications in Selling**
  - Salespeople know that commercially worthwhile ideas are the best way to strengthen their relationships with customers and the best way to prevent inroads by competition.
- **Suggestion in Selling**
  - If you have an in-depth understanding of your customers' needs and they trust that you will act in their best interests, the use of suggestion can achieve your joint objectives more efficiently.
- **Summary**
  - To practice need satisfaction selling effectively, you need to master problem solving, creativity, straight and devious thinking, and suggestion.
- **Topics for Thought and Discussion**
- **Application Exercises**
  - Appendix I   Determining Differential Competitive Advantage
  - Appendix III   Rules for Brainstorming
  - Appendix XXII   Salesperson's Example of Logical Analysis in Selling
  - Appendix XXIII Suggestion versus Reasoning
  - Appendix XXIV Exercise in Creative Selling
  - Appendix XXV   Call Checklist and Presentation Checklist
  - Appendix XXVI Guide for Observing Sales Performance

1. PROBLEM SOLVING

You must be a creative problem solver in your relationships with your customers and prospects as well as within your own firm. In a competitive marketplace, buyers will place their orders with the salesperson who can furnish worthwhile answers to questions and suggest ways to enhance profitability and competitiveness. They often view the salesperson as "external staff," a trusted business consultant. In a survey of purchasing executives, idea productivity by the salesperson was cited as an important reason for patronage. Salespeople are expected, as part of their work, to be problem solvers and to provide valuable new ideas.

In addition to this creative and problem-solving relationship with each account, salespeople must often function in a similar capacity for their own companies. They are in a unique position to discover new uses for their firm's products and services. They encounter firsthand any difficulties or problems in using the firm's offering. They are often able to suggest modifications, improvements, and additions to the line of products and services their company markets. Further, they can observe the strengths and weaknesses of competitive offerings. They, more than any others, have a current picture of competitive strategy and tactics. Thus, salespeople also have an "internal staff" function as their company's "eyes and ears" in the marketplace.

While many companies maintain marketing research departments to uncover and evaluate market opportunities, salespeople are a prime source of information regarding areas for investigation. Moreover, in numerous companies, their observations and recommendations guide the implementation of marketing strategies.

You should consider the question, "What do I sell?" When you analyze it, it is evident that you sell *your products, your services, your prices, your company's image,* and *yourself* as well as your support *team.* The acronym—TIP-IT—captures the essence of most offerings. There are Tangible (T), Intangible (I), Pricing (P), Image (I), and Team (T) factors in most transactions. Your challenge then is to tip the sale in your favor by matching the elements of your offering with your prospect's unique requirements. (These ideas were developed in detail in Chapter One.) If a particular prospect thinks that the competing products and services are of equal merit, that prices are equivalent, and that the companies are equally prestigious, what is left to make the difference? Clearly, it is you, the salesperson—the services you render in conjunction with other members of your company's team, the problems you solve, the ideas you produce, and the suggestions you make. You are evaluated on your knowledge, reasoning, problem-solving ability, creativity, and suggestions. These furnish customers with the "value added" factors that make doing business with you profitable. Of course, excellent communication skills are required to ensure that customers understand your points.

Exploring the problem-solving process is imperative, then, so that you can enhance your ability to contribute "value added" to your customers.

Issues in Logical Reasoning

Distinguish between Fact and Opinion

Reasoning begins with inputs in the form of facts and opinions. You need to distinguish between these two types of information.

What is a fact? If problem solving is to be effective, you need to have a clear meaning for this word. *A fact is any information, the reality of which is independent of the reporting source.* Facts are, by their very nature, objective and reliable. Thus, other things being equal, the people with the relevant facts at their command can expect to be more adept at problem solving than those who are less well informed.

In a similar vein, what is an opinion? *An opinion is any information, the worth of which is dependent on the reporting source.* The value of an opinion is no better or worse than the person giving it. Thus, the effectiveness of the problem solver often depends on knowing trustworthy sources. You have to know "who knows what." Having the weighted opinions of a few experts is better than the superficial opinions of hundreds of people. Robert Mueller, a longtime student of networking, suggests that one of the key elements in building communication channels for information and influence is to develop and maintain a special "guys-who-really-know" (GWRKs) file.

Because perception and memory are subjective and feelings color our thoughts, everyone is prejudiced to some degree. The effective problem solver attempts to keep an open-minded attitude and to minimize prejudgments. This is also an important consideration in evaluating opinions as well as their givers. Generally, worthwhile opinions come from those who are not opinionated.

A retailer may tell a salesperson that a new line of products will not sell. This is an opinion. However, if the retailer places an order, and the salesperson returns to find all the merchandise on hand, it is now a fact that it did not sell. The reasons for it may be fact or opinion. The slow-moving merchandise may have been poorly displayed—a fact. Whether the display caused the problem is an opinion.

While facts are preferable, they are not always available, and you are forced to use opinions. Opinions are not necessarily low in validity, but you must be cautious when cross-examination is not feasible.

Identify the Central Issue

Dealing with the real problem rather than symptoms is important. Clear thinking must cut through the petty details and come to grips with the fundamental problem. Usually, when the basic problem is under control, the details take care of themselves. In the preceding example, the salesperson could easily be drawn into a discussion of the merits of the merchandise and its likely turnover. This, however, is not the real problem. If the retailer can be persuaded to provide adequate display, factual evidence will soon exist as to whether the merchandise is salable. As long as the real issue is clouded, no progress is likely.

Evaluate Assumptions

Opinions are always based on assumptions, either warranted or unwarranted. They may also be relevant or irrelevant. Good reasoning depends on good assumptions. For example, the assumption is warranted and relevant that the sale of merchandise in a retail store is related to the size, position, and nature of the display. If enough data are collected from a variety of stores and properly analyzed, the assumption may achieve the status of a fact. To assume that charcoal will sell better in the summer is a warranted assumption but not relevant to the problem of display. To assume that doubling the display will increase sales 10 times is relevant, but probably not warranted. Unless assumptions are evaluated and used according to their relevance and apparent validity, confusion rather than clear thinking will follow.

Estimate the Value of Authority

Often evidence is based on the authority of a third person or organization. Therefore, you must judge the qualifications of the person or organization to decide what weight to accord the evidence. If the merits of an exercise machine were an issue, the opinions of professional athletes and doctors would seem appropriate. The opinion of an investment counselor would seem to be of little value. Conversely, if the merits of a particular stock or bond issue were under consideration, the relative value of the opinion sources cited would be reversed.

Assess Unverifiable Data

Many times the information offered will be of dubious value not only because it is opinion rather than fact but also because you cannot verify the information. It may or may not be true, but you must use caution in drawing conclusions based on it. A good example of unverifiable data is the statement "A picture is worth a thousand words." Why not a "hundred" or a "million" words? No possibility of verifying it exists. Another example, relevant to sales activity, is the arbitrary statement "80 percent of a person's information comes through seeing, 20 percent through hearing." Again, there is no way of verifying the statement, so you must evaluate it very carefully.

Determine Adequacy of Data

People often make decisions without adequate data. Sometimes, complete data is unavailable, so assumptions and opinions must be used. However, making a decision without all the relevant and warranted data available is a failure of good reasoning. You use equally poor reasoning deferring a decision on the basis of not having sufficient information when more and/or better data are unlikely.

To return to our display example, here are some of the data that probably are available and worth considering:

- Size of display.
- Department in which display is set up.
- Results of previous displays.
- Elapsed time since last display.
- Competitive activity in the shopping area.
- Season of the year (especially for seasonal merchandise).
- Sale price in relation to regular price.

When you consider the preceding data as well as any other available information, you will not only come up with a better solution to the problem, but you will also create a more authoritative impression and be more likely to obtain customer agreement.

Recognize Bias and Emotion

Many opinions do not reflect the giver's best thinking. The person may be emotional about the situation, may have a prejudice that interferes with clear thinking, or may be unclear about your requirements. If you accept such biased opinions, you are unlikely to arrive at a high-quality solution.

For example, customers who dislike particular suppliers and only use their products when no satisfactory substitute is available are likely to be biased. Their dislike of the suppliers may cause them to misjudge products/services and make unwarranted statements. Another example of poor judgment due to bias centers around the profit motive. Retailers are almost always concerned with profits and the markup on merchandise. Many times, however, the desire to carry prestige merchandise will overcome the profit motive and can result in biased estimates of the true potential of products.

While the preceding set of considerations applicable to logical reasoning is not exhaustive, you must take precautions when trying to solve problems with less than complete factual information.

Restrictions and Restraints

When you have reached the best possible solution in terms of clarity of thinking, you have not necessarily solved the problem. Restrictions may make the solution unacceptable. The principal restraints are company policy, time, money, and talent.

Unless an exception is justifiable, most business problems need to be handled within policy. For example, a problem may arise with an account where a solution involves policy on terms of payment. Allowing an exception makes it likely that the customer will seek more exceptions.

A second restriction involves time. You must invest time proportionately to the problem's commercial importance. Further, the salesperson faces not one but many problems. Time needs to be allocated among them. Finally, often a deadline exists for the solution. Having a workable solution by the deadline may be better than having the "perfect solution" a day late. This consideration is of obvious importance with proposals or bids.

Money certainly constitutes an important restriction. Manifest as well as hidden outlays are involved here. Examples include free samples, commitment of technical help without charge, and travel.

Talent is not as clear a restriction as the preceding, but it is equally real. Talent may be a restriction because it calls for skills not available in the organization. Ordinarily these skills could be obtained, but in so doing the restrictions of time and money may appear. (For an example of a restriction, see Figure 7.1.)

Logical Methods of Problem Solving

Now that we have examined certain important issues involved in logical reasoning and some of the restrictions in reaching solutions, we need to consider four systematic approaches to problem solving. They are (1) observation, (2) application of old solutions to new problems, (3) logical analysis, and (4) experiment. Obviously, the experimental method does not hold much promise for salespeople in solving sales problems. The other three approaches will be examined in detail.

Observation

One way to solve a problem is to observe all aspects of it and draw a conclusion as to a proper solution. *Inductive reasoning* involves doing this on a formal and systematic basis.

As noted in Chapter Two, Section 2, the common definition of inductive reasoning is *reasoning from the specific to the general.* Put in other terms, by observing a series of specific instances, you may be able to find a general statement or common denominator that solves the problem at hand and other like problems. The conclusion reached is a *generalization* and is expected to hold in a majority of

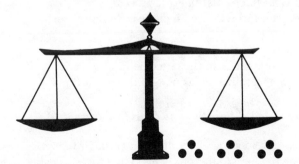

Figure 7.1 You have nine steel balls, identical except that one is slightly heavier than the rest, but not enough heavier as to be perceptible when held in your hand. You have a simple balance scale. Find the heavier ball using the scale only twice. For the solution, see Figure 7.4.

cases. It need not be a perfect solution and work 100 percent of the time to be helpful. By contrast, the term *generality* refers to a vague statement with no precise reference or application. Unfortunately, in sales work, generalities are used too much and generalizations not enough.

Before *inductive reasoning* may be applied, specific instances must be observed, analyzed, and classified. These specific instances could be a series of sales calls on a particular customer, or they could be a series of sales calls on a series of customers. The problem will determine what kind of specific observations to make.

A salesperson had a customer who placed orders on some calls but not on others. The customer seemed pleased with the merchandise, so the salesperson saw no apparent reason for the failure to buy on every call. Application of inductive reasoning called for noting and keeping a record of each call to find the factors common to successful calls and to those that were not. Analysis of this data showed that the customer seldom bought during the middle of the day. As this did not solve the problem, the salesperson made further observations. It now became apparent that a business partner often sat in on sales presentations during the lunch hour and seemed to be the inhibiting factor. Now the problem was solved. All that was necessary was to avoid the partner. By avoiding the lunch hour and the partner, the salesperson obtained orders regularly.

A stationery supplies salesperson, in analyzing one of her accounts, discovered that orders had been substantially larger on calls made during the third week of the month than at other times. Her smallest orders occurred in the first week of the month. Inquiry revealed that the customer had a considerable amount of charge business and took advantage of cash discounts on all purchases. The salesperson concluded that any orders she wrote with this account were likely to be proportionate to cash on hand. She then planned her future calls during the third week of each month.

In each of these examples, a generalization is derived from particular, similar occurrences. Inductive thinking, then, involves going from the particular to the general. It is an inferential thought process.

Three good rules to follow on inductive thinking are:

1. Never generalize on a single instance.
2. Keep an open mind as to the outcome of observations.
3. Refine each generalization as new evidence warrants.

Application of Old Solutions to New Problems

When you have developed a generalization through inductive reasoning, you may use it to solve other similar problems. The process—called *deductive reasoning*—is described as *reasoning from the general to the specific.* Following are some examples.

A sales engineer confronted with a price objection knew from experience with the product that labor costs outweigh equipment costs 10 to 1. He, therefore, asked the prospect what estimated labor costs were. He then showed that the equipment provided a substantial reduction in labor-hours and the savings more than offset the higher price.

A direct selling company found that the likelihood of an order is 3 in 10 on the first call, 1 in 10 on the second, and almost negligible on subsequent calls. It has a policy that a salesperson is to make no more than one callback if an order does not result in the first attempt.

If the salesperson mentioned earlier runs into another situation where a business partner is present at sales presentations, he or she will quickly note any inhibiting effect the person may have and solve the problem immediately. If a close similarity exists in the second case, the earlier solution will have high transfer value. This is called *deductive reasoning*.

In many instances, the solution is not so obvious because it was derived by analysis of a different kind of problem or in a different field of study. When a problem is solved by application of a solution from an essentially different environment, it is called reasoning by *analogy*. You can solve many problems by reflecting on experience without having to study each new problem in painful detail.

The principal sources of information for solving sales problems by analogy are careful questioning of other salespeople and reading in the behavioral sciences—psychology, sociology, and cultural anthropology. Ignoring these sources is comparable to trying to build an automobile without reference to the experience of Toyota or Daimler-Benz. More specifically, a growing body of research exists on seller-buyer relationships. You can gain additional insights if you review the research on teacher-pupil and supervisor-employee relationships and apply it by analogy.

Logical Analysis

Logical analysis involves the systematic application to a problem of all that is known. It is used primarily for complex problems where experience does not readily suggest a solution. (See Figure 7.2 for an example.)

This classic puzzle can be solved by logical analysis. There is no "catch" in it, but every fact is important.

On a train, Green, Black, and Gray are the fireman, brakeman, and engineer—but *not* respectively. Also aboard the train are three businesspersons with the same names: Mr. Green, Mr. Black, and Mr. Gray.

1. Mr. Black lives in New York.
2. The brakeman lives exactly halfway between Philadelphia and New York.
3. Mr. Gray earns exactly $20,000 per year.
4. The brakeman's nearest neighbor, one of the passengers, earns exactly three times as much as the brakeman.
5. Green beats the fireman at billiards.
6. The passenger whose name is the same as the brakeman's lives in Philadelphia.

What is the name of the engineer?

Figure 7.2 Who is the engineer? See Figure 7.5 for solution.

The overall process has five steps.

Step 1. Defining and Bounding the Problem.   You must break down the problem as initially posed into "subproblems." Each of these in turn breaks into still smaller elements until no further reduction is possible. An analogy might be drawn from chemistry. A molecule represents the problem as initially thought about or stated. The atoms making up the molecule are the first group of subproblems. Each atom in turn contains still smaller particles that may consist of subparticles. Similarly, each problem is composed of smaller problems. In turn, each small problem contains smaller problems. In summary, problem definition consists largely of breaking up the big problem into smaller elements.

As this process develops, inputs and restrictions interact. For example, when defining a problem, it is commonplace to need more facts or additional opinions. Also, as problems involve specific policy, time, and/or monetary questions, unanticipated restrictions may arise.

Once you have defined the problem by breaking it down into elements, you take each smaller problem in turn through the next steps. When you have solved all the small problems, the big problem is also solved.

Step 2. Establishing Criteria for Evaluation of Alternative Solutions.   Before attempting to solve a problem, it is important to consider how to evaluate alternative solutions. This is especially true if others are involved in the task. Failure to do this at the outset may result in the choice of a poor solution if you are working alone and disagreement on the solution if you are working with other people.

Certain restrictions mentioned earlier become criteria. Thus, time and money expenditure may impose limits. Good commercial judgment dictates that the investment of time, effort, and money not exceed the commercial worth of the problem's solution. Often the sales engineer has to guard against solving a problem with a tool or component more precise or versatile than is warranted. One sales manager of an industrial firm calls this "Michelangeloitis"—using the perfect device for an application where a far less costly one would have sufficed.

Also *risk* is often important. Generally, choose a solution that minimizes risk, in case of negative results. For example, in helping a customer solve a problem, you would seldom want to place the account in jeopardy if your proposed solution is not successful. *Loss* is another consideration. Failure to attempt to cope with some problems may be more costly than to try almost any reasonable solution.

Additional specific criteria peculiar to each problem might be necessary. Think about what they are before proceeding to the next step.

Step 3. Think of Alternative Solutions.   This step is largely the domain of creative thinking. It challenges the ingenuity of the problem solver. (Section 3 discusses the nature of the creative process, so the treatment here is limited to procedural points.)

It is tempting to accept the first potential solution that you identify. If you are to be an effective problem solver, however, you should consider other possibilities.

In fact, if you can only generate one solution, chances are you are wrong. Most significant business problems have multiple causes and can usually be solved in several different ways. If time permits, you should allow ideas to gel. Often a second or third attempt at solutions reveals alternatives that you otherwise would have missed. Jot down the alternatives as they occur; otherwise, you may forget them. As soon as you have formulated an exhaustive list of alternatives, you can undertake the next step.

Step 4. Evaluation of Alternatives. Weigh each alternative in turn against the Step 2 criteria. As evaluation proceeds, additional criteria will often suggest themselves. Also, in applying the criteria, you may modify the relative weight you give each one. Some criteria may be rigid and admit of no exception; for example, policy. Others may encompass only desirable but not mandatory factors. You should evaluate each alternative on each criterion and calculate a "score" for each potential solution.

Step 5. Selecting the Best Solution. The "best" solution is that alternative among those considered that best meets the differentially weighted criteria. The quotation marks around *best* are a reminder that a superior solution might have been overlooked.

Figure 7.3 portrays the steps in the problem-solving process. Appendix XXII illustrates their application to a sales problem.

Results of Logical Analysis

You cope with problems to accomplish worthwhile results. Thus the output of the process is some combination of *recommendations, decisions,* and *actions.* Recommendations are directed either to your own company personnel or to appropriate persons in accounts. Remember that the form in which you make the recommendation may markedly influence its acceptance by the other person. (Chapter Two deals with principles and methods that help ensure acceptance.)

Decisions stemming from the solution of a problem have to be considered in terms of initial inputs and restrictions, especially policy. If a decision is to be a good one, it must stand the test of time. You have to live with it. Decisions must also be equitable to those affected by them. Further, decisions must be implementable.

The actions resulting from problem solving often involve commitments by you to accomplish certain matters within a prescribed timetable. To maintain good account relations, commitments once made must be binding.

Dynamics of the Process

The steps in problem solving seem orderly and clear. Often, however, backtracking occurs; for example, the search for more facts or the need to consider additional criteria. Further, few persons can handle all the problems facing them

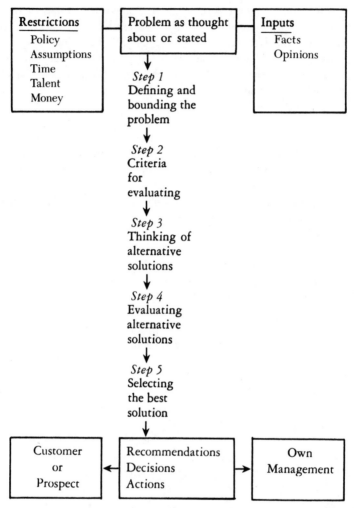

Figure 7.3   Solving problems through logical analysis using the steps presented in the text.

without enlisting the help of others. Indeed, in many selling situations, you may need your company's technical specialists.

When other people join in the process, different opinions and approaches are bound to occur. You must be skilled in drawing out the ideas of others without, at the same time, making a commitment to follow such suggestions uncritically. It is important to brief any other person entering the process on the background and restrictions impinging on the solution. Often, technical people are "thing" oriented and need insight into the "people" factors that influence the situation. In fact, you may have experienced this situation when you have taken a staff person into an account with you.

To conduct the experiment, divide the nine balls into groups of three each. Put one group of three on one side of the scales and another group on the other side. If the two groups balance, the heavier ball is in the third group. Now weigh any two of the three remaining balls. If they balance, the heavier one is the unweighed one. If not, you can pick the heavier ball. If however, the first two groups do not balance, take the heavier group and weigh any two of the three balls. This experiment illustrates the concept of restraints. If no restraints were set, it would be simple to weigh each pair of balls in sequence until the heavier ball was detected. Similarly in a sales situation, restrictions and restraints may be imposed on the easy answer.

Figure 7.4 Explanation of the experiment in Figure 7.1.

Facilitating Factors

The most important influences on logical analysis are the following:

1. An open-minded attitude. Prejudgments or prejudices prevent a fresh approach.
2. The problem solver must have a positive viewpoint. This is illustrated by a sign in an office that reads: "The difficult we do immediately; the impossible takes a little longer."
3. As mentioned earlier, the problem solver must be a "knower" and aware of who the other "knowers" are.
4. The problem solver must be able to fail successfully. This does not mean that you condone failure in yourself and others. Rather you learn from your failures and try not to make the same mistake twice.
5. You are not so tied to precedent that you are unwilling to try the new. The effective problem solver takes a calculated risk in innovating.

The brakeman, who lives halfway between Philadelphia and New York, also lives near Mr. _____, who earns three times as much as he does. Mr. _____ cannot be Mr. Black, as Mr. Black lives in New York. He cannot be Mr. Gray, as Mr. Gray's $20,000 a year isn't divisible by three. Therefore, the brakeman's neighbor must be Mr. Green.

The passenger whose name is the same as the brakeman's lives in Philadelphia. He cannot be Mr. Black because Mr. Black lives in New York. He cannot be Mr. Green because Mr. Green is a neighbor of the brakeman, who lives halfway between Philadelphia and New York. Therefore, he must be Mr. Gray.

Therefore, the brakeman's name is also Gray.

Green beats the fireman at billiards, so the fireman must be Black. Therefore, the engineer is Green.

Figure 7.5 Solution to the problem in Figure 7.2.

6. You provide yourself with enough psychological privacy to think in an un-
   hurried, orderly fashion. Problem solving under duress often results in
   half-baked thinking.
7. You maintain a commercial perspective in terms of time, talent, and money
   invested. The key question is: "What is the value of the solution?"

2.   REASONING IN SELLING

Peter Drucker's famous challenge to business leaders, "Innovate or perish," can
also be directed to salespeople. When competing products, services, prices, and
company reputation approach equality, one source of differential competitive advantage remains—the creative problem-solving ability of the salesperson. However, even if you have done your homework and developed an appropriate solution
for the prospect's problem, many times the prospect will openly state an objection
or difference of opinion.

The technique for changing the mind of a person who has openly stated a
conflicting opinion is *reasoning*. You must assemble and present the information
necessary to support the desired point of view. If the prospect will accept facts at
face value and use the rules of logic, reasoning will be a simple matter. In that
case, a straightforward presentation will suffice. Unfortunately, *devious reasoning* is likely on the part of the prospect; hence, you will need to counteract this
tendency. This may involve presenting information so that prospects can apply
their biases or prejudices and still agree with you. In any event, you must be prepared to deal with openly stated conflicting points of view as well as fallacious
reasoning. To do this, you must master the techniques of *straight thinking* for
yourself and develop the capacity to change the opinions of others who may not
have the ability or the desire to think straight.

Reasons You Should Think Straight

You should master the principles of straight thinking for three compelling reasons. The first reason is to more accurately extract the meaning from both
written and spoken messages. How many times have you expressed your opinion only to learn later you have been misunderstood and misinterpreted? Most
written or spoken messages have a definite meaning that can be extracted by
a careful reader or listener. If not, the message is confused and you should
seek clarification. Poor attention or a noncritical approach will also result in
drawing an erroneous conclusion. When a salesperson and prospect misunder-
stand each other, a disagreement results that must be resolved before a sale
is likely.

The second reason for mastering the principles of straight thinking is to be
able to recognize and deal with blind forces—deception, ignorance, emotions,
and prejudices. For example, prospects who feel they have been insulted by a
former company representative constitute emotional problems and must be
dealt with accordingly. Prospects who are prejudiced in favor of long-standing

companies may prefer their products even though they are less innovative. Some buyers deliberately try to confuse and impede you. This situation calls for special understanding and treatment.

The third reason for mastering straight thinking is to overcome the difficulties generated by a failure to grasp the correct meaning of messages. When you encounter a misunderstanding or erroneous point of view for any reason, you need to change that viewpoint before you can make a sale. You must counteract the existing point of view and supply new information so as to make it acceptable to the prospect.

To counteract an existing point of view you must know what the point of view is, as well as why the conclusion is at variance with the facts. You need to know the mental process that reached the conflicting opinion. This means that to be well prepared you must be familiar with the principles of straight and crooked thinking so that you can discover the techniques the prospect used to reach an unwarranted position.

The major portion of this section describes common methods of devious reasoning. Each method is examined from two points of view: First, how it might influence another person unfairly, and second, how you can defend yourself from such devious reasoning if it is used on you. Mastery of these techniques will enable you to deal effectively with prospects who refute your claims through devious reasoning and will help you to present your point of view appropriately. We emphasize that we offer this material for use in making sales that are mutually beneficial to the buyer and the seller and abhor its use to gain an unfair advantage.

Kinds of Devious Reasoning

The following are some of the more common methods of devious reasoning. They are also the ones that salespeople are most likely to encounter. While there are a variety of ways to arrange them, we have presented each method as a customer or prospect might use it for sales resistance, followed by a suggestion for counteracting the devious reasoning.

In this sense, you have a defensive tool. However, you can readily appreciate that you can use the same technique on the customer when you need to present your message in a less straightforward manner.

Use Emotionally Toned Words

This is illustrated by the use of "cur" or "mongrel" when referring to a dog. In the field of selling, "dog" might be used to refer to a slow-moving product. Another example is "peddler" to describe a salesperson.

The defense against the technique is simple. Simply restate the sentence with the proper, rather than the emotionally toned, word and ask whether that is the intended meaning. For example, a customer might say, "You peddlers are all alike." A reply might be, "I consider myself a salesperson. Is that the same as a peddler?"

Imply "All" When "Some" Is True

An illustration would be "Red-headed people have bad tempers." This implies that all red-headed persons have bad tempers. Actually, some may have bad tempers. As a salesperson, you may be told "Your products are terrible." This again implies that *all* the products are terrible.

The defense is to put the ideal "all" into the statement to show that it is false. For example, "Do you mean that every one of our products is terrible?" The next step would be to say, "Let's take them one at a time and analyze them." As soon as one satisfactory product is discovered, the fallacy in the statement is obvious.

Divert the Discussion to a Side Issue

When customers deny the ability of a product to meet specifications and switch to complaints they had with the previous salesperson or some other dimension of the seller-buyer relationship, the discussion has been diverted to a side issue. They may be right about the previous salesperson and hope that through this device they will appear right about the specifications.

The antidote in this instance is to point out that there are now two issues under discussion. You should be willing to take up either issue, but not both at the same time. Make it clear that a resolution of one issue will have no bearing on the soundness of the other.

Recommend a Compromise Solution

Politicians are noted for taking a middle road out of conflicts rather than arriving at sound decisions and standing by them. Customers may do the same. When you recommend 100 units and the customer has in mind 50 units, he or she may suggest a compromise and place an order for 75.

To show that this kind of reasoning is unsound, you must demonstrate that compromise is a faulty method for discovering the truth. Any position can be made to fall between two extremes. If, in the preceding instance, the customer feels 50 units are proper, you need only select 150 as your objective to make the middle ground 100. If your recommendation is based on experience and correct arithmetic, there is no reason to compromise. Other reasons might exist for not placing an order of the proper size, but isolating the true ones is better than arriving at an unsound conclusion that might hurt future calls.

When you know that a customer is prone to use compromise, you have the alternative of trying to show the fallacy in this approach or going along with it. If you decide to go along, you must inflate your objective so that a compromise will result in a proper size order.

Block Further Progress by Insisting on an Extreme Position

A customer can stall a presentation by making a demand that the salesperson cannot possibly approve and one that would not be approved by the home office or met by a competitor. An example would be to request a discount or an unrealistic delivery schedule.

The remedial step would be to explore and, if possible, point out that the demand is not necessary from the buyer's standpoint, nor is it in keeping with industry practices. A further step is to demonstrate an awareness and understanding of the technique and request that the prospect drop it so that the presentation can continue.

Make Reference to Unqualified Authority

A person may be prominent as an expert in one field, but that expertise cannot necessarily be applied in every field.

When a customer refutes a sales point by reference to an unknown "authority," ask for a statement of the person's qualifications before accepting the rebuttal.

Avoid the Issue by Provoking Anger

By directing criticism to the person rather than to the issue under discussion, you can sometimes cause the person to lose self-control and attempt to defend him- or herself. In the process, he or she inevitably loses the argument.

Your response to this method is to point out that you have no personal interest other than to carry out your company's policy. You can then restate the basic issue and try to continue your presentation.

Cause a Person to Overstate a Position on a Particular Point, Then Reject the Entire Proposition

When a salesperson shows enthusiasm for some aspect of a product or service, a customer may appear interested and bait the salesperson into overstating the likely performance. The customer then forces the salesperson to back down on that point, implying that the entire proposition is unsound.

You must be cautious and objective in the claims you make for your offering. You must resist the temptation to exaggerate or even to agree with the prospect's exaggeration. If you have fallen into this kind of trap, you should concede your overstatement on the particular point and proceed to show that the rest of your presentation is sound and warrants consideration.

Profess Inability to Understand the Proposition

On the basis that a salesperson cannot expect people to buy something they cannot understand, some customers act as though they do not see the application to their problem.

In such an instance, you must repeat your presentation in simpler terms and use questions that cause prospects to state the relationship between their needs and the features and benefits of the offering. If this approach does not work, you must decide whether to abandon the attempt or to challenge the prospects' deliberate failure in understanding. Reference to Chapter Five and related appendixes may be useful in this instance.

Use an Inappropriate Analogy

Suppose a salesperson is selling a machine tool as capital equipment on the basis that it will pay for itself in lowering production costs. The customer rejects the proposition by remembering a salesperson who "sold" her on a new accounting system and—while some labor cost was saved—extra costs were incurred in the form of specialized programming.

You can refute this by distinguishing between capital expenditures and expenditures for expense items and showing that examples of one are not a valid basis for evaluating the other.

Demand a Formal Definition Where None Is Needed

This is most likely to happen where abstract values are involved. For example, a chemical additive may be designed to increase or improve the effectiveness of a basic product. A request for a definition of "improve" is difficult and will not necessarily clarify the proposition.

Under these circumstances, you should refuse to attempt a formal definition but proceed to explain what you feel can be accomplished by adding your product. You can also offer to give "yes" or "no" answers to specific questions the prospect may wish to ask, such as "Will your product allow me to claim _____?"

Be Ambiguous So That It Is Difficult to Point up an Issue

A discussion as to whether a third person has an "inferiority complex" is almost certain to result in confusion because the term is ambiguous. Each person gives it a different meaning. Unless the speakers agree on the exact meaning for the purpose of the discussion, nothing can be accomplished.

You should ask for a clarification of word meanings or phrases and be willing to use the customer's meaning during the actual sales presentation. You must be flexible and use words that the customer understands. This may mean using a different definition with each customer.

Attribute a Specific Prejudice to a Person and Act as Though All Arguments Advanced Are Unsound

There are very few people who do not have a strong enough preference in some area to cause another person to label it prejudice. It may be in as common an area as politics or religion or in an area such as a minority group or a method of doing business. In any event, a customer may come up with a statement to the effect "If you are as one-sided about your proposition as you are about _____, I had better give this some more thought." You can take two steps to combat this method of argument. First, minimize the prejudice or deny it if appropriate, and second, show that the prejudice is a personal matter with you while the proposition reflects the best thinking of your company executives and is not affected by your personal opinions.

Confuse the Listener through the Use of Trade Jargon

Asking for *acetylsalicylic acid* when you want an *aspirin* illustrates this method. Every business and industry develops words and phrases that have a special meaning to that particular group. An example is the word "spiff," used to denote a special sales commission in the jewelry and related fields. When buyers use these terms on a salesperson who has not yet mastered them, they are trying to evade a direct discussion.

When this happens, you should ask for a definition or explanation of any unfamiliar term.

Try to Achieve Plausibility and Acceptance through Repetition

Repeating a lie does not make it true, but uncritical persons may lose their perspective in the face of repetition. Fifty years ago, Hitler's constant claims about the "master race" lulled many persons into this belief but did not result in creating a different type of person. More recently, Communist leaders claimed their totalitarian systems would bury capitalism, but in truth the standard of living of their people declined and many regimes have been overthrown.

A customer who constantly finds fault with a product or service, such as the retailer who repeatedly states "It won't sell," may cause uncritical salespeople to accept the claim and reduce their sales effort.

To refute any constant but *untrue* claim, point out the claimant's technique and try to assess the accuracy of the statement rather than repeat it. If the statement is true, it will not need repetition. If it is unwarranted and you stress your awareness of the technique of repetition, it will diminish the likelihood of repetition and eliminate the likelihood of its acceptance.

Confuse the Issue by Making the Change Seem So Slight It Is Not Worthwhile

Air conditioning is designed to control heat and humidity so that employees can devote their energy to work rather than have it drained off by uncomfortable weather. Assume that the average temperature of a locality is 73 degrees and the salesperson gives 72 degrees as the proper indoor temperature. The prospect may say "Is it worth all that money to change the temperature one degree?" Put that way, air conditioning is not warranted.

The purpose of air conditioning, however, is not to combat the average temperature, but to offset the 80+ temperatures of the summer months.

Appendix XXIII is an exercise for developing skill in meeting sales resistance through reasoning and suggestion. ("Suggestion" is covered in Section 5.)

3.   THE CREATIVE APPROACH TO PROBLEM SOLVING

Creativity in thought or action has two ingredients, what is thought about or worked on and the life values of the person. For example, three artists might be furnished identical palettes and asked to paint the same sunset. The resulting pictures would have discernible differences, for the artists themselves have different value systems, and hence each would perceive the sunset somewhat differently. So it is with salespeople. They may follow similar selling principles as other salespeople, but the implementation reflects each unique individual.

Creativity has an emotional or feeling ingredient. It comes from the gut as well as the mind. Rarely are people creative in matters about which they do not feel strongly. Creative persons in any field, including selling, have to like what they are doing. Commonplace evidence of this is the disturbance you feel when an idea of yours does not get the reception from others you feel it warrants. Another bit of evidence is the irritation you experience at being interrupted when you feel you are in the midst of creating something.

The creative thought process is relatively unpredictable and undisciplined. It is difficult to know when an idea is going to emerge. Further, the flow of ideas can suddenly dry up. Creative thoughts cannot be forced or coerced. Everyone has experienced times when they have been unable to think creatively. An inventor we know reports that weeks often go by unproductively, then suddenly a new flow of ideas begins.

Generally, people are likely to produce ideas in their fields of knowledge or expertise. Here they have more potential inputs, more grist for their mental mills. Yet sometimes it pays to be ignorant. A person may come up with a new approach, concept, or method, because of not being hidebound by the existing body of knowledge. The aforementioned inventor was able to solve a reproduction problem in the office-equipment field by mechanical redesign. The problem had been identified as chemical, and the chemists were stumped by it. The inventor, however, knew no chemistry, and saw it in a different way.

You may be creative in other fields and contribute ideas to other parts of the business, but your greatest opportunity for producing ideas of value is in your own field—professional selling—especially in the handling of customers and prospects.

Steps in the Creative Thought Process

The creative thought process begins with *stimulation*. Something seen, heard, or remembered impinges on consciousness. Examples in selling might include observing an unusual use of a product, hearing a colorful way to make a sales point, seeing a new method of packaging, or exchanging ideas with another salesperson. Whatever the stimulus, the mind begins to add elements from the past and present to it.

The second step is *ideation*. Often this step is far from logical and straightforward. Rather, it involves unstructured, free association. Each successive thought leads to another. *Branching* is an important characteristic of this second step. For example, as this is being written in a garden in Italy, the word *price* enters consciousness as the stimulus. There follows: value, money, lira, ECU, hotel bill, bank. . . . Money branched into lira, the currency of Italy, and then to the new European Monetary Unit, the ECU. This ideation step is sometimes referred to as "brainstorming." If the person engaged in it attempts to evaluate the flow or to analyze it, brainstorming stops. If two or more persons "brainstorm," it is imperative not to evaluate or question the contributions as they occur. Appendix III provides a set of rules to follow in brainstorming. Each person's contributions stimulate those of others. This "hitchhiking" on the previous thought can often generate more ideas than if a person works alone. However, the research evidence on this is inconclusive, so you must decide for yourself whether you are more productive working alone or enlisting the help of others. Sooner or later the flow of ideas stops. This marks the beginning of the next step.

At any moment of time, the barest fraction of a person's experience is present in consciousness. Furthermore, as indicated in Chapter Two, only a small percentage of the environment that is sensed reaches conscious perception. These elements from the past and present are stored in the subconscious.

The third step in creative thinking is *incubation*. The ideas arrived at in the second step intermix with other elements in the mind. The person is unaware that it is going on, for example consider the expression: "Let me sleep on this and perhaps I'll have some more ideas tomorrow." When human subjects learn new material and the amount of learning is measured immediately, and then later, they often know more after the mind has a chance to gel what has been learned.

The fourth step is *illumination*. Suddenly ideas emerge from the subconscious, and these in turn provide the stimulus for additional ideation. One of the psychological factors in illumination is *insight* or, as W.J.E. Crissy has called it, the *aha!* feeling. A new perception is gained. You can demonstrate this for yourself by following these instructions with regard to Figure 7.6: Without taking your pencil off the page, intersect all nine dots with no more than four straight lines. If you do not accomplish the task in one sitting, leave it and return to it. Illumination will eventually occur—the problem is soluble. Verify the solution in Figure 7.7.

Figure 7.6   Draw four continuous straight lines that will pass through all nine dots in this design (for solution, see Figure 7.7).

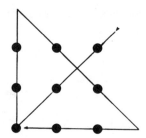

Figure 7.7 Solution to the problem in Figure 7.6. The normal approach to this problem is to stay within the area bounded by the dots. The creative element in the solution lies in the recognition that, to solve the problem, the lines must go beyond the self-imposed boundaries suggested by the dots.

Evaluation and application is the fifth step, taking place only after completion of ideation (Step 2) and later, illumination (Step 4). Any creative thought becomes valuable only when put to use. As noted in Section 1, creative thinking has its major application in problem solving, especially in generating alternative solutions. This fifth step necessarily involves evaluation of ideas to select the best one for application.

Dynamics of the Process

"Success breeds success" certainly applies in the case of creative thinking. Because the ideation step is free flowing, initially use a stimulus that easily elicits associations. This is analogous to warming up in sports. Once the mind starts clicking, you can think about more complex matters. You should jot down creative thoughts when they occur. Many ideas are lost because they are not recorded.

Sometimes you discard an idea because of status or timing. You may say to yourself, "Who am I to think of that?" or "This is not the time to consider that." These two considerations often lead to the rejection of other people's ideas too. Creative individuals act relatively independent of their environments. They do not hesitate to "stick their necks out." They are not locked to the status quo. Jules Verne wrote about travel in the ocean's depths long before today's submarine.

Charles F. Kettering, an automotive engineer and prolific inventor, made an interesting observation about creative thinking in his field. He said that we need to "think the way the machine thinks." Inventors have to project themselves into the situation and not be blocked by an "it ought to work this way" attitude. A frequently told story that illustrates this observation involves the bee. Considering the weight of its body relative to its wing span and other aerodynamic characteristics, engineers have determined that it should not be able to fly. However, no one has told the bee this, so it keeps on flying.

Reasoning by analogy is also critically important in the creative thought process. Kazuo Inamori, head of the spectacularly successful Kyoto Ceramics, which had a reputation for making delicate components for industry, was given a particularly challenging assignment by Sony. His company was asked to formulate a ceramic base the size of a pencil eraser, about 0.5 millimeters thick, with a groove in the middle as well as two holes. Because the part was so thin, known manufacturing processes failed. If the part could be made, however, Kyoto would be the recognized leader in its field. One day after many false starts and much brainstorming, Inamori thought of spaghetti: "They would mix the powders like dough and press it through tubes as if it were pasta and slice the chips off rather than press them down." The process was simple and it worked. Susumu Yoshida, a Sony executive, said it was "the most primitive state-of-the-art technique he had ever seen."

Levels of the creative thought process can be distinguished in terms of likely frequency of occurrence. The rarest is where the initial stimulus or germ of an idea is developed into a completely new concept. Next in occurrence is the translation of a concept from one field into a new setting or application. More frequent is the adaptation, modification, or refinement of an existing concept. The one that occurs most often is a change in the use of an existing idea. These latter two categories certainly are a part of the everyday life of the salesperson.

Some years ago, a Bell Laboratories study provided additional insight into the dynamics of the creative thought process. When engineers were confronted with novel situations, those who were more creative had not only a greater number of ideas, but also proportionately more of their ideas were positive than negative. In contrast, the less creative engineers had fewer ideas and proportionately more of them were negative. Creative people think, "How it will work," not "This is why it won't work."

Factors Influencing Creativity

The following factors are determinants of creativity:

1. Because idea flow is relatively unpredictable, you must be flexible enough to devote yourself to creative pursuits when your productivity warrants it and to shift to other tasks when "dryness" sets in.
2. Keep in mind that evaluation curtails ideation. If at all possible, allow for a time lapse before evaluating ideas.
3. Idea productivity is likely to be greater when you are "up" mentally, emotionally, and physically such as at the beginning of the workday, on weekends, or during a relaxed evening. The cumulative harassments during the day cause "psychological fatigue" and inhibit freewheeling thought processes.

4. To be creative, you must like what you are doing. Ego involvement is critical in any creative task. If individuals have no "feel" for their work, they let it become stereotyped and routine.

5. The work climate, physical and social, must seem empowering and acceptable. As a salesperson, you are fortunate in this respect since you generally have considerable control over your work schedule and manner of operating. Further, you frequently have a more varied work environment than most other employed persons. If, however, you perceive your firm's policies as restraining and your supervision as oppressive, you are unlikely to have many original ideas.

6. Individuals must provide themselves with an occasional "change of pace" and new experiences to stimulate their creative output. An engineering professor at MIT requires his students to read *Alice in Wonderland* for this reason.

7. While creativity is not contagious, you can stimulate it by interacting with other creative people. Conversely, seeking the company of those who accept the routine and mediocre tends to curtail creativity.

Profile of the Creative Person

Research indicates that creativity is not a universal trait or characteristic. A person may be creative in one field but not necessarily in others. To show genius in several areas is rare—very few of us are like Leonardo da Vinci, who achieved immortality as a painter, sculptor, architect, and scientist. Further, creativity is not an "all or nothing" characteristic. Individuals in a particular field vary in the degree of creativity they possess.

The relationship between intelligence and creativity is by no means close. A person does not have to be the brightest in the field to come up with new ideas. As indicated in a previous section, a person who has a breadth and depth of knowledge is likely to be more creative than the less sophisticated person. Andrall Pearson, former president of PepsiCo, says, "I firmly believe the best backdrop for spurring innovation is knowledge—knowing your business cold."

Creative persons characteristically display *curiosity* and *constructive discontent*. They wonder why things are as they are and why people do what they do. They seek a "better way." They are not complacent. Yet, their quest for the new is not destructive of the worthwhile old.

They have a *drive to achieve*. They seek to put their personal stamp on their accomplishments, to display their values and talents to others. The mediocre will not do. They strive for excellence and distinctiveness in what they say and do.

Creative persons are *intense* in their pursuits. Because they are ego involved, they make the task part of themselves. They see it through to culmination even though intermittent "dryness" occurs. This manifests itself as enthusiasm for work. They do not give up easily. This is why creative persons sometimes appear "odd" to those who are more willing to accept things as they are and who are less persevering in accomplishing the new.

They are likely to be *self-confident*. They view change as a challenge, not as a problem. They perceive themselves as able to cope with their environment.

Conversely, less creative persons find comfort in things as they are: the status quo. They find security in the present environment and resist change.

4. APPLICATIONS IN SELLING

Salespeople have numerous opportunities to apply their ability to reason, solve problems, and think creatively. In the marketplace, the primary focus for their talents is on their *present accounts*. They know that commercially worthwhile ideas are the best way to strengthen their relationships with customers and the best way to prevent inroads by competition. They are also aware, however, that they often generate a *new account*, not through product, service, or price advantage, but through their ability to solve problems and suggest improvements in some phase of the prospective customer's operations. The third target for their ingenuity is *their own company*—its products and services, its marketing efforts, and its methods of doing business. Finally, their fourth and most frequent application of problem solving and creative thinking is to their own *selling methods* and techniques. A salesperson should eagerly seek new and better ways to achieve objectives as well as improve personal productivity.

Present Customers

Customers buy more than products; they buy ideas and services. They favor the salesperson whose ideas and services are *different* and *better*. Just as every salesperson seeks profitable sales, so every customer wishes to make profitable purchases.

Professional salespeople know they need to penetrate each account in sufficient depth to understand every step their products and/or services go through as they are used. Their mission is dual—to prevent trouble and to facilitate profitable usage. They realize that competing salespeople are eager to find any difficulties and to capitalize on them. You might well review each of your customers in terms of the following checklist. Additions can be made peculiar to your own selling situation and to each of your accounts.

1. *Marketing.* How might customers market their products and services more effectively? To what degree are they taking full advantage of your company's marketing efforts? How does your offering strengthen the relationship between your client and their customers?
2. *Research and Development.* How effective is the liaison between each customer's development work and relevant research in the company? What suggestions might you make for improving and refining the customer's operation and product line?
3. *Financing.* In the case of capital purchases, how appropriate is the financing? Leasing? Rental? Better money source?
4. *Production Processes.* How advantageously is the product being employed? What problems are being encountered? What bottlenecks must be overcome?

5. *Materials Handling.* What difficulties occur in moving the product? How can labor savings be realized by employing better methods?

The following are some specific examples of how salespeople contributed solutions to customers' problems.

Convenience in Use and Storage

A machine-tool salesman designed a rig for suspending a machine attachment in the space above the machine. Previously, it had been stored in the toolroom. His idea made the device more accessible to the operator and utilized space that otherwise would have been wasted. In addition, it reduced machine down-time and saved labor costs. Whatever product you sell, you should be alert to ways to add to the customer's convenience.

Efficiency in Use and Maintenance

With many products, the creative salesperson can work out ways to ensure that the company's products are used more efficiently and maintained in better condition. When salespeople provide such ideas, they increase the goodwill felt toward themselves and their company and virtually ensure first crack at the replacement sale when the time comes.

Product Resale

The industrial salesperson who sells to the distributor and dealer and the consumer goods salesperson who sells to a variety of resellers, including retailers, have the task of not only selling their products but, equally important, also assisting in resale. The latter may include such contributions as conducting imaginative sales meetings, helping individual wholesalers' salespeople with problems in their accounts, and sparking ideas for local advertising. A steel salesman gained deeper penetration in several wholesaler accounts by working out a training program for the sales personnel who handled telephone inquiries. He was alert enough to enlist the aid of his own company's telemarketing manager in this project. A candy saleswoman knew that a community in her territory was celebrating its centennial. With her firm's cooperation, she offered a "centenary special" to her retail customers there. This not only increased business but also built considerable goodwill for the company and its products in the city.

Prospective Customers

Virtually every statement about problem solving in customer accounts can be applied with little change to generating new business. There are, however, several differences. First, in most instances, you do not intimately know the details and the problems in the account. Hence, part of your challenge is to learn enough about the account to use your ingenuity and originality. Second, because you are an outsider, you must generate ideas that the prospect perceives are *different* and *better* to gain entry. Thus any idea, any suggestion, any solution to a problem must be distinctive from the present practice. Third, your investment of time, talent, and money will be speculative until you write the first order. Therefore, guard against commitment beyond what good business judgment dictates. Despite these restraints, your ideas and solutions to problems may be the means of obtaining a share of the business. What are the recurrent opportunities to explore a prospect account? The short answer is the dimensions of differential competitive advantage, developed in Chapter One and detailed in Appendix I.

You have the objective of translating your firm's total offering—TIP-IT—Tangible, Intangible, Price, Image, and Team components into a need-satisfying system that is *different* and *better* than others from the buyer's standpoint. The starting point, therefore, is to use the concept of differential competitive advantage as a diagnostic tool. By determining where the prospect recognizes significant differences between your own and competitive offerings, as well as noting evidence, you have the foundation for designing a customized sales strategy.

The Salesperson's Own Company

Creative salespeople contribute worthwhile ideas to their own companies. They are in a favorable position to do this, seeing the products and services in actual use. Further, they observe competitive offerings and are able to make comparisons.

Products and Services

You have a vested interest in doing everything you can to make your company's products and services the best available. While many companies maintain departments directly responsible for product development and improvement, even here you may be the catalyst for change. Your suggestions for improvements may cover the following aspects:

1. *Size.* New size needed? Old size not selling?
2. *Shape.* Square? Squat? Round?
3. *Weight.* Lighter? Heavier?
4. *Color.* Brighter? Duller? Contrast?
5. *Package.* Stronger? Reusable? Recyclable? More distinctive?
6. *Assortment.* New combinations? Deals?
7. *Ingredients.* Additions? Deletions?
8. *Form.* Solid? Powdered? Crystalline? Liquid?
9. *Flavor.* Sweeter? Dryer?
10. *Aroma.* Flowery? Odorless? Pungent?

Your ideas for better service may be in such areas as:

1. *Speed.* Order processing? Delivery? Handling complaints or adjustments?
2. *Efficiency.* Control checks? Handling?
3. *Coordination.* Between sales and field service? Sales and headquarters?
4. *Individualization.* At the request of _____? Specifically for _____?
5. *Accuracy.* Attention to detail? Available information?

Marketing Efforts

Each day you have the opportunity to observe the impact of your company's advertising, sales promotion, merchandising, and other marketing efforts. You are in a unique position to contribute useful ideas on all of these. For example, with regard to advertising:

1. *Theme.* Appeals? Benefits?
2. *Wording.* Understandable? Interesting? New words?
3. *Illustrations.* Prestige user in territory? Product in use?
4. *Media.* Local newspapers? Radio? TV?
5. *Timing.* Local tie-in with special events? Seasonal emphasis?

Company Policies and Practices

It is not your prerogative to tell your management how to conduct the business's affairs. Nevertheless, constructive suggestions from the sales force help to ensure that the firm's policies and practices maintain a favorable position in the competitive marketplace. In particular, you might consider the following as having a direct impact on customers and prospects:

1. *Delivery.* Carriers used? Drop shipments?
2. *Billing.* Form? Timing? Terms?
3. *Credit.* Amount? Extension? Dating?
4. *Plant/Facility Visitation.* Treatment on premises? Authority to invite?
5. *Trade and Industry Relations.* Participation in associations? Expositions? Shows? Conferences?
6. *Executive Level Contacts.* Frequency? Scheduling? Clearance?
7. *Cooperative Advertising and Promotion.* Amount? Arrangement?
8. *Technical Assistance.* Caliber? Commitment?
9. *Contract Purchasing.* Terms? Minimum amounts?
10. *Adjustments.* Guarantees and warranties? Other?

The Salesperson's Own Selling Methods and Techniques

The most recurrent opportunity for applying creative thinking and logical problem solving in selling is to your own selling knowledge and skill. You have four key sources or inputs to consider. First is a critical review of *your own performance*.

You must ask yourself: What worked or did not work on the call? In the management of each account? A careful analysis of both successes and failures is bound to lead to improved selling ability. (Appendix XXVI provides detailed discussion of observing sales performance.)

Second, you can add to your knowledge and skill by *studying on your own.* (Chapter Nine, Section 3, suggests sources to tap for continuing self-development.)

The third source of ideas is the individual application of principles, methods, and techniques covered in the *company's sales training program.* An open-minded "ready to learn" attitude toward ideas set forth in group sessions, as well as in two-person calls with the supervisor, is essential for continuing improvement.

Fourth, you can gain many ideas from carefully studying what seems to be *successful for other salespeople,* including the competition. When you encounter a difficult prospect, you may find it useful to learn how the competitive salesperson established such a strong account relationship.

Specifically, you might review the following factors and ask yourself how you might improve each phase of your selling.

Prospecting

Every salesperson realizes the need to create new accounts. Prospecting involves *seeking out* potential customers from the following sources and *screening* them for likely business:

1. Company furnished.
2. Customer generated.
3. Trade and industry press.
4. Newspaper, radio, and TV announcements.
5. Noncompeting salespersons.

In screening leads, are the following being used to the fullest?

1. Company's credit department.
2. Trade and industry directories and reports.
3. Letter or telephone call designed to arouse need.
4. Reference to a known problem.
5. Personal contact through community, trade, professional, or industry activity.

Approach

You are likely to see key personnel easily in accounts where you have established relationships. In contrast, you may have difficulty gaining entry to prospective accounts. "Getting the door open" is a challenge, and you should review these potential sources of entry:

1. Satisfied customer recommendation.
2. Introduction by mutual friend.

3. A letter or phone call demonstrating a need.
4. Reference to a known problem.
5. Professional contact through community, trade, professional, or industry activity.

Presentation

Chapter Two is devoted to effective communication in selling. Creative salespeople might think of their presentations in the following terms:

1. Question technique.
2. Ability to listen.
3. Colorfulness of language.
4. Emphasis on meeting customer needs.
5. Aptness of examples, comparisons, and illustrations.

Appendix XXV provides a model presentation checklist. To ensure consistent effective presentation, you should develop your own checklist, customized to your unique situation.

Demonstration

Salespeople have many occasions to reinforce their sales story with visuals, including the actual product or service in use. Chapter Two points out that the sales message is more likely to be understood if you enlist several senses simultaneously. The phenomenon involved is *spatial summation*. The following points comprise a good checklist for the demonstration:

1. Timing and synchronization with presentation.
2. Appropriateness to the customer's situation.
3. Attention getting devices.
4. Understandability.
5. Ease of use.

Objections

A call seldom occurs without an objection being raised. Chapter Four discusses specific tactics for handling objections. They are analyzed as negative-voluntary reactions, that is, signals that the customer or prospect is disagreeing and letting you know it. The tactical principle suggested is to shift radically to something that is bound to elicit a favorable response. If you are eager to improve yourself in coping with objections, you might jot down the most recurrent and difficult ones you have encountered and note from experience the best way to answer each one. *Understandability, believability,* and *acceptance* are the prime considerations.

Closing

Everything you say and do during the call focuses on achieving a successful outcome—in most cases, a sale. The closing signal suggested in Chapter Three is the *positive-voluntary* reaction, where the customer or prospect is responding favorably and letting you know it. You are cautioned not to let the opportunity go by but rather to seek an order then and there. A review of successful and unsuccessful calls is likely to yield a list of specific tactics that work for you. *Persuasiveness* and *conviction* are fundamental to successful closing.

Appendix XXIV provides an exercise to apply the points covered in this chapter to a particular customer or prospect. Try it!

5.   SUGGESTION IN SELLING

If you have an in-depth understanding of your customers' needs and they trust that you will act in their best interests, the use of suggestion can achieve your joint objectives more efficiently. One caution is in order: Suggestion is not a shortcut to the need satisfaction process. It is an alternative method for reducing the time required to conduct need fulfillment. Without a clear understanding of the customers' needs, your use of suggestion is likely to backfire.

Suggestion is defined and used in this volume as "uncritical acceptance of an idea." It means that one person acts in accordance with the wishes of another without considering the implications of his or her act. The opposite of suggestion is critical reasoning—a process that requires a person to consider the advantages and disadvantages before taking action.

Another way of distinguishing *suggestion* is to compare it with a *recommendation*. When salespeople say, "I suggest you take three of these," they are recommending a quantity. They are not using suggestion. Note that the use of the word "suggest" does not make the statement a suggestion in the technical sense.

Some examples of suggestion may help to clarify the concept. Many persons order wine in restaurants. Diners who are familiar with wines make their choices from the wine list without difficulty. Other diners may need help from the wine steward. Rather than explaining all the qualities of all the wines to help diners make a selection on a logical or reasoned basis, the steward is more apt to say, "This wine is just right for your meal" or "We sell a lot of this wine." These are attempts to get the wine order uncritically or by suggestion.

One sales force had a product packaged in three sizes. It was easy to sell the small package as well as the large one to stores. The mid-size package, however, met resistance for a variety of reasons. After training, which included the technique of suggestion, the company's salespeople discovered that the simple statement, "You don't have any mid-sized packages on the shelf" produced many sales.

Reasons for Using Suggestion

The preceding example shows the advantages of using suggestion. One benefit is the *saving of time*. Obtaining an order without discussion clearly takes less time than exploring all aspects of a situation.

Another advantage is the avoidance of friction between you and the prospect. In the process of presenting all the facts and advantages of a proposition, the buyer will in all probability take exception to some points and interrupt you for more detailed information at other places. This situation may call for forceful presentation, which carries with it the possibility that buyers will feel they are being dominated or pressured into buying.

A third advantage of suggestion is that the alternate course involves bringing up the proposition's disadvantages as well as advantages, which may give the prospect reasons for resistance. You should not go out of your way to make your job more difficult.

The Nature of Suggestion

Basically, suggestion takes place in two separate instances: (1) when thinking is inhibited or (2) when it is dissociated.

Inhibition of thinking may have a physiological basis—fever, fatigue, or use of controlled substances. Psychological states—fear, awe, anger, elation—can also cause inhibition.

Dissociation means that more than one course of thought or action is taking place at the same time. At the extreme, amnesia, somnambulism, and split personality of the Dr. Jekyll/Mr. Hyde type illustrate dissociation. At the more normal level, driving a car while on the phone and carrying on a conversation while playing a game are examples. The essence of dissociation is that a stimulus other than the suggester causes the responses that the subject is aware of.

You can easily see how you might use suggestion with people whose thinking is inhibited. Because of their agitation or listlessness, they do not fully consider the proposition. In the case of dissociation, the prospects are fully alert but are more attentive to some other activity than to the salesperson. A pharmacist filling a prescription while talking to a salesperson is an example. Any time a prospect continues an activity while purporting to talk to you, he or she sets up an opportunity for you to accomplish the call objective through suggestion.

If you are tempted to use suggestion to obtain orders that are not in your customers' best interest, you should remember that before the orders are delivered, customers will have ample opportunity to think about their purchases and cancel them. Suggestion is meant to be used to effect smoother selling-buying relationships, not transactions that would not normally take place.

Individuals vary in suggestibility. Research has indicated some of the factors that cause this variation. They are:

1. *Prejudice.* Any strong prejudice tends to interfere with the ability to think clearly. You should discover the nature of the prejudice and submit the

proposition so that it is in keeping with the prejudice. This will reduce the tendency to look at the proposal from all points of view. A prospect with an "isolationist" view politically may seek out products "made in America."

2. *Ignorance.* A synonym for ignorance is "a specific lack of knowledge or information." This is not a reflection on general knowledge or ability but often crops up when a customer must purchase a product or service for the first time. For example, a home owner elects to install a sprinkler system for the lawn. Facing a multitude of decisions, most of which cannot be made on the basis of experience, the home owner is likely to be suggestible in this area.

3. *Low Intelligence.* In such cases, prospects lack the ability to acquire information and relate it to their situations. They cannot resist persuasion or suggestion because they may not be able to verbalize their feelings. They either have to place orders without understanding the proposition or stubbornly refuse to buy. Only after listening to several detailed presentations can they comprehend all the relevant ideas. Patience rather than suggestion will pay dividends with this type of buyer.

Comparison of suggestion with command will throw further light on the nature of suggestion. A person of authority, for example, is normally obeyed uncritically. Technically, this is the same result as that created by suggestion. The only difference is that the speaker has the authority to back up his or her intentions while a salesperson uses skill to achieve compliance. If the person seeking results holds authority, his or her request must be labeled "command." If the company president says to a purchasing agent, "That _____ might work well," the remark is by definition a command, because the authority to compel compliance is associated with the position of the president. If a salesperson made the same statement, it would be a suggestion.

While the mechanics of command and suggestion may be identical, you must recognize that, in the case of command, vague or indirect comments may be acted upon where suggestions would be ignored.

Kinds of Suggestion

Two dimensions of suggestion need clarification to ensure proper use and understanding. Suggestion can be direct or indirect, and it can be positive or negative.

In direct suggestion, the person receiving the suggestion can see the objectives of the person who makes it. The suggestion spells out what is to be done. "Try a dozen of these" is an example. If the suggestion does not reveal the desire of the suggester and does not spell out the desired action, it is indirect. An example would be, "A dozen of these should solve your problem."

Indirect suggestion is more subtle, hence in many ways more desirable than direct suggestion. Another important consideration is that if indirect suggestion does not work, either because the person receiving the suggestion does not get the point or does not care to comply, the suggester can resort to direct suggestion, which is more forceful.

For example, the following series of statements starts with one that is relatively indirect and progresses to some that are more direct.

- This product is very effective.
- Other customers swear by this product.
- This should solve your problem.
- Order some of these.

Another clue to the use of direct or indirect suggestion is to note the basis for suggestion. If inhibition is involved, direct suggestion is appropriate. When dissociation is present, indirect suggestion is in order.

A positive suggestion indicates a straightforward course of action, while a negative suggestion strives to accomplish a result by favoring something. "Order this today" is in positive form, while "Don't put off ordering this" is in negative form. Both suggestions are designed to produce the same result; namely, prompt action.

Negative suggestion is more complex than positive suggestion because it has two elements. It contains an idea to be avoided as well as one to act on. For example, a parent might tell a child, "Come right home after school." This is positive. If the parent says, "Don't play on the way home from school," the form is negative and gives the child the potentially distracting idea of playing.

Applied to selling, negative suggestion may cause the prospect to react to the negative rather than the positive step. This is tantamount to furnishing the basis for rejecting the proposition.

Principles of Suggestion

Suggestions Should Be Indirect Rather Than Direct

The indirect suggestion does not spell out the actual desired response. Therefore, if customers act on the suggestion, they feel it was their own idea. This increases the likelihood of making the sale and decreases the likelihood of antagonistic ideas arising to create sales resistance. The use of analogous cases or third party endorsements are good examples of indirect suggestion. A statement that another person profited from a similar purchase may be more effective than a direct suggestion that the prospect can profit from a purchase.

Suggestions Should Be Positive Rather Than Negative

Whenever possible, keep suggestions positive. They are simpler and easier for the person to follow.

The Prestige of the Suggester Is an Important Consideration

The greater the prestige of the persons making suggestions, the less the likelihood of their suggestions being considered critically. Many factors contribute to prestige. One of these is the reputation of the company. The salesperson may possess others, such as social standing, financial resources, physical size, age, and educational attainment. The suggestion that a certain stock is a good investment is less likely to be questioned when coming from a person known to be a successful investor than from a person with no comparable record of achievement. You may be able to use this type of suggestion by quoting prestigious people. These can be executives in your company, persons well known in the trade, or people from public life.

Several Persons Suggesting the Same Thing Are More Potent Than a Single Person

In a difficult sales situation, other company personnel may need to back up the salesperson's suggestions. A joint call with a sales executive, a company engineer, or another person of authority will increase the likelihood of success.

Attention Level Is a Factor in Suggestion

Devoting a high level of attention to the subject at hand enhances the probability that your suggestions will be followed. Persons become so concerned over a problem that their ability to weigh the pros and cons objectively diminishes. (This supports the idea that stepping back—relaxing attention—to get a fresh view is an aid to clearer understanding.)

While there is little experimental evidence on the subject, it may be that the other end of the scale—inattention—also increases the likelihood of suggestions being acted upon. This is based on the idea of dissociation. Suppose you call on a prospect who is completely immersed in thinking about a problem. You may present your proposition, but the prospect never really shifts attention to you. If you make the sale, you have done so without the prospect attending to, or critically evaluating, the proposition.

If the preceding reasoning is correct, then suggestion is most likely to be effective when the customer is either barely attending to, or completely engrossed in, the problem. At the middle level of attention, the prospect is most likely to think critically about the proposition.

Absence of an Opposing Idea Increases the Effectiveness of a Suggestion

Early writings on psychology often include the statement that every idea that enters the mind will be acted upon unless an antagonistic item is present (William James is credited with this concept). One way, then, to minimize opposing ideas is to keep the desired idea in mind. The more time a prospect devotes to the desired idea, the less time he or she can devote to inhibiting ideas; hence, an idea kept before a person long enough will be acted upon.

Repetition of a Suggestion Increases the Likelihood of Its Being Acted On

When an idea is repeated often enough over a period of time, buyers tend to forget its origin. They may eventually accept it as their own. When this happens, it helps the salesperson because it is easier for buyers to act on their own ideas than on those of the salesperson. Because an idea planted through company advertising often will benefit the salesperson, it is helpful to coordinate advertising and selling. The advertising copy and the salesperson's presentation should be couched in the same style as far as possible. This allows the salesperson to make maximum use of the advertising as a preselling device.

Ignorance of the Topic under Discussion Increases the Likelihood of Adopting a Suggestion

The reason for this result is that the person lacks information through which to disagree. For example, how does a person having a home built know what material to use on the exterior? He or she must choose among wood, concrete, brick, and a variety of metals, such as stainless steel and aluminum, as well as various combinations of the same materials. The contractor "suggests" a material, and, lacking any prior knowledge of the materials, the person may adopt the contractor's ideas. The contractor, in building his or her own house, might very well end up with the same kind of material. The difference would be that the contractor would select the material after a process of reasoning rather than as the result of suggestion.

A Disturbed State Increases Suggestibility

Any physical disturbance (fever, fatigue, substance abuse) will reduce people's ability to think clearly and, hence, leave them more open to suggestion. People make purchases under the influence of alcohol that they would not make otherwise. While perhaps less dramatic, the purchases made under other forms of disturbances are equally likely to be unsatisfactory.

Should you find that you are dealing with a person who is in no condition to make a satisfactory evaluation of the proposition, you face an ethical problem. If you feel that the person can really profit from the transaction and you elect to complete the sale, you should provide reasons the prospect can use to justify the purchase. Otherwise, you may find the purchase is returned when clearer thinking prevails.

Previous Performance of an Act Increases the Likelihood of Suggestion

Any novel act is likely to require a conscious effort and be accompanied by critical thought processes. As far as selling is concerned, this would indicate that you should not expect to achieve your first sale to a customer by suggestion. Initial contacts require undivided attention and a full presentation. Later, after developing your relationship with the customer, you may accomplish sales by suggestion and without full attention.

Of course, more than suggestion accounts for the ease of the second sale to a customer over the first one. Other factors are satisfactory service from the first purchase as well as your increased knowledge of the customer's needs.

Wording of the Suggestion Affects the Likelihood It Will Be Acted Upon

Evidence shows that leading questions, definite rather than indefinite articles, and positive rather than negative phrasing influence the individual's reply.

For example, "Did you see the horse?" is more likely to produce an affirmative answer than "Did you see a horse?" If you want to suggest a dog was dark-colored, you could do it more readily by asking, "Was the dog dark-colored?" than by asking, "What color was the dog?"

Another way that you can employ language for suggestion is to use technical terms. A liberal sprinkling of such terms, especially if they are spoken easily and habitually, may influence the listener. Dramatic effect through the use of colorful words, intonations, and gestures will also increase suggestion.

Seeing an Act Performed by Another Person Increases the Likelihood of Suggestion

People have a tendency to imitate the actions of others unless some inhibiting factor is present. Any audience can illustrate this: One person's cough will trigger a whole series of coughs. A salesperson who realizes this will be alert to perform any motor act, the imitation of which will bring the prospect nearer to any affirmative buying decision. For example, an order form calling for the signature of the customer might contain a space where the salesperson could also sign. The salesperson should sign the form first as a way of reducing the resistance of customers to signing.

Other Applications of Suggestion

Salespeople are not the only ones who can profit from the study and application of suggestion. Following are a few examples from other fields. Noting these applications may suggest more effective techniques.

Reassurance is a method you can use in much the same way it is used by psychiatrists. The doctor, among other things, reassures patients that they are going to improve. The constant reassurance (frequent repetition) serves to minimize the patients' troubles. In a similar manner, salespeople can constantly assure the prospect that their products and services will render better service than the competitors' products. Salespeople can also, where they have made a sale, reassure the customer that they will receive very satisfactory service.

Closely related to reassurance is the technique of appearing highly *self-confident*. Certainly, if the doctor or the salesperson has any doubt, the patient or customer will detect it. This destroys confidence and lessens the suggestion value of the salesperson or doctor. Salespeople should be sold on their product or services and their company so that they can appear completely confident that their products will fill the needs of customers.

Techniques of suggestion used by advertisers are testimonials and guarantees. The value of testimonials depends on the prestige that the customer accords the person furnishing the testimonial. That some individual has used the product or service and is satisfied suggests the offering has merit. You should take care that the person providing the testimonial is a logical and genuine user of the product. The indiscriminate use of movie stars and athletes for testimonials has reduced their effectiveness in many instances.

A *guarantee* is evidence that a company has faith in its offering. This display of faith has suggestion value. Not only does it imply the product or service is good, but it also reduces the risk in purchasing it.

Comparison or *contrast* is another technique that facilitates suggestion. You can build drama into a demonstration so that a product will appear favorable either by comparison or contrast. Salespeople who either compare or invite comparison of their products with the competition are suggesting that the customer will find the superiority claimed.

SUMMARY

An important aspect of your position involves problem solving and creative thinking for customers and prospects as well as for your own company. The problem-solving process starts with thinking about a particular problem or issue. Inputs needed are relevant facts and opinions. Restrictions include policy, talent, time, and money. The five steps in the process are problem identification, establishment of criteria, thinking of alternative solutions, evaluating alternatives, and reaching a "best" solution. Many factors influence your effectiveness: your own attitude, your knowledge, your willingness to try the new, and your ability to enlist the help of others.

In addition to understanding straight thinking, you must identify and combat devious reasoning to practice effective need satisfaction selling.

Creativity has two inputs—what you are thinking about or working on and your life values. The creative thought process is relatively undisciplined and cannot be forced. Five steps occur: stimulation, ideation, incubation, illumination, and application. No single characteristic earmarks the creative person. However, generally speaking, the creative person has more intelligence, breadth and depth of knowledge, curiosity, attitude of constructive discontent, drive to achieve, capacity to work, and self-confidence.

As a creative problem solver, you have four prime targets: customer accounts, prospect accounts, your own company, and your own selling skills. Suggestions and checklists have been presented for exploring each of these target areas and for stimulating a flow of ideas.

If you have an in-depth understanding of your customer's needs and a strong relationship with the customer based on trust, you may elect to provide a full presentation of your offering. Alternatively, you may use suggestion to improve your efficiency. This method reduces the time required to conduct need fulfillment when the customer does not desire to explore all ramifications of your offering. Suggestions may be direct or indirect and may or may not be backed up by authority. Twelve common principles of suggestion were presented, together with examples of their uses in enhancing productivity.

To practice need satisfaction selling effectively, you need to master problem solving, creativity, straight and devious thinking, and suggestion.

TOPICS FOR THOUGHT AND DISCUSSION

1. Illustrate the difference between fact and opinion from a recent experience.
2. Give an example of how each of the following factors has restricted the way you have had to cope with a problem: policy, time, money, and/or competition.
3. Which step in problem solving is most difficult to accomplish? Why?
4. What additional factors in problem solving should be considered?
5. What factors might cause a customer or prospect to engage deliberately in devious thinking?
6. How can you improve your ability to think clearly?
7. Think back over sales calls where you were unsuccessful because of the prospect's devious reasoning. How would the suggestions in Section 2 have helped you?
8. What "big idea" have you had? Where did it come from?
9. Who is the most creative person you know? How does this person fit the profile of the creative person presented?
10. What are your most frequent professional opportunities for thinking creatively?
11. What are some of the reasons you might come up with an idea that has escaped a prospect?
12. What new uses have you found for your firm's products/services?
13. Describe your most creative sales presentation.
14. What suggestions do you have for improving your company's marketing? Products? Services?
15. What are the ethical considerations in using suggestion?
16. Laboratory evidence has not verified the fifth law of suggestion, dealing with attention level. What is your opinion of the validity of the law?
17. What are the greatest advantages to you in mastering suggestion?
18. Testimonials are a form of suggestion. What is their relative value in advertising as compared with personal selling?

EIGHT

Guiding Buying Behavior

The art of teaching is the art of assisting discovery.

MARK VAN DOREN

In this chapter:

- **The Nature of Learning**
  - You have a dual stake in knowing how people learn—for your own use and for influencing customers and prospects.
- **Learning Applied to Selling**
  - To make a sale, you must supply information so the customer can "learn" to buy from you.
- **Learning Channels**
  - To use the sensory channels—hearing and seeing—to best advantage, you must understand how they operate.
- **Remembering and Forgetting**
  - If salespeople learn (1) the nature of forgetting and (2) ways to improve memory in customers and themselves, they can be more effective.
- **Summary**
  - The effective salesperson is able to convey ideas to others in a form and manner that ensures learning and retention.
- **Topics for Thought and Discussion**
- **Application Exercises**
  - Appendix X   Work Sheet for Making a Trait Description
  - Appendix XXVII Analysis of Learning Channels

1. THE NATURE OF LEARNING

To make a sale, you must often "teach" the prospect, that is supply information so the buyer can "learn."

Before you can teach, however, you have to learn the information yourself. Teaching and learning are two aspects of the same process of transferring information from one person or source to another. Therefore, this chapter could be written from either point of view: *how to teach* or *how to learn*.

This chapter is presented in how-to-teach form so that you can use the suggestions with customers directly. Keep in mind that when you practice the need satisfaction theory of selling, learning occurs largely in the need fulfillment phase.

Basic Ways of Learning

Learning takes place in three basic ways. The first is by *association*. New ideas are added to those the learner already holds. The second is by *trial and error*. Here new ideas are acquired by using alternative approaches and finding out which ones work. The third way of learning is by *insight*. The learner picks up bits and pieces of knowledge, which suddenly become organized into a whole or "Gestalt."

Learning by Association

Pavlov conducted the basic experiments on learning by association showing that a response elicited by a stimulus may subsequently be made in response to a new one, provided that the two stimuli are presented together a sufficient number of times.

Whenever you learn a new idea or behavior by relating it to something already known, it represents associative learning. When a new price list is issued, you normally compare it with the present list and note the differences. You can then easily tell which prices changed upward or downward. The relationship between the two lists is obvious: hence association is simple.

Suppose you are given new sales responsibilities. How would you learn about your new market? customers? prospects? competitors? To the extent that you can make comparisons with your old responsibilities, you can use association to master the new assignment. Where previous experience does not apply, you will need different techniques to master the new situation. People who cannot learn other than by association are at a disadvantage. They will need help frequently.

Learning by Trial and Error

The basic findings on trial and error learning have come from using laboratory animals in a variety of situations. Putting rats in a maze and recording the number of trials and errors for each test run has contributed much of the information important to trial-and-error learning. Take the price list again. If you had never seen the earlier list, you could not learn the new list by association. You would have to read through the list, remove it from sight, and try to repeat the details from memory. This is called recitation. If you could not recall certain points, you would continue memorizing and reciting until you could repeat the list without a single error. The list would then have been learned by trial and error.

Learning by Insight

Kohler, a German psychologist and a pioneer in Gestalt psychology, performed experiments with a chimpanzee that led to an awareness of the importance of insight. He placed the chimpanzee in a cage and put a banana outside it, beyond the reach of the animal. He furnished a potential tool in the form of sticks that could be joined together like a fishing pole. A single part would not reach the lure, hence the chimpanzee needed to get "insight" to see that by joining the pieces of the stick, the food could be reached.

In a new territory, for example, you have many opportunities to use associative learning by comparing new accounts with the familiar ones. Mastering new accounts can also be accomplished by trying different tactics on each call until you are successful. You might also learn how to handle new accounts through insight.

The routing problem provides an example. You are not likely to solve it satisfactorily by either association or trial and error. The possibility of traveling the territory in a variety of ways is not feasible in terms of time, cost, and risk. The only realistic approach is insight. Armed with customer and prospect lists, as well as maps and perhaps a computer program, you can simulate and evaluate various solutions until you reach the best combination of calls. Insight is necessary to solve routing problems.

Suggestions for helping another person learn through association, trial and error, and by insight are provided later in the chapter.

Principles of Learning

The next step is to take a broader view of the principles that apply to a variety of learning situations: effect, primacy, recency, and frequency. Different ways of learning depend on different principles. Hence, a law that is appropriate for one way of learning may be irrelevant or in apparent conflict with principles for another way of learning. In addition, what appears to be a conflict may disappear when more complete information is available.

Effect

The principle of effect states that pleasant experiences are more apt to be retained than unpleasant ones. According to the law of effect, your objective is to ensure that your customers associate pleasant experiences with you. Risking unpleasant experiences is dangerous.

Primacy

With the principle of primacy, the first stimuli brought to a person's attention are the ones most likely to be learned or retained. In learning a list of names, the ones at the beginning of the list are the ones most easily remembered. In a sales call, the points you bring out at the beginning of the interview are best retained.

Recency

The principle of recency would seem to be in opposition to the primacy principle because it holds that those items at the end of a list or the points at the close of an interview would be best retained. Actually, both laws hold and you can use them by putting the most important points first and last (see Figure 8.1).

Frequency

The principle of frequency suggests that other things being equal, the points that are repeated the most will be best retained. You should see a relationship between this principle and summation as treated in Chapter Two. This means you should work the key points into a presentation several times and repeat them near the end of the interview. This procedure will increase the likelihood of retention. Repetition without changing the phrasing becomes monotonous, so change the wording with each repetition.

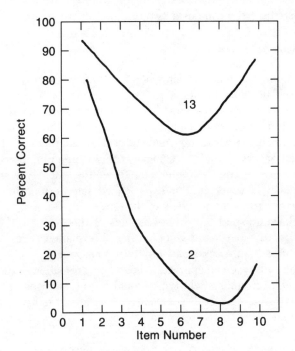

Figure 8.1 Primacy and recency. The laws of primacy and recency are illustrated by showing that material at the two ends of a sequence are mastered before the middle items. The vertical scale shows the percentage of correct answers. The horizontal scale shows 10 items to be learned. The numbers on the curve are the numbers of the trial. The implication is that on the second trial, the first item had been 80% learned; the eighth item, 2%; and the tenth item, 17%. By the thirteenth trial, the same items had been mastered at the rate of 93%, 61%, and 88%, respectively. It took many more trials to master the items in the center of the material. The curves in this and the following diagrams are deliberately smooth rather than representations of actual data. All that is intended is to show general outlines.

Guides to Efficient Learning

In addition to the basic principles of learning discussed in the preceding section, you should consider the following factors in designing efficient learning experiences.

Spaced versus Massed Learning

In general, when you must cover a significant amount of material, the spacing of learning periods is preferable to trying to accomplish the task in one sitting. Of course, you must consider the complexity of the material, the time available, and the physical or mental challenge involved. In addition, you must take into account the practical implications of time, distance, and access. The question you must answer is whether it is better to spend all the time available in one session or to distribute the time over two or more meetings.

Whole versus Part Learning

This is a very important consideration when a person is learning new material, especially in a self-teaching situation.

To illustrate, assume you have just been hired as a salesperson. Should you start by making calls (whole), or should you start by attending sessions (part) at the company factory or office? Aside from practical considerations—the complexity of the product or service and the company training program in effect, for example—whole to part learning is preferable. To see the whole, you should make bona fide calls with a supervisor or experienced salesperson. You should be merely an observer getting an overview of the job.

When you have grasped the overall aspects of the position, then you can proceed to master the parts—product/service information, sales techniques, market data, competition assessment, territory management, and so on. After you have been on calls, you can appreciate how the information in the parts will be used. If feasible, frequent field trips should be interspersed with the part learning. Such trips increase both your understanding and motivation.

Take the game of golf. A person who only played 18 holes according to the rules would not make as much progress as someone who practiced particular strokes between rounds. Further, a person who only practiced specific shots without understanding their function on a golf course would find little interest or motivation to continue practicing.

If part learning were in effect from the beginning, you would see no application of the content of the training program and you would find yourself on the job but lacking the "big picture" essential to success. Follow-up training (learning on the job) would include field supervision that would spot weaknesses in performance and result in more part training.

For shorter tasks, learning is more efficient when the whole is grasped before the parts are attempted. Introducing a new product promotion to a retailer is an example. You must give the retailer a quick explanation of the whole program before you discuss the details. If you start the interview by explaining how merchandise can be returned, it will make much less sense to the retailer than if you provide an overview of the promotion.

With a large task, such as installing a new production line in a factory, you may need to go from the part to the whole because the whole may be too complex and abstract to master readily. Some of the points you may need to take up separately are costs, structural changes in the building, the mix of humans and robots to be used, anticipated production schedules, and the recruitment and selection of employees.

Generally speaking, when tasks are very long or very difficult, they should be broken down and mastered part by part. When the overall task can be grasped readily, you should start with the whole and proceed to the parts.

Recitation

If the learner cannot understand or remember the material, continuing the learning process is pointless. The way to determine whether progress is being made is to try to recall the key points or, in some cases, to repeat the text of the material verbatim. This recitation can be self-administered or, in the case of a sales interview, you can ask questions to note the prospect's degree of understanding and retention.

In addition to ensuring understanding and retention, recitation utilizes the law of frequency and brings repetition into the learning process. Hence, recitation ensures future retention as well as provides a check on the immediate grasp of the material.

Special Effects in Learning

Some interesting effects take place in the process of learning. They are not obvious to the teacher or learner at the time, but laboratory research has shown that they exist and you should take them into account when planning a learning session.

Latent Learning

A synonym for *latent* is *hidden*. It means that learning can take place without being apparent. This might occur because no reason existed to use the information at the time it was learned. A simple example is an advertisement that has been seen or heard innumerable times. If a need for that particular product or service exists, the advertisement may be recalled. It was learned at the time of exposure, but as the product or service was not needed, no recitation or application took place, so the learner was not aware that learning had occurred.

Laboratory evidence for latent learning is interesting. Rats were allowed to work their way through a maze and a reward was established, such as food or a member of the opposite sex. Almost immediately their performance improved greatly, so much so that it could only be explained on the basis of the learning that took place while the rats were wandering aimlessly through the maze (see Figure 8.2).

When you make a presentation to a customer, you must recognize that the customer's immediate need could be so weak that the customer sees no point to what you are explaining and, accordingly, shows little interest in the message. This should not disturb you. You now know that a strong possibility exists that the customer will recall the information when it is needed. You may have had the experience of a customer recalling details of an earlier conversation that you thought had been lost or wasted. Many orders result from belated use of information presented by you and other salespeople.

Overlearning

When you have mastered material to the point of perfect recitation, you are considered to have learned it. If you then put aside the task and try a recitation at a later date, quite likely some forgetting will have occurred. This means that the learning process must be resumed to consider the material mastered.

Obviously, it would be desirable if you could recall material, once learned, at any time. This is seldom the case, but by understanding and applying the concept of *overlearning*, you can obtain some improvement.

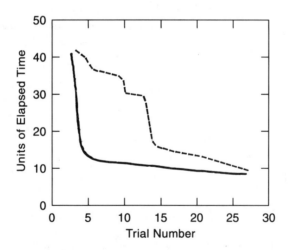

Figure 8.2 Latent learning. The solid line shows a typical learning curve. In this example, the vertical scale shows elapsed time. It could also represent errors or some other units. The horizontal scale is the trial number. Each trial shows an improvement in that each took less time than the previous one. By Trial 5, most of the learning had taken place. By contrast, the dashed line portrays a case of latent learning. At Trial 13, a reward was given; note the dramatic improvement. This shows that some knowledge had been acquired (latently) and was available when needed.

Overlearning is any practice or recitation that takes place after achieving one perfect recitation. It consists of continuing to learn after the prospect is believed to have mastered the details. When the buyer finally comprehends the advantages of a product or service and feels disposed to place an order, you should not terminate the interview. Your success depends on teaching the prospect enough about the proposition to make an adequate presentation to other decision makers in the company. When the time comes to get approval, if the prospect forgets some of the detail and cannot influence others to feel as strongly about the product as he or she originally felt, no sale will result.

You can reduce this problem and possibly eliminate it through the principle of overlearning. Research has shown that up to 50 percent of the time required to reach a perfect recitation of the facts can be used efficiently to maintain the learning level or reduce forgetting. Specifically, if a child needed 10 trials to learn a multiplication table, another 5 drills would help ensure recall at a future date (see Figure 8.3).

Obviously, you cannot expect the prospect to recite the way a child does, but with a little ingenuity, you can find ways to review and repeat the outstanding sales points and thereby increase the prospect's retention level for use at a later time.

Inhibition

In the field of learning, inhibition means that the presence of extraneous material can reduce or interfere with learning or retention of some particular material. More specifically, it means that learning one set of facts can interfere with the learning of another set.

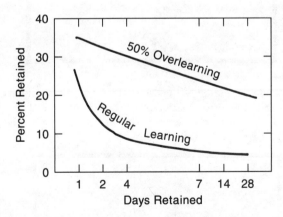

Figure 8.3 Overlearning. This curve shows that 50% overlearning resulted in retention of a higher percentage of the material than that achieved by regular learning. Although the difference is notable after one day, the rate of forgetting is slower for the material that was overlearned, and after 30 days retention of the overlearned material is markedly superior.

This interference can work two ways. Assume two separate learning tasks, 1 and 2. After learning Task 1, the person turns immediately to Task 2. He or she now forgets some of Task 1, particularly the part most recently learned, because of confusing it with the initial part of Task 2. Furthermore, the learning of Task 2, particularly the initial part, is less effective because of the residue of Task 1. The effect that Task 1 has on Task 2 is known as *proactive inhibition* because it works ahead. The effect Task 2 has on Task 1 is called *retroactive inhibition* because its effect is backward.

For example, if a student doing homework immediately turns to history after completing an English assignment, the retention of both subjects will be reduced or inhibited, history proactively and English retroactively.

The obvious way of reducing the inhibition is to pause between assignments. A 10- or 15-minute break will allow the consolidation of the English material. The student can then start the history assignment without the same likelihood of inhibition (see Figure 8.4).

As far as you are concerned, whenever you switch topics in a sales interview, you introduce the possibility of inhibition in the customer's learning. Take a break between major topics or successive interviews. The alternative is to plan another call.

Transfer of Learning

Material or behavior that a person learns in one situation can augment the ability to learn new material or behavior under different conditions. For instance,

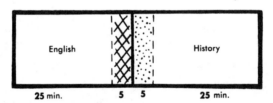

The crosshatch in the period of English study is retroactive inhibition, and the dotted area in the history period is proactive inhibition. If the student were to take a 10-minute break between studies, inhibition would be largely eliminated. This is shown in the next diagram.

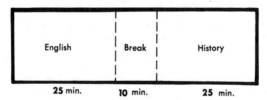

This schedule would result in as much or more total learning and reduce the fatigue of the learner.

Figure 8.4 Inhibition.

learning either ice-skating or roller-skating will facilitate the acquisition of skill in the other sport. People who master several languages report that, generally speaking, each successive language is easier to learn. This is because transfer of learning takes place.

The practical significance of this transfer is that you can use this knowledge to step up your customer's acquisition and retention of new ideas. While some transfer of learning will take place anyway, you can enhance its value by presenting ideas so that their similarity to other ideas already possessed by the customer is obvious. You can describe a new product by showing its similarity to an existing product that the customer knows well. If a new process is involved, you can describe a similar process in another customer's company.

The relationship between transfer and inhibition should be clarified. The greater the similarity between two different tasks, the greater the transfer that can be expected, but also the greater the likelihood that inhibition will take place. The solution to this paradox lies in analyzing your objectives. If you intend to impart general understanding, such as the overall desirability of opening a new account with you, similarity and transfer of learning are appropriate. Alternatively, if you are communicating precise and specific information that the customer can clearly distinguish, you should avoid inhibition. Hence, you should minimize similarity and transfer when presenting the topic.

Participation

Learning is essentially an active process. The learning discussed under latent learning is *passive* learning. It is not as efficient as deliberate and intentional learning. When a person takes the initiative, active learning occurs. If the customer sits back and lets you expend all the effort, some learning might take place, but it is insignificant compared with what the person could accomplish by participating in the discussion. Hence, you should resist the temptation to give lectures. Instead, develop the technique of breaking the presentation into small sections and drawing the customer into the conversation through questions. With this technique, the customer will retain more information. First, in answering the questions, the learner verbalizes key thoughts enhancing ownership. Second, the procedure utilizes repetition and the law of frequency.

Learning Plateaus

Learning is not a smooth process. It usually takes place in spurts and then levels off. The leveling off or mere maintenance of the existing level is called a plateau. Figure 8.5 shows the type of curve that is frequently encountered in learning a skill such as word processing. At some point "a," the learner makes a significant effort and succeeds in increasing word processing ability. Learning levels off again, and at point "b," the learner repeats extra effort.

Customers experience plateaus. A plateau is a comfortable situation, and customers tend to maintain it. For example, a retailer might achieve the goals set for a promotional program and feel no further compulsion to expand sales.

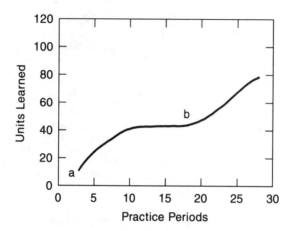

Figure 8.5 Learning plateaus. This curve shows the learning of a simple task. The subject made fairly rapid progress until the twelfth period. From then to the twentieth period, a plateau or slowdown in learning occurred. At the twentieth period, something caused the subject to try harder, and more learning took place.

Normally, to overcome the plateau, you will have to create both dissatisfaction with the present results and teach new skills and/or information that will result in higher performance. Once you recognize a plateau, you can think through how to persuade the retailer to commit to higher sales goals as well as to implementing the programs that will achieve higher sales volumes.

Motivation in Learning

As implied in the preceding paragraph, teaching requires more than presenting information. It must be organized and presented with both the principles and special effects of learning. In addition, the learner must be motivated to acquire the information. The following paragraphs discuss several factors bearing on this challenge (see Figure 8.6).

Knowledge of Results. If you want to motivate customers to learn, you should keep them informed. If a service program includes laboratory tests, the results should be reported back to the customer as soon as practical. The customer's interest in the matter and motivation to learn more about the issue will drop proportionately to the length of time required to get the answer.

Intention to Use the Information at a Later Date. As far as you are concerned, this is the strongest motivation you can offer customers for learning what you have to say. If customers can see that they will need the knowledge or that it will be helpful at a later date, they will attend to and participate in discussions with you.

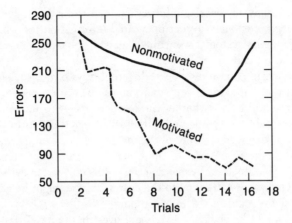

Figure 8.6 Motivation in learning. This graph represents the kind of learning that you can expect from two comparable subjects. One is motivated; the other has no particular motivation to learn. The dotted line shows the performance of the motivated subject; the solid line represents the nonmotivated subject. As the trials progressed, the number of errors decreased, particularly for the motivated subject.

Take the simple act of finding a telephone number in a directory. If you expect to use it one time, you will forget the number as soon as you have made the call. If you know that you will call the number many times in the future, you will file it or program it into your phone system.

Before going too far in your presentation, you should try to establish its degree of importance and what use the customer is going to make of it. The better you understand the potential use of your material, the more efficient your teaching will be.

When a product changes substantially or is discontinued, it triggers a change in buying habits. The customer whose present inventory is exhausted must make a decision and thus will be motivated to pay attention to your presentation because the information is now critical.

Likewise, a company planning to move or to build an additional plant will likely suspend various purchasing activities at some point. Nevertheless, buyers for the company will continue collecting information to use when full operations resume.

Evidence of Learning

Most sales jobs require more than one call to convert a prospect to a customer and then repeat visits or communication with customers. Thus, on the second and subsequent calls, one of the most important functions is to discover what information the customer has retained from previous calls. Three reasons exist for this.

First, you must supply any missing information to create a desire for the product or service. Second, customers resent being told information they already know. Third, if you know the customer's learning capacity, you can guide yourself more effectively on future calls.

Experts on learning have developed different ways of measuring the degree of learning, but these are largely for classroom use. However, one, *recognition* — information presented to see whether the learner can recognize or identify the material—is applicable in selling and is the safest way for you to test the customer's retention. You need a record of the major points covered previously or an unusually good memory yourself. In the opening stage of the second or subsequent interview, you can casually mention the points covered in earlier meetings. By paying extremely close attention to the customer, you might be able to detect whether he or she recognizes the information.

Some clues might be obvious—"We went over that before," or "I remember that." Such responses indicate good memory. If the responses are "Not so fast," or "I don't remember that," the degree of learning was poor and, for all practical purposes, you must repeat the points from the earlier interviews in their entirety.

Often the clues will not be as obvious as the spoken words illustrated here. You might, for example, encounter silence if the customer feels embarrassed at not remembering the content of the first interview. You must watch for more subtle signs, the *involuntary reactions* developed in earlier chapters. You might see signs of boredom if the customer recognizes material or a quizzical or startled expression if you imply the customer should have remembered the topics you are discussing. Your success depends on being very attentive and getting to know the customer as an individual so that you can better interpret buyer behavior.

2. LEARNING APPLIED TO SELLING

Using the preceding outline of learning principles as a foundation, you can now focus on applying the knowledge to selling. Keep in mind that in many cases you can expect to make several calls before obtaining an order; hence, you must envision learning as taking place over a series of calls as well as within a single call. You must also consider the differences between a call on one buyer and a presentation to two or more buyers in the prospect company.

Selecting a Basic Learning Pattern

The first step in presenting information to a customer is to decide which of the three basic ways of learning is most applicable, *association, trial and error,* or *insight.*

Several factors bear on this choice. The most important ones are knowledge possessed by the customer, learning capacity of the customer, difficulty of the material, and the skill of the salesperson.

Knowledge Possessed by the Customer

The larger the customer's fund of information, both general and specific to your proposition, the more appropriate association becomes as the basic teaching method. You can relate the new information to existing knowledge. A new chemical that is similar to one already in use can be explained to a chemist in terms of similarities and differences with respect to a product with which the chemist is familiar. To explain a chemical to a purchasing agent, new in the job and unschooled in chemistry, is an entirely different matter. The buyer has little knowledge on which to base association. Trial-and-error learning would seem more practical.

Learning Capacity of the Customer

Customers with a large capacity for learning will acquire knowledge readily by any of the three methods. The prime consideration in dealing with such people is to avoid talking down or boring them. With persons at the other end of the scale, the danger lies in going too fast for them to grasp the points.

Fast learners prefer to decipher things for themselves; hence, insight learning is best for this group. You can provide them independent bits of information until they see the relationship between the pieces—and *get insight*. This will enable them to feel they solved the problem for themselves, perhaps giving them some degree of ownership in the solution if it fits their needs. When they have many associations to build on, fewer bits of information are required. For example, if a bright retailer were given the expected markup and turnover rate of an item, computing the return would be a reflex action.

With slow learners, insight learning will not be successful. You should utilize all possible associations, then proceed on a trial-and-error basis. You can break the information into small bits and see that one is mastered before proceeding to the next. In this case, doing the calculations together is advantageous.

Difficulty of the Material

As the material becomes more difficult, insight learning becomes less likely. After using all possible associations, you should adopt rote learning or trial-and-error learning.

Before installing a local area network, a number of people in the prospect company have to acquire considerable knowledge so that many other system components can be modified. Most of the information needed is abstract and complex and might require considerable effort on the part of both the prospects and the salespeople. Unless someone at the prospect company has considerable experience with networks, the buyers will have little, if any, associations. Insight learning will be difficult because that also depends to a degree on a fund of background information. Trial and error is usually the best method for learning difficult new material.

Your Skill as a Salesperson

Insight learning requires the highest level of skill on the part of the salesperson, followed by *association* and *trial and error*. To use insight properly, you must have a grasp of the subject far superior to that of the customer. You must carefully select apparently isolated bits of information to convey to the customer in view of preceding events in the interview.

In the case of learning by association, you must discover the extent of the prospect's information so that you can build on that knowledge. This requires possession of information by you plus skill in determining the amount and accuracy of that held by the prospect. When you use the need satisfaction theory of selling effectively, the quantity and quality of the prospect's information is automatically determined.

If you are just starting to develop your teaching skills, trial-and-error learning is the simplest and hence most attractive method. All that you need is a simple presentation of information and enough feedback to determine when the prospect has retained it. It resembles the use of the selling-formula or stimulus-response theory of selling, except that those theories do not necessarily entail feedback. Without feedback, we would not dignify the process as one where the term *teaching* is warranted.

The One-Call Sale

When you expect a decision on a single call, you need to ensure that the prospect acquires enough information to desire placing an order. After learning the customer's needs—or assuming them where need satisfaction selling is not practical—you should decide on your key points. Ordinarily, you should consider no more than four; otherwise, it is better to make a series of calls.

The *laws of learning* are very important in this situation, especially *primacy*, *recency*, and *frequency*. The laws are applied by ranking the sales points in order of importance to the prospect. Assume three points. Presenting them in 1-2-3 rank order of importance fulfills the law of primacy. The 3-2-1 order acknowledges the law of recency. By making the order 1-2-3-2-1, you recognize both laws and, in addition, include the law of frequency. This approach would seem soundest. If the law of *effect* can be worked in by tying the points to some pleasant experience, all the better.

The questions of *whole-or-part* and *massed-or-spaced* learning have less application in a one-call sale. Little opportunity for spacing exists. If the material cannot be handled by the whole-to-part approach, more than one call is needed. You can implement the whole-to-part concept by giving a quick overview of the proposition, then proceeding to make the individual points. When you use need satisfaction selling, the need awareness phase is the proper place for presenting the whole picture.

Recitation, too, is relatively less important in a one-call sale because you are seeking an immediate decision. Recitation is most effective when you use it at intermediate steps of a multicall selling process to check learning points covered in the present call and again at the beginning of a call to review the points covered in earlier ones.

The only special effect that is pronounced in a one-call sale is *participation*. By drawing the prospect into the discussion, you receive feedback on your major sales points. In this way, you can determine when the prospect understands them and move to the next point. Participation has other important advantages for you. It functions as an informal type of recitation allowing you to gauge your effectiveness. It also increases the learning efficiency of prospects. Prospects are more convinced by what *they* say than by what you say. Unless the message is very brief and simple, and the prospect highly interested, you cannot afford to leave the prospect out of the discussion.

In a one-call sale, the best motivational procedure is to analyze the prospect's situation (need development) to ensure that you select sales points of genuine interest. When you have done this and have made an effective presentation, the prospect should be sufficiently motivated to ensure a favorable decision. Compliments on the buyer's ability to understand the proposition might also be in order.

As the goal of the interview is an immediate order, you do not need to test the level of learning other than to ensure that the prospect grasps the separate sales points as the interview progresses. Normal participation is adequate for this purpose.

The Multicall Sale

The multicall sale results from one or a combination of the following factors: the need to communicate a complex message, a large expenditure that calls for special budgeting, a final decision by a buying committee rather than an individual, a buying decision that affects present processes or more than one department of the company, and the need for information on which to base a proposal. The list could be extended, but you can see a number and variety of reasons why all sales cannot be made on a single call.

While one-way communication might be adequate for some one-call sales, this is improbable in multicall sales. Therefore, this section uses the need satisfaction approach throughout because the selling-formula and stimulus-response theories would not accomplish the desired results. Need satisfaction should be interpreted as a broad process that can take place over a series of calls as well as within a single call.

The Overall View

From an overall standpoint, you should consider the questions of spaced versus massed and whole versus part presentations early in the sale. If you are making a multicall sale, the first question is automatically answered in favor of spaced. You have no real need to be concerned with this concept within the individual call.

It is more difficult to decide the problem of whole versus part. If you are using whole-to-part learning, you might have to devote the major part of the first call to establishing the overall objective and describing how it can be accomplished. When you have outlined the overall problem, you can then consider the individual parts or points. Before discussing each part, you should place it in perspective to the whole.

If the problem is so complex that you select part-to-whole learning, you can consider the individual points as fast as time allows. The second and subsequent points can be related to the preceding ones. The possibility that the prospect will get insight at any time and supply the remainder of the missing points exists. If this happens, a close is in order. After the order is signed, you can briefly cover the omitted points to be sure that the customer understands all aspects of the proposition.

Arranging Sales Points

You can easily apply the laws of *primacy, frequency,* and *recency* in a series of calls. The first points discussed draw on the law of primacy. By repeating them at the end of the call, you can attain recency as well as frequency.

You must decide through questioning in the need development phase how many and which product features and customer benefits you must teach to ensure that the prospect has to desire to buy. This might take several calls, so the learning part of the sale, as far as the buyer is concerned, does not start until you have determined the sales points. After you have established the points, you can lay out a program for communicating them.

Suppose you need to cover five important points. Two points may be safely covered per call. This would demand a minimum of three calls. You could cover two points thoroughly on each of the first two calls. On the third call, you could present the fifth point and review the previous four points. Start each call with a review of previous calls and end calls with a review of all calls to date. On the last planned call, more thorough review is in order as it is the logical buildup to a close.

In planning such a series of calls, two considerations are practical rather than theoretical:

1. How should you rank sales points?
2. When should you use the most important point?

No precise spot can be pinpointed without knowing the number of points, the number of calls, the learning capacity of the prospects, and their personality. Your skill as a salesperson is also a consideration. In spite of these complexities, we can offer some guidance.

The most important sales point should *not* be presented first nor at the first of a series of calls. You need time to size up and adjust to the prospect. You need to gauge the prospect's learning capacity and interest in the proposition. If the prospect is logical and methodical, the most important sales point can be properly placed in terms of a smooth flow of information because the prospect will accept the pace you provide. If, on the other hand, the prospect is impulsive, a close could take place at any time. You should be alert to this possibility and retain enough flexibility to vary any predetermined order.

The most important point should not ordinarily be left until last because, if the close fails, any further discussion will be anticlimactic. Without having any specific situation in mind, the key point should be scheduled about 75 percent of the way through the overall presentation as planned. On this basis, you might make a close at this point. If not, the presentation can continue, and after a review of all the points, you can attempt another close.

When you anticipate making several calls on a prospect, the law of *effect* becomes important. Not only do pleasant experiences facilitate learning, but unless the contact with you is pleasant, the prospect will not wish to continue the association. This type of pleasantness is primarily a matter of you adjusting to the personality of the prospect. Following the methods for analyzing individuals covered earlier in Chapter Five and Appendix X, you must demonstrate enough flexibility in your own personality to make the adjustments necessary to communicate with the prospect. For example, if the prospect is inhibited and needs a long period to warm up to the point of discussing business, you should adjust to this quality and not create an unpleasant situation because you do not feel the need for a warm-up.

Positive Steps to Increase Learning

You can do several things to improve the quality of learning by the prospect. The more important ones are (1) gain participation and recitation if possible, (2) encourage overlearning, and (3) facilitate transfer of learning.

As we pointed out earlier, learning is basically an active process. This means that learning takes place very much in accordance with the learner's effort and participation. You have a great interest in the outcome of the sales presentation; hence, you must motivate the prospect to learn. You must encourage both participation and recitation. Your first goal should be to get the prospect to participate in the discussion. Use questions to get the prospect to contribute pertinent information to the conversation. Demonstrate to the prospect by questions that further information is needed, and try to get the prospect to ask for it rather than presenting information as one-way communication. If you have developed a solid relationship with the prospect, you might be able to get the prospect to feed back the information. This form of recitation not only achieves participation but also reveals the accuracy and completeness with which the prospect learned your sales points.

A multicall sale is similar to a continued story on a TV serial. The media use the "cliff-hanging" technique to sustain interest until the next installment. You do not need to be this dramatic, but it is wise to close an intermediate interview with some unfinished business that makes a logical opening for the next call. This approach uses the idea of providing immediate results, which we developed in Section 1 in the discussion of motivation. One of the best devices is to make a return call with the answer to a technical question that was raised in the previous call.

Another motivational strategy for causing the prospect to participate and hence to improve the quality of learning is to show that the topic of discussion is of value to the prospect regardless of the interview's outcome. Intention to use information increases the likelihood of learning and retaining it.

Encouraging Overlearning

Discovering on your second call that the prospect has retained very little information from the first call is discouraging. (The reason more salespeople do not experience this type of discouragement is that they do not bother to determine how much knowledge has been retained.) The way to reduce and possibly prevent this loss of memory is to use the principle of overlearning.

Even though the prospect appears to grasp the points as you make them, research and experience show that retention is unlikely. Most individuals are inefficient listeners. You can expect 50 percent of your presentation to be forgotten immediately, and a startling 75 percent after 48 hours. Alternatively, the prospect is likely to retain 25 percent of your presentation after two days. Hence, you should find a way to use, for review and repetition, up to 50 percent of the time that it initially took for the prospect to grasp the idea.

Although it will take considerable ingenuity to find alternate words and ways to go over the material that is apparently understood, it will pay great dividends in time saved on future calls.

Facilitating Transfer of Learning

A final step to maximize learning is to tie the new information to knowledge presently held by the prospect. This is transfer of learning and falls under the broad concept of associative learning. One of the basic principles of the need satisfaction theory of selling is that it is necessary not only to find out the prospect's needs but also the amount and kind of information the prospect possesses about the proposition. Whenever you discover related information, it can be helpful in presenting new information.

When you reach the need fulfillment or teaching phase of the presentation, you can refer to the prospect's present knowledge and existing experience and present the new information as an addition rather than as unfamiliar and abstract material. To actually do this in practice, you must have an in-depth understanding of the prospect's needs. To facilitate communication, you should use the prospect's own vocabulary to describe how your offering will satisfy his or her requirements. You should acquire this information in the need development phase of the interview.

Avoid Discouragement When No Progress Is Apparent

Even in the best-managed interviews, you will encounter times when it appears that you are making no progress. Some aspects of learning theory account for this; hence, you need not be concerned unless the apparent stalemate continues over several meetings. The phenomena that account for the apparent lack of learning are latent learning and learning plateaus.

Latent learning is learning that takes place without either the learner's or teacher's awareness. This is primarily because the learner sees no application in what is being learned and hence furnishes no feedback. Information that you feel is essential to a particular case may strike the prospect as being useless and meaningless. The prospect shows no interest and appears to have missed the point. Actually, the prospect could have acquired the information yet not realize it. The best procedure is to continue the presentation and, at a point where the previous points are pertinent, give the prospect an opportunity to demonstrate mastery of the material.

A good chance exists that the prospect will retain the essential information. If the prospect does not recall it readily, you can review that portion of the presentation. Two factors now work for you. First, the customer can now see the need for the information and can actively participate in the interview; and second, having gone over the information previously, can learn it much faster.

The preceding point is consistent with our earlier recommendations to the effect that learners are motivated by an intention to use the information being presented. You should constantly explain not only the sales points but also why the points are important to the overall presentation.

Learning plateaus are another reason that learning often seems to be at a standstill. Learning does not take place as a smooth progression but occurs in spurts separated by plateaus. The plateaus are discouraging both for the teacher and learner.

Awareness of the nature of plateaus should give you insight into the problem and the encouragement to keep going in the face of no apparent progress. If the prospect seems discouraged at not understanding the material, you might mention that as soon as you have presented all necessary information, the relationships will be clear. This is undoubtedly true, and when the learning takes place, there will be a new plateau at a higher level. You must then repeat the learning process.

You should keep in mind that lack of obvious learning progress is as embarrassing and distasteful to the prospect as to you. You should also remember that you have the responsibility for the outcome, and you must often work in the face of difficulty. "If the learner has not learned, the teacher has not taught." Constant reassurance and increased effort might be necessary to get past the apparent stumbling blocks.

The Pitfalls in Learning

While many factors can impede learning, most are beyond your control. Poor physical surroundings are an example. You often call on prospects who are hostile for a variety of reasons. The problem of time haunts all persons in business and can be a drawback to learning. You cannot be held responsible for all these factors, but you can control one impediment to learning. It, therefore, warrants further consideration.

Inhibition, both proactive and retroactive, is probably the biggest barrier to learning over which you have nearly complete control. Inhibition can occur not only within the sales presentation but also as a result of the activities preceding and following your interview.

The first inhibition you have to contend with is the proactive inhibition resulting from the prospect's activity preceding your call. The topics from the previous project or interview are still on the prospect's mind, reducing the ability to acquire the information that you present. The solution is quite simple. Ask the prospect to comment on the preceding activity. Then you can judge whether the prospect is still thinking about that topic or is ready for new business. A presentation can accomplish little when the prospect is actively thinking about another subject. If appropriate, try to help the prospect resolve the issue. If this is not feasible, try to make social conversation until the prospect is ready for a new topic.

If you plunge into a discussion of your proposition while the prospect is still considering another subject, you reduce the prospect's grasp of that subject through retroactive inhibition.

The same thing can happen to your presentation. If your interview is terminated while the prospect is actively considering the proposition, the next caller or activity can interrupt the thought processes and undo much of your work. The best defense is to prolong the interview to allow the prospect's mind time to consolidate the ideas without being inhibited by the next subject. If necessary, converse before leaving to reduce the retroactive inhibition of the next activity. Many such pauses are already built into many business activities. For example, if you pick a prospect up for lunch, use the driving time for chatting before the meeting and a similar period following. Depending on the timing, these breaks insulate various segments of conversation from each other.

In summary, efficient learning in the sales process requires insulating the sales presentation from past and future activities through the use of elapsed time and small talk. As inhibition can take place within the sales presentation, consider the proper conduct of the individual interview.

Normally, you need to make several major points in a presentation. Many ways exist for arranging their order, such as by importance, logical relationships, and so on; but for present purposes, the concern is with separating and insulating the points so retention of one does not inhibit or retard the retention of other points. Finish a sales point, give the prospect ample time to reflect on it, and ask questions before taking up the next point. It is better to cover a few points thoroughly and have the prospect retain them than to jam them together so that none of the points can be clearly and accurately recalled.

Presentations to Groups

Chapter Six covers the challenges of communicating successfully with groups. The emphasis here will be the application of learning principles to groups as contrasted with individuals.

The primary difference in presenting information to groups is the reduced opportunity to monitor feedback and hence to determine the effectiveness of the presentation. While feedback in the form of recitation is unlikely, opportunities may evolve for participation, depending on the size of the group and the formality of the occasion. You should encourage participation. It gives clues to each member's grasp of and attitude toward the topic under discussion. By carefully noting the attitude of other members of the group toward the person or persons entering into the discussion, you can gain additional insight into the effectiveness of the presentation.

The perennial advice, "Tell them what you are going to tell them, tell them, and then tell them what you told them," is sound in view of the law of frequency. This enables the speaker to repeat points without seeming to talk down to the group. You can observe the laws of primacy and recency by placing the more important points at the beginning and end of the presentation rather than in the center. The judicious use of humorous stories and a good-natured open manner with the group can create a pleasant feeling, an application of the law of effect.

With a large audience, direct participation might not be feasible. Alternatively, you can achieve simulated participation by frequent use of rhetorical questions, personal references, and interjections such as "as you know" or "as you are well aware." Another possibility is to have the audience seated in table groups of five to seven with a designated chairperson who is responsible for providing feedback. A third way of obtaining feedback is through a question-and-answer period following the address. If you use this method, preparing some "pump primer" questions and placing these with persons scattered through the audience might be helpful.

In small groups of two to seven people, you might want to pause after each point and have comments or questions from members. Careful planning of the presentation can ensure that you take into account several special effects of learning. Inhibition of learning is a major problem. Arrange for a pause between major points to minimize it. An informal discussion provides an opportunity to review the information and get it firmly in mind before going on to the next point.

These pauses with repetition of the basic ideas also recognize the principle of overlearning, but as no formal recitation to establish the exact point of learning is likely, overlearning must be assumed.

You can also take transfer of learning into consideration in planning the presentation. Grouping similar ideas facilitates this transfer.

Motivating the individual learner in a group is difficult. Praise of one person's efforts is useful up to a point, but with mature adults, praise in a group situation might prove embarrassing to everybody; hence, it could have an undesirable effect.

When one or more top executives are present in the group, other members might be motivated to make a favorable impression on the executives. In this case, you can ask for a comment from one of the lower ranking members of the group, and then ask one of the executives to comment on it. This can motivate the lower ranking members to pay careful attention, but it is hazardous for three reasons. It is a negative rather than a positive form of motivation and hence is dangerous in general. It also might embarrass someone. If hostility develops, this could lead to efforts to undermine your objectives. Another hazard is that the executives might not have the correct information and attitude as far as you are concerned.

3.   LEARNING CHANNELS

Most learning takes place through the visual and auditory sensory channels. The senses of touch, smell, and taste may have utility in presenting some products and services, but this section is limited to the two major senses—seeing and hearing.

The goal of this discussion is not to decide which sense is most important, but to analyze the unique characteristics of the senses so that you can attain maximum effectiveness when communicating ideas to buyers. The senses have greater impact when they reinforce each other. Therefore, discovering their proper sequence and combination of use is important.

To use the sensory channels to best advantage, you need to understand how they operate. Receptor cells in the eyes and ears transform incoming stimuli to nerve impulses that are carried to the appropriate part of the brain. The eye responds to light waves; the ear to sound waves.

Which sense is more effective depends on a variety of conditions such as (1) the format, length, and difficulty of the material to be presented; (2) the learning capacity of the receiver or learner; and (3) the sequence in which the material is presented (material can be presented simultaneously or sequentially).

Analysis of the Channels

Visual and auditory channels can be compared in terms of a variety of factors.

Sequence of Presentation

Using the auditory sense, you have complete control over the sequence in which you present information. The prospect can hear things only in the order in which you speak them. When the visual sense is used, you lose some control over the sequence because the prospect might not look at the particular point on which you are commenting. On a catalog sheet, the buyer might study the price while you are discussing the construction of the product or vice versa.

Speed of Presentation

In the auditory sense, your rate of speech limits the rate of presentation. By comparison, a chart, diagram, or table can show at a glance what might take several minutes to relate. This assumes the buyer has the capacity to understand or decode the visual presentation and will arrive at the conclusions you desire. Actually, as noted earlier, you give up control of the sequence in which information is received when you use the visual channel. In Chapter One, we used charts to visualize the differences between the three theories of selling (see Figures 1.8–1.10). Presenting the differences in words took much longer.

Resistance to Fatigue

Eyestrain is a common condition, but not ear strain. In practice, the length of time and amount of material that a person can absorb visually has a limit. The ear never experiences fatigue as a receptor organ. Exhaustion may occur at the brain level resulting from either seeing or hearing, but as far as the receptor cells are concerned, the auditory sense is less susceptible to fatigue. When you make presentations late in the day, you should take this into account.

Communication of Dimension

The auditory sense is temporal or sequential, and the visual sense is capable of discerning two dimensions on charts or graphs and three dimensions where actual models are used as visual aids. The product or service discussed will indicate the need for multidimensional representation. The depiction of dimension has been greatly facilitated by the computer's ability to accurately simulate everything from molecules to what the pilot sees out of the cockpit window.

Capacity for Achieving Repetition

When you make a statement that is not grasped by the prospect, you must repeat it. In oral conversation, unless you change the terminology, repetition will be boring to both parties. If you present a chart or diagram, however, and it is not understood, go over it again without changing it. Following the repetition when no changes occur is easier. Thus, while repetition can be achieved through hearing, it can ordinarily be achieved more easily and effectively through the visual sense.

Flexibility

While the preceding factor seems to favor the visual sense, you will often have the problem of adjusting a message for a prospect who has trouble grasping the information. More opportunity exists for variation and flexibility in presenting the message through the auditory channels. Perhaps only part of the message needs repetition. You can easily achieve this orally, while a chart or graph might lose its sense if you omit something.

Variety of Stimuli

In the visual sense, there is almost limitless opportunity for getting a point across. Pie charts, bar graphs, cartoons, photographs, computer simulations, or regular text are only a few of the possibilities. By contrast, the auditory sense is for all practical purposes limited to the voice.

Economy of Learning

In an oral presentation, the customer can select those points of greatest interest. In comparison, in a visual presentation, the customer might have to go through a lot of detailed information of little interest. The visual presentation is more in the nature of the formula approach to selling, while the auditory channel is closer to the need satisfaction method. This does not mean that an oral presentation cannot be canned, but by contrast, a visual presentation is difficult to rearrange if it is poorly organized. The inherent power of an oral presentation, or the need satisfaction approach, is that it is designed to give the customer the information of greatest utility.

Inability to Avoid Stimuli

The auditory channels are easier for the speaker to control. While prospects can close their eyes or turn their heads, they have no comparable way of avoiding an oral message. Undue dependence on visuals can be disastrous for this reason.

Closely related to the ability to avoid stimuli is the matter of sensory defect. You are quite likely to notice a defect in hearing, especially if you use the need satisfaction theory of selling. On the other hand, a prospect could have a pronounced uncorrected visual defect, unknown to you. An otherwise effective presentation could be rendered worthless if too much dependence is placed on visual acuity.

Inducing Emotion

The human voice has more capacity for arousing emotion than any other stimulus. The extended crying of a baby compared with reading about it or seeing it through a soundproof glass panel demonstrates the point. As a slight emotional tension facilitates learning, you can use your voice to good advantage.

Comparison of the Channels

The easiest way to compare the two sensory channels is to list the advantages and disadvantages of each. With such a comparison, you can analyze a sales presentation and determine the right combination of oral and visual stimuli.

Advantages of the Visual Sense

1. Several bits of information can be presented simultaneously if desirable. For example, you can project a picture of a product simultaneously with detailed drawings or enlargements of particular parts. Computers with

windows are illustrative. You can present several graphs in a series without removing the previous ones. If the visuals are quite simple and are presented one at a time, you achieve considerable control over the sequence.

2. You can show visuals a second time if necessary. This facilitates repetition and thus lessens the necessity of ensuring perfect understanding the first time you raise a subject. If the customer has difficulty grasping the point, you can say, "Let's leave this now and come back to it after we talk about _____."

3. You can transmit ideas in a greater variety of ways through the visual sense. Maps, charts, photographs, computer simulations, and computer graphics are a few of the useful ways of transmitting ideas. The oral sense is limited to your voice.

4. Visual material can be presented more rapidly because the auditory channel is limited to the rate a person can speak. Most persons can read faster than they can speak. Therefore, a visual in the form of a chart, graph, or map can supply much more information in far less time.

Disadvantages of the Visual Sense

1. When you present material simultaneously, you lose control over the order in which the customer attends to the various points. Furthermore, simultaneous presentation might breed confusion if you are discussing one point and the customer is attending to another.

2. Unless the prospect has a good reading vocabulary and has been trained in the use of charts, graphs, and so on, he or she can miss the point of the presentation unless you reinforce it orally.

3. A person studying a visual is more easily distracted than one engaged in conversation. In addition, you have no way of knowing how much attention the prospect is giving to the presentation unless you engage the person in conversation (in which case you are using the auditory sense).

4. Fatigue and/or sensory defects may cause the prospect to miss part of the presentation. As in the preceding point, oral questioning is necessary to determine the degree of attention.

5. As light waves travel only in straight lines and often depend on artificial illumination, your relative position to the prospect and the prospect to the visual are very important. If slides or some other projected visuals are planned, smooth walls or a screen as well as an electrical outlet are necessary but inconvenient. You might also find it difficult to darken a room to the degree necessary for good projection. Quite simply, many conference and/or meeting rooms are poorly designed for educational purposes.

Advantages of the Auditory Sense

1. You have complete control over the sequence in which the customer receives the components of the message. This provides for an orderly building of

knowledge and gives you more control over the final attitude of the customer. It also makes you aware when the prospect does not appear to understand a particular point. You can then make a decision whether to continue with the presentation or rephrase the point.

2. You have limitless possibilities for varying the message to adapt it to the needs of the customer. You can also modify, repeat, and review the message as necessary to get it across when the customer appears to be having difficulty understanding you.

3. You can more easily hold a customer's attention with an oral presentation than with a purely visual demonstration. The nature of the voice allows variation of the volume and pitch to avoid the monotony that can creep into a strictly visual presentation. Social convention also encourages buyers to attend to you because it is discourteous to ignore a person speaking directly to you.

4. The auditory sense is resistant to fatigue compared with the visual channels. The buyer can always hear your words.

5. You can generate more emotion with the human voice than through visuals. When it is necessary to disturb the homeostasis of a prospect or generate a slight emotional condition to facilitate learning, your voice is the best known device.

6. You have more flexibility in the choice of physical conditions surrounding the sales interview when you use auditory channels. By contrast, visual channels depend on controllable light and adequate room for positioning the visual stimuli.

Disadvantages of the Auditory Sense

1. Many messages are more effectively transmitted by simultaneous presentation of several elements. This is not possible through auditory channels.

2. Your speaking rate limits the rate of presentation. This is relatively slow compared with the study of diagrams or pictures. The minds of untrained listeners may wander.

3. The voice is the sole form for presenting the message. In the visual sense, an infinite number of devices ranging from models to drawings and charts of all kinds exists.

4. Referring back to a point made earlier in the presentation is more difficult. When you use visuals, you can repeat the stimulus; while an oral presentation requires recalling and repeating a relatively large portion of the presentation. A slight change in the oral repetition can be confusing to the prospect.

With the foregoing advantages and disadvantages for each sense, you can now draw some guidelines that will indicate the most appropriate channel for a given purpose. Assuming that both senses are used in all effective presentations, the intent here is to show the channel that should take precedence for a particular problem.

Factors Favoring Visual Channels

1. *Complex Material.* As the material becomes more complex, use of the visual channel is more justified. Visual presentation along with oral presentation introduces repetition or the law of frequency. Enlistment of both these senses demands more attention than an appeal to one alone. When two or three dimensions are involved, visuals have a great advantage over a simple oral presentation.
2. *Colors.* The capacity of a color presentation to outdo a verbal description of a color is unarguable.
3. *Time Limitations.* Material can be presented more quickly in printed form than in oral communication. Most persons can read a printed message faster than another person can speak it. Also, with visuals such as charts, you can present two or more ideas simultaneously. When time is of the essence, the visual channel is preferable.

Factors Favoring Auditory Channels

1. *Preferred Sequence.* When you feel that controlling the sequence of ideas presented to a prospect is important, an oral presentation is more effective. When you introduce visuals, the prospect might leaf through the presentation book while you try to focus attention on a particular page. Projected visuals also set up difficult situations with regard to controlling the attention span of the prospect. However, you can retain focus partially by using simple visuals containing core ideas that build one upon another.
2. *Hold Attention.* With an oral presentation, you can induce the prospect into participating in the discussion. This not only improves learning but also keeps the prospect's attention on the subject.
3. *Sensory Defects.* Prospects, like other people, are more apt to gloss over their sensory defects than to bare them and ask for help in compensating for them. With an oral presentation requiring the prospect's participation, you are almost certain to discover and overcome any communication problem caused by poor hearing and vision. In a visual presentation, you must depend on assumptions as to what the prospect has understood from the material displayed. Whenever accuracy is vital to a sales presentation, the auditory sense is preferable.
4. *Need to Generate Emotion.* The human voice is the best possible stimulus whenever you want to rouse a prospect from a state of homeostasis or generate enthusiasm for a proposition. The human voice is unquestionably a powerful tool for developing emotion in listeners.

With the preceding considerations in mind, you should be able to analyze your message and your prospect and to plan a presentation that utilizes the sensory channels in the proper sequence and with proper emphasis.

Visuals

The reason for the analysis and discussion of the auditory and visual sensory channels is to assist you in the proper use of visual, audiovisual, and computer technology that is available to you. Appendix XXVII provides a work sheet for the Analysis of Learning Channels.

A number of pitfalls can be encountered in using visuals and you should be aware of these before making final plans for your presentation. Perhaps the greatest problem is that *distraction* enters the sales interview if the prospect continues to show interest in a visual after you have finished your reference to it. To get the material out of the prospect's hands and to continue the presentation is sometimes difficult.

This raises another problem with visuals. The prospect might wish to keep the materials, yet you, for a variety of reasons, need them back. This can lead to a situation where you must risk offending the prospect by firmly requesting the return of the materials. In addition to eliminating the potential distraction, there are other reasons for wanting the visuals returned: (1) They might fall into the hands of competitors; (2) their value might be greater than can be charged off to goodwill; or (3) permanent possession might reduce the likelihood of a sale.

Visuals, most particularly computer-generated audiovisuals, are not foolproof. Many times they do not work properly, and the confusion in adjusting them detracts from rather than adds to the basic message. In addition to the intricacies of the systems, the problems of finding convenient electrical outlets and achieving the correct lighting effects are troublesome, to say the least.

A final seldom-recognized weakness is that more preparation and more competence are needed to use the visuals effectively. First, if the equipment fails, you must be prepared to give a credible presentation. The second point is that a visual can raise as many questions as it answers; hence, you must know the background of the chart or visual and anticipate all the questions, objections, and ramifications it might engender. If a graph suggests to the prospect a question you cannot answer, it can hinder rather than advance your presentation. Third, you must arrange the visuals in foolproof order. You should, for example, be able to reach into your briefcase and withdraw a piece of material without taking your eyes from the prospect or interrupting your oral presentation in any way. If the materials are in a binder, you should be able to find the proper page with no delay.

With these cautions in mind, principles for proper use of visuals can be established.

Visuals should be developed only for situations where words cannot adequately express the point in question, where more than one dimension must be portrayed, or where complex relationships need to be explored. A simple statistic such as the percentage increase in sales or profits does not usually require a chart. If you want to relate profits of a particular company to profits in an industry or a variety of other measures, a chart is almost mandatory.

Simplicity is another virtue in selling aids. Any complicated device is apt to get out of adjustment and/or fail completely. As the devices become more complex, their effectiveness depends on your knowledge and skill. Their failure will reflect on the product or service being offered when in reality your ability is the problem. As noted, you should have a complete backup presentation to use in the event of equipment failure.

To the extent it is feasible, you should limit visuals to a single point or topic. This helps to avoid interference with the sequence you wish to follow in building your presentation. Also, you can easily remove a visual or cover it with another when it is limited in application.

4.   REMEMBERING AND FORGETTING

As soon as the learning process stops, the forgetting process sets in. Material that is not forgotten is "remembered"; hence, memory is the difference between learning and forgetting. One way to increase what is remembered is to learn more thoroughly; another approach is to slow down the forgetting process.

Forgetting

With the exception of the phenomenon of reminiscence, forgetting starts as soon as learning stops. Forgetting takes place very rapidly at first, then slows down. The typical forgetting curve is shown in Figure 8.7.

The concept of reminiscence is that, in many instances, more material is available from memory a short period after the learning process has stopped than at the actual end of the learning session. Factors that contribute to reminiscence are meaningfulness of the material, effort expended in trying to recall, and rapidity

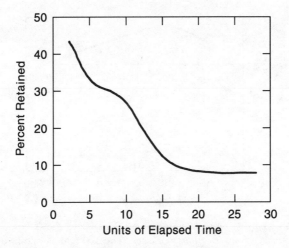

Figure 8.7   Forgetting. Note the resemblance of this curve to the typical learning curve of Figure 8.2. This graph shows that as units of time pass, less material can be recalled.

with which material was learned. The first two items are readily understandable. The third, rapidity of learning, indicates that when material is learned rapidly, more reminiscence will be present than when material is learned slowly and over a long period of time. In cases of slow learning, reminiscence will be noticeable after a few months rather than after a few days or a few hours. This situation of delayed reminiscence is of less practical value because your interest is in either inducing a buying decision as part of the interview or having the prospect possess maximum information when making the buying decision, usually soon after your visit. The longer the time to the buying decision, the more leisurely your presentation should be. If several months are to elapse, several calls should be made at intervals (Figure 8.8 depicts the forgetting curve when reminiscence is involved).

Forgetting can take place either actively or passively. With the exception of reminiscence, as time elapses loss of memory will occur, as suggested in Figure 8.7. This is a passive process. When inhibition (either proactive or retroactive) takes place, forgetting becomes an active process, as has been explained in previous sections.

Some of the other factors that affect learning and hence forgetting have also been covered in earlier sections. They are *associations with material already learned* and *pleasantness of the learning experience.*

Another factor affecting forgetting is whether recall is attempted in the same surroundings in which learning took place. Other things being equal, a person will retain more when attempting recall in the environment in which learning occurred.

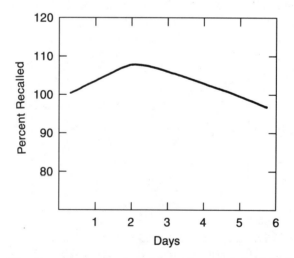

Figure 8.8 Forgetting and reminiscence. This curve shows how someone typically learns a prose or poetry passage. The 100% at the point of origin of the curve represents the learning at that point after several trials. *It does not mean a perfect recitation.* The curve shows that the rate of retention improved for two days; after that, forgetting set in.

Whether the material is used or not also affects forgetting. When ideas are used or referred to often, forgetting will not take place as easily as if they are completely dormant. This is why phoning, faxing, using E-mail, or writing a prospect who is considering a proposal is good tactics. Even if you do not review the entire proposal or add new material, the contact will prolong the retention of the material. If a review of the proposal can be included, so much the better.

Once a prospect makes a decision to buy or not to buy, the detailed bases for the action tend to be forgotten with the press of other activities. Of course, if a purchase has been made, the product or service itself might be a reminder. In contrast, if the decision was not to buy, the prospect is unlikely to remember much about the proposition. In the latter situation, you might have to be more careful and courteous than on a first call because you may have to overcome inertia or resistance if the prospect feels uncomfortable, realizing how much he or she has forgotten.

In our discussions of pleasantness of the law of effect we have implied that pleasant material is learned more easily. Not only is this true, but unpleasant material, in addition to being more difficult to learn, is more quickly forgotten. One of the psychological defense mechanisms similar to projection and rationalization is *suppression*. This mechanism allows a person to ignore unpleasant facts. It is a means of actively forcing information out of the conscious or thinking mind. When a customer acts as though you never presented the information, you may have a case of suppression. When you encounter such a situation, avoid saying "we went over that," and start over as though the material were brand-new. If the prospect later admits that the information is familiar, you can quickly make a suitable adjustment.

Closely allied to suppression is the prospect's modification or change of the information you provide. Material might not be unpleasant enough to forget completely, but might be changed to agree with the prospect's prejudices or to fit strongly felt needs. If the change does not reduce the likelihood of a sale, it is of no real importance to you. However, if it takes the form of rationalization that would mean loss of a sale, you must deal with it. Briefly, you must discover the value to the prospect in distorting the information and present the information in a new light so that the distortion can still be applied but will result in a favorable decision. (For a more detailed treatment of handling objections, refer to Chapter Four, Section 2.)

The following case of an insurance call is an example of changing the salesperson's meaning. Assume you have shown a prospect how he can create a sizable estate for his wife and for his children's education. You included various ways of achieving the objective, together with the premiums involved. After serious thought, the prospect decided he did not wish to provide as large an estate as you had recommended. Instead of telling you he wished to reduce the size of the estate, the prospect assumed you gave him an all-or-nothing proposition, and he now says he cannot afford it. He has distorted the information you presented.

Trying logical reasoning will be of no use. Only if you discover the prospect's true feelings, will you be able to suggest a suitable type and amount of protection.

Relearning

Even though you make what you consider to be an effective presentation, there are three instances in which you might need to renew your efforts to achieve a sale. First is the situation where, through inhibition (active) or disuse (passive), the prospect no longer retains enough information to desire the product or service. Second, the prospect has distorted your message to fit personal needs and prejudices, your assumption being that these result in no sale (otherwise the prejudices would not be of interest). The third consideration involves suppression. The prospect has deliberately forced the message out of consciousness. Therefore, the message is not a factor in the prospect's thinking.

One other area exists in which to use relearning. The prospect is currently dealing with a competitive supplier. The prospect has "learned" to buy from that source and must be "taught" the advantages of dealing with a new supplier. This is an example of habit change or relearning.

Inhibition or Disuse

This is the simplest of the relearning situations. You become aware that the prospect has forgotten a significant part of the previous interview and proceed to use questioning to pinpoint the weak areas. You then supply key points until the prospect has reached the original degree of knowledge. The presentation can then proceed as though nothing has happened.

This approach assumes that the prospect is interested in pursuing the proposal and cooperates in reviewing the previous discussion.

Distorted Memory

As soon as you recognize that the opinions held by the prospect are at variance with those you tried to develop on previous calls, you must proceed very cautiously. Possibly an innocent misinterpretation has occurred. If so, the prospect's opinion will change as you supply the correct information. Also, in some instances the prospect distorts the information to make a buying decision easier. This situation presents no problem.

It is more likely, however, that the prospect will cling to the distorted view. Trying to correct the information on a logical or straightforward basis is pointless. This is emotional resistance that must be handled in accordance with the principles presented in the section on handling objections. Basically, you must discover the psychological value the distorted view has for the prospect. When you discover this, you will know what you must do to correct the situation.

Suppose you are a chemical salesperson and you are calling on the purchasing agent of a prospect company. On the first call, the purchasing agent examines the specifications, and while they are not identical to the product currently in use, you succeed in demonstrating that your product would work satisfactorily. Furthermore, you are in a position to reduce the cost of the finished product. You leave with a promise that the purchasing agent will talk with the chemists about approving your product. On the return visit, the buyer takes the position that your product does not meet specifications and that further discussion is pointless. Resorting to logical argument at this point would only antagonize the prospect.

On the other hand, if you appear to back down and take the position that you are sorry that you cannot do business because it would have been mutually beneficial, the purchasing agent might confide that if the chemists were not so bullheaded, everything would be in order.

Now you can take the side of the purchasing agent and ask for a replay of the conversation with the chemists. You might quickly discover that the purchasing agent did not have a sufficient grasp of the subject to answer the objections they raised. In the second discussion with you, the purchasing agent distorted the message to save face and avoid revealing ignorance. The purchasing agent did not understand the proposition well enough to present it to a third party.

You have now discovered the psychological value of the distortion to the buyer and have a choice of two courses of action. You can attempt to educate the purchasing agent to make an adequate presentation to the chemists, or you can request permission to call on the chemists either alone or in the company of the buyer. Your relationship with the buyer, considering such things as ego, the capacity to understand the product, and the relationship of the chemists and the buyer, will determine your next step.

Suppression

You may be shocked to call the second time on a prospect and find the person acting as though no significant discussion had taken place on the first call. Psychologically, this is similar to the distortion of a message, but to a more extreme degree.

In the example in the preceding section, the salesperson discovered that the purchasing agent had made a presentation to the chemists but failed because of not mastering the necessary information. The recollection of the facts was distorted to protect the purchasing agent's ego. The purchasing agent then tried to blame the chemists for the situation.

Assume that the purchasing agent had not made any presentation to the chemists, even though you had agreed to it in the first sales interview. On the second call, the buyer is embarrassed and, finding this an unpleasant situation, decides to save face by denying that the product was to be discussed with the chemists.

This is readily understandable. What is perhaps more difficult to understand is that the purchasing agent could do this and actually forget about it. This is suppression in the psychological meaning of the term.

You cannot expect to deal with such a person with any real hope of success. If you can recognize this type of adjustment in prospects and avoid expending large amounts of time on a relatively hopeless cause, you will have made a great leap forward.

However, as sales managers might not be sympathetic to a call report that lists "suppression" as a reason for not getting an order, you must ordinarily make several calls before abandoning the prospect. Until you recognize the situation as suppression, you will treat it as a simple case of forgetting, as outlined in the preceding discussion of inhibition or disuse. When you discover no likelihood of the prospect cooperating in recalling the previous discussion, you must search for the psychological value the suppression has for the buyer, as was outlined in the preceding section. The only real difference is that few clues will guide you, hence the process will take longer.

In a true case of suppression, no likelihood of making a profit on the sale exists. With the time and effort required to understand and persuade such a customer, you could very likely have closed several other sales. You must be alert to avoiding ego involvement with a prospect who proves unprofitable for you and your company.

Changing Habits

Even though William James said, "Habit is thus the enormous fly wheel of society, its most precious conservative agent," there may be times when you wish to change the habits of a buyer.

The buying pattern of a customer can be viewed as a habit that will continue until something occurs to change the pattern. This behavior was earlier described as a circle response. When you get credit for the business, you see it as a desirable habit. Competitive salespeople see it as a habit that they would like to change.

The best way to change a habit is to call more often and present a clearer picture of your proposal's benefits than competitors communicate about theirs.

Improving Memory

Improving memory is no mystery. The principles of learning are well disseminated throughout the educational system. Most instructors give good advice on how to study, which results in effective learning and hence good memory. Books on "how to read" or "how to study" are helpful for schoolwork, but not everything in such books is applicable to salespeople.

In addition to general principles of learning, you can use some specific techniques usually referred to as mnemonic devices. Webster defines mnemonics as the "art of improving the efficiency of memory." The inclusion of the word *efficiency* indicates that the objective is to increase the retention of material in relation to the time and effort expended in learning.

The ideas presented in this book are written so that you can use them to improve the efficiency of the prospect's memory, hence the efficiency of your own selling. You will recognize that the ideas are equally helpful for improving your own memory.

General Ways of Improving Memory

Aside from basic intelligence, the most important ingredient of a good memory is *interest*. A brief discussion with someone interested in baseball or horse racing will frequently reveal prodigious memory feats revealed in the statistics of the sport. The main reason such people are able to retain the large amount of data is that they are interested in it.

To be successful in getting prospects to retain your sales message, you should generate interest in the discussion. Interest results in knowledge. A person who knows nothing about baseball is unlikely to be successful in memorizing league standings or batting averages. If the person learns the rules of the game and understands the statistics, the increased knowledge might kindle interest. No one can guarantee that interest will follow knowledge, but certainly without knowledge, no real interest can exist.

Your first task then is to supply information and knowledge. As the prospect absorbs the information, interest can develop. When this occurs, he or she will probably request more information. When you reach this stage of interest, you need not fear the loss of memory.

You may have fallen into the trap of supplying information to customers without stimulating interest. Think about it! You supplied information in which you were interested rather than information of interest and value to the customer. The mechanism of projection involves assuming needs rather than developing them as part of the sales interview.

When the prospect is a logical user of your product or service, you should be able to discover needs and opinions, then proceed to provide information that will enable the buyer to generate interest in the proposal.

Understanding is another important factor in memory. Material that is not understood is seldom retained. On the contrary, failure to understand leaves an unpleasant feeling that discourages learning and contradicts the law of effect. While the failure to understand might be due to low learning capacity, the prospect is more likely to see it as a weakness of the salesperson. If this happens, the prospect will not look forward to another interview and might actively avoid it. In addition, if the interview does take place, the prospect's message can be distorted or suppressed.

When you sense that the prospect does not understand the proposal, you should do one of several things. You can try harder to present the message so that it can be understood (review Chapter Two). You can seek out another person in the prospect company to consider the proposal, or you can decide to abandon the attempt. If the prospect cannot understand your message, a satisfactory sale is not likely.

A common weakness in memorizing and retaining information is that the person undertakes too great a task, which results in a fuzzy rather than a clear image of the message. This can be illustrated by comparing the mind with a fine camera. The camera must be focused. You can focus it on nearly anything within its range, but as you focus it on one object, other objects may become

blurred. The same goes with the mind. To be effective in retaining information, it should be focused clearly.

You should not be content with giving the prospect an overall view of your
proposition. You should select the key points (needs you have developed) and
focus on them. You should look at these points from several angles until they are
finally fixed in the mind of the prospect. *Selection* and *concentration* are important factors in good retention.

One other principle of good memory is *ego-involvement.* Many times you
see a sale as a personal challenge rather than a company objective. In such a
situation, not only do you work harder to accomplish your objective, but you
also retain a clear picture of all that has taken place in the interviews with the
prospect.

The same idea can work with prospects. If you can present your proposition
as a challenge, you not only will have the prospect working with you, but you can
also be sure he or she will remember all necessary information. Some possible
areas of ego-involvement are ability to understand the product or service, authority to make the purchase, authority to change company procedures to utilize a
new product or service, and authority to change or deviate from specifications.

SUMMARY

You have a dual stake in knowing how people learn—for your own use and for
influencing customers and prospects. Three basic ways of learning exist: by association, by trial and error, and by insight. Fundamental learning principles are
effect, primacy, recency, and frequency. Additional guides to learning include
spaced versus massed, whole versus part, and recitation. Special effects in
learning include latent learning, overlearning, inhibition, transfer, participation,
and plateaus. Motivation in learning and evidence were also noted.

The principles of learning were applied to selling. As a first task, the salesperson must decide which of the three basic ways of learning is more applicable in
each situation. "One-call" versus "multicall" sales were analyzed in terms of applicable learning strategies. Finally, presentations to groups were discussed, especially the prime importance of participation.

The senses of hearing and seeing were analyzed and compared in terms of
conveying information in sales presentations. Suggestions for developing and using visuals followed the analysis of the two senses.

Memory is the difference between learning and forgetting. If salespeople
learn (1) the nature of forgetting and (2) ways to improve memory, they can be
more effective. Specific suggestions were made for coping with forgetting and
for improving memory. Applications were made to influencing customers and
prospects.

*The effective salesperson is able to convey ideas to others in a form and
manner that ensures learning and retention.*

TOPICS FOR THOUGHT AND DISCUSSION

1. Recall entering your current job and identify what you learned by each of the three basic ways of learning—association, trial and error, and insight.
2. Review typical sales presentations you make and note the use or absence of the laws of learning—effect, primacy, recency, and frequency.
3. How might you improve your presentations?
4. What have you overlearned that is part of your basic sales presentation? What should you overlearn? How would overlearning affect your presentation?
5. What can you do on second calls to test the retention of ideas you presented in the first call?
6. Try to recall a situation where you misjudged the learning capacity of the buyer. Was your error one of overestimating? Underestimating? How did you adjust? What have you learned from the text that would help you adjust in the future?
7. What have you learned from the text that would improve your skill as a salesperson?
8. In terms of learning principles, how does a one-call sale differ from a multicall sale?
9. In terms of learning principles, how would a presentation to a group differ from a presentation to an individual?
10. What is the significance to you of the fact that light waves travel only in straight lines while sound waves travel in any direction?
11. What is the importance of controlling the sequence in which you present ideas to a buyer?
12. In your particular sales position, what is the relative importance of auditory and visual channels? Compare this with other sales positions with which you are familiar.
13. Considering the content of Section 3, design the ideal visuals for your job. (Appendix XXVII will be helpful.)
14. What action might you take to utilize the concept of reminiscence with your customers and prospects?
15. Distinguish between "active" and "passive" forgetting. How could you cause a buyer to "forget" a presentation made by a competitive salesperson?
16. How might you use social imitation and reconditioning to change habits in your customers and prospects?
17. Devise some mnemonic devices to improve your customers' retention of your name or your company name.

NINE

The Seller as a Self-Manager

Most powerful is he who has himself in his own power.

SENECA

In this chapter:

- **Your Selling System**
  - With a managerial outlook, you view each customer as a business asset to be appreciated over time. You also see each prospect as an asset to be acquired.
  - Many competent, dedicated professionals fall victim to the Activity Trap.
  - An example of how salespeople are using micro-computers appeared in *Marketing News* titled, "Marketer uses his computer to become a sales champion."
- **Implementing the Planning Process**
  - As part of your strategic planning process, goal setting is critical.
  - Effective objective setting must be based on current and contemplated reality.
  - The essence of improving is action that adjusts the operation of your selling system to match your objectives.
- **Self-Management**
  - You must assume the major responsibility for your own welfare and conduct.
- **Summary**
  - The most critical managerial assignment in the company is yours— running your area of responsibility at maximum efficiency.
- **Topics for Thought and Discussion**
- **Application Exercises**
  - Appendix II   Salesperson-Oriented Product Manual
  - Appendix XXV   Call Checklist and Presentation Checklist
  - Appendix XXVI   Guide for Observing Sales Performance
  - Appendix XXVIII Work Sheets for Setting Objectives
  - Appendix XXIX   Account Improvement Planning Guide
  - Appendix XXX   Factors for Defining Selling Jobs

1. YOUR SELLING SYSTEM

Every salesperson's managerial assignment is to profitably operate a territory or area of responsibility. This assignment is, in effect, an "operating subsidiary" of a larger business unit called a district or branch, which, in turn, is a subsidiary of a still larger business unit—a division or region. Finally, the latter is an "operating subsidiary" of the total marketing effort of the firm. Figure 9.1 illustrates these relationships.

The salesperson's company can achieve its goals only when each of the smaller units is effectively managed. In a real sense, then, the most critical managerial assignment in the company is that of salespeople—running their territories or areas of responsibility at maximum efficiency.

Selling: The Critical Managerial Assignment

Why is the salesperson's managerial assignment the most important in the company? First, he or she is responsible for nurturing the company's most critical asset, the customer base. The effective salesperson manages selling-buying relationships for mutual benefit. Profiteering in the short run will undercut the value of the customer base and limit its appreciation potential. On the other hand, undirected investment in customers and prospects, or market share, makes little sense. The salesperson plays a key management role in balancing the allocation of resources between short- and long-term marketing objectives.

Second, the salesperson plays a central role where resellers or intermediaries are part of the marketing channel. The salesperson is captain of the selling team when it includes other representatives of his or her company. If you achieve a high degree of interfunctional coordination and each member of your

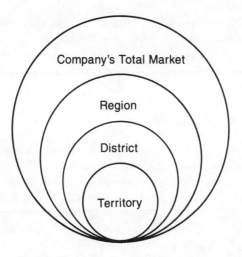

Figure 9.1 The territory as a business.

team can communicate the relevant parts of your program to the reseller, you become a powerful agent for increasing reseller sales.

In many respects, your role is similar to that of an outside consultant. If the reseller is more effective, then you have an opportunity to sell more products or services. The economics of vendors and resellers are typically dissimilar: Consider the differences between paper mills and paper houses or industrial equipment manufacturers and machinery dealers. The vendor who does not determine what the reseller needs to capitalize on market opportunities or improve performance will have little likelihood of increasing sales.

Third, the salesperson's responsibility is to continuously match products and services to markets. Few if any products or services occupy an unassailable market niche in today's highly competitive environment. Therefore, you have an ongoing challenge to create an offering that is different and better. In this role, you frequently make decisions under tight time constraints. No one else in the organization operates for extended periods in this environment. The achievement of the firm's objectives depends on your continuously differentiating your offering in the eyes of prospects and buyers. The challenge to create a competitive edge is particularly acute in high technology and global markets. To maintain effectiveness, you must overlearn your product or service to ensure that you have appropriate information available on demand in the sales encounter.

Fourth, if the selling effort fails, every other function of the firm is in jeopardy. The firm depends on effective selling for its livelihood. A salesperson typically generates revenue to support between 15 and 20 employees in the other areas of the firm.

Fifth, selling is a critical source of future management talent. Marketing is a significant source of corporate leadership because salespeople learn the fundamentals of creating and servicing a customer base. Once you understand the fundamentals of the sales transaction, you have mastered one of the most critical elements in business.

Firms need high-level performance in their other major functional areas to be successful, but the salesperson's managerial assignment is central in achieving corporate purposes. The importance of the salesperson can be summed up in a statement by a major corporation: "We don't train salespeople; we train future chairs of the board."

What Do You Manage?

Much of your success depends on your competence as a manager. Consequently, you must know as much as possible about the process itself. When asked what they do, most salespeople typically discuss their customers, their prestigious accounts, their competitors, their markets, products or services, as well as many other facets of the selling process. Each of these is important, but a more powerful perspective considers the whole and how the elements that make it up relate to one another. You are the manager of a selling system. This approach not only includes the elements listed earlier, and their interrelationships, but also provides a framework for assessing your managerial effectiveness. The systems approach is one of the most important ideas developed in the last century. The systems approach:

- Allows you to focus quickly on your greatest opportunities.
- Deals with all the elements of the sales process in an integrated whole.
- Requires you to keep your objectives, outputs, activities, inputs, and feedbacks in mind.
- Is a powerful tool for improving sales performance.

Figure 9.2 depicts the major components of the system.

Every sales assignment has two cardinal managerial *objectives*. The first is to have your offering perceived as different and better than others available from your competition. The second is to link customers to your firm in a sustained, mutually profitable relationship. Your selling effort should be allocated to prospects and customers with the greatest potential for recognizing the value added in your offering. These managerial objectives have important implications for you in the daily conduct of your business.

With a managerial outlook, you view each customer as a business asset to be appreciated over time. You also see each prospect as an asset to be acquired. For each account, current and potential, you set specific objectives for value added, profit, margin, growth, share of business, and service level. Your managerial responsibility is to conduct the business to achieve your cardinal objectives.

Your objectives are results desired; *outputs* are the results achieved. Output is what actually results from the combination of activity and input in a given situation. The output may or may not be consistent with your expectations, objectives, and plans. If the mix of results achieved has greater value in the marketplace than the cost of all the inputs and activities employed, selling has

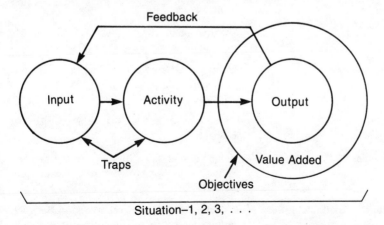

Figure 9.2 The systems approach. (Adapted from materials devised by George S. Odiorne and reproduced with his permission.)

created profitable differential competitive advantage. Conversely, if the customer places value on the output that is less than direct or indirect cost, you have made unprofitable sales and your company loses money on those transactions.

In selling, outputs are multidimensional, consisting of a mix of profitable and unprofitable sales as well as nonsales. Additional results are reflected in such categories as the mix of current and past-due receivables.

Activity is what you do to transform inputs into outputs that your customers and prospects will perceive as valuable.

You should create a master plan for each account based on your knowledge of the actual and potential business available as well as the extent and kind of competition. You should also consider the key decision makers as well as the benefits and uses that customers can derive from your offerings.

In addition to market potential and competitive conditions, selling results depend on your skill in performing a number of important roles. An old saying suggests, "You are only as good as your situation." The relative importance of each role varies both between individual customers and over time. To be effective, you must be proficient as a manager, tactician, problem solver, creative thinker, transactor, follow-upper, and monitor of market intelligence. Table 9.1 provides examples of performance in each of these roles.

The primary *inputs* managed are time, money, talent, and information. Inputs are either used up, or they facilitate system performance. For example, the

Table 9.1   Roles Frequently Performed by the Salesperson

Selling Roles	Illustrative Examples of Role Performance
Manager	Objective setting; planning/programming; execution, evaluation, improvement
Tactician	Adjusting to customer's changes in mode of doing business; taking remedial action as delays in delivery occur
Problem solver	Enlisting aid of R&D in solving a difficult application problem involving one of the firm's products
Creative thinker	Assisting resellers in improving the effectiveness of their marketing programs; suggesting improvements in company literature
Transactor	Consummating a sale; suggesting a financing plan leading to a sale
Follow-upper	Making a joint call with field service at start-up of equipment; assisting resellers with display of company products
Monitor of market intelligence	Reporting competitive activity; estimating each competitor's market share; obtaining customer's reactions to advertising

time you commit to selling is consumed and, if properly employed, will become manifest in customer satisfaction, sales, requests for proposals, a high income, or other desired results.

Effective *time* management is critically important in maximizing your contact with customers and prospects. Time is your prime input. The first step in managing time is to run a time log to determine where you are actually spending your time. The next step is to review how you would like to allocate your time to improve your productivity. At the heart of any time management analysis is a series of questions related to the cells in Figure 9.3:

- What is most important?
- What is least important?
- What is most urgent?
- What is least urgent?

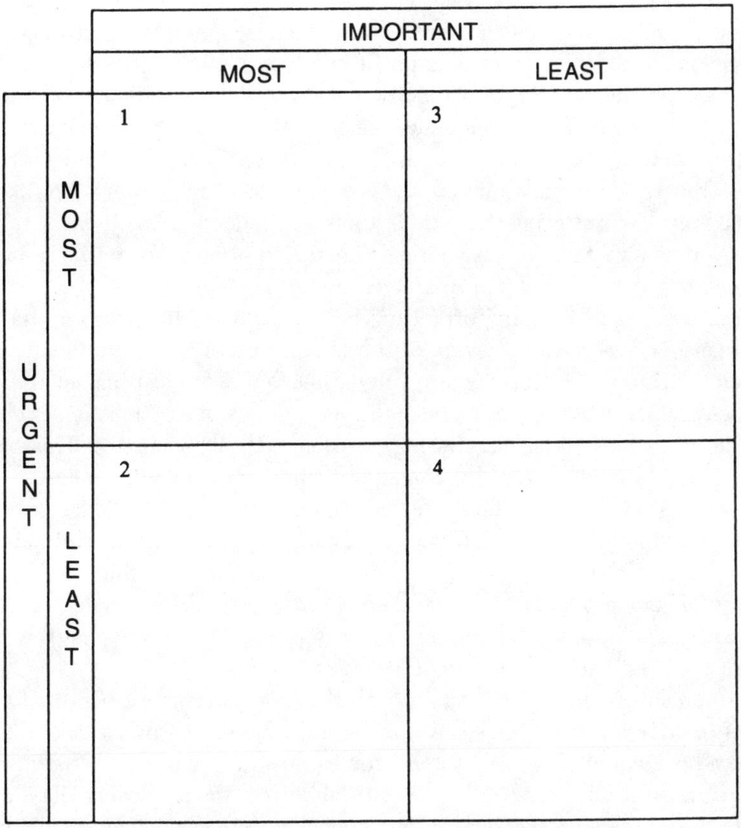

| | IMPORTANT | |
	MOST	LEAST
MOST (URGENT)	1	3
LEAST (URGENT)	2	4

Figure 9.3 Basic time management.

Clearly, you should do first what is both most important and urgent (Cell 1). What should you do second? Upon reflection, the most important and least urgent (Cell 2). The most urgent and least important (Cell 3) should not be done at all, nor should you allot any time to the least important and least urgent (Cell 4).

Once you have analyzed where you are investing your time as well as where you would like to invest it, you have the basis for improving your productivity.

Money is required to make most selling systems productive. If you total your company's inventories and receivables and divide by the number of persons in the selling positions, you have just calculated what the cost would be for you to "buy" your job. Because most selling positions are supported by working capital, usually ranging from $50,000 to $300,000 per position, understanding how you impact your company's profitability is critical to your long-term success.

The easiest sale in business is where the prospect takes your products or services and has no intention of paying. If you sell to persons who pay within terms, you conserve working capital that can be invested in more inventory or new lines. If your nominations for new products or services are carefully thought out and have justified market potential, your firm will invest fewer dollars in slow-moving or low-profit programs.

You should understand the three basic financial statements: profit and loss, balance sheet, and cash flow. The profit and loss is a historical document that captures operating results for a specific period of time, usually one month, one quarter, or one year. The balance sheet reflects the condition of the business at a particular date in time; and the cash flow statement is the "window on the future," forecasting probable market and corporate events together with the likely financial results. Mastering these three tools and understanding them in the context of your company as well as your customers will provide you with the insights you need to create mutually profitable relationships.

Your own *talent* is an important ingredient in your selling system. As a systems manager, you must be aware of the dimensions of your own talent so that you can allocate your efforts where you will have the greatest impact. You must also look at your talent in a dynamic light. As your customers' businesses change, their methods for making purchasing decisions will likely change. This process is being accelerated by rapidly changing technology, globalization, and many other factors. Hence, you should seriously consider what knowledge and skills you require to be successful tomorrow as well as today. At a minimum, you should evaluate your competence in five general categories: selling skills, understanding of your products or services, competitive knowledge, understanding of the market, and administrative knowledge. Your personal development is so important that Section 3 of this chapter covers it in depth.

No employer can supply you with all the *information* you need to be successful in your profession. Because having information is so critical, you must design a personal intelligence system. You can begin by asking, "What information do I need to succeed?" "What is available from my employer?" The difference between the answers to these two questions defines what you must obtain. You can develop much of the information on the job: buyers' needs, "who's who" and "what's what" in buyer and prospect accounts, as well as an understanding of your own firm's products, services, and capacity to respond to clients. Information about your markets, competition, and technology may be available from management, colleagues, or the marketing plan. Alternatively, you may have to develop your own market intelligence from various data bases as well as from your personal participation in the market.

You must build a network of relationships throughout your own organization, inside customer and prospect accounts, and with a wide spectrum of other participants in your industry. To have the information you need when you need it requires connections, like tentacles, reaching people who really know. Successful salespeople build hundreds of connections that enable them to achieve their objectives. Establishing reliable relationships with a diverse set of people is a significant task that never ends because change requires continuous development of new relationships.

The *feedback* loop at the top of Figure 9.2 indicates the return flow of information about the performance of your system measured against previously set objectives. Based on analysis of your successes (or failures), you can adjust your inputs and/or activities to provide an output more appropriate to the situation you face.

The situation completes the model, because outputs are valuable only for particular situations. The value attributed to your offering depends on the market conditions—buyers' needs and competition—on any specific day. To appreciate that the value of output depends not on what has gone into it, but on the customer's judgment of its worth at a particular time, simply keep in mind that of every two new products or services brought to the market, only one is a success.

To effectively manage your selling system, you need to know who your customers are (or should be), where they are, and what constitutes value for them. In addition, you must attend unremittingly to your objectives, employing inputs and activities productively. As a system manager, you strive to achieve profitable differential competitive advantage in a continuously changing business environment.

Profitable accounts occasionally require unprofitable orders; you must sometimes make investments to acquire expertise in new target markets; and some historically sound customers will become unprofitable. These examples suggest that you must strive continuously to obtain a better mix of profitable and unprofitable outputs. On balance, you are an effective manager when you provide value-added buying opportunities for your customers and prospects and earn targeted profits for your company.

This brief introduction to selling systems provides you with the basic concepts you need to be an effective manager. Figure 9.2 also identifies the traps awaiting the unwary. When you become emotionally overattached to one or more elements in the system, you neglect other elements and the system becomes unbalanced, or less effective in delivering value to your customers than it should be. Typical pathologies include the following:

1. Input-focused salespeople may spend too much time, for example, on the wrong prospects or too little on the right ones. Similarly, they may be underqualified or overqualified for the prospects they are expected to

serve. Similarly, some salespeople become so interested in profiling their clients, they never get around to selling them while others put enormous energy into selling but are unaware of the financial consequences of their actions.

2. Output-centered salespeople fail to consider whether the inputs are adequate or the activities realistic. Their "results at any cost" approach may work for awhile, but long-term results are undermined by squandering inputs and activities. Productivity usually declines.

3. Activity-obsessed salespeople frequently become enmeshed in activity for the sake of the activity itself rather than for the results the activity was designed to produce. Many competent, dedicated professionals fall victim to this malady. From a professional selling perspective they are "hobbyists" who have lost sight of Disraeli's dictum, "The secret of success is constancy to purpose."

The Activity Trap in Selling

Ineffective salespeople get so involved in the activity that is supposed to produce a result that they lose sight of the objectives they set out to achieve. This is especially fatal in managing selling systems because competitive conditions and account requirements change frequently, requiring continuous adjustment of inputs and activities to accomplish objectives. If you fail to adjust inputs and/or activities in terms of the new realities, you may end up pursuing irrelevancies.

Activity traps are pervasive. Salespeople who strive to make more calls without adjusting call content are in this category and frequently their results get worse. If you are already working a full day, the issue is not how to do more or how to work harder, but how to achieve more of the desired results. Usually, this requires changes in inputs as well as in activities. One way to facilitate adjustment is to eliminate the things that do not need to be done. A starting point is for you to ask yourself, "What am I *not* going to do next week?" and stick to it. This frees resources for reallocation. You must "unload" less important work before you can take on the more important tasks that would improve your productivity. A crucial lesson from our Japanese competitors who use just-in-time concepts is that the organization of work can be improved. We must redesign the way we sell to become more productive.

Systems of the activity trap are reflected in Figure 9.4 (an actual case, illustrating what happened when a salesperson became enmeshed in the activity trap). Of the accounts currently served, 44 percent are unprofitable, and of the orders processed, 40 percent are unprofitable. (The discrepancy indicates unprofitable accounts sometimes submit profitable orders.) Fifteen percent of sales are unprofitable. The startling fact is that if the unprofitable business were *not* sold, profits would be 31 percent higher. In addition, substantial selling, delivery, storage, handling, office, and administrative capacity would be available for redeployment. When questioned about the unusually high percentage of unprofitable accounts and orders, the salesperson replied sincerely that he was "working on it." When one of the authors suggested he limit his nonprofitable accounts to three, he was

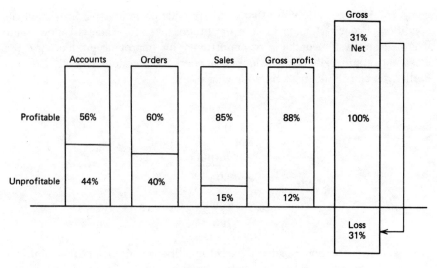

Figure 9.4 Symptoms of the activity trap.

horrified. Without commitment to concrete objectives and without adjustment of activities and inputs, this salesperson will remain in the activity trap, generating subpar profits.

An indicator of how widespread activity-centered thinking has become is the volume of strictly "motivational" materials, urging salespeople to greater effort, that inundate the salesperson. In all probability, the popularity is inverse to the long-term results achieved because after forgetting the inspirational message, the salesperson has no new insights or analytic tools to cope more effectively with selling problems and opportunities. The basic questions are left unanswered:

- "How should I adjust my selling system for greater customer satisfaction?"
- "How can I improve my productivity?"
- "How should I adjust my selling system for greater profit?"

In a rapidly changing environment, more activity alone is not likely to produce the sales results desired next month. Perhaps the other vital sign typical of the activity-centered selling systems is the belief that growth in gross volume will solve basic problems. In most cases, the desire for more "volume" or "motivation" is symptomatic of the need for careful analysis of how effectively you are managing your selling system.

Analyzing Your Selling System

You owe it to yourself to become an expert in managing your selling system. The ultimate purpose of the system is to produce an output that a significant number of prospects will perceive as valuable with a competitive cost structure. One way to analyze your system is to look at partial ratios to sample what is going on. Any one ratio will usually only provide an interesting insight on the condition of your system, but a number of ratios taken together will allow you to diagnose any system problem or opportunity for improving productivity. You can create appropriate ratios by looking at your selling system in detail. Conceptually, you can think about the following ratios:

$$\frac{\text{Output}}{\text{Input}}$$

$$\frac{\text{Output}}{\text{Activity}}$$

$$\frac{\text{Activity}}{\text{Input}}$$

given specific situational factors: market conditions and competition. You may develop your personal ratios by creating questions that help you define system parameters. For example:

- How many new leads do you need per month to achieve your sales objectives? Of what quality?
- How much business per month will come from current accounts? How much new business per month do you require?
- What should your expense-to-sales ratio be? What is it? Why?
- How do your sales skills stack up compared with what is required to serve your customers?
- What percentage (how many) of your accounts are nonprofitable?
- For your area of responsibility, what is your market position?

Based on your personal experience, you can create many additional questions. Once you have a fairly exhaustive list, focus on the 10 most insightful questions and eliminate the rest. Using these questions, you can now develop ratios that fit your own situation.

Analysis of your key ratios should give you insights on how your time allocation, interpersonal skills, and effectiveness stack up relative to leaders in your company and/or industry. These analyses give you the marketing intelligence you require to manage a superior selling effort.

For improving productivity longer term, you can also look at your selling position as a unique collection of measurable roles. Table 9.2 provides illustrative operational measures of role performance. You can compare your current effectiveness on each of these measures against what will be required in the future. The gaps can become an ingredient in your productivity improvement plan. The ancient Japanese tradition of Zen suggests that the greatest improvements in productivity come not from learning something new, but from doing better what we already know how to do well.

Table 9.2 Measures of Roles Frequently Performed

Selling Roles	Operational Measures of Role Performance
Manager	Percentage of market potential covered
	Mix of profitable/unprofitable accounts
	Average order size relative to breakeven order size
	Allocation of time relative to norm
Marketing tactician	Index of ability to monitor feedback
	Determination of key decision makers
	Organization of presentation
	Adjustment to unforeseen and unexpected factors
Problem solver	Knowledge of industry
	Grounding in products/applications
	Technologies associated with products
	Systems view of each account
Creative thinker	Improved product usage
	Mobilization of supportive personnel as needed
	Suggestions concerning customer's products
	"Promotional consultant"
Transactor	Negotiating skill
	Legal and ethical "company in the flesh"
	Commercial judgment on commitment
	"Closer"
Follow-upper	Product conformance with original specifications
	Customer kept information of shipping dates
	Provision of promised information
	Scheduling of installment and start-up
Monitor of marketing intelligence	Relationship of selling effort to account potential
	Assessment of competition
	Changes in customer/prospect needs, wants, expectations
	Other factors influencing demand

Selling in the Information Age

Of the many developments in technology that you can use to improve your selling system, one of the most important is the information technology available for use both by the company and by individual salespeople. In particular, the advent of the personal computer offers new ways to improve the selling process at the individual level.

The primary benefit offered by the computer is information management. Enormous amounts of data about customers and company products are available but not used by many salespeople. One reason for this lack of use is the difficulty in compiling all these data in a readily available and easily understood form. Data are not so important; information is. Data are defined as facts and figures about the environment. Information is defined as data organized in such a manner that it helps a person to make decisions.

The computer has the capability to store huge amounts of data. With appropriate software or programs, you can organize these data so that you can easily extract specific data in the form of usable information.

Your ability to use a computer-based information system for information collection and dissemination can greatly improve your performance. Inputs to such systems come from three sources: the company, the customer, and the salesperson. Activities that you can perform with computers are limited only by your imagination. Computers allow people to undertake different activities rather than just allowing them to perform the same activities more efficiently.

An example of how salespeople are using microcomputers appeared in *Marketing News* titled, "Marketer uses his computer to become a sales champion." The article reported how a salesperson for Xerox Corporation went from 228th in sales to number 1 in the nation in one year. In that year he more than quadrupled his quota.

The basic elements of his program are:

1. A prospect management system that finds, adds, deletes, and edits entries about prospects in an information data base. It also indexes the data base to allow for selective searching of prospect entries by various criteria such as product type or profitability. Finally it prints out either a complete listing of prospects or any partial listing based on these search criteria.
2. An activity reporting system to which the salesperson can add accomplished activities. At the end of the week, the salesperson can use the system to print out a finished report.
3. A daily time management system to keep track of activities, list them according to priority, and delete those that are completed.
4. A master account management system that adds current accounts to the file, searches by account type, and displays a master list.
5. A sample generation system that allows the salesperson to automatically print customized or generic mailings to selected customers.

6. A correspondence system to write the letters and print out mass mailings and envelopes. The computer program also includes a "callback tickler system" to help the salesperson keep in touch with prospects.

This salesperson developed his own programs to accomplish his specific goals, but many commercial programs have also been developed specifically for salespeople and companies. You do not need to have an expensive customized program, however, to derive benefits from the computer. Many off-the-shelf programs are available, usually defined in terms of functions rather than in terms of solutions for salespeople. Among the functions included are word processing, spreadsheet software, data base management, graphics, and communications. Examples of spreadsheet software and data-base management software are included in this chapter. In addition, Chapter Ten focuses on the use of data-base management to improve selling in depth.

Spreadsheet software has been particularly beneficial in allowing salespeople to do things they were previously unable to do. A common presentation is the financial ramifications of a purchase.

Using a microcomputer and spreadsheet software, a salesperson can build the basic *relationships* that are relevant for any number of alternatives into what is known as a template. As part of the template, graphs can be defined to represent the data pictorially in a variety of ways. During the presentation, the salesperson can demonstrate two or three alternatives by entering numbers and displaying the results on the screen. If the customer has an alternative he or she wishes to see, that can be entered as well, with the results instantly displayed.

The salesperson can store data in a loose-leaf binder or file cabinet if desired. However, if data are stored in a computer data base that ties them to the individual customer, then the salesperson has a much improved method for accessing the information. All information is stored in one location, the computer; and the data-base program makes it possible for you to select information about the sales call, the customer, the account, or whatever level of analysis you might wish to pursue. Studying the information at the customer level—reviewing particular needs, personality traits, motivations, and customer-specific strategies—will enable you to effectively plan for maximum impact in the sales encounter.

The disadvantage of the computer is the time required to master it. Unlike some other information technology tools, the computer requires an investment of time and effort before you can see the benefits. Is it worth it? As a partial answer to that question, consider what the competition is doing. Will staying at the current level of knowledge and expertise allow you to continue to generate differential competitive advantage with your clients?

2. IMPLEMENTING THE PLANNING PROCESS

An individual salesperson can benefit from strategic planning. How can you apply functions of the business unit to yourself? Although the goals and strategies of the business are specified, what are appropriate goals for you? As part of your strategic planning process, goal setting is critical.

Goal Setting

Effective objectives or goal setting must be based on current and contemplated reality. Before you can set objectives and formulate plans, you need to ask yourself:

1. Where am I now?
2. If I do not do anything differently, what results can I expect next month, next year? Do these results equal my expectations?
3. What results would I like to achieve?
4. How can I measure my progress?

The salesperson with a sense of purpose wants to improve, to do better, and to do more. If your actual performance satisfied your aspirations, you would have no need to manage. Managing implies change—not just following trends but also making them. If you desire to achieve more, you begin by formulating objectives to attain at specific times in the future.

Setting Objectives

The first step in managing is setting objectives. These are expectations regarding future results the person wants to achieve. The effective sales planner sets objectives that meet certain criteria.

1. They are potentially achievable in terms of the salesperson's talent, time, money, resources, and information.
2. They are commercially worthwhile. In addition to providing value for the customer, their achievement will contribute to the profit and growth of the enterprise.
3. They are concrete and definite. The salesperson is less likely to strive to achieve objectives expressed in vague terms.
4. They are clear and understandable. For example, the objectives set for an account must be equally understandable to the salesperson and his or her supervisor.
5. To be effective, the objectives must be congruent or in step. This means that the goals a salesperson sets for each account and for his or her territory are complementary to and in agreement with the objectives the district manager has set for the district.

No process at any level of management is more critically important than setting objectives. In your work, you have many occasions to set them. You set objectives for each call; you set objectives for each transaction; you set objectives for each buying-selling relationship or account; you set objectives for your total territory or the market segment for which you are responsible. You set objectives for allocation of your personal time. The process of setting objectives follows.

An illustrative hierarchy of objectives—innovative, problem solving, and regular—for the salesperson is presented in Figure 9.5.

Regular objectives define your responsibilities and are frequently stated in terms of measures of output per unit of time: sales volume/month, gross profit/line/month, and so on. Increasingly, attachable input costs are being included in the statement of regular objectives, making it possible for salespeople to improve their contribution to profitability. For example, specific expense budgets are frequently developed to foster the efficient use of support personnel as well as the optimal routing of salespeople in their territory.

Regular objectives must be stated as ranges rather than point estimates. In an uncertain world, to expect salespeople to commit to and achieve a specific sales volume is unrealistic. When single-number objectives are achieved, they are frequently "self-fulfilling prophecies." Where possible, therefore, establish a range of acceptable performance for each major objective. Your pessimistic estimate of sales volume for the next period might be $1.0 million, the optimistic appraisal $1.4 million, and the balanced expectation $1.2 million. Results within the range of $1.0 million to $1.4 million would indicate acceptable achievement of your volume objective.

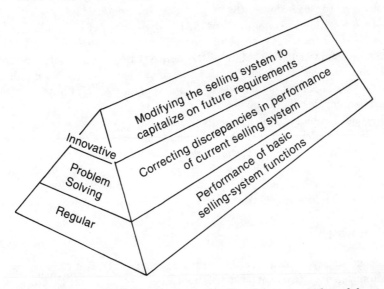

Figure 9.5 A hierarchy of objectives for the salesperson. (Adapted from materials devised by George S. Odiorne and reproduced with his permission.)

Where your performance is measured on a number of interrelated objectives and each is stated as a range, you have latitude to react to changing environments. Stating objectives as a range provides you with maximum freedom to fulfill responsibilities consistent with the achievement of overall company objectives.

You set problem-solving objectives to take advantage of opportunities to improve or correct the performance of the selling system. You should focus your efforts on two or three high-priority problems or opportunities—where there is a significant discrepancy between the present condition and what you would like it to be.

For example, you might recognize that you are allocating your selling effort to customers according to how your sales manager "feels" about the relative profitability of the accounts. In many instances, you are making an allocation without any factual data or on data that are several years old. You might decide that you can improve this performance by classifying your accounts according to the likelihood that they will purchase within the next time period as well as according to their profit potential. Consequently, you summarize the present situation and detail what you would like conditions to be.

Set innovative objectives to better capitalize on future situations. You should ask what innovations, changes, or improvements you must make in your selling system to cope with future markets. For example, when a leading maker of industrial machinery announced that several new lines of much larger and more expensive products would be introduced over the next 5 years, an alert salesperson thought through how she would change her selling to accommodate the new line. In this instance, the new product line required dealing with a new set of buyers within the organizations. As the size of the potential sale increases, the authority to purchase moves upward and involves more individuals in the customer organization. As captain of the selling team, you must do a better job of coordinating the efforts of the other members of your selling team to impact favorably on the corresponding buying team. Appendix XXVIII provides a set of work sheets for developing objectives.

Regular, problem-solving, and innovative objectives are specific commitments for salespeople to fulfill through the management of their selling systems in the year ahead. Equally important, salespeople need to set strategic objectives to be achieved beyond the first year, as depicted in Figure 9.6. To ensure the survival and growth of your selling system, you must adopt a multiyear perspective and develop long-range plans.

Planning

The second step or element in effective management is planning or programming. Here, for each objective, you must map a series of steps or events that must occur to achieve your objective. Effective planning requires that the steps laid out are definite, clear, and understandable. They must also be placed in proper sequence so that one leads logically into the next. You need to allocate the time to be

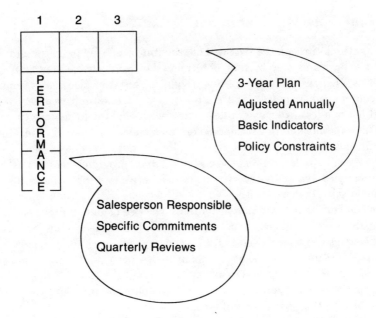

Figure 9.6 Strategic goals. (Adapted from materials devised by George S. Odiorne and reproduced with his permission.)

devoted to each step in advance. Once you have formulated the total program, you can determine the timing to achieve each objective.

Contemplating Execution

The third step or element in managing is contemplated execution. For each step in the program you need to determine in advance the answers to questions such as "Who will do this?" For example, one step in your program might require a joint call on the account with the district manager.

Another question is, "How will I perform this step?" For any single step, several alternatives usually exist. Thus, in planning, there is a premium on reviewing relevant experience for cues and ideas on the best way to execute your plan.

You also need to determine in advance, "What will I need to accomplish this step?" This may include information, selling aids, and samples.

Another relevant question is, "Where is the best place to accomplish this?" For example, part of the plan might be to arrange for a plant visit with the account's production manager. Part of your managerial assignment is to select situations beneficial to the achievement of your objectives.

Finally, in contemplating execution you need to ask, "Whom must I inform?" For example, certain steps in a plan may involve notifying the service department. Others may require you to inform a supervisor.

Contemplating Evaluation

Once you think through the best way of executing each step in the program, you need to go back and, step by step, determine the cost in time, talent, and money as well as what new information you require. This step places a premium on good commercial judgment. If the cost of a particular step is excessive, you must think of a less extensive or less time-consuming way to achieve the objective. The contemplated investment of your own talents or those of others in your company must be proportional to the results you hope to achieve.

Once you have determined the cost of the total program, you must ask yourself a final question. With one eye on your objective and the other on the cost, you should ask, "Is it worth it?"

Several comments are in order on the subject of planning. First, planning is not usually as clear and orderly as outlined here. For instance, once you have set your objectives and have moved to the formulation of a program to achieve them, you may need to look back and change them in view of the number of steps needed or the amount of time required to achieve your original goals.

Second, as you examine the best way to execute the program, you may also need to change the program itself, especially when you examine the answer to the question, "What is needed for each step?"

Third, when you evaluate costs, you may go all the way back to the program and make modifications there, or you may make modifications to your contemplated execution. You may say in answer to the question "Is it worth it?" that "No, it is not worth it; I should change my objective."

The essence of good planning is in replanning. The mark of the mature manager is that he or she is willing to revise original ideas as many times as he or she can find ways to improve them. People of lesser stature and experience sometimes start action before they have thought through the consequences of their plans. This frequently leads to waste and confusion. Figure 9.7 illustrates the planning process with a sample plan that has been filled in to show how to use the Account Improvement Planning Guide in Appendix XXIX.

Executing Plans

Until you have effectively executed plans, no payoff occurs. What are the characteristics of this managerial process? For effective execution of your plans, you need to organize your information and materials and have them ready for smooth and effortless use. The condition of materials in your briefcase, for example, may critically influence your calls. A salesperson who has to fumble through a briefcase for an item loses the prospect's attention and irritates him or her.

Successful salespeople do not spend time; they invest it. They manage their daily and weekly schedule to maximize face-to-face time with customers and prospects. They have on tap some worthwhile tasks to perform as segments of time unexpectedly become available. They do not depart from the timetable of their program without good cause. They avoid being diverted from the activity at hand.

OBJECTIVE: To improve dealer relations and save money by designing a new inventory check sheet.

CONTEMPLATED ACTION

Program	Who?	How?	What?	Where?	Inform Whom?
A. Revise inventory sheet	Myself	Study existing sheet and make obvious changes	My time plus Secretary	My territory between calls	Get OK from J.M Jones S.M.
B. Confer with dealers	Myself and dealers	Show revised sheet and ask for any suggestions	A few minutes of time on each call	In territory as parts of call	Dealers whose opinions are being sought
C. Draft revised form	Myself and Secretary	Combine ideas into new form	A block of my time plus 18 hours for secretary	Collate ideas at home on weekends	Sales Manager should see revised form
D. Put plan into effect	Myself and dealers	Sit down with dealers and go over form	30 minutes per call with each dealer	At stores	

CONTEMPLATED EVALUATION

Time	Talent	Money
40 hours piece-meal	Myself and secretary	$600 full cost ($120 out-of-pocket)
10 hours piece-meal	Myself	$120 time
4 hours alone and 2 hours with steno 18 hours for secretary	Myself and secretary	$72 time and $120 steno
24 hours of my time	Myself and dealers	$288 time

RECAP: With estimated savings of $2,000 per year, plus more effective effort that should yield improved dealer relations, the initial cost of $600 is well justified.

IS IT WORTH IT?

Yes. Form will show dealers advantages of longer, better balanced inventory. Initial sales will more than pay the cost.

Figure 9.7 Account improvement planning guide.

Good salespeople do not hesitate to ask for help with their work when they need it. They are self-sufficient, however, and do not run to their supervisors when a difficulty arises or a change in plans is necessary. They sustain a steady pace throughout the total execution of the plan and avoid marked ups and downs in the interest and energy directed toward it.

In selling, perhaps more frequently than in any other area of management, modifications in the execution of any plan are the norm. Frequently, a competitive salesperson does the unexpected or unforeseen with an account, which in turn forces modification in the plan for that account and the manner of its execution. Another commonplace example is the frequency with which delays occur through no fault of the salesperson. Who is not familiar with "wait time"?

Evaluating Performance

Outputs, activities, and inputs as well as their interrelationships are considerations in the evaluation process. Objectives are statements of the results expected based on a current ability to perform to which the salesperson is committed. Talent, time, information, and money are four inputs of the selling system. The central valuative question is: "Am I achieving objectives profitably?" To be effective as an evaluator, you must pause periodically in the execution of your plans to ask, "How much is this costing in relation to what I planned?" In short "Is it worth it?" The longer the plan's time horizon, the more you need to build in checkpoints.

Mañana-itis, that dread management disease, afflicts many people. Successful evaluators, however, avoid it by scheduling time to assess their progress in execution. They also check the monetary costs in relation to their estimates. Avoid being stingy in the investment of talent, time, and money in relation to the worth of your objectives. On the other hand, avoid being profligate in the use of these valuable inputs.

Information is central to effective evaluation. For you to answer the question, "How am I doing?" you require valid feedback that is immediate and specific so that you can adjust the allocation of your resources. In a larger sense, to set meaningful objectives in the first place, you need appropriate information. The effectiveness of your selling effort hinges on having a sound information base. Indeed, objective setting, planning, execution, and evaluation all require relevant information. As the manager of a selling system, you must be concerned with how the data you have available for decision making relate to reality. Are the data valid? Are they reliable? Are they accurate? Are they complete? Are they timely? Are they usable?

Evaluating offers an additional benefit. If you do it periodically, you can more easily spot either the need to modify the program or to modify the mode of executing it. (This is what was referred to previously as replanning.) Thus, you prevent trouble before it begins. This procedure keeps the plan workable and within the bounds of the available time, talent, information, and money budget.

Improving Performance

Evaluating is valuable in proportion to the constructive remedial action that you take as a result. Where evaluation shows that you are not achieving the expected objectives, that information is inadequate, or that you are investing too much time, talent, or money, corrective action is necessary. An attitude of constructive discontent is desirable if you are to improve your performance.

The essence of improving is action that adjusts the operation of your selling system to match your objectives. This might mean polishing skills in objective setting, planning, execution, and/or evaluation. Improvement is rarely based on the adjustment of any one element in isolation because each ingredient involves and impacts the others as shown in Figure 9.8.

For the salesperson to think that no improvements will be required is naive. Effective management of a selling system is based partially on expectations about future conditions that only infrequently occur as predicted. Therefore, opportunities for improvement arise even in well-managed territories.

On the one hand, you want to profit from experience, but on the other, you should not be hidebound to it. Selling is a creative assignment, so where appropriate, you must seek new and better ways to do things. Newness for its own sake, however, is not worthwhile.

One final note. A widespread belief demands debunking. That everybody should "do his own thing" and that controlling your life somehow reduces freedom provide the basis of a popular theory. Nothing could be farther from the truth. Dedication to improving your performance allows you to achieve more. In

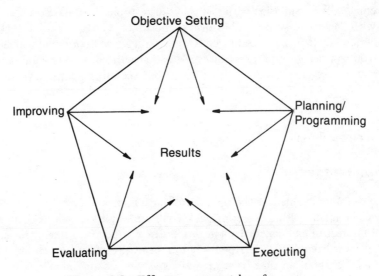

Figure 9.8 Effective managerial performance.

a mature sense, freedom is not an absence of management, "taking a random walk," but achieving a significant portion of your life objectives through managed improvement. Freedom is the result of responsible self-management. *"Free" salespeople are the ones who have managed their responsibilities so well and so promptly that their managers have had no cause to interfere.*

3.   SELF-MANAGEMENT

In addition to the areas of management covered in the preceding sections, you need to devote time and energy to managing yourself. Although your employer naturally has some interest in helping you as a person, you must assume the major responsibility for your own welfare and conduct. The most crucial areas to consider are *physical well-being, appearance, mental attitude,* and *improvement in job skills.*

Physical Well-Being

Obviously, if you are not in good health, you cannot perform your job at peak efficiency. You cannot depend on a spouse, mother, or employer to assume responsibility for your well-being. You must see to it yourself.

One important detractor from the health of a salesperson is irregular hours. A certain amount of irregularity is inevitable. However, in planning your routine for daily and weekly territory coverage, you need to plan for your health as well as for meals, lodging, and for your customer and prospect calls.

Fortunately, recent advances in our understanding of nutrition, exercise, and their interaction make planning for good health relatively straightforward. For example, in consultation with your physician, you can set measurable objectives with regard to your aerobic fitness, body fat, cholesterol, HDL, LDL, triglyceride, chylomicrons, and so on. Once you have written down your objectives, you can design a program of exercise that will earn 30 or more aerobic points every week combined with a diet that monitors your intake of fats, cholesterol, protein, carbohydrates, fiber, salt, alcohol, and caffeine to allow you to achieve your peak selling performance.

You know the challenges you face in your market, so you should be sure to include physical well-being in your plans.

Appearance

Your appearance influences the opinions of customers and prospects about you and your company with a direct effect on sales. Do not lose sales because of a lack of interest in and concern about proper dress. Budgeting money for an appropriate wardrobe is not an expense but an investment. You can obtain appropriate advice about apparel from magazines as well as any reliable store. The first step, however, is to recognize the importance of good appearance.

Mental Attitude

Your mental attitude affects customers and prospects and, therefore, has a bearing on your success. "Laugh and the world laughs with you; cry and you cry alone" is one guide to the proper attitude. Customers have their own troubles and would rather spill them to you than listen to yours. Hence you need to be cheerful and self-sufficient. Other things being equal, people prefer to buy from the salesperson who sticks to business. If you discuss personal problems at all, they should be the customer's, not yours.

Salespeople generally fail to make calls due to a lack of (1) courage, (2) determination, or (3) industriousness. Where you have had a poor reception in the past or when you anticipate one, you should evaluate the situation. The first consideration is whether your product or service is one that the customer or prospect can logically use. If the answer is "no," you should delete the call from your schedule. If the answer is "yes," you should be assertive and make a fair presentation and evaluation.

Your ethical values are manifested in your mental attitude, which in turn affects your sales efficiency. You are in a unique position with respect to values. On the job, company policies provide a guide for personal conduct, decisions, and action. However, free-time activities are also of concern. In many instances, you will find yourself alone in a strange city. You must learn to use your free time constructively. You can do this positively by using the time for personal development or you can use it neutrally with movies, TV, or escape reading. On the other hand, you should not use the time negatively by developing bad habits and acquaintances which will ultimately lower your ethical standards and your sales volume.

Character development is beyond the scope of this book. Whether companies should provide such training to salespeople is even questionable. Low moral standards will likely preclude promotion and may even result in dismissal. We merely point out that you must manage your free time just as carefully as your selling time. This practice will ensure that you work toward better sales performance as well as a more rewarding personal life.

Improvement in Job Skills

While companies train salespeople in the basic requirements of their job, two potential weaknesses exist in most training programs. First, they may omit one or more essential ideas. This can happen in any company, either in the planning stage or in the actual training program. This observation is particularly true where the company emphasizes informal on-the-job training and provides little formal classroom training. The second weakness is that salespeople do not retain what they have been taught. For these reasons, you can improve your job skills by assuming some of the responsibility for your own training and development.

The first step you should take to improve your job skills is to review your performance against your job description and thereby identify your strengths and weaknesses. If the company does not have a formal job description, you should prepare one for yourself. Appendix XXX is helpful for this purpose. If you must prepare your own job description, you should check it with your supervisor to be sure that the duties you listed are what the company expects. When all are in agreement as to the duties, you can then ask for a performance review that will point out your strong and weak areas (see Appendix XXVI for a discussion of observing sales performance).

The next step is to review the knowledge you obtained from the training program and company publications to correct any weaknesses or gaps in your information. You can now plan a program that will make you more effective.

You can take additional steps to identify your strengths and weaknesses. Discussions with fellow salespeople in the company can help you evaluate your performance relative to others. Customers' comments and attitudes also provide clues. You may find other trade or industry people who can give you feedback. If you make it clear that you are interested in constructive criticism, you will find many people willing to help you.

Reading trade publications, especially reviews of new books in the field, is a good way to keep abreast of developments. Many of these books are worth reading. Programs planned by companies or by trade associations are usually devoted to recent developments or a review of major problems in the industry. Trade shows are also a source of information that you can use in your everyday work.

Outside the trade or industry, college bulletins offer possibilities for self-development. Note the course offerings to see whether some of them suggest areas or topics that would be helpful to you. If you cannot register for a particular course, you may be able to get the name of the textbooks used and study them on your own.

The task of self-improvement can be simplified by recognizing that improvement will probably fall under one of the following three headings:

1. More and better product/service information.
2. Improved sales techniques.
3. General improvement in terms of a larger fund of general information and increased ability to reason critically.

More and Better Product/Service Information

Your company is your basic source of product/service information. If your product or service is not sufficiently technical to pose a problem, you need to have a knowledge of allied information. Merchandising consumer goods is a good example. Here a knowledge of merchandising is as important as the actual product knowledge. You should study all company literature and ask for clarification of points that you do not understand or that appear to be in conflict.

The next best source of information is customers. You cannot take all complaints or compliments at face value, but you should check them out with company technicians—engineers, chemists, product managers, or other specialists. In this way, you can serve your customers better by helping them get better results from your products and services. At the same time, you can add to your fund of knowledge in a way that lets the company know you are doing a good job of training yourself and serving your customers.

Improved Sales Techniques

Advice on the subject is so varied that developing a program of self-improvement is difficult. To complicate the problem further, most of the available information is opinion rather than fact.

Reading is, of course, the most obvious way to gain information. To read wisely, survey the books available and determine which will help. The books fall into the following categories:

1. *Textbooks on Selling.* These are usually written by college professors and consist of a systematic coverage of what is known about the field of selling.
2. *Trade Books.* The usual pattern is for successful salespeople to tell how "they did it." Bear in mind that the author probably has a unique personality, a specialized product or service, and a specialized clientele. Advice will be helpful to the extent that your situation is similar.
3. *Books on the Psychology of Selling.* Most of these are written by people with scientific training who draw on the entire field of the behavioral sciences. They stress interpersonal aspects of selling. One word of caution: Just because the title of a book contains the word "psychology," you cannot assume the contents are based on established psychological theories. Note the author's background and the references given. If the book does not include references to standard psychological works, consider it a trade book.
4. *Sales Stories.* These are interesting reading but not necessarily educational. Like trade books, they must be considered critically rather than applied blindly because each salesperson performs in a unique market niche.
5. *Related Books.* Books on advertising, speech, psychology, and so on can all be helpful if you use them cautiously rather than accepting them at face value.

Speakers are the next most prevalent source of sales techniques. Most speakers on sales topics are good salespeople themselves, so if you are uncritical, you may adopt a suggestion that works for the speaker but will not necessarily work for you. Listen to speakers whenever you have the opportunity, but with reservations, and only adopt those suggestions that fit your particular job. Studying the technique of the speaker is as valuable as listening to the content of the speech.

In the area of sales techniques, identifying some important skills needed by salespeople may prove helpful.

1. *Opening Remarks.* These are questions and comments that will focus the buyer's attention on the crux of the matter as soon as the "small talk" is finished.

2. *Answers to Objections.* All salespeople should compile a list of the objections they encounter and ask their supervisor to help them formulate company-approved answers.

3. *Organized Product/Service Information.* The manner in which a salesperson uses product/service information in a sales call differs from the way most company literature is prepared. A salesperson needs information organized in terms of feature-benefit tables, sales points (including need-developing questions and alternate phrasings), and handling objections. Do this outside of face-to-face situations rather than improvising under pressure. Appendix II provides a model salesperson-oriented product manual.

4. *Call Checklist.* This is discussed in Chapter Seven, Section 1; and Chapter Ten, Section 2 ensures that you consider all important steps in a call, even if you do not actually execute them (see Appendix XXV).

5. *List of Suggestions.* Often you can make a point more effectively by suggestion than by logical reasoning. As with product or service information, develop these before rather than during the call.

6. *Customer Personality Analysis.* Every customer is unique. The way to appreciate and utilize this uniqueness is to analyze him or her in terms of the personality traits outlined in Chapter Five of this book.

7. *Customer Motivation Analysis.* Whereas a personality analysis reveals "how" to handle a customer, a motivational analysis, along the lines of Chapter Five, will show "what" key points to stress.

8. *Principles of Logic and Argument.* Although emotional appeals are used more often than logical reasoning, occasionally you will need to engage in the latter. To do this effectively, you need to study books on straight thinking and related subjects (see Chapter Seven, Section 2).

You should develop yourself in the above areas in your off-selling time to improve your performance in face-to-face situations. After you have developed each of the preceding topics, keep the information available in a computer data base or manual file for reference in the planning phase of a call.

General Improvement

Any information can be helpful to you at one time or another, if for no other reason than for talking with customers about a special interest or hobby.

The following list discusses some areas of general improvement that will be beneficial to you:

1. *Logic.* The elements of straight thinking and logic can keep you from succumbing to customers' fallacious reasoning. Principles of debate might be included here. Mathematics, especially geometry, puts a premium on clear thinking and may be helpful. Any laboratory science is good training in clear thinking. Most experiments require identification and control of

the variables and a write-up that forces an analysis of the cause-and-effect relationship.

2. *Literature.* Reading provides two areas for improvement. First is the improvement of vocabulary and general verbal facility, which will enable you to express yourself more completely and colorfully. The other area is in the understanding of people. The classics are full of characters who analyze and influence each other. An alert salesperson can learn much about human nature by a critical analysis of how authors depict each character's behavior so that it leads to the successful completion of the book's theme.

3. *Psychology.* This field contains most of the research on understanding people. Through reasoning by analogy, you can sometimes use the various research studies to solve sales problems.

4. *Speech.* This includes both speech exercises to improve diction and training in public speaking and conference leadership. A salesperson who is poised and composed when speaking before a group has a tremendous advantage, not only in individual sales but also in opportunities to become better known in the industry.

In addition to the preceding fields, the individual salesperson who is truly concerned with self-development should be able to find more detailed advice within the company or community.

SUMMARY

You have a professional managerial assignment with your company. The profitable operation of your area of responsibility is critical to the success of your company.

You are the manager of a selling system. The objectives of the system are to create profitable differential competitive advantage (value added) and to manage a set of selling-buying relationships for mutual profit. Your selling system is made up of three basic elements: outputs, activities, and inputs. Inputs consist of time, money, talent, and information. In well-run selling systems, customers see value added in what you do. Most of your activities and inputs are focused on creating an appropriate output. You can improve system performance by analyzing the relevance of every activity and input to the desired output. Progress can be monitored by measuring feedback. Frequently, systems become unbalanced and salespeople focus on favorite activities or inputs rather than on the desired results. These pathologies are called traps. The most pervasive is the activity trap. The antidote for unbalanced systems is ratio analysis that isolates specific areas for improvement.

The advent of the personal computer makes it feasible to manage the information you require to run your selling system, improve its productivity, and provide better customer service.

Once you define opportunities for improving system performance, you can develop a plan to achieve your sales performance objectives. You must master five interrelated processes: objective setting, planning, execution, evaluation, and improvement.

To be effective, you must first be able to manage yourself. You must set up rules of conduct to ensure good physical health. You should recognize the importance of appropriate appearance to the kind of impression you wish to make on your accounts. You will realize that a positive, optimistic viewpoint, backed by courage, determination, and healthy moral values, will be manifested in your mental attitude, which in turn has a direct bearing on the impression you create on your accounts and your personal productivity. Self-improvement, too, is an important objective. Becoming better informed about your products, service, markets, competition, and sales techniques, as well as the broader area of general information, will make you a more knowledgeable, interesting, and effective salesperson.

The most critical managerial assignment in the company is yours—running your area of responsibility at maximum efficiency.

TOPICS FOR THOUGHT AND DISCUSSION

1. Why is your managerial assignment one of the most important in the company?
2. What do you manage?
3. "You are the manager of a selling system." What does this concept mean to you?
4. Why is the systems approach one of the most important ideas developed in the past century?
5. What objectives are you seeking when you use the systems approach?
6. What are the elements of the systems approach?
7. Define the primary inputs to the system.
8. How might you use the concept of networking?
9. One salesperson asserted: "Situation is the most important variable in systems theory!" Why do you agree? Disagree?
10. What are the principal pathologies found in system performance?
11. What is the activity trap in selling? How can you avoid it?
12. What must you do before you can improve your productivity?
13. What benefits does the computer provide for the modern salesperson?
14. What will you have to do to grow with your clients?
15. How can the systems model be applied in the analysis of successful and unsuccessful sales performance?
16. Discuss some examples where the input/activity relationship tends to be ignored. How does self-improvement fit this relationship? Time management?
17. How much of an investment is required to learn to use computer technology? Is it worth it? Why?

18. What strategic questions should you ask before setting objectives? How does your answer to this question relate to the concept of situation in the systems model?
19. What criteria should objectives meet?
20. What is the importance of the hierarchy of objectives?
21. What are the primary components in the effective management process? How are they related?
22. What is your opinion of the relationship between planning and control?
23. Draw up a list of criteria for assessing your professional conduct.
24. Develop a checklist of health, appearance, and mental attitude factors that should be considered by all salespeople. Note the factors you should be focusing on.
25. Draw up a plan for your own self-improvement.
26. Notice the quality of speech of persons you meet. How much of your "first impression" is based on speech? What type of first impression does your speech make on others?

TEN

Managing in Depth: An Analysis for Effective Action

But I have promises to keep.
And miles to go before I sleep.

ROBERT FROST

In this chapter:

- **Managing Your Selling System with the Computer**
  - By considering the call, the transaction, the account, and the territory, you can effectively analyze your situation and improve your productivity.
- **Managing Each Call**
  - You might be outstanding in performing every other duty and yet fail dismally if you are unable to fulfill the primary function of making sales calls successfully.
- **Managing Each Transaction**
  - Maximizing the effect of the individual sales call will not necessarily result in a sale.
- **Managing Each Account**
  - One of your objectives is to increase business from existing accounts and to acquire new business from those who are not now customers.
- **Managing the Territory**
  - If you manage each call, each transaction, and each account effectively, you have gone a long way toward managing your territory effectively. However, the task of fitting the plans made for each account into a master plan for the territory remains.
- **Maximizing Territory Coverage**
  - Your objective in simplest terms is to sell the full line to the full marketplace.
- **Summary**
  - Viewing your responsibilities from the four perspectives—the call, the transaction, the account, and the territory—provides you with a framework to analyze your work and improve your productivity.

- **Topics for Thought and Discussion**
- **Application Exercises**
- Appendix XXV   Call Checklist and Presentation Checklist
- Appendix XXXI   Advertising Analysis Checklist
- Appendix XXXII   Account Potential Planning Guide
- Appendix XXXIII Territory Potential Planning Guide

1. MANAGING YOUR SELLING SYSTEM WITH THE COMPUTER

You manage a selling system that can be viewed from four perspectives: the call, the transaction, the account, and the territory. By considering each of these, you can effectively analyze your situation and improve your productivity.

Your primary focus is to manage each sales call so that you trigger the maximum differential competitive advantage in the mind of the customer. However, managing an individual call will not necessarily maximize your results at the broader system levels. To understand why, consider how the four perspectives are related.

At the most basic level, your primary focus is the sales call itself. Your goal is to create differential competitive advantage with your customer. You must manage your time, information, expenses, and so on, to create a perception of added value. Inputs to the system include information about the customer, his or her needs, position in the company, unique characteristics that impact the sales call, and specific issues to be addressed. Additional inputs come from the nature of your offering, its features and benefits, and comparisons with the competition. Activities at the sales-call level center around the preparation and execution of the sales call to create maximum impact for the given situation. The results of the call can range from a customer's commitment to listen to a signed purchase contract.

Often one sales call will not generate a sale. When you anticipate a set of sales encounters to consummate a transaction, you must analyze more variables and consider a longer time horizon. In many cases, you will have to organize a team of people to call on their counterparts in the target account who will be involved in the buying decision. You may identify a primary decision maker, but other influencers such as the user of the product or service, financial analysts, and other "experts" can be involved. In your company, customer service, production, engineering, and even current customers may be used to influence the customer.

Additional inputs to the system include your company's history with the account. What calls have been conducted? What problems have been overcome? With whom do you have an edge? With whom do you need to conduct additional calls? At the transaction level, you are concerned with arranging and conducting effective sales calls, meetings, demonstrations, and other communications with the appropriate buyers in the organization to produce favorable buying decisions.

The critical difference at the transaction level from the sales-call level is that while the different sales calls have provided different levels of output, you have aimed their combined impact to make a sale. You focus the set of sales calls with assistance from your associates to effect the transaction.

In professional selling, individual transactions provide the basis for profitability, and account management generates a stream of repeat purchases over time to develop a profitable relationship. If, in addition, you wish to maximize the value added of all sales calls in your territory, you must allocate your calls among accounts for the greatest total effect. Maximizing the effect of a single sales call will generally *not* accomplish this objective. Different customers require varying numbers and types of sales-call activity. The goal at the territory level is to maximize the total profitability of the accounts under your management. Of course, you are constrained by time.

Management at the territory level is aimed at evaluating accounts for inclusion or exclusion to achieve the greatest overall profitability. Accounts that are profitable today may be unprofitable tomorrow. You must cultivate new business to maintain a profitable set of accounts that you can efficiently handle.

Applying Computer Technology

Improvements in technology enable you to better control your selling system. The primary benefit is an enhanced ability to measure precisely the inputs, activities, and results of your system at each of the four levels so that you can develop appropriate strategies and tactics. Previously, salespeople could develop a feel about customers and, if they were organized, write it down. For more complex transactions with multiple calls, trying to maintain information on past calls as well as information about the company's capability and willingness to buy was frequently neglected and seldom current. Rigorous analysis of the data was so time consuming that it was seldom done.

Times have changed. Now maintaining up-to-date information about individual customers and tracking sales calls, transactions, and account information to analyze territory profitability and your personal productivity is feasible. Information is power! A data-base program and a computer can provide this information.

The Data-Base Management System

With the development of microcomputers and the improvement of data-base management programs, the advantages of readily accessible and organized information are directly available to you.

Following is a brief review of the components of a relational data base: tables, records, and fields. The table presents a set of data. Information about sales calls would be presented in a table. A complete set of information about one sales call is a record. Individual items in the record about the sales call are fields. An example of the fields that could be captured for a single sales call (record) is presented in Figure 10.1

Sales Call #: _____ Date: _____ Time: _____

Customer: ▼_____

Customer: ▼_____

Company: _____

Address: _____

_____

_____

Call Type:_____

Goals: _____

_____

_____

Results: _____

_____

Next Visit: _____ With Whom: ▼ _____

Figure 10.1 A sales-call table.

Sales Call #, Date, Time, and so on are all fields. The completed set of fields is stored as a record. Associated with fields are indexes that can be used to sort and search for specific types of data. For instance, individual sales calls can be sorted by date to produce a chronological history of calls. Calls can also be sorted by company and date to get a chronological history of calls for each company.

Note the ▼ mark next to the name. The ▼ indicates additional information about that field is available in a separate table about customers. Thus, the mark represents a defined relationship between the two tables. The term relational data base comes from these defined relationships. Using the information in the customer table, you can develop a clearer picture of the sales-call activities for that customer. The calls could also be sorted by the next call date to provide a basis for future sales-call planning.

The preceding example illustrates a basic data base. To manage your area of responsibility, however, you would need to have tables about sales calls, individual customers or prospects, transactions, accounts, and information summarizing your results. Each of these tables contains multiple records of information that are associated with the records in other tables through the defined relationships. Continuing the example, you could develop productivity ratios, such as average sales per call, gross margin per order, time per call, gross margin per hour, and so on. Ask yourself, "What measures do I need to identify to improve my productivity?"

The informational advantage of the data base becomes apparent as you prepare for a sales call. On your computer you select the customer table. Through the relationships defined to sales calls, you can review the sales history for that company and analyze the number of calls, total volume of sales, and other pertinent information. You can also directly review the information you have about the customer analyzing such items as individual traits, needs, and so on. Armed with this information and additional analyses you can run on the computer, you are ready to develop a well-planned sales call.

2.   MANAGING EACH CALL

The individual sales call is the cornerstone of effective selling. You might be outstanding in performing every other duty and yet fail dismally if you are unable to fulfill the primary function of making sales calls successfully. What is involved in managing each call?

The Three Phases of Every Call

As an experienced professional, you are aware that the call involves more than what happens when you are face-to-face with the customer or prospect. You know that each call has three phases—*Before, During, and After.*

Before the Call

This is the planning phase in which you set the call objectives and lay out the program for achieving them.

Customer Calls.   On customer calls, you review the previous buying history; you note who the competitors are; you translate the amounts of business you presently enjoy into the share of the business you have compared with competitors. You check your last call to see whether there were any unanswered questions or incomplete items that must be part of your agenda on the next visit. You should remind yourself that the best way to improve your position with the account is either to sell a larger quantity of what is now being bought or to sell items that are not presently being purchased.

You review what you know about the individuals you plan to see—their outstanding characteristics and any idiosyncrasies that you should recognize in dealing with them.

With these considerations in mind, you can plan for your next call.

Prospect Calls.   Obviously, you do not have as much detailed information on a prospect call to use as inputs for your plan as you would on a customer call. In fact, the key objective on prospect calls may be to obtain the information you need to develop a customer, if that is warranted. Despite the relative lack of information, however, planning is critical. The quality of your plan may be the big difference that gives you an edge in opening a new account. The prospect may perceive you as knowledgeable and efficient and, as a result, desire to do business with you.

The importance of planning to acquire needed information on a prospect account calls for further emphasis. One of your objectives is to create an impression in the mind of the prospect that you and your company can be of help. The most effective way you can do this is by obtaining the kind and amount of information that will back up your suggestions to the prospect to induce purchase. If you suggest a purchase, the prospect can hardly take you seriously unless you show convincingly that you understand what is needed. On the other hand, if your suggestions fit what the prospect needs, your proposal should receive serious consideration. Plan what you are going to ask as well as you plan what you are going to say.

During the Call

This is the execution phase of the sales call. The better you have planned the call, the more smoothly it is likely to go when you and the customer or prospect are face-to-face. Seldom, however, does a call go exactly as planned. So your task is to adjust to the unforeseen or unexpected in the interview.

The factors that might influence the need to adjust the plan may be classified into three groups: (1) "people," (2) "things," and (3) "competition."

1. People. Some of the more common "people" factors include finding the person you call on to be in an unanticipated mood, not being able to see the person, having to make the presentation in the presence of additional and unexpected persons, or finding the prospect interested in something else (Chapter Five, Section 5).
2. Things. "Thing" factors might include a difference in the size of the inventory from what you anticipated, unexpected problems in using your materials, internal changes within the account that influence the needs satisfied by your product or service, and/or unanticipated technological requirements.
3. Competition. "Competitive" factors might include price advantages granted by a leading competitor, unanticipated purchases made from one or more of the competing firms, or a shift in competitive strategy.

In the "during" phase of the call, you should remind yourself that your task is twofold—to understand the customer or prospect and to influence that person's behavior in a favorable way. Paying close attention is important. Observe not only what he or she says and does, but how it is said or done. You must adjust your behavior to the other person's and be willing to take up problems that interest the prospect rather than the points you originally planned for the presentation.

In most sales jobs, fortunately, common steps occur in the process of each call, even though you will have to make modifications in individual call plans during their execution. For example, when calling on retail stores, as part of every call, you may have to check storeroom stock as well as shelf stock. This step has to precede any suggestions you make with respect to the next order. As another example, an industrial salesperson often learns from the inventory control clerk or other informed employee the state of both stocks and ready-use inventory prior to an interview with the purchasing executive. Hence, to bring about the greatest influence on purchasing behavior, it is important to perform, in proper sequence, activities that are part of virtually every call (see Appendix XXV for an example of a call and presentation checklist used by a company that merchandises through drugstores and supermarkets).

The more complete the planning, the easier you can make changes in executing it. Good planning includes consideration of a large number of possible customer reactions together with appropriate responses. It reduces the "surprise" element in the call and allows you to keep your poise and composure.

Rigidity in following your plan will lead to conflict with your customers. Insistence on taking the same steps in the same order on each call is unrealistic as well. The essence of effective planning is to ensure that you have taken all necessary steps in a manner that is most conducive to achieving your ultimate objective—inducing your customer to buy. As Dwight D. Eisenhower once stated, "Plans are nothing; planning is everything."

After the Call

This is the evaluating and improving phase of the call. Once you leave the prospect, you need to invest your time and review what has occurred—to check out the "hits, runs, and errors." You must do this while your information is fresh. Evaluate the extent to which you met your objectives, the effectiveness with which you followed your plan, and where modifications are necessary. You should put this information in your data base in the results section of the call table.

The evaluating step pays off in two ways. It provides, in effect, the beginning of the planning phase of the next call on that account. As you consider your results, part of the evaluation should be the appropriate objectives for the next call and the timing. Entering the timing of the next call in the data base allows you to later list pending calls in chronological order to help you plan your daily activities. Evaluating also enables you to discover ideas and thoughts that you can use with other accounts. By being a good evaluator, you will spot things to do and things to avoid, which is the basis for improving productivity. Careful evaluation will lead to improvement in future calls on other accounts as well as the specific one you are evaluating.

3. MANAGING EACH TRANSACTION

Maximizing the effect of the individual sales call will not necessarily result in a sale. For many selling situations, the ultimate sale or transaction will occur only after multiple sales calls. In such cases, multiple sales calls may involve contacts with different buyers in the account and even with other sales, service, and production personnel within your company. Not every company has accounts and/or sales situations that require an in-depth analysis for each transaction. However, for those that generally do, the additional level of analysis is worthwhile. Substantial volumes of business are commonly concentrated in a few accounts. By focusing your attention on every potential transaction your company could make with the customer, you should cover any potential business.

As with the sales-call selling system, you need to construct a data-base table of the inputs at the transaction level. Figure 10.2 gives an example. As you can see from the table, inputs include people from your organization, buyers, and previous sales calls. Highlighting the block next to sales calls will allow you to

Trans. ID: _____ Transaction: _____

Account: ▼ _____

Primary Decision Maker: ▼ _____

Influencer 1: ▼ _____

Influencer 2: ▼ _____

Influencer 3: ▼ _____

Coseller 1: _____ Phone: _____

Coseller 2: _____ Phone: _____

Coseller 3: _____ Phone: _____

Goals: Dollars _____

      Units _____

_____

Sales Calls ▼ ☐

Figure 10.2 A transaction table.

view sales calls that have been assigned to this transaction. You can then review past calls and plan for the next type of call that will most effectively accomplish the transaction.

At the center of the transaction selling system is the recognition of multiple sales calls and multiple personnel involved in the selling process. The concept of multiple sales calls is discussed further at the account level. Here the focus is on the effect of "team selling." As a member in the team selling process, you will often be responsible for coordinating and conducting sales calls with other personnel in your company.

Team Selling

In your ongoing relationships with prospects and customers, you will sometimes find it desirable to utilize other personnel from your firm for reasons such as these: (1) to reinforce your own efforts with an executive-level buyer (in this case you might bring along your immediate supervisor or, in some instances, one or more headquarters executives); (2) to provide technical information to people in the account (in this case you might take along a technical staff member or perhaps an executive from the company who has the specialized knowledge needed); or (3) to help someone in your own company gain necessary information concerning the product in use. For example, a member of the research and development group might wish to see a particular application of one or more of the company's products with a view to refining and improving it.

On such joint calls, you need to remember that you are the transaction manager or team captain. It is your customer and you must carefully plan the visit. You have the obligation to brief the other person(s) thoroughly on all facets of the account history. You also need to provide background on the individual or individuals whom you will see. All too frequently a salesperson limits the briefing to the product or "thing" side of the relationship and omits the details of the idiosyncrasies of the people who will be present.

The data base can provide important information in this briefing. First, the individual buyer table contains information about each of the decision makers involved in the transaction (Figure 10.3). Note the fields for individual traits, buyer position, and unique needs. Information maintained in these fields will allow you to quickly review your relationship with the buyer and to share that information with other members of your selling team.

Second, the sales-call table displays past and planned calls to the buyer under consideration. By highlighting the sales-call field in the buyer table, you can obtain a list of sales calls to this particular buyer.

Reinforcing the Selling Effort

If your primary reason for initiating a joint call is to have help in getting an order, additional considerations apply. First, you must inform the accompanying executive of the exact proposition made on your previous visit. You must come

ID: _____   Business Phone: _____

Last Name: _____

First, MI: _____

Title: _____

Company: _____

Address: _____

_____

Significant Traits: _____

Buyer Position: _____

Unique Needs: _____

_____

Sales Calls ▼ ☐

Figure 10.3 An individual buyer table.

to a meeting of the minds with the executive on what concessions, if any, should be made on this call.

Second, you both must be clear about your respective roles and responsibilities. Third, prospects may be inclined to direct most, if not all of their attention, to the accompanying executive. Consequently, as subtly as you can, you should remind the executive of this possibility in advance and arrange with him or her to redirect the prospect's questions to you whenever appropriate. In this connection, certain cues agreed on between you and the executive can provide each of you with forewarning that you are about to shift attention to the other person.

Fourth, you might want to have the accompanying executive make a few courtesy visits on other personnel in addition to the one who is the prime focus of the joint call.

Providing Technical Information

Here, too, you should cover certain points in advance if your call is to be effective. First and obviously, you must inform the other person in detail about the issues to be resolved. You need to let the technical person know the level of sophistication and understanding of the various buyers. Use the data base to review your experience with each of the decision makers.

Second, keep in mind that technical people are not salespeople and may not be sales oriented. You need to let the technical person know as politely and firmly as possible, at the advance briefing, that he or she is making the call as a source of technical information and as a problem solver for the prospect, not to try to sell the account.

Third, technical people are likely to revert to their own specialized language and jargon. You must, therefore, be alert to statements that the buyer may not understand. Your task is to interject explanatory comments. You do not want the buyer to feel ignorant.

A special case, worth serious attention, is taking service people on a joint call. Rarely do service personnel have an opportunity to call on happy customers or to see equipment that works well. Consequently, they are likely to see only problems and defects. You need to remind service people how rare it is to encounter difficulty with equipment in the field and discourage them from expounding on all the technical problems and shortcomings that they have been able to overcome for other customers. Unwittingly, they can give the impression that the product line has serious shortcomings.

Helping Company Personnel Gain Knowledge

When the objective of the joint call is for you to help someone within your own company gain information concerning your products or services, you must settle several matters in advance. First, the second person's role is to be an attentive observer and listener. Second, the customer is doing you a favor by sharing knowledge and information. On this kind of joint call, it is important to get clearance in advance for the visit and to let the customer know exactly what information you seek. Third, guard against undue demands on the time of the account's personnel, and be sure to thank the people for their assistance.

On joint calls, taking time for evaluation is even more important. A postcall discussion with the accompanying person gives you a unique opportunity to get someone else's perception of the account, the people, and challenges encountered in it. Further, this evaluation does much to ensure that subsequent joint calls on this or other accounts will be more effective. Indeed, this review also subtly educates other company personnel in the need satisfaction process.

Multiple Buyers in the Transaction

If you are to sustain and improve your position, you must avoid three unwarranted assumptions: that each member of the decision-making group is equally satisfied with the present buying-selling relationship, that each person in the account has the same view of the company needs, and that each person's influence on the buying decision remains constant with time.

Decision Makers Equally Satisfied.   Gauging the depth of each person's satisfaction with the present relationship is important. You can do this with judicious questioning and by noting the enthusiasm and conviction expressed. Your strategic objective with those well satisfied is to make them internal salespeople within the account. In the case of those less satisfied, your objective is to increase satisfaction.

Views of Needs Vary.   Because each person in the company is likely to have his or her notion of company needs and how they are being satisfied, your task is to determine, for each member of the buying group, that person's version of what would be most beneficial to the company. For example, a director of research might be concerned with the benefits of buying proven products or services and his or her influence on the buying decision would center mainly on a professional judgment concerning quality. The treasurer could be expected to look at the firm's profit picture, direct and indirect cost savings, and the advantages of dealing with a financially sound supplier. The same company's marketing director might be most interested in the value added that your product would provide for the firm's customers.

Exhibit 10.1 shows how one company (Ideal) solved the problem of getting its salespeople to analyze the persons or groups that influence decisions in each account by providing a Guide for a Complete Sales Call. Your task is to keep abreast of the needs of each individual or group. You must be equally attentive to actual or potential difficulties occurring within each group. Further, you must evaluate the extent to which each competitive salesperson is aware of the needs and how he or she is attempting to fulfill them.

Thus, if you are to "lock in" each member of the buying group, you must systematically analyze each member's perception of the needs of the enterprise as well as each person's peculiar role in the final decision-making process. Your strategy then, is to show that your offering meets two sets of criteria: those each member of the "who's who" sees a paramount to the firm's well-being and those that relate to each member's function in the customer organization. With the present account, this means basically that you must provide a continuing rationalization for each member of the influence group vis-à-vis the present situation. To the extent that you accomplish this, you give each member a sounder basis for buying from you than from alternative sources. Stated differently, you help each person reinforce his or her feelings as to why the present state of affairs should continue. If you have done your task well, should any member of the group waver, other members can provide him or her with reasons for continuing the present buying-selling relationship.

Buying Influence Varies.   The impact a particular member of the influence group has on a decision whether or not to buy varies with time and with the transaction. For example, if the customer account is having difficulty filling its own orders while working two shifts, the production manager's opinion may be most influential. In contrast, if the company is encountering competitive problems in

	PRODUCTION	PURCHASING	RESEARCH	MARKETING	MANAGEMENT
NONUSERS USES NO PRODUCT	1. Ask reasons for not using IDEAL. 2. Point out advantages of IDEAL. 3. Discuss formula changes if IDEAL is adopted. 4. Show simplification in procedures and anticipated cost savings. 5. Furnish names of users and use testimonials if appropriate. 6. Show sample.	1. Point out low cost of IDEAL when expressed in unit costs. 2. Point out expected labor savings. 3. Point out ease of obtaining IDEAL.	1. Check level of information. 2. Show advantages of IDEAL. 3. Describe technical service available. 4. Discuss new items and formulas on which the prospect is working. 5. Present latest technical information.	1. Discuss sales curves. 2. Show evidence of sales increases by other users. 3. Discuss ways of reducing returns. 4. Show possibilities of a new advertising campaign with an improved product. 5. Point out new claims that could be made if IDEAL were adopted.	1. Point out labor savings. 2. Point out possibility of simplified procedures and increased production. 3. Demonstrate potential improvement in quality. 4. Explain all services available. 5. If appropriate, ask the prospect to authorize a demonstration.
USES COMPETITIVE PRODUCT	1. Evaluate present formula. 2. Compare present product with IDEAL. 3. Discuss added benefits of our service. 4. Demonstrate IDEAL. 5. Emphasize simplified procedures. 6. Point out items in which IDEAL can be used.	1. Discuss relative unit cost. 2. Discuss relative delivery costs. 3. Explain service available. 4. Point out inventory convenience.	1. Draw comparison with IDEAL. 2. Describe technical service available.	1. Discuss sales curves. 2. Discuss possibility of reducing returns. 3. Compare consumer benefits and appeals with that of competitive products. 4. Try to find points of dissatisfaction with present products.	1. Discuss relative costs in terms of quality and unit cost. 2. Compare IDEAL service with competitors. 3. If appropriate, ask the prospect to authorize a demonstration.

	PRODUCTION	PURCHASING	RESEARCH	MARKETING	MANAGEMENT
PART USERS	1. Find out whether the customer has tried IDEAL in other items. 2. Show samples of these items with IDEAL. 3. Show advantage of using IDEAL in additional items. 4. Discuss production problems in general. 5. Show new formulas.	1. Remind user of cost advantage. 2. Ask for help in arranging demonstrations for other products. 3. Explain service available. 4. Explain new products available. 5. Point out any savings available if larger orders are placed. 6. Check satisfaction with present service.	1. Discuss other products available. 2. Point out new applications of our products. 3. Offer technical laboratory service on current problems. 4. Supply new literature and other information. 5. Pinpoint next logical area of research.	1. Discuss sales curves. 2. Discuss possibility of reducing returns in other products. 3. Point out product claims that could be made on basis of present use. 4. Discuss sales promotion on seasonal items.	1. Make sure user is aware of present usage and attending benefits. 2. Call user's attention to other products available and other areas of application of present products. 3. Show appreciation for present patronage. 4. If appropriate, ask user to referee disagreements of key personnel.
TOTAL USERS	1. Reinforce proper usage. 2. Supply new formulas. 3. Supply latest technical information. 4. Show samples of new items using IDEAL.	1. Review latest price list. 2. Check satisfaction with deliveries. 3. Discuss ordering procedures. 4. Supply new literature or information developed since last visit.	1. Furnish new formulas. 2. Supply new technical data and literature. 3. Offer technical laboratory service on current problems.	1. Discuss unique items and their marketing value. 2. Compliment them on their product line. 3. Encourage them to advise consumers about advantages of product. 4. Point out product claims that could be made on basis of present use.	1. Show samples of new items. 2. Review contacts with department heads. 3. Show appreciation for present patronage. 4. Reassure the customer that our products are good items. 5. Offer suitable entertainment, if appropriate.

Exhibit 10.1 Guide for a complete sales call.

the marketplace, the vice president of marketing may have a key influence on purchasing decisions. You should never assume any constancy of influence on the part of any individual in the customer account. Rather you should be sensitive to any changes that may dictate a shift in emphasis on your part with the various members whose opinions are important.

Using Advertising and Telemarketing

Your company's overall marketing strategy defines various ways of communicating with customers—personal selling, advertising, and telemarketing. While this book is primarily about personal selling, practiced in face-to-face and/or telephone interviews, you should also understand how what you do relates to advertising and telemarketing.

While effective sales calls are usually necessary to generate transactions, you can enhance the impact of your calls by coordinating them with your company's other demand-cultivating programs such as advertising and telemarketing.

If we view the market as having three phases, *pretransactional, transactional,* and *posttransactional,* advertising fits mainly in the pretransactional phase as a market-cultivating force. It may also enter into the posttransactional phase by providing a rationalization to the purchaser. Only in rare instances does it accomplish the transaction itself. In contrast, selling is important in all three phases (Figure 10.4).

Advertising readies the market for your personal efforts. Even with carefully selected media and well-conceived advertising, the strategy employed must be relatively general. In selling, not only can you formulate strategy for each transaction, each account, and each decision maker but you can make tactical adjustments on the spot to influence these transactions.

Even if you are not directly involved in planning or formulating your firm's advertising campaign, you must be aware of its advertising plans, the media in

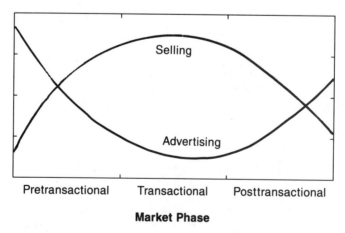

Figure 10.4 Relative importance of advertising and selling.

which the advertisements are appearing, and what objectives your firm is seeking. Having customers refer to advertisements of which you are unaware is embarrassing. In addition, you should also be aware of your competition's ads. The latter often provide an important input for your own selling strategy (see Appendix XXXI).

To coordinate demand cultivation, the content of your firm's advertising and your presentations to customers and prospects must be congruent.

Many companies accomplish the mutual reinforcement of advertising and selling by furnishing their sales force with reprints of advertisements from the printed media. In this case, you can reinforce your oral presentation with advertising copy. Videotapes and other promotional material sent to customers should also be available for you.

In addition, you are in a prime position to gauge the advertising's effectiveness with customers. You can provide useful feedback to management in this regard.

Your company may increase the effectiveness of both its advertising and personal selling programs with telemarketing. While the roles of advertising and personal selling in marketing strategy are well understood, telemarketing is continuing to evolve as a communications channel. Innovative new applications are reported almost daily. Fundamentally, telemarketing is the planned use of the telephone with traditional marketing tools. Telemarketing utilizes special facilities, advanced telecommunications systems, computerized data bases, and trained telemarketing representatives to substitute or supplement other communications media. As information technology advances, the power of telemarketing is enhanced and its uses multiply. Undoubtedly, however, the linchpin of the system is the interactive data base that allows companies to provide customized service to prospects and customers. Properly conceived and well-executed telemarketing can increase sales and reduce selling costs.

Depending on your specific sales assignment, you may substitute telemarketing for face-to-face selling. While you might be able to make five to seven face-to-face calls per day with an average cost of $250, a telemarketer can average 30 calls at about $25 per call in the same time. The numbers appropriate to your situation will undoubtedly vary from those used here, but the ratio of the cost of the face-to-face to telemarketing calls is about 10 to 1 and the ratio of the calls made by the telemarketer to the outside salesperson is roughly 5 to 1. If all calls were equal, the telemarketer would have a 50 to 1 advantage. All calls are not equal, but the data suggest that telemarketing may improve the productivity of your selling effort.

As competitive conditions continue to put pressure on margins and sales costs, you can improve your productivity by using telemarketing. For example, you might serve small accounts and/or accounts in outlying areas by assigning them to a telemarketer.

You can also supplement your selling efforts with telemarketing by asking what mix of face-to-face and telephone calls is required to serve each account in your territory. You may find ways to improve your service to your customers yet reduce expensive face-to-face selling time by handling more of your business over the telephone. You can make the calls yourself or delegate them to a telemarketer, freeing up more of your time for face-to-face activity, spreading your cost and the cost of the telemarketer over a significantly larger volume.

These examples of telemarketing services barely scratch the surface of what can be done with this powerful media. Ranging from the simple to the complex, telemarketing can also:

- Provide product information.
- Respond to promotions.
- Service customers.
- Sell add-ons and upgrades.
- Qualify leads.
- Manage marginal accounts.
- Practice need satisfaction selling.
- Manage the total territory.

Your use of telemarketing is only limited by your ingenuity and creativity. Figure 10.5 shows the probable relationship of the eight major telemarketing strategies to the phases of the selling process—pretransactional, transactional, and posttransactional.

4. MANAGING EACH ACCOUNT

Because you are the manager of a business, your own territory, or market segment, one of your objectives is to increase business from existing accounts and to acquire new business from those who are not now customers. You have, therefore, an objective to strengthen the selling-buying relationship with each customer to gain an increased share of the available business. You also have an objective to win a share of the business available in prospective accounts. For every account, therefore, you should have immediate, intermediate, and long-range objectives.

Within each account, you should make profitable use of the talent, information, and material resources available to you. In fostering account relationships,

	Pre-transactional	Transactional	Post-transactional
Manage Total Territory	X	X	X
Practice Need Satisfaction Selling	X	X	X
Manage Marginal Accounts	X	X	X
Qualify Leads	X	–	–
Sell Add-Ons and Upgrades	X	X	–
Service Customers	–	X	X
Respond to Promotions	X	–	X
Provide Product Information	X	–	X

Figure 10.5 Eight major telemarketing strategies related to market phase.

you must take into consideration your company's advertising effort, its direct marketing programs, the merchandising aids it makes available, and perhaps its field services and other marketing forces and resources. All of these demand-creating forces exist for one purpose—creating and recreating customers.

To attain your objectives and make the most efficient use of your time and efforts, you should analyze both customer and prospect accounts.

Analyzing Customer Account Potential

Figure 10.6 (and Appendix XXXII) presents nine factors that you must define if you are to do an effective job of analyzing each customer account. In the column labeled "Situation Up to Now" the first question to be answered is, "How much business has been available for all sources—for the competition as well as myself?" Depending on the field of sales work, this can be reported in dollars, units, and/or both. The next square in the column calls for an answer to the question, "What are my sales in dollars or units with this account for that period under consideration?" Finally, in the third square of this column, your present share of the account's business is indicated by dividing the volume of business you enjoy by the total business available.

<u>OO634</u>
Account

<u>*J. H. Wills*</u>
Salesperson

<u>9/2/xx</u>
Date

	Situation up to Now	Future Situation	Trend
Industry (Competition and My Company	Market: Dollars or Units *$5,000 sealing compound per year.*	Potential market: Dollars or Units *With expansion best estimate is $7,000 per year.*	Market up or down *+40%*
My Company	Sales: Dollars or Units *$1,500 of type "K" sealing compound.*	Potential sales: Dollars or Units *$3,000 of type "K" because new machines require it.*	Sales up or down *+100%*
My Company's Share	Sales / Market *30%*	Potential sales / Potential market *43%*	Penetration *2½ times*

Figure 10.6 Account-potential planning guide (for customers).

The next column, "Future Situation," puts the emphasis on the time up to the next sales call, the next fiscal period, or some other appropriate time period. The first square requires the answer to the question, "What is the best forecast of potential business for all vendors from this account for the period under consideration?" This is the market potential of the account. The second square in this column asks you to give your best prediction of the amount of business you will get from the account during the period ahead. This is your sales potential. Finally, the third square calls for your potential share by dividing your expected business (Square two) by the total potential business (Square one).

The final column is labeled "Trend." Looking across the first row, if the future figure is larger than the past figure, the trend is upward, and there is an anticipated increase in business, which can be expressed as a percentage. In this example, the $2,000 increase is divided by the base of $5,000 to arrive at the 40 percent increase. If, in a given account, the potential is less than business up to now, the trend is downward, so a percentage decrease is computed. The percentage increase or decrease that you expect is entered in the second square of the last column. Finally, the third square contains the ratio of your sales trend to the marketplace trend in the particular account. In the example, the salesperson expects to penetrate two and one-half times relative to the trend in total business available (100% divided by 40%).

Analyzing Account Potential for Coverage

The second step in analyzing account potential is to compare each account with other accounts in your territory. You must determine the appropriate number of calls to make on each account to maximize the productivity of the account.

Accounts are analyzed on two dimensions: account attractiveness and competitive position. Attractiveness is the account's need for and ability to purchase your product or service. This opportunity is essentially available to firms in your market niche. Competitive position is your position relative to competing firms—given that a prospect will purchase a product or service, what is the probability that it will purchase from you? You can use these two dimensions to classify your accounts into a four-cell grid (Figure 10.7).

Key Accounts

These are the accounts that will return the highest sales and profits to the company. They are the critical accounts in the short run as they will in large part determine short-run profits. You must pay special attention to these companies due to their high potential for sales and the high probability that you can close those sales.

Prospect Accounts

These companies represent your future. They are investments for long-term profitability. These companies are highly attractive, but for whatever reasons

COMPETITIVE POSITION

	HIGH	LOW
HIGH **ACCOUNT ATTRACTIVENESS** **LOW**	**Cell 1** **KEY ACCOUNTS STRATEGY** High level of calls to maintain current position and maximize profits.	**Cell 2** **PROSPECT ACCOUNTS STRATEGY** High level of calls to develop accounts into profitable, key accounts.
	Cell 3 **STABLE ACCOUNTS STRATEGY** Moderate level of calls to maintain position but recognize limited growth opportunity.	**Cell 4** **WEAK ACCOUNTS STRATEGY** Minimal level of calls. Consider options of telephone sales or elimination of account.

Figure 10.7   Sales portfolio.

you do not currently have a competitive position with them. They may not know much about your offering, they may have strong loyalties to competing firms, or their needs may be new and undeveloped. Your returns from these companies will generally be low in the short run because a high investment of time and effort is required to develop these accounts and gain a competitive position with them. If you disregard these accounts, however, your future sales and income will suffer. This segment is most critical to your long-term growth and success.

Stable Accounts

These are companies that may have limited opportunity for growth or large sales; but what they do purchase, they generally purchase from you. They often are accounts that you have had for a long time. A common misallocation of effort is to spend too much time with these. You may be tempted to call on these accounts because they are "old friends." However, the number of calls can usually be lowered with little or no decrease in the volume of sales, freeing up time for reallocation. Less frequently, you may realize that you are spending too little time with loyal accounts. You should increase your calls on these before the account surprises you by selecting a more attentive salesperson.

Weak Accounts

These accounts are prime candidates for elimination from your portfolio. Accounts in this category may come from any of the other cells. You may recognize that accounts you first considered to be Prospects do not need your products or services. Changes in the account or in competitive offerings may result in Key Accounts or Stable Accounts changing their purchasing patterns.

The objective in managing your accounts is to develop as many Key Accounts as possible. Key Accounts will primarily come from Prospects. Over time these can become less profitable and thus become Stable Accounts. Those that become less profitable through lack of opportunity as well as through loss of strength or position become the Weak Accounts. As mentioned earlier, Prospects may not have the potential you initially believed, so they are reclassified as Weak Accounts. Changes in the business environment may enable Stable Accounts to become Prospects for your offerings and to become Key Accounts. Even Weak Accounts may become Prospects due to changes in their needs, their capability to buy, or changes in your own product offerings. You need, however, to understand the status of your accounts for the present and immediate future so that you can develop appropriate strategies for calling on them.

Applying the Portfolio Concept to Accounts

To classify your accounts, you must obtain information on the attractiveness of and your competitive position in each account. One tool for evaluating your accounts is a set of questions (Figure 10.8). These questions were developed for a company in the industrial equipment industry. Based on your knowledge and experience of your industry, you can develop a similar set of questions.

Once you have developed the questions, you can use them to evaluate your accounts (Figure 10.9). Experience suggests seasoned salespeople have little difficulty developing the information but new salespeople may have to consult with their managers.

Notice that after the scores on each measure are entered, they are summed to generate an overall account attractiveness score (27) and a competitive position score (26). In this example, each measure is weighted equally. Depending on your industry and how your products or services are purchased, you may wish to use different weights for the questions.

To classify your accounts, you must determine the appropriate "break points" for account attractiveness and competitive position. Usually, you will have an idea where the break points should be, and you can develop the individual measurement scales so that the midpoint on each scale represents the appropriate break point. Thus the midpoint on the overall dimension would then be the appropriate break point for classifying the accounts.

For the preceding example, assume the appropriate break points are the midpoints of the scores. The potential scores on the measures range from 1 to 6 with a midpoint of 3.5. The midpoint for the sum of the scores, therefore, would be 17.5 ($5 \times 3.5 = 17.5$). The example is above 17.5 on both dimensions so would be classified as a Key Account.

A major reason for classifying your accounts is to determine how much time you should allocate to each account. Two approaches are available. The first is

Account Name ─────────────────────────────────

Attractiveness

1. Extensiveness of the account's equipment maintenance program.

Extensive   6   5   4   3   2   1   Limited

2. Strength of the account's position in its market.

Strong position   6   5   4   3   2   1   Weak position

3. Growth rate of account.

High growth rate   6   5   4   3   2   1   Low growth rate

4. Financial ability of the account to purchase capital equipment.

Financially strong   6   5   4   3   2   1   Financially weak

5. Tenure of the account in distributor's market area.

Well established   6   5   4   3   2   1   New in the market

Competitive Position

1. Account's overall attitude towards distributor's brand of equipment.

Very positive   6   5   4   3   2   1   Very negative

2. Previous business experience with account.

High experience   6   5   4   3   2   1   No experience

3. Distributor's familiarity with the people and operations of account.

Very familiar   6   5   4   3   2   1   Not familiar

4. Distributor's relationship with the people who make equipment purchasing decisions for the account.

Good relationship   6   5   4   3   2   1   Poor relationship

5. Distributor's relationship with the account's equipment users.

Good relationship   6   5   4   3   2   1   Poor relationship

Figure 10.8   Account evaluation form.

Account ID: _____   Name: _____

Sales Calls Past 12 months _____

Total Sales Past 12 months _____

Attractiveness Factor

		Score
1.	Extensiveness of maintenance program.	5
2.	Strength of account's position in market.	6
3.	Growth rate of account.	4
4.	Financial ability to purchase capital equipment.	6
5.	Tenure of account in market area.	6
	Score	27

Competitive Position Factor

		Score
1.	Attitude toward distributor's brand of equipment.	5
2.	Previous business experience with account.	6
3.	Distributor's familiarity with people and operations.	5
4.	Distributor's relationship with decision makers.	5
5.	Distributor's relationship with equipment users.	5
	Score	26

Goal-based work load estimate:	12
Category classification:	1
Recommended classification work load:	12
Individual work load estimate:	13.5

Figure 10.9   Account information table.

to estimate how much effort you think is necessary to accomplish your objectives in each account.

A second approach is to manage your accounts by category. For instance, Prospect Accounts might be assigned a relatively high level of call activity because the strategy is to develop them into Key Accounts. Key Accounts would receive a high level of attention to ward off competitors and maintain current profitability.

Stable Accounts and Weak Accounts would receive significantly less attention. For example, the average number of calls per year might be: 12 for Key Accounts, 8 for Prospect Accounts, 6 for Stable Accounts, and 2 for Weak Accounts.

Just because call levels are suggested for accounts does not mean that all accounts in the category would receive the same level of activity. You may adjust for individual differences, depending on your knowledge of the account.

The benefit of account analysis is the recognition that accounts differ in sales potential, likelihood of purchasing, and in the effort required to obtain and service them. Using the two-dimensional account classification, you can analyze how many accounts should be in each category. A common problem is to find you have too many Stable or Weak Accounts and not enough Prospect Accounts to ensure your future income. You must cultivate more new accounts to replace attrition and to grow.

After you have determined reasonable guidelines for how many calls to make on each category of account, you can check the actual calls made versus your objectives. Frequently, Stable Accounts receive too much or too little attention. Prospect Accounts are avoided many times because they are not well known, relationships have not been established, and the probability of a sale is uncertain.

Accounts in your territory will generally change over time. Hence, you should reanalyze each account on a timely basis. Additional analysis will indicate how effective you are at converting Prospect Accounts to Key Accounts and increasing your business with your Key Accounts.

Key Accounts: Gaining Penetration

In each Key Account, your continuing objective should be to increase penetration. You must seek to tailor your company's products and services to the needs of the customer; to get to know the decision makers better than before, both as individuals and as a group; and to learn more about how your products and services are used.

Homeostasis

You face strategic challenges in your customer accounts that differ from those in your prospect accounts. With the former, your goal is to maintain homeostasis; that is, keep your company, its goods and services, and yourself locked in. You may strive for a larger share of the business by either selling more of your current products or services or increasing business through the introduction of new ones. However, even in accomplishing this, you seek to manage the account in a manner that will minimize the likelihood of competition.

Conversely, with prospect accounts, your goal is to disturb homeostasis, to upset the status quo, and thus make the prospect receptive to consideration of your products and services. To achieve this, you must somehow demonstrate that your company, products, services, prices, and team provide a different and better overall offering than those available from your competition.

People

A second strategic difference is your handling of key people in customer accounts versus prospect accounts. In both categories of business, it is vital to identify members of the decision-making group. With customer accounts, however, you must pay particular heed to those persons who have reservations or doubts about the present business relationship. You must strengthen these weak people-links. The best assumption you can make about competitive activity is that entry will be sought through one or more of these people whose homeostasis is easiest to disturb. In the case of prospect accounts, in contrast, you are seeking to locate those weak people—links that may exist in the people cycle. Through them, you have the best opportunity to initiate business. Because decision makers change with time, you must also be alert to determine who is becoming more influential and who is no longer important in buying decisions.

Products and Services

In both customer and prospect accounts, you must also know the steps through which the products and services move from the initiation of the order to the final application. Here too, as with people-links, the strategy is different for customer accounts and prospect accounts. In the case of customers, your strategic objective is to prevent trouble or difficulty. By observation and inquiry, you must trace your products through the various steps and prevent problems from occurring. Your best assumption is that the competition will be on the lookout for these problems and capitalize on them as a way of making entry. In contrast, in prospect accounts, your key objective is finding trouble. Locating the difficulty or problem and helping to solve it may present your best means for initial penetration of the account.

Additional Considerations in Effective Account Management

To manage each account successfully, you must keep an up-to-date data base. The discipline of entering call data while it is still fresh in your memory is a primary ingredient of viable account records. The cumulative history that call records provide enables you to predict the trend in each account. In keeping each account record, noting the people information is also important. By reviewing these tables periodically, you will make sure you do not neglect any important decision maker.

One practice you must guard against is investing your time in each account with the people whom you like and who like you. Rather, the criterion of time investment with individuals in each account should be their relative importance in making buying decisions. In the case of customer accounts, you must reinforce yourself, your products and services, and your company with those people *least* satisfied with you. Competition is likely to use such weak links as entry points. In the case of prospective accounts, you must spot the people who are least satisfied with the existing situation and use them as a place for initial penetration.

5. MANAGING THE TERRITORY

If you manage each call, each transaction, and each account effectively, you have gone a long way toward managing your territory effectively. The task of fitting the plans made for each account into a master plan for the territory remains however. Further, you will in all probability perform certain other duties related to but not directly involved in calling on accounts. These may include describing, analyzing, and predicting total business and business potential for the whole territory; representing the company at trade shows and in trade associations; conducting, assisting with, or complementing specific market research projects; working with dealers and dealers' salespeople; and providing various services, such as adjusting and starting up equipment once it has been installed and/or services contracted. The following sections examine the managerial aspects of some of these related activities.

Predicting Total Business in the Territory

To predict total business in the territory, you will probably need to use both primary and secondary sources of information. Primary sources include your own observations and information on each account stored in the data base you have personally created, plus company-furnished market research data. Secondary sources, depending on the nature of your sales assignment, may include industry surveys, government reports, and special studies and assessments. The task of predicting will be easier if you divide it into three parts; namely, existing business, prospective business (prospects called on one or more times at the time of analysis), and other potential business.

If you have done a careful job of analyzing each customer account, the first part of the project is an easy one, available on your computer, and the estimates are likely to be more valid than those based on staff-generated marketing research information. Your estimates for the second part, prospective accounts, may not be as accurate. Here the company's market research information, plus data from secondary sources, is usually of greater validity than your own observations. Finally, for the third part, you must rely on market research data and information from secondary sources for your description, analysis, and prediction. Once you have made the three estimates, you can summarize them as shown in Figure 10.10 (and Appendix XXXIII) to complete the territory picture.

In preparing the forecast, keep the following in mind. You should make as accurate an estimate as possible (in percentage form) of the number of customer accounts that will be lost during the period despite your best efforts. This gives the minimum number of new accounts that you must generate simply to hold your own. If one of your objectives for the territory is growth, then you will have to

No. 17
Territory

J. H. Wills
Salesperson

9/2/xx
Date

		Situation up to Now	Future Situation
Customers	Total Market (Competition and My Company)	$800,000	$1,000,000
	Total Sales (My Company)	$100,000	$130,000
	Share	12.5%	13%
Prospects	Total Market (Competition and My Company)	$1,950,000	$2,250,000
	Total Sales (My Company)		$225,000
	Share		10%
Other Potential Business	Total Market (Competition and My Company)	$60,000	$70,000
	Total Sales (My Company)		$7,000
	Share		10%

Figure 10.10 Territory-potential planning guide.

determine how many additional prospective accounts you must convert not only to make up for the lost accounts but also to add to your total. For example, one consumer-goods firm has found that, on the average, each salesperson can expect a 15 percent account mortality rate per year. In the average territory, a salesperson handles about 50 accounts. Thus, each salesperson for this company must plan to generate at least seven or eight new accounts per year just to remain even. In this particular company, each salesperson is expected to show a 10 percent increase in the number of accounts sold each year. Thus, in effect, each salesperson must generate at least 12 to 13 new accounts per year to attain the expected goal.

Trade and Industry Relations

One of your duties may involve representing your company in various trade and industry associations. This may entail attendance and participation at meetings, manning company exhibits at trade shows, demonstrating the product line or describing services at conventions, and similar activities. Here, as with other job duties, planning is highly beneficial.

As a professional, you must consider the potential benefits, relative to your investment of time, effort, and money. Your first decision may be which associations to join and which shows and exhibitions to attend. The wider the product line, the more diversified the marketplace, the more difficult it is to make proper choices. Generally speaking, however, selecting a few and deriving full benefit from them is better than joining everything and getting little return from your investment. The likely time demand in relation to the payoff in profitable business is a prime criterion.

We cannot overemphasize the necessity of preplanning for a trade show. Besides verifying the number of potential prospects attending and establishing goals to achieve while there, you must have a follow-up plan in place before the show begins. How will you handle the leads generated after this show? In addition, the need satisfaction process applies to trade show and conference environments, but it should be modified to allow for communicating with large numbers of people in relatively short encounters (Exhibit 10.2). Given the expense and potentially high impact of trade shows, you should consider simulating trade show conditions and role playing before the show to warm up your team.

For each meeting or show you attend, you should set objectives. These may include:

- To generate a specific number of qualified leads.
- To launch a new product or service.
- To learn more about a particular competitor's product/service.
- To meet with key distributors.
- To obtain feedback on key uses of your product/service.

Wasting time at a convention or show is easy. So, once you have the determined objectives for attending, establish a timetable for each day. Each night, review the day's activities, evaluate accomplishments, and revise plans, if necessary, for the next day. You can use mealtimes for a dual purpose: to entertain people who are important to you, and to accomplish matters that might be difficult to handle in the hustle-bustle of the convention with its many interruptions.

You may face the problem of controlling the distribution of samples, pamphlets, and so on. You certainly want to place these in the hands of people who should have them, but, on the other hand, you want to avoid promiscuous distribution to "collectors," curiosity seekers, and those seeking entertainment. Some companies merely have specimen materials at the exhibit and provide a means to mail the appropriate materials to qualified prospects. The request for a business

SALES MODEL APPLICATIONS

1. Accord Uniqueness

   There is no such thing as a typical prospect. Every person is a unique individual.

2. Questioning Technique

   Know what you are going to say—*prepare* and *rehearse.*

   Start dialogue with an open-ended question requiring more than a one-word answer.

   Develop open-ended questions that are framed around some factor that is interesting, unusual, humorous, or dramatic about your products and services.

   Plan questions that enable you to quickly qualify the prospects and learn key information.

3. Communicating—Sending cues and monitoring feedback

   20%—What you say—the content.

   65%—Nonverbal—good eye contact critical.

   15%—How you say it—tone, volume, voice, and pitch.

   Greet prospects at the booth's perimeter by welcoming them to our organization's environment.

   Establish level of knowledge/interest in your products and services.

   Show product knowledge by *succinctly* answering prospect questions.

   Weave prospect's own words into the conversation.

   Pause and allow prospect to respond or ask questions.

   When qualifying, find the need, determine how strong the need is, and present *briefly* how you can satisfy the need.

   Try to connect with several prospects, not just the one with whom you started the conversation.

   Don't be afraid to say "I don't know." Find out and follow up.

   Speaking up shows confidence. Speak clearly and slowly.

4. The Close

   Determine the status of each lead.

   Write lead information on back of lead card immediately while prospect is still with you.

   Prioritize the leads.

   Put "Follow Up Plan" into action.

Exhibit 10.2   Trade shows and the sales model.

card is one easy way to screen the request and expedite shipping. Another is to use a lead card and well-prepared questions to get the basic information you need to quickly qualify the prospect and determine the priority of the lead.

If you are to make a presentation at a meeting, remember that you are placing the company's reputation before the audience. Careful preparation and a dry run will do much to ensure a successful effort. If you intend to use visuals, check them out in advance. If possible, look over the room or hall where you are to make the presentation, and check the layout, acoustics, and lighting. Finally, adhere rigidly to the prescribed timetable.

Market Research

You are the company's eyes and ears in the marketplace. Through your observations and inquiries, your company keeps abreast of and, ideally, ahead of the competition. You, therefore, have a major responsibility to channel significant information to your management. You should do this task promptly and on a relatively continuing basis. In addition to this day-to-day market intelligence function, you may occasionally assist with specific research projects. For example, you might help with such activities as:

- Placing prototypes with selected customers for field testing.
- Providing entry for staff personnel to customers and prospects.
- Collecting specific data on company products and/or services as well as on competitive offerings.
- Obtaining customers' and prospects' answers to specific questions.
- Using the territory as a test market for a new product or service.

Selection for such assignments indicates the company's confidence in your business acumen, resourcefulness, and knowledge. While these tasks may be time consuming and encroach on your already-crowded schedule, you should undertake such extra assignments with enthusiasm and a professional managerial attitude. Research projects are useful for the company and developmental for yourself.

Such a project should never jeopardize ongoing account relationships. As the territory and account manager, you are probably the best qualified to answer such questions as: Which accounts should be approached? What is the best way to arrange for needed cooperation? When is the best time to make arrangements?

In market research, a professional body of knowledge exists, just as it does in selling. You may not perceive the full significance of a particular project. Some of the directions for it may seem unimportant or silly. But, the research should be executed exactly as designed if the results are to be worthwhile to your company. "Second guessing" or modifying the arrangements is a serious mistake.

Working with Dealers and Dealers' Salespeople

If you call on dealers, distributors, or other resellers, you have to be a consultant and teacher as well as a salesperson. (Note: If you work for a wholesaler, you should read this section to determine what to expect of suppliers' salespeople.) Selling the account is not enough; you have an obligation to help the account sell products and services to its marketplace. Often you face the additional task of inducing the dealer and the dealer's sales force to push your product line in preference to a competitor's.

Your general objective in this phase of your work is to help each dealer to be a good businessperson. The first step in achieving this goal is to use care in choosing dealers to represent your company. You should assess each dealer's present market share for the sale of relevant products as well as the future or potential market share. You should check each dealer's reputation, credit rating, business acumen, and general standing in the community. Finally, you can develop a more comprehensive list that is customized to your particular situation.

Assuming that you have selected the best dealers, what is the next step? You should then become well enough acquainted with each dealer and his or her marketplace to suggest specific ways to be of help. These may include: allocating a definite number of "work with" days for helping the dealer's sales force, participating in sales meetings, making calls with the dealer on high-potential accounts, demonstrating the product line at meetings, suggesting inventory controls and procedures, and apprising the dealer of useful marketing information.

As with any other duty, effective performance depends in large measure on careful planning. For example, if you are to participate in a dealer's sales meeting, the suggestions for presentations before trade groups apply. You should also specify definite objectives for the session, determine the content and coverage of the meeting, and decide on the methods of presentation. Providing for real or simulated participation by the dealers' salespeople is important. Remember, the impression that you make, as a person, on the audience can markedly influence whether your message is heeded and applied or not.

As another example, in planning a "work with" day, you must remember that you are going to the dealer-salesperson's accounts. Your manner in giving advice and suggestions is going to determine whether the dealer's salesperson and his or her accounts accept you. The challenge is to meet the dealer-salesperson's learning needs. These may involve technical and product information as well as selling principles, methods, and techniques. You should conduct yourself so that the dealer's salesperson sees you as a helpful assistant, not as a show-off flaunting superior knowledge. You must remember that you are now in the position of the extra person described in the Joint Call discussion and should act accordingly.

The Salesperson-Oriented Product Manual described in Chapter One would be a valuable tool for training dealer sales personnel. While compiling one on your own may be beyond your resources, you should recommend such a procedure to your management.

Other Functions

In addition to the continuing role of consultant and problem solver for each account, your job may involve specific customer services. Some examples of these are:

- Being on hand at the start up of machinery purchased by a customer to supervise the installation and make necessary adjustments.
- Assisting customers in setting up displays for special events or initiating the seasonal marketing effort.
- Helping accounts recruit and select sales and other personnel.
- Collaborating on special sales by demonstrating products or services, setting up cooperative advertising, and so on.

An important consideration here, as with other "nonselling" duties, is sensible time allocation, both in relation to the time required for direct selling activities and in relation to the actual or potential business in the account. Sometimes, because these service duties are so tangible and interesting, salespeople engage in them to the neglect of other aspects of their jobs. On the other hand, some salespeople neglect these services, erroneously assuming that they do not contribute directly enough to sales.

6. MAXIMIZING TERRITORY COVERAGE

The territory is a business that you manage. Any business, including a sales territory, achieves growth only from two sources-increased share in existing accounts, and the generation of new ones. Thus, your objective in the simplest terms is *to sell the full line to the full marketplace.*

The strategy outline in Section 4 for handling the decision makers within each account has its parallel within the territory in many fields of selling. The principles to follow with the external "who's who" are much the same as those for influencing the people-cycle in the company. For example, in pharmaceutical sales work, the sales representative who wants to reinforce existing accounts and create new ones must deal with an external people-cycle that includes the physician, the wholesaler, the retailer, and the various professional groups within buying organizations, perhaps within each hospital. In industrial sales work—for instance, in the sale of air-conditioning equipment—the sales engineer has an external influence group consisting of the financial interests, the architects, the consulting engineer, and the contractors.

The first step, then, in increasing territory coverage is to know who influences whom with regard to purchasing decisions in the various communities comprising the territory. In the case of accounts where business presently exists, these external people-links need continuing reinforcement. Where you seek new business, you must make new contacts.

It is a sound assumption that these people are being cultivated by competitive salespeople. The stronger your relationship with each of them, the more likely you will retain present accounts and increase the share of business. Where you are seeking new accounts, disturbing homeostasis in these external spheres of influence is your strategic objective. Your task is to get to know each influential person as intimately as possible and to convince him or her of the soundness of your company, its products and services, its prices, and its people. Further you must show the product's benefits to the person who is recommending your offering to decision makers.

Prospecting

In most sales situations the creation of new accounts is so critical that analyzing the process in some detail is worthwhile. This phase of sales work, prospecting, has two facets—finding and screening potential customers. For example, in the case of some leads furnished by customers, the information is sufficient to warrant classifying the prospects as bona fide. Others are only suspects and you must find ways and means to screen them by generating additional information.

Generating Leads

One sales executive describes customers as the unpaid sales force. Effective salespeople take every opportunity to generate new leads from present customers. The more satisfaction customers derive from their present buying-selling relationships, the more likely they will willingly assist you to find new business. Third-party testimony and cooperation can be powerful sales weapons. They are key factors in increasing territory coverage.

In most sales territories, individuals or firms exist whose buying behavior is directly imitated by others. To achieve full territory coverage, you must take every opportunity to identify and cultivate such accounts. Indeed, making expenditures of time, talent, and money beyond the worth of the business might be wise to gain influence with opinion leaders. Research in the pharmaceutical field corroborates this observation. The prescribing habits of certain leading physicians are imitated by others. In the industrial marketplace, smaller firms often look to larger ones to determine what to buy and with whom to deal.

Noncompeting salespeople constitute another important source of information about potential business. You are likely to find this source useful in proportion to your own ability to generate leads for others. It is a reciprocal relationship. Here, as in the case of leads from customers, you may be able to classify some as prospects; others may need screening. Occasionally, the noncompeting salesperson may furnish direct entry either through a joint call or by permission to use his or her name. If you attempt this, however, you must be certain that the other salesperson has a good relationship with the particular account. Otherwise, the reference will boomerang. Generally, leads from noncompeting salespeople are suspect. You need additional information to determine if business is available.

Acquaintances and friends in the business community are also important sources of new business. Networking is important! Bankers, executives of the Chamber of Commerce, and trade and industrial groups can also apprise you of new businesses and shifts in existing firms. You must respect confidences to cultivate these sources.

Telephone, mail inquiries, and responses to advertising are still other sources of leads. Your company may also use telemarketing, either alone or in combination with other direct response media, to generate leads. Here, a premium is on your doing a careful job of screening with a minimum investment of time, effort, and out-of-pocket expense. You should experiment with various screening techniques to ensure that your response is related to the probable commercial value of the lead.

In some fields of selling, special directories, reports, and open-to-bid announcements can provide leads. This category varies in importance and quantity from industry to industry. Each salesperson should investigate whether such a source is available and, by experience, determine its worth.

Salespeople in some fields discover new business by cold canvass. To use this method effectively, you should apply some crude criteria or yardsticks before investing time and effort on interviews. These may involve observations such as the size of the establishment, traffic flow in the case of a retailer or wholesaler, amount and kind of inventory in sight, and the general appearance and condition of the plant. Should you feel it worthwhile to call, you must be armed with a quick method of screening in the form of a repertoire of questions that you can use to qualify the prospect.

Evaluating Leads

Screening leads from every source involves generating information on the following factors:

1. *Financial Ability.* Can they pay for the product and/or service?
2. *Volume of Business.* How much business is required for a viable relationship?
3. *Special Requirements.* Is the product or service in its standard form directly usable by the prospect? If not, what special services or modification will be required?
4. *Continuity.* Is an ongoing buying-selling relationship likely to develop?
5. *Location.* Can the potential account be serviced with reasonable cost?

You can obtain information on financial strength through observation, questioning, references, Dun & Bradstreet and other credit reports, and, in many cases, your company's credit department. Whatever the assistance available, ultimately your sound commercial judgment must prevail. More often than not, when you do not follow sound credit criteria, problems ensue. The easiest sale is one where the customer takes your product and has no intention of paying.

With regard to the volume of business, you need to think about your company's best interests first. Fixed costs are associated with servicing any account regardless of size. Invariably, some accounts will be too small to cultivate. Most firms are subject to the 80–20 rule, 80 percent of the business occurs in

20 percent of the accounts. However, you may well develop new customers with the thought that they have every chance of growing to a profitable size.

With respect to special requirements, remind yourself that your task is to sell your company's products and services in the form in which they are produced, unless you represent a job shop or custom house. Presumably, product design is based on optimizing use with a defined target market. Each time you modify your offering, not only have you incurred extra costs for your company, but also your action might be construed as indicating a shortcoming in the offering. You must weigh any request for special products or services against the efforts and costs that you are likely to incur.

For many companies, continuity of the business relationship is an important consideration. Often achieving break-even on one or even several transactions is unlikely. For example, one specialty chemical firm estimates that a profitable relationship in a new account is not achieved until the fourth order is written. Thus, your task is to size up the chances for continuing business.

Location, the fifth factor, is likely to be a consideration in those fields of selling where buying may be done in one office but shipments are made to the new customer's various sites. When a considerable amount of follow-up service and personal contact work is involved, you must balance the attendant cost for these services against the likely volume of goods moving to each of the locations.

While prospecting is vital to increasing territory coverage, never do it at the expense of increasing your share of business in your existing accounts. Further, to do prospecting efficiently, you must systematize it so that you do not invest undue amounts of time in it. You should estimate the time that you need to devote to cultivating new accounts. Some firms have written policies on this point. Moreover, you can do much of the background and investigative aspects of prospecting during hours when you cannot call on customers and prospects.

Time Management

As noted in Chapter Nine, effective time management is critical in maximizing communication with customers and prospects. Time is your prime investment.

The basic time-management challenge most salespeople face is selling to a number of customers and prospects, each of whom is in a different phase of the sales cycle. You can readily visualize taking one lead through the complete sales cycle to closure, but when you must work 5, 25, or 50 leads, you need a new perspective. When you are responsible for more than a few clients, how are you to prospect, qualify leads, develop needs, determine need awareness, handle objections, close sales, and follow up effectively?

The sales funnel is an excellent conceptual tool for managing your time while practicing the need satisfaction selling process (Figure 10.11). It will help you focus your energies for greater productivity and long-term success. Use of the funnel helps you sort prospects and track their progress. Based on your analysis of where prospects are in the funnel, you can concentrate your efforts on the sales work required to keep each prospect moving toward the close.

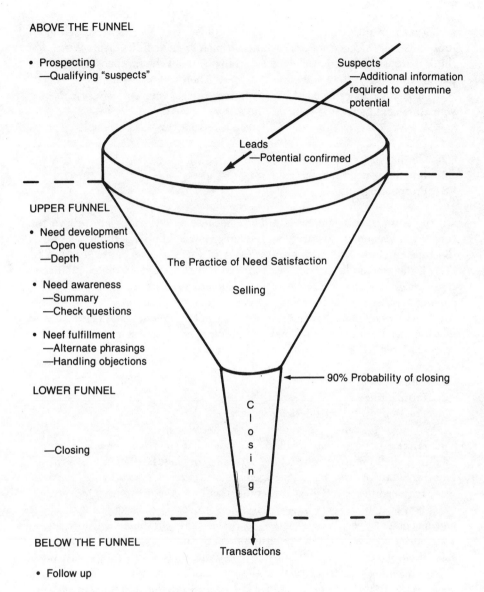

ABOVE THE FUNNEL

- Prospecting
  —Qualifying "suspects"

Suspects
—Additional information
required to determine
potential

Leads
—Potential confirmed

UPPER FUNNEL

- Need development
  —Open questions
  —Depth

The Practice of Need Satisfaction

Selling

- Need awareness
  —Summary
  —Check questions

- Neef fulfillment
  —Alternate phrasings
  —Handling objections

LOWER FUNNEL

—Closing

90% Probability of closing

C
l
o
s
i
n
g

BELOW THE FUNNEL

Transactions

- Follow up

Figure 10.11   The sales funnel.

Above the funnel you are prospecting and qualifying leads. If you have one piece of data suggesting you might be able to do business with a prospect, the prospect is a suspect. When you have confirming evidence, a second data point, you can consider the suspect to be a qualified lead and put it into the top of the funnel. If your prospecting is successful, a number of leads will enter the funnel. It takes many leads to generate one transaction. At this point, the need satisfaction model takes over. In the upper part of the funnel, you develop needs and move prospects toward need awareness and ultimately need fulfillment. When you think there is a 90 percent chance of closing, you put the prospect in the lower part of the funnel. Next you close the order. Then you follow up.

The funnel concept has three main uses: setting your objectives, managing your time, and increasing your productivity.

When asked how they would allocate their time, most salespeople respond:

1. Closing.
2. Practicing need satisfaction.
3. Prospecting.

On the surface, this ranking is rational because as prospects move down the funnel you learn more about them, reducing your level of uncertainty as well as the time to close. Make no mistake about it, when prospects are ready to be closed, they should be closed. The problem is that because of the possibility of rejection, prospecting can be a very uncertain and intimidating process. Hence, a natural tendency exists to avoid prospecting and to spend too much time in the need satisfaction model. When this occurs, you tend to enter an uneven flow of qualified leads into the funnel and, as a result, have unnecessary fluctuations in sales. The remedy is to set different priorities:

1. Closing.
2. Prospecting.
3. Practicing need satisfaction.

This ranking ensures that you close sales and that you have a steady stream of qualified leads entering your selling system, reducing the "boom and bust" effect frequently observed in unmanaged selling systems. In addition, all the sales work required to convert leads into orders will be done more productively.

Many customers remain loyal, but others are lost because of changing needs and/or competitive inroads. Hence, to replace lost customers and to increase your business, you must continuously prospect and execute each phase of the sales cycle more effectively than your competitors. To do this, you must think about allocating your time. Look at the total sales work you have to do at each stage of the funnel. For example, if you have just developed a number of high-quality leads, you might allocate 20 percent of your time above the funnel, 60 percent to the upper funnel, and 20 percent to the lower funnel. Of course, as the distribution of your work load changes, you must reallocate your time to keep your selling system in balance. Undoubtedly emergencies will interrupt your schedule, but scheduling is not planning. You must plan your time to achieve your objectives.

To increase your productivity, you need to develop a quantitative picture of how your funnel operates. You begin by coding leads by their source: unsolicited, trade show, sales executive, research, competition, telemarketing, advertisements, and so on. For each source you should track the number of leads and develop qualitative definitions of what differentiates a suspect from a lead. Once leads enter your system, how many make it through the upper part of the funnel? How many proposals are written? Of the leads you put into the lower part of the funnel, how many close? Of those closed, how many become repeat customers? How many clients are lost? Ultimately, you want to know:

- How can you improve the quantity and quality of leads?
- How many leads are needed weekly (monthly, yearly) to sustain your selling system? To increase it?
- Which sources are most productive for you?
- How can you move qualified leads through the system more effectively?
- What can you do at each phase to improve productivity?
- How many cases have a 90 percent probability of closing in the near future? How many should you have?
- How can you improve your closing rate?
- How many leads (by source) do you need to produce a transaction?
- What can you do to improve your operating characteristics?

When you have the answers to these questions, you can set objectives for how much work should be in process at each phase of the model. By comparing your results to your objectives, you will inevitably discover gaps. In-depth analysis of the gaps should suggest opportunities for further increasing your productivity.

The preceding discussion of time management focuses on a "macro" view. An explanation of the "micro" perspective follows.

Despite your best efforts, you are going to have some "wait time," and you must plan to invest it well if you are to be an effective territory manager.

Frequently, the best usage is to devote such time to observations and inquiries about the account where the delay is occurring. The company's products or literature may be on display. You can question the receptionist if he or she seems available. Noncompetitive salespeople who are also waiting can be a fruitful source of information. Alternatively, you may use this time to review carefully what you know about the account and to refine your call plan. If this is not the first contact with the account, you may ask yourself, "What has occurred up to now?" If none of these activities seems feasible, you may use the time to complete your review and reporting of the day's previous calls, perhaps entering relevant data on your laptop computer.

Still another possibility is to review other calls you intend to make at the completion of this one. Often, "wait time" provides an opportunity for you to access business and trade magazines as well as newspapers. Whatever you do with such time, the important point to remember is that you should invest it, not waste it.

A second aspect of effective time management that influences territory coverage is to relegate those job duties that do not involve face-to-face or telephone contact with customers and prospects to hours that cannot be used for actual communication. To do this, you must know the work habits of your customers and prospects well enough to pattern your calling time to the hours most desirable from their standpoint.

For best results, you should invest some time early in the morning or in the evening to complete your data base, reports, correspondence, and the like before forgetting occurs. Data base management and paperwork vary from job to job, but some is always present. Such material serves as both a historic record and as a planning device. You must do it well to achieve effective territory coverage.

Complete, up-to-date data saves your time during actual communication with prospects and customers. You can quickly relate your present mission to previous visits. Further, being "on top of" your account is bound to have a favorable impact on customers or prospects. It saves them time too.

Time management is also related to routing, which is treated in the next section. Proper routing ensures that you do your traveling without losing prime selling time.

Routing

To use your time effectively, you must pay particular attention to the sequencing of calls. In many fields of selling, you need to incorporate alternate calls in the routing plan so that, if you cannot complete the primary calls, you do not lose time. It may prove useful to have a large map of the territory on which you can plot the locations of customers and prime prospects. This management tool enables you to call in a specific sequence and to decide on the best places to stop overnight or to use as a hub for the ensuing day's work. Research indicates that, for many kinds of sales work, the successful salesperson invests proportionately more total time in face-to-face interviews than does the less successful one. Undue wait and travel time can be a major impediment to full coverage of your territory.

Almost any systematic routing plan is superior to a haphazard coverage of the territory. The size of the territory, concentration of business, number of accounts, call frequency, the likely duration of each visit and mode of transportation are factors that you must consider in deciding the best method. The commonly accepted routing plans are as follows (Figure 10.12):

1. *Circular* (concentric circles or spiral). This is appropriate when accounts are distributed uniformly, few limitations exist on accessibility, and call frequency is relatively the same for all accounts.
2. *Cloverleaf.* This is desirable when accounts are concentrated in specific parts of the territory. The salesperson uses a hub point in each area and plans calls in loops. Alternative calls and those made less frequently can be placed on the agenda for each segment.
3. *Leapfrog.* When frequency of call on each account is an important consideration, this pattern is feasible. The salesperson starts at a distant point in the territory and works back to his or her office or home, making calls en route.
4. *Straight Line.* If business is scattered, the salesperson makes a straight line routing through each cluster of business, then changes direction to move through the next concentration.

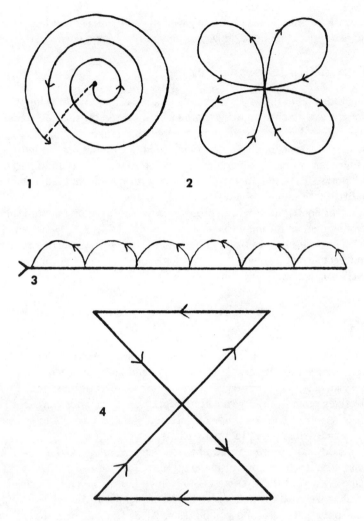

Figure 10.12 Routing plans.

5. *Skip Stop.* This is a combination of (3) and (4). When call frequency is the key consideration, none of the other patterns may apply. Illustratively, if "A" accounts are called on monthly, "B" accounts bimonthly, and "C" accounts trimonthly, the salesperson may have to work out a more complex routing pattern.

The preceding plans are designed to ensure efficient coverage of the cities in a territory. Planning the coverage of accounts in a city or metropolitan area is equally important. Because the distance between accounts is shorter, the total distance covered is usually less important than the time spent between calls. The same routing plans are helpful in covering a city, but you will also need to consider the potential of the account, your plans to entertain at lunch or dinner, as well as the location of parking facilities in planning a day's work.

Your Attitude toward Selling

Your attitude and enthusiasm for selling as a rewarding career is highly relevant to your success. You are an image builder both on and off the job. You are likely to have personal contact with more people than any other employee of your company, and your conduct can do much to build respect for the selling profession. Your conduct is the key to demonstrating that selling is an important managerial profession, vital to the success of every company and essential to a competitive free enterprise system.

You can contribute to your profession by encouraging talented and ambitious young men and women to consider careers in selling. Few careers provide such rich opportunities to master oneself, interact with widely diverse individuals, understand rapidly changing technologies, learn about how businesses work, and serve customers.

SUMMARY

The sales call is the cornerstone of effective selling. A collection of calls may lead to a transaction, transactions can be looked at as an account, and all your accounts amount to a territory. Viewing your responsibilities from these four perspectives provides you with a framework to analyze your work and improve your productivity. The computer and related software are the tools that make the analysis feasible on a practical basis.

The sales call involves three phases—*before, during,* and *after.* The planning and strategy development undertaken before the call markedly influence the effectiveness of the time and energy invested in the call. During the call, you must make modifications in your plan to adjust to the unexpected influences of people, things, and competition. After the call, you should make an immediate analysis and enter it in your data base as an aid in planning the next call on that account.

The joint call is desirable to reinforce your own efforts, to provide technical information to the account, and to help the company get information on the application and performance of its products and services. The joint call demands even more careful and thorough planning than the regular sales call.

One of your objectives is to track all the potential transactions you could make in each of your customer and prospect accounts. This perspective should make you very sensitive to any losses to competitors and help you to focus your selling team.

As a business manager, you are interested in profitable growth. To evaluate the opportunities and to invest your time, effort, and money in proportion to the potential return, you must analyze both customer and prospect accounts. The plan presented in this chapter is useful for achieving a more accurate and objective forecast as well as for allocating your efforts to accounts. Also, in the interests of profitable growth, selling the optimum mix of products and services to existing accounts is important. Developing additional business from existing accounts is less expensive in time and effort than opening new ones. Nonetheless, new accounts are important, too, due to inevitable mortality among customers. In the interests of minimizing customer loss and expanding your volume, you must penetrate your accounts sufficiently to identify the real decision makers and to invest time in them in proportion to their importance to your business.

To manage a territory is to be in control of every aspect of selling. If you are an efficient manager, you will budget your time to accomplish each of your duties.

In addition to your direct selling responsibilities, you need to focus on such nonselling ones as making a careful analysis and forecast of the business potential in your territory. You must also recognize the value of trade and industry relations, the phases of marketing research in which you can assist, and the importance of working with dealers and dealers' salespeople. You should allocate time to these activities in proportion to the value of their potential return. You must be mature enough to allocate time in relation to the commercial worth of each duty, not in accordance with your personal likes and dislikes or the amount of interest each provokes.

You stimulate business growth by increasing the share of business in existing accounts and by generating new ones. To build volume in your territory, you must cultivate the external "who's who" in the territory, those spheres of influence that impact the buying decisions of others.

Key sources of new business were discussed with suggestions and actions for handling each. Five yardsticks were suggested for screening leads.

Investment of personal time is a key factor in full territory coverage. The chapter presented specific timesavers as well. Routing in systematic fashion was seen as time and cost saving.

In all companies, you make a general contribution to business by creating a favorable image of your company, by generating useful ideas, and by promoting a favorable attitude toward selling.

Viewing your responsibilities from the four perspectives—the call, the transaction, the account, and the territory—provides you with a framework to analyze your work and improve your productivity.

TOPICS FOR THOUGHT AND DISCUSSION

1. Review the Guide for a Complete Sales Call (Exhibit 10.1). What information do you need to make a complete sales call? Create your own matrix.
2. What information do you need to manage your calls, transactions, accounts, and the territory?
3. What kind of a personal information system do you need to manage your territory?

4. How much of the information you need is provided by your company? If you detect gaps, how will you close them?
5. What are the main considerations in each of the three phases of the call?
6. How can you use information from previous calls to greatest advantage in planning for future calls?
7. In view of the material on joint calls, what steps can you take to ensure greater success in future joint calls?
8. Examine the Sales-Call Table (Figure 10.1) in this chapter. What changes might you make to customize it to your position?
9. How could you use telemarketing to enhance your productivity?
10. For one of your best accounts, develop your immediate, intermediate, and long-range objectives. Be sure the objectives are specific enough for you to measure the progress you are making in the account.
11. Select three accounts that are widely separated in volume. For each account, estimate the time, money, and effort expended. How profitable is each account to you? To your company?
12. What are some situations that may justify spending more time, money, and effort than would appear to be warranted on a given account?
13. What are some signs that an account cannot be sold at a profitable service level?
14. What steps do you take in customer accounts to keep abreast of changes among the people who influence buying decisions?
15. What methods do you use to identify the decision makers in each prospect account?
16. Select a customer account and list the steps one of your products goes through from the time the order is placed until it is finally used. Indicate potential trouble spots.
17. For your industry, what are some possible off-premise opportunities to contact persons in the buying process?
18. Review your previous experience to determine the number of accounts you can expect to lose through normal turnover.
19. Draw up a list of factors you feel your management should consider in assessing your trade relations as opposed to your profitability to the company.
20. Outline your company policy for the use of samples, and estimate the degree to which you comply with that policy.
21. If you sell to dealers who have a sales force, draw up a list of points each dealer salesperson should master.
22. Who are the 10 persons in your territory who exert the most influence on business? Tell what you know about each one.
23. Which of the sources of leads described in the text do you find most useful? Least useful?
24. How many leads are required to produce a transaction?
25. What are your personal methods of ensuring effective time management?
26. What routing plan is most effective in your territory? Why?
27. What is required to develop selling as a profession?

Bibliography

Chapter One. High-Performance Selling for the 1990s

1. The Cardinal Objectives for Professionals

Cases: Cumberland Metal Industries HBR 9-580-104 and Raymond Mushroom Corp. HBR 9-584-093.

Drucker, P. F., *Management,* New York: Harper and Row, 1974, pp. 74–94.

Garda, R., "Comment," *Journal of Marketing,* 52 (October 1988), pp. 32–41.

Hayek, F. A., "The Use of Knowledge in Society," *The American Economic Review,* 35 (September 1945), p. 519.

Kotler, P., *Marketing Management,* 7th ed., Englewood Cliffs, N.J.: Prentice-Hall, 1991, pp. 6–8, 289–309.

Stalk, G., Jr., and T. M. Hout, *Competing against Time,* New York: The Free Press, 1990.

2. Need Satisfaction: Theory and Practice

Cash, H. C., and W. J. E. Crissy, *The Psychology of Selling* (Educational Edition) Garden City, N.Y.: Personnel Development Associates, 1977.

Cash, H. C., and W. J. E. Crissy, *The Psychology of Selling* series, Vol. 1, "A Point of View for Salesmen," Flushing, N.Y.: Personnel Development Associates, 1973, pp. 1–20.

Grikscheit, G. M., H. C. Cash, and W. J. E. Crissy, *Handbook of Selling: Psychological, Managerial, and Marketing Bases,* New York: Wiley, 1981.

Strong, E. K., Jr., *The Psychology of Selling and Advertising,* New York: McGraw-Hill, 1925, pp. 348–49.

3. Improving Your Productivity

Fisher, R. and W. Ury, *Getting to Yes: Negotiating Agreement without Giving In,* New York: Penguin Press, 1983.

Goldratt, E. M., and J. Cox, *The Goal: A Process of Ongoing Improvement,* New York: North River Press, 1986.

Hanan, M., *Key Account Selling,* 2nd ed., New York: Amacom, 1989.

Luck, D. J., O. C. Ferrell, and G. H. Lucas, Jr., *Marketing Strategy and Plans,* Englewood Cliffs, N.J.: Prentice-Hall, 1989.

Munter, M., *Guide to Managerial Communication,* 2nd ed., Englewood Cliffs, N.J.: Prentice-Hall, 1987.

Odiorne, G. S., *Performance Driven Sales Management,* Chicago: Dartnell, 1991.

Sellers, P., "How to Remake Your Sales Force," *Fortune* (May 4, 1992), pp. 98–103.

Chapter Two. The Communication Process in Selling

1. The Nature of Communication

Berger, C. R., and S. H. Chaffee, eds., *Handbook of Communication Science,* Newbury Park, Calif.: Sage, 1987.

Berlo, D. K., *The Process of Communication,* New York: Holt, Rinehart and Winston, 1960.

Grikscheit, G. M., and W. J. E. Crissy, "Improving Interpersonal Communication Skill," *MSU Business Topics,* 21, No. 4 (Autumn 1973), pp. 63–69.

Huebsch, J. C., *Communications 2000,* 2nd ed., Durban: Butterworths, 1989.

Leavitt, H. J., *Managerial Psychology,* 4th ed., Chicago: University of Chicago Press, 1975.

Leavitt, H. J., L. R. Pondy, and D. M. Boje, *Readings in Managerial Psychology,* Chicago: The University of Chicago Press, 1989.

Nirenberg, J. S., *Getting Through to People,* Englewood Cliffs, N.J.: Prentice-Hall, 1977.

2. Analysis of Human Processes in Communication

Douglas, L. M., and E. E. Smith, "Concepts and Concept Formation," *Annual Review of Psychology,* 35 (1984), pp. 113–138.

Elsendoorn, B. A. G., and H. Bouma, *Working Models of Human Perception,* San Diego, Calif.: Academic Press, 1989.

Freedman, W. J., "The Physiology of Perception," *Scientific American* 264, No. 2, (February 1991), p. 78.

Gruneberg, M. M., P. E. Morris, and R. N. Sykes, eds., *Practical Aspects of Memory,* New York: Wiley, 1988.

Hilgard, E. R., *Psychology in America: A Historical Survey,* San Diego, Calif.: Harcourt Brace Jovanovich, 1987.

Klivington, K. A., *The Science of Mind,* Cambridge, Mass.: MIT Press, 1989.

Osherson, D. N., and E. E. Smith, *Thinking,* Cambridge, Mass.: MIT Press, 1990.

Skinner, B. F., "Outlining a Science of Feeling," in *Emotions and the Family,* edited by E. A. Blechman, Hillsdale, N.J.: Lawrence Erlbaum, 1990.

3. Developing Real-Time Skills

Bostrom, R. N., and E. S. Waldhart, "Memory Models and the Measurement of Listening," *Communication Education,* 37 (January 1988), pp. 1–13.

Christensen, C. R., D. A. Garvin, and A. Sweet, eds., *Education for Judgment: The Artistry of Discussion Leadership,* Boston: Harvard Business School Press, 1991.

Evans, D. R., M. T. Hearn, M. R. Uhlemann, and A. E. Ivey, *Essentials of Interviewing,* Pacific Grove, Calif.: Brooks/Cole, 1989.

Hargie, O., C. Saunders, and D. Dickson, *Social Skills in Interpersonal Communication,* 2nd ed., London: Brookline Books, 1987.

Kleinfield, N. R., "Carving a Career Out of Chats," *The New York Times* (December 23, 1990), H 41 and 43.

Main, J., "How to Sell By Listening," *Fortune* (February 4, 1985), pp. 52–54.

Nichols, R. G., and L. A. Stevens, "Listening to People," *Harvard Business Review,* 35, No. 5 (September–October 1957), pp. 85–92.

Van Ments, M., *Active Talk,* New York: St Martin's Press, 1990.

Chapter Three. Strategy and Tactics for Conducting the Sales Call

1. Sales Strategy for Control of the Interview

Cash, H. C., and A. A. Witkin, *Tools of Personnel Selection*, Peoria, Ill.: 21st Century Marketing Management International, 1976.

Churchill, G. A., Jr., *Marketing Research*, Hinsdale, Ill.: The Dryden Press, 1987.

Crapo, R. F., "Questioning: The Epitome of the Art," *Training and Development Journal* (January 1988), pp. 46–50.

Mears, P. "Surviving a Deposition," *Business Horizons,* (January–February 1991), pp. 62–70.

Oldfield, R. C., *The Psychology of the Interview*, 4th ed., London: Methuen & Co., Ltd., 1951.

Strong, E. K., *The Psychology of Selling and Advertising*, New York: McGraw-Hill, 1925.

2. Filling Needs

Buskirk, R. H., and B. D. Buskirk, *Selling: Principles and Practices*, New York: McGraw-Hill, 1992, pp. 66–100.

Jackson, D. W., Jr., W. H. Cunningham, and I. C. M. Cunningham, *Selling: The Personal Force in Marketing*, New York: Wiley, 1988, pp. 314–317.

O'Shaughnessy, J., *Why People Buy*, New York: Oxford University Press, 1987.

Pederson, C. A., M. D. Wright, and B. A. Weitz, *Selling Principles and Methods*, Homewood, Ill.: Irwin, 1988, pp. 170–173.

3. The Importance of Timing

Boff, K. R., L. Kaufman, and J. P. Thomas, *Handbook of Perception and Human Performance*, New York: Wiley 1986, pp. 7–4, 14–22 to 14–26.

Jackson, D. W., Jr., W. H. Cunningham, and I. C. M. Cunningham, *Selling: The Personal Force in Marketing*, New York: Wiley, 1988, pp. 95–103.

Zimbardo, P., *Psychology and Life*, 10th ed., Glenview, Ill.: Scott, Foresman, 1979, pp. 352–354.

4. Prospects' Reactions and Sales Tactics

Feldman, I., "The Pros Don't Close," *American Salesman* (July 1986), pp. 3–5.

Grikscheit, G. M., and W. J. E. Crissy, "Improving Interpersonal Communication Skill," *MSU Business Topics*, 21, No. 4 (Autumn 1973), pp. 63–69.

Jackson, D. W., Jr., W. H. Cunningham, and I. C. M. Cunningham, *Selling: The Personal Force in Marketing*, New York: Wiley, 1988, pp. 230–242, 303–308.

Pederson, C. A., M. D. Wright, and B. A. Weitz, *Selling Principles and Methods*, Homewood, Ill.: Irwin, 1988, pp. 393–423.

Chapter Four. Managing Sales Resistance

1. The Nature of Sales Resistance

Bergler, E., *Money and Emotional Conflicts*, Garden City, N.Y.: Doubleday, 1951.

Doyle, K. O., "Toward a Psychology of Money," *American Behavioral Scientist*, 35, No. 6, (July–August 1992), pp. 708–724.

Jackson, D. W., Jr., W. H. Cunningham, and I. C. M. Cunningham, *Selling: The Personal Force in Marketing*, New York: Wiley, 1988, pp. 324–332.

Miller, R. B., and S. E. Heiman with T. Tuleja, *Strategic Selling*, New York: Warner, 1985, pp. 100–113.

Strong, E. K., Jr., *The Psychology of Selling and Advertising*, New York: McGraw-Hill, 1925, pp. 326, 434.

2. Handling Objections

Buskirk, R. H., and B. D. Buskirk, *Selling Principles and Practices*, New York: McGraw-Hill, Inc., 1992, pp. 252–311.

Hersey, P., *Selling: A Behavioral Science Approach*, Englewood Cliffs, N.J.: Prentice-Hall, 1988, pp. 78–82.

Chapter Five.   Strategy with Individuals

1. Understanding Personality

Cattel, R. B., and R. M. Dreger, *Handbook of Modern Personality Theory*, New York: Wiley, 1977.

Jackson, D. W., Jr., W. H. Cunningham, and I. C. M. Cunningham, *Selling: The Personal Force in Marketing*, New York: Wiley, 1988, pp. 143–153.

Mischel, W., *Introduction to Personality*, 3rd ed., New York: Holt, Rinehart and Winston, 1980.

Mowen, J.C., *Consumer Behavior*, 2nd ed., New York: Macmillan, 1990, p. 183.

2. Describing an Individual's Personality and Planning Strategy

Allport, G. W., *Personality*, New York: Henry Holt, 1937, Chapter 11.

Allport, G. W., "Traits Revised," *American Psychologist*, 21, (1966), pp. 1–10.

Cash, H. C., and W. J. E. Crissy, "Sizing Up People," *Supplement to The Psychology of Selling No. 2*, Garden City, N.Y.: Personnel Development Associates, 1977.

Cattell, R. B., *Description and Measurement of Personality*, Yonkers, N.Y.: World, 1946, pp. 219–232.

McAdams, D. P., *The Person: An Introduction to Personality Psychology*, San Diego, Calif.: Harcourt Brace Jovanovich, 1990.

Snow, A. J., *Psychology in Personal Selling*, New York: McGraw-Hill, 1926, pp. 182–185.

3. Understanding Motivation

Bonoma, T. V., "Major Sales: Who Really Does the Buying?" *Harvard Business Review*, 60, No. 3 (May–June 1982), p. 112.

Herzberg, F., "One More Time—How Do You Motivate Employees," *Harvard Business Review*, 49 (January–February 1968), pp. 53-62.

Herzberg, F., B. Mausner, and B. Snyderman, *The Motivation to Work*, 2nd ed., New York: Wiley, 1959.

Hilgard, E. R., *Psychology in America: A Historical Survey*, San Diego, Calif.: Harcourt Brace Jovanovich, 1987.

Kotler, P., "Behavioral Models for Analyzing Buyers," *Journal of Marketing* (October 29, 1965), pp. 37–45.

Maslow, A. H., *Motivation and Personality*, New York: Harper and Brothers, 1954.

McClelland, D. C., "Achievement Motivation Can Be Developed," *Harvard Business Review*, 43 (November–December 1065), pp. 7–24, 178.

McGregor, D., *The Human Side of Enterprise*, New York: McGraw-Hill, 1960, pp. 33–34.

Odiorne, G. S., *Performance Driven Sales Management*, Chicago: Dartnell, 1991.

4. Analyzing Customers' and Prospects' Motivations and Planning Strategy

Jackson, D. W., Jr., W. H. Cunningham, and I. C. M. Cunningham, *Selling: The Personal Force in Marketing,* New York: Wiley, 1988, pp. 153–158.

Kassarjian, H. H., and T. S. Robertson, *Perspectives in Consumer Behavior,* Englewood Cliffs, N.J.: Prentice-Hall, 1991, Part 3.

Leavitt, H. J., L. R. Pondy, and D. M. Boje, *Readings in Managerial Psychology,* 4th ed., Chicago: The University of Chicago Press, 1989, Section 1.

Muchinsky, P. M., *Psychology Applied to Work,* Pacific Grove, Calif.: Brooks/Cole, 1990, Chapter 10.

5. Understanding Background and Improving Your Ability to Adjust to Others

Evans, D. R., M. T. Hearn, M. R. Uhlemann, and A. E. Ivey, *Essential Interviewing,* 3rd ed., Pacific Grove, Calif.: Brooks/Cole, 1989.

Hall, E., *Beyond Culture,* Garden City, N.Y.: Anchor, 1977.

Muchinsky, P. M., *Psychology Applied to Work,* Pacific Grove, Calif.: Brooks/Cole, 1990, pp. 124–128.

Chapter Six.   Strategy and Tactics with Groups

1. Analyzing Individual Members of Groups and Planning Strategy

Johnson, D. W., and F. P. Johnson, *Joining Together: Group Theory and Group Skills,* 3rd ed., Englewood Cliffs, N.J.: Prentice-Hall, 1987.

Leavitt, H. J., L. R. Pondy, and D. M. Boje, *Readings in Managerial Psychology,* 4th ed., Chicago: The University of Chicago Press, 1989, Section 7.

Pederson, C. A., M. D. Wright, and B. A. Weitz, *Selling: Principles and Methods,* Homewood, Ill.: Irwin, 1988, pp. 121–129.

2. Maximizing Participation by Group Members

Hackman, J. R., *Groups That Work (and Those That Don't),* San Francisco: Jossey-Bass, 1990.

Larson, C. E., and F. M. J. LaFasto, *Teamwork,* Newbury Park, Calif.: Sage, 1989.

Parker, G. M., *Team Players and Teamwork,* San Francisco: Jossey-Bass, 1990.

Varney, G. H., *Building Productive Teams,* San Francisco: Jossey-Bass, 1990.

3. Communicating with Groups

Odiorne, G. S., "The High Cost of Unproductive Meetings and How to Cure Them," *The George Odiorne Letter,* XXII, No. 10 (May 22, 1992), pp. 1–3.

Chapter Seven.   Logic, Creativity, and Suggestion in Selling

1. Problem Solving

Albion, M. S., and E. J. Hoff, *Business Decision Making with 1-2-3®,* Englewood Cliffs, N.J.: Prentice-Hall, 1988.

Katzer, J., K. H. Cook, and W. W. Crouch, *Evaluating Information,* New York: McGraw-Hill, 1991.
Odiorne, G. S., *MBO II: A System of Managerial Leadership for the 80s,* Belmont, Calif.: Fearon Pitman, 1979, pp. 141–152.
Rubinstein, M. F., *Tools for Thinking and Problem Solving,* Englewood Cliffs, N.J.: Prentice-Hall, 1986.

2. Reasoning in Selling

Deardsley, M. C., *Thinking Straight,* New York: Prentice-Hall, 1950.
Meyer, H. E., *Real-World Intelligence,* New York: Weidenfeld & Nicolson, 1987.
Odiorne, G. S., *Management and the Activity Trap,* New York: Harper and Row, 1974, pp. 102–113.
Thouless, R. H., *Straight and Crooked Thinking,* rev. ed., London: Pan Books, 1974.

3. The Creative Approach to Problem Solving

Evans, J. R., *Creative Thinking in the Decision and Management Sciences,* Cincinnati: South-Western Publishing, 1991.
von Oech, R., *A Whack on the Side of the Head,* New York: Warner, 1983.

4. Applications in Selling

Foster, R. N., *Innovation: The Attacker's Advantage,* New York: Summit, 1986.
Odiorne, G. S., "Pumping Up Your Personal Creativity," *The George Odiorne Letter,* XXII, No. 11 (June 5, 1992), pp. 1–3.
Samli, A. C., L. W. Jacobs, and J. K. Wills, "What Presale and Postsale Services Do You Need to Be Competitive?" *Industrial Marketing Management* 21, (1992), pp. 33–41.
von Hippel, E., *The Sources of Innovation,* New York: Oxford University Press, 1988.

5. Suggestion in Selling

Jackson, D. W. Jr., W. H. Cunningham, and I. C. M. Cunningham, *Selling: The Personal Force in Marketing,* New York: Wiley, 1988, pp. 226–230.
Schramm, W., *The Process and Effects of Mass Communication,* Urbana: University of Illinois Press, 1965, pp. 210–212, 417–422.

Chapter Eight. Guiding Buying Behavior

1. The Nature of Learning

Burris, R. W., "Human Learning," M. D. Dunnette, ed., *Handbook of Industrial and Organizational Psychology,* Chicago: Rand McNally, 1976, Chapter 4.
Cherrington, D. J., *The Management of Human Resources,* 3rd ed., Needham Heights, Mass.: Allyn and Bacon, 1991, pp. 321–339.
Christensen, C. R., D. A. Garvin, and A. Sweet, *Education for Judgment: The Artistry of Discussion Leadership,* Boston: Harvard Business School Press, 1991.

2. Learning Applied to Selling

Christensen, C. R., *Teaching and the Case Method,* Boston: Harvard Business School, Division of Research, 1987.
Gragg, C. I., "Teachers Also Must Learn," *Harvard Educational Review,* 10 (1940), pp. 30–47.
Hobbs, C. R., *The Power of Teaching with New Techniques,* Salt Lake City, Utah: Deseret, 1973.

3. Learning Channels

Boff, K. R., L. Kaufman, and J. P. Thomas, *Handbook of Perception and Human Performance,* New York: Wiley, 1986.
Elsendoorn, B. A. G., and H. Bouma, *Working Models of Human Perception,* San Diego, Calif.: Academic Press, Inc., 1989.
Zelazny, G., *Say It with Charts,* Homewood, Ill.: Dow Jones-Irwin, 1985.

4. Remembering and Forgetting

Cherrington, D. J., *The Management of Human Resources,* Needham Heights, Mass.: Allyn and Bacon, 1991, pp. 333, 334.
Gruneberg, M. M., P. E. Morris, and R. N. Sykes, *Practical Aspects of Memory,* New York: Wiley, 1988.
Mowen, J. C., *Consumer Behavior,* 2nd ed., New York: Macmillan, 1990, Chapter 3.

Chapter Nine.   The Seller as a Self-Manager

1. Your Selling System

Bagozzi, R. P., *Principles of Marketing Management,* Chicago: Science Research Associates, 1986, Chapter 1.
Odiorne, G. S., *Management and the Activity Trap,* New York: Harper and Row, 1974, Chapters 1 and 2.
Schoderbek, P. P., *Management Systems,* New York: Wiley, 1971.
"The Computer in Sales and Marketing," *Sales and Marketing Management* (August 15, 1986), p. 71.

2. Implementing the Planning Process

Aaker, D. A., *Developing Business Strategies,* 3rd ed., New York: Wiley, 1992.
Sujan, H., B. A. Weitz, and M. Sujan, "Increasing Sales Productivity by Getting Salespeople to Work Smarter," *Journal of Personal Selling and Sales Management,* 1988, pp. 9–20.

3. Self-Management

Churchill, G. A., Jr., N. M. Ford, and O. C. Walker, *Sales Force Management: Planning, Implementation, and Control,* 2nd ed., Homewood, Ill.: Irwin, 1985.
Pederson, C. A., M. D. Wright, and B. A. Weitz, *Selling: Principles and Methods,* Homewood, Ill.: Irwin, 1988.
Sauers, D. A., "Behavioral Self-Management as a Supplement to External Sales Force Controls," *Journal of Personal Selling and Sales Management* (Summer 1990), p. 17.
Weitz, B. A., H. Sujan, and M. Sujan, "Knowledge, Motivation, and Adaptive Behavior: A Framework for Improving Selling Effectiveness," *Journal of Marketing* (October 1986), pp. 174–191.

Chapter Ten.   Managing in Depth: An Analysis for Effective Action

1. Managing Your Selling System with the Computer

Kauffman, R. S., *Futuresell: Automating Your Sales Force,* Boulder, Co: Cross Communications, 1990.

McCann, J. M., *The Marketing Workbench: Using Computers for Better Performance,* Homewood, Ill: Dow Jones-Irwin, 1986.

Shapiro, B. P., and R. T. Moriarty, "Support Systems for National Account Management Programs: Promises Made, Promises Kept," *Working Paper Report 84–102,* Cambridge, Mass.: Marketing Science Institute, 1984.

Wallis, L. A., "Computer-Based Sales Force Support," *Conference Board Report No. 953,* New York: The Conference Board, 1990.

2. Managing Each Call

Grove, S. J., M. C. LaForge, and P. A. Knowles, "Improving Sales Call Reporting for Better Management Decisions" *Journal of Business and Industrial Marketing* (Summer 1992), p. 53.

Lambert, D. M., H. Marmorstein, and A. Sharma, "The Accuracy of Salespersons' Perceptions of Their Customers: Conceptual Examination and an Empirical Study," *Journal of Personal Selling and Sales Management,* (Winter 1990), pp. 1–9.

Weitz, Barton A., "Relationship between Salesperson Performance and Understanding of Customer Decision Making," *Journal of Marketing Research,* (November 1978), pp. 501–516.

3. Managing Each Transaction

Brock, R. T., "Sharpening Your Telemarketing Edge through Automation," *Sales and Marketing Management* (May 1990), pp. 156–157.

Coppett, J. I., and W. A. Staples, *Professional Selling: A Relationship Management Process,* Cincinnati, Ohio: South-Western Publishing, 1990.

Dwyer, F. R., P. H. Schurr, and S. Oh, "Developing Buyer-Seller Relationships," *Journal of Marketing* (April 1987), pp. 11–27.

"Making the Team," *Sales and Marketing Management* (February 1, 1992), p. 54.

Moncrief, W. C., C. W. Lamb, and T. Dielman, "Developing Telemarketing Support Systems," *Journal of Personal Selling and Sales Management* (August 1986), pp. 43–49.

4. Managing Each Account

LaForge, R. W., D. W. Cravens, and C. E. Young, "Improving Salesforce Productivity," *Business Horizons* (September–October 1985), pp. 50–59.

LaForge, R. W., D. W. Cravens, and C. E. Young, "Using Contingency Analysis to Select Selling Effort Allocation Methods," *Journal of Personal Selling and Sales Management* (August 1986), pp. 19–28.

LaForge, R. W., B. C. Hamm, and C. E. Young, "Increasing Sales Productivity through Improved Sales Call Strategies," *Journal of Personal Selling and Sales Management* (November 1983), pp. 52–59.

5. Managing the Territory

References in previous section are adequate.

6. Maximizing Territory Coverage

Cravens, D. W., T. N. Ingram, and R. W. LaForge, "Evaluating Multiple Sales Channel Strategies," *Journal of Business and Industrial Marketing* (Summer/Fall 1991), p. 37.

George, W. R., J. P. Kelly, and C. E. Marshall, "The Selling of Services: A Comprehensive Model," *Journal of Personal Selling and Sales Management* (August 1986), pp. 29–37.

Appendixes

APPENDIX I

Determining Differential Competitive Advantage

This appendix is referenced on pages 4 and 193.

Step 1

Customer _____
Salesperson _____
Date _____

Factor	Does the customer/prospect recognize significant differences between my own and competitive offerings?		What evidence do I have supporting my choice?
	Yes	No	
Tangible Superiority	( )	( )	
Intangible Superiority	( )	( )	
Price Superiority	( )	( )	
Image Superiority	( )	( )	
Team Superiority	( )	( )	

Step 2

Does the customer/prospect recognize significant differences between my own and competitive offerings?	What evidence do I have supporting my choice?	Your Company	Competitor 1 _____ Name	Competitor 2 _____ Name
	Tangible Superiority	Buyer's ranking of competitors on elements of offering (1 = high)		

Tangible Superiority

	Yes	No			
Versatility	( )	( )			
Efficiency	( )	( )			
Storage	( )	( )			
Handling	( )	( )			
Appearance	( )	( )			
Design	( )	( )			
Mobility	( )	( )			
Packaging	( )	( )			
Life expectancy	( )	( )			
Adaptability	( )	( )			
Additional elements	( )	( )			
_____	( )	( )			

Intangible Superiority

	Yes	No			
Delivery	( )	( )			
Inventory	( )	( )			
Credit	( )	( )			
Training	( )	( )			
Merchandising	( )	( )			
Installation	( )	( )			
Advertising	( )	( )			
Financial	( )	( )			
Maintenance	( )	( )			
Guarantees and warranties	( )	( )			
Additional elements	( )	( )			
_____	( )	( )			

Price Superiority

	Yes	No			
Price	( )	( )			
Discounts	( )	( )			
Freight	( )	( )			
Terms of payment	( )	( )			
Future delivery	( )	( )			
Warranties	( )	( )			
Packaged pricing	( )	( )			
Installation	( )	( )			
Extra products/ services	( )	( )			
Additional elements	( )	( )			
_____	( )	( )			

Step 2   (continued)

Does the customer/prospect recognize significant differences between my own and competitive offerings?	What evidence do I have supporting my choice?	Your Company	Competitor 1 ___ Name	Competitor 2 ___ Name
		Buyer's ranking of competitors on elements of offering (1 = high)		

Image Superiority

	Yes	No
Time established	( )	( )
Industry standing	( )	( )
Marketplace reputation	( )	( )
Community image	( )	( )
Location	( )	( )
Labor relations	( )	( )
Size	( )	( )
Source of supplies	( )	( )
Financial soundness	( )	( )
Policies and practices	( )	( )
Additional elements	( )	( )
_____	( )	( )

Team Superiority

	Yes	No
Personal knowledge and skill	( )	( )
Knowledge and skill of supportive personnel	( )	( )
Integrity and character	( )	( )
Availability for emergencies	( )	( )
Sophistication on buyer's industry	( )	( )
Standing in community	( )	( )
Flexibility of call schedule	( )	( )
Mutual friends	( )	( )
Interpersonal skills	( )	( )
Cooperation	( )	( )
Additional elements	( )	( )
_____	( )	( )

Step 3

(A) Number of Times Ranked:	Your Company	Competitor 1	Competitor 2
First			
Second			
Third			

(B) Summary of Your Competitive Position

Strengths	Weaknesses

(C) Final Rating of Your Competitive Position

Rating	Description	Observation
		Buyer perceives your offering is:
( )	Excellent	Significantly different and better than competitor's
( )	Good	Slightly different and better than competitor's
( )	Average	No different or better than competitor's
( )	Poor	Slightly inferior to competitor's

APPENDIX II

Salesperson-Oriented Product Manual

This appendix is referenced on pages 21, 23, 24, 73, 76, 108, and 270.
The tables in this appendix use this book as an example.

Feature Benefit Table

Features		Benefits
1. The authors are highly qualified. A, H	A	The material is credible to salespeople. 1, 5, 6, 8
2. All necessary information (practical and theoretical) is in one volume. G	B	By using appendixes over a period of time, salespeople can advance in skill. 2, 3, 9, 10
3. The appendixes have training exercises. B, C, D, E, F, G	C	Salespeople become more effective in the interview part of the sales job. 3, 4, 7
4. Interpersonal skills are emphasized. C, D, H	D	Communication between salespeople and sales trainers/managers is improved. 3, 4, 5
5. The book has a scientific basis for the recommendations and a vocabulary to facilitate communication in training programs. A, D, H	E	Salespeople can be assigned sections of the book in keeping with their strengths and weaknesses. 3, 9, 10
6. The book is written in general terms rather than those of one industry. A	F	Salespeople can be asked to concentrate on a particular unit (section or chapter), which reduces resistance to voluminous reading. 3, 9, 10
7. Much of the material is unique—there is no real competition. C, H	G	Minimum amount of material for salespeople to physically handle. 2, 3
8. The material has been tested in previous publications. A, H	H	Salespeople can take pride in acquiring skill. 1, 5, 7, 8
9. The book is organized into sections and chapters that are relatively discrete. B, E, F		
10. The book is heavily cross referenced, including appendixes. B, E, F		

Sales Points

I. The authors are highly qualified. One is a professional psychologist; one has extensive experience as a salesperson; and one is a computer expert. All have advanced academic degrees and experience teaching in-company and on-campus selling programs. The book was written after working with a variety of companies in many industries and revised after extensive use of the original material. Such qualifications should be compared with authors lacking a background in psychology, selling, business, and computers and having experience limited to a single company or product.

A. Need developing questions

1. How does the authors' background compare with that of other writers on selling?

2. How would an academic background in the behavioral sciences affect sales advice?

3. What is the ideal background for an expert on sales training?

B. Alternate phrasings

1. The authors have teaching experience in college as well as industry.

2. The authors have studied all relevant scientific literature.

3. The authors are intimately familiar with salespeople and sales jobs.

II. All necessary information (practical and theoretical) is in one volume. The authors have consolidated all their pertinent previous publications. This eliminates the need for using much unbound material.

A. Need developing questions

1. What is the danger in loose-leaf training materials?

2. What respect is given to printed as compared with merely word-processed material?

3. How do you feel when salespeople lose training materials?

B. Alternate phrasings

1. There is no need to handle a variety of materials with different shapes and sizes.

2. The hard cover means the book will last.

3. The book is durable and can be reassigned to other salespeople if you wish.

III. The appendixes have training exercises. The exercises provide a plan for practicing the procedures recommended in the book. Such practice is necessary to apply knowledge in actual sales situations.

A. Need developing questions

1. What practice exercises do you now give your salespeople?

2. How does practice affect retention of selling skill?

3. How do your salespeople hone their sales skills?

4. How do your salespeople develop their product knowledge?

Sales Points (continued)

    B. Alternate phrasings

        1. The appendixes make the book practical as well as theoretical.

        2. The appendixes furnish a basis for salespeople practicing outside sales calls.

        3. All recommendations are backed by practice exercises.

  IV. Interpersonal skills are emphasized. The thrust of the book is on psychological factors that make or break the sales interview. The balance of the material is focused on management as well as improving productivity through use of the computer.

    A. Need developing questions

        1. What are the most important areas of the selling process?

        2. How do you distinguish between product knowledge and sales skill?

        3. What is the relative importance of effective sales technique compared with product knowledge?

        4. What does it take to manage the sales process in today's competitive environment?

    B. Alternate phrasings

        1. This is the only book on selling that treats the interview as the most important part of the sales process.

        2. This is the most complete treatment of the face-to-face or on-the-phone part of the sales process.

        3. All standard psychological principles that will help salespeople are considered in the book.

  V. The book has a scientific basis for the recommendations and a vocabulary to facilitate communication in training programs. The recommendations are based on generally accepted psychological literature. A bibliography is provided. A glossary of psychological terms is also included. This permits exact communication in training and supervisory sessions.

    A. Need developing questions

        1. How does your medical vocabulary compare with your doctor's? Your understanding of medicine?

        2. What makes recommendations credible?

        3. How does knowledge of technical terms affect your understanding of the stock market (e.g., warrant) or space exploration (e.g., yaw)?

    B. Alternate phrasings

        1. The vocabulary of the book allows senior salespeople to verbalize their experience and pass it on to new recruits.

        2. More precise discussion of sales skill is possible after reading the concepts in this book.

        3. Adoption of this book's terminology increases the training potential for the entire sales force.

Sales Points (continued)

VI. The book is written in general terms rather than those of one industry. Hence, salespeople can gain insights from a broad sampling of real sales experience and can adopt the advice to their unique situation. By offering a broad variety of examples from different companies and industries, salespeople will find examples with which to identify.

   A. Need developing questions

   1. To what extent do your salespeople think their job is different from other sales jobs?

   2. What type of sales advice turns your people on? Off?

   3. What is the likelihood of finding sales material of this quality with all the examples from your industry?

   B. Alternate phrasings

   1. Salespeople prefer examples from their field and resent advice from others. Using general terms is one solution.

   2. Having examples from a variety of industries is more effective.

   3. You would have to commission your own book to find one better adapted to your needs.

VII. Much of the material is unique—there is no real competition. As far as is known, no other accredited psychologist has undertaken a systematic and complete review of the field with the intention of applying the findings to the sales process in conjunction with writers experienced in field sales and computers.

   A. Need developing questions

   1. How will improving the productivity of your company's sales force affect your share of the market?

   2. What field is best qualified to provide effective sales advice?

   3. How many psychologists apply themselves primarily to the field of sales training?

   B. Alternate phrasings

   1. There is no other known psychologist who has applied his or her knowledge to sales skill.

   2. Most psychologists who claim to be interested in selling are limited to personnel selection.

   3. Understanding the power of computer data bases is the biggest innovation for salespeople in this century.

VIII. The material has been tested in previous publications. The original book was published over 20 years ago and has sold more than a quarter of a million copies. All the ideas in the book have been successfully defended in sales training discussions.

   A. Need developing questions

   1. What can you conclude from evidence that a book has had a good sales record?

Sales Points   (continued)

---

2. How long would you expect sales training materials to remain valid?

3. What do authors do with materials that do not work as intended?

B. Alternate phrasings

1. Using ideas that have stood the test of time is always good practice.

2. Large repeat sales of books are a good recommendation.

3. After 20 years, the ideas are still sound. Now they are presented in a better format.

IX. The book is organized into sections and chapters that are relatively discrete. To acquire sales skill, several separate subskills must be acquired and integrated for use in an actual sales situation. Each chapter and section deals with a separate skill.

A. Need developing questions

1. How many separate skills does a salesperson need? Name some.

2. Why do golfers practice with one club at a time on a driving range, rather than just play the course?

3. What do you know about whole versus part learning? Should sales training go from the part to the whole or the whole to the part?

B. Alternate phrasings

1. You can select a specific skill for concentration.

2. There is no need to study the book in the order presented. Sections are self-sufficient.

3. Pick the sections where your salespeople are most in need of training.

X. The book is heavily cross referenced, including the appendixes. While sales subskills must be acquired separately, they must often be applied concurrently. The cross referencing brings out this relationship. The appendixes, which are also cross referenced with the text, show the type of practice needed to develop a particular skill.

A. Need developing questions

1. How much time are you willing to spend hunting through a book for an idea you remember reading?

2. How can authors make reference books easier to use?

3. How could authors show the relationship between separate sales skills?

B. Alternate phrasings

1. Cross references allow a reader to use the book starting at any point.

2. The text is cross referenced to the appendixes; this blends the practical with the theoretical.

3. The organization of the book allows the reader to undertake one sales skill at a time. Cross references show how the skills are integrated at the point of sale.

Handling Objections

1. Objection	The book looks too formidable.
Answer	The book is divided into discrete subsections for purposes of study.
Question	a. How does the breakdown by chapter and section affect the readability of the book?
	b. How does the size of the appendix affect the amount of reading?
Answer	Salespeople only study one portion at a time.
Question	How long would it take to read a typical section?
Answer	The alternative is to have a variety of pamphlets.
Question	How many different items would you need if each skill were treated separately?
2. Objection	Practice and experimenting may lose some sales. I want my salespeople to stick to what they know.
Answer	Temporary setbacks are quickly matched by increased skill.
Question	What happened when you switched from manual typewriters to word processing?
Answer	Your competitors may gain on you if you are not making progress. The status quo does not usually last long.
Question	What usually happens when progress stops?
3. Objection	Training is an extra expense.
Answer	The quickest way to a greater share of the market is through better marketing. Training costs are negligible compared with the research necessary to improve your product(s) technically.
Question	How do training costs compare with the basic research effort to develop a superior product?
Answer	Training is as necessary an expense as travel.
Question	Why don't you eliminate travel to save money?
4. Objection	I only use training materials from my industry.
Answer	Your trade association is not likely to provide material of this quality.
Question	How do the qualifications of your association executives compare with those of the authors as sales trainers?
Answer	Trade associations usually wait until members pressure them before they attack a problem. By then, the leaders have gained a head start.
Question	a. Do you want to be considered a follower or leader in sales training?
	b. What good is a training program if all your competitors also have it?
5. Objection	I have no one to teach the material.
Answer	The authors can recommend consultants and trainers.
Question	Why not contact the authors about available services?
6. Objection	I have another consultant.
Answer	If his/her program is similar, repeating it in another format is excellent.

Handling Objections   (continued)

Question	a. How does the content of your present program compare with this one?
	b. How much can your people remember from a single presentation?
Answer	If your present program does not concentrate on the face-to-face part of the sales call, you are missing an important element.
Question	How does your present program treat the interpersonal part of the salesperson's job?
7. Objection	My people are already thoroughly trained.
Answer	There is always room for improvement. Look at world athletic records.
Question	Why does the *Guinness Book of Records* need to be updated frequently?
Answer	The best people are attracted to leading companies. They will leave if your competitors offer them better training and opportunities.
Question	What caliber of salesperson (best or weakest) welcomes training?
8. Objection	Training takes people away from work.
Answer	Home study can be arranged.
Question	How could the exercises in the appendix be used for home study?

Note: When a product or service is sold in different markets, the salesperson-oriented product manual may need to be modified. For example, this book could be used by salespeople or students. The salesperson-oriented product manual in this appendix is designed for use by salespeople selling the book to business buyers. Salespeople calling on the academic market would use a revised version, reflecting differences in terminology as well as in the buyer-seller relationship.

APPENDIX III

Rules for Brainstorming

This appendix is referenced on pages 22 and 187.

1. *What Kind of Topic Should You Brainstorm?* The topic should be specific rather than general. A big topic should be broken into smaller elements and each of these "brainstormed" in turn.
2. *Who Should Participate?* Those likely to be both interested in the subject and competent to generate ideas on it should be included. However, sometimes an inexperienced person may have a novel slant so one or two relatively unknowledgeable people might be included.
3. *What Is the Leader's Job?* The leader's role is to set the mood and to keep the session moving. The leader snould *not* participate in the idea flow and might have someone assist in recording the ideas.
4. *How Is a Session Conducted?* Because spontaneous contributions are sought, definite signals are needed to alert the leader when an idea is available: (a) A raised hand with full palm indicates a new idea. (b) A raised hand with index finger up, other fingers down, signals a "hitch hike" or branching of the previous ideas. The leader develops one branch before beginning a new one. The leader uses the word "Ban" to indicate a contribution is inappropriate.
5. *Is a Warm-Up Desirable?* The group should practice on any easy topic to start an idea flow. This also familiarizes them with the signals and other mechanics.
6. *What Are the Guide Lines?* Four are imperative. The leader's task is to see that they are followed:
   a. *Rule out Evaluative Statements.* The leader calls "Ban," if one is made.
   b. *Welcome Freewheeling.* Ideas should flow as they occur and without critique.
   c. *Branch First, Then Develop New Ideas.* Creativity depends on this. Each individual contribution stimulates the others and frequently generates new insights that would not occur without the interplay of members.
   d. *Record Ideas in Front of the Group* (e.g., on a flip chart or electronic recording device). This serves two purposes: stimulation and reassurance. Ideas in sight trigger additional ones. As the number increases, the group "tastes success."

338

Work Sheets for SOPM

This appendix is referenced on pages 22, 82, and 108.

Work Sheet for Feature-Benefit Table

Features	Benefits
1.	A.
2.	B.
3.	C.
4.	D.
5.	E.
6.	F.
7.	G.
8.	H.
9.	I.
10.	J.

Work Sheet for Listing Sales Points, Need Developing Questions, and Alternate Phrasings

I. Sales point

    A. Need developing questions

        1.

        2.

        3.

    B. Alternate phrasings

        1.

        2.

        3.

II. Sales point

    A. Need developing questions

        1.

        2.

        3.

    B. Alternate phrasings

        1.

        2.

        3.

Work Sheet for Handling Objections

1. Objection

    Answer

        Question

    Answer

        Question

2. Objection

    Answer

        Question

    Answer

        Question

3. Objection

    Answer

        Question

    Answer

        Question

APPENDIX V

Comparative Analysis of Competing Products/Services

This appendix is referenced on page 26.

Comparative Analysis of Competing Products/Services

Your product/service to be analyzed _____

INSTRUCTIONS: Insert the name of your product/service, and list its three most important features in the space provided in Column 1. Translate the features into benefits and uses that accrue to your buyers. Now, in Row 2, list the product you find most competitive. List the features you think you would stress if you were selling that product/service. Fill in the uses and benefits as with your own product/service. Repeat this analysis for the next most competitive product/service.

By noting the claims most likely to be made by competitive salespeople, you should be able to formulate your replies if buyers offer these claims as objections to your product/service. (When the products/services being analyzed have more than three important features, develop an extended form.)

Company's Product/Service _____

Features	Benefits and Uses
1. _____	a _____
	b _____
	c _____
	d _____
2. _____	a _____
	b _____
	c _____
	d _____
3. _____	a _____
	b _____
	c _____
	d _____

342

Comparative Analysis of Competing Products/Services   (continued)

Competitor A's Product/Service _____

      Features   Benefits and Uses

                                        a _____
                                        b _____

1. _____   c _____
                                        d _____

                                        a _____
                                        b _____

2. _____   c _____
                                        d _____

                                        a _____
                                        b _____

3. _____   c _____
                                        d _____

Competitor B's Product/Service _____

      Features   Benefits and Uses

                                        a _____
                                        b _____

1. _____   c _____
                                        d _____

                                        a _____
                                        b _____

2. _____   c _____
                                        d _____

                                        a _____
                                        b _____

3. _____   c _____
                                        d _____

Factors Influencing Communication

This appendix is referenced on page 45.

Customer _____

Salesperson _____

INSTRUCTIONS: Select a customer or prospect you know well. With this buyer in mind, fill in the spaces below. (This should make your next call more effective in terms of your ability to communicate.)

1. PERCEPTION
   a. What are the key elements in the background and experience of the buyer that may affect his or her perception?

   b. What are the likely needs that will affect his or her perception? (These needs should be verified in the next interview before action is taken.)

   c. What are the most likely differences between the buyer's perception and your own?

2. COGNITION
   a. What are the most likely facts the buyer knows and what ones will you need to communicate in order to make him or her want to place an order?

Facts Probably Known	Facts to Be Communicated on Next Call
1.	1.
2.	2.
3.	3.
4.	4.
5.	5.
6.	6.

3. FEELINGS
   a. What feelings about your product/service need to be changed?

   b. What are some irrelevant feelings that the buyer might express?

   c. What are some aspects of your proposition that may trigger emotional reactions?

APPENDIX VII

Work Sheet for Compiling Examples of Prospect Reactions

This appendix is referenced on page 93.

The text suggests that you should develop a thorough command of your questions and alternate phrasings so you can devote your attention to the reactions of the buyer.° Some recommendations follow about what you can observe.

An alert and attentive salesperson can classify each reaction of a buyer. (If the buyer chooses to ignore a stimulus, that, too, is a reaction.) One classification would be whether the reaction brings you closer to or farther away from your objective. These reactions are defined as *positive,* closer to the objective, and *negative,* farther away from it.

At the same time, the reactions can be classified another way: whether the buyer intended to reveal his or her opinion or attitude or whether you made an assumption about the buyer's feelings. Again, by definition, if the buyer wanted you to know his or her position, the response was *voluntary.* If you had to make an assumption, the response was *involuntary.*

The accompanying work sheet enables you to organize and classify the reactions you encounter in your regular calls. By listing prospects' reactions in the appropriate boxes, you can then prepare suitable responses to move the interview toward a successful close.

° To simplify and clarify this discussion, we will use *reaction* to refer to the *buyer* behavior and *response* to *salesperson* behavior.

	POSITIVE	**NEGATIVE**
VOLUNTARY	Example of Speech	Example of Speech
	Example of Behavior	Example of Behavior
INVOLUNTARY	Example of Speech	Example of Speech
	Example of Behavior	Example of Behavior

APPENDIX VIII

Sample Sales Interview: Observing the Prospect's Reactions

This appendix is referenced on page 93.

The exercise in this appendix shows you how the closing technique discussed in Chapter 3 works in practice.

In the following sample sales interview, in the left margin indicate the appropriate classification for both the salesperson's responses and the customer's reactions. Code them as follows:

1. Positive–Voluntary (PV).
2. Positive–Involuntary (PI).
3. Negative–Involuntary (NI).
4. Negative–Voluntary (NV).

and the salesperson's responses can be noted as follows:

1. Close the sale (CS)
2. Provide more information (PI)
3. Change the sales point (CP)
4. Change the entire approach (CA)

Salesperson	What profit do you consider necessary to stock a new product on your racks?
Customer	There are many factors besides profit to consider in stocking a new product.
Salesperson	I imagine that the amount of advertising and the manufacturer's reliability are just as important as profit.
Customer	I know your company name should help sell a cold product and your advertising schedule looks good. However, we now stock many brands of cold tablets and we just don't have room for a new item.
Salesperson	To avoid carrying too many items, you have to choose just the brands that are the best sellers, right?
Customer	That's right.
Salesperson	Actually, to make the most profit these brands should be the three or four best sellers.

Customer   How do we know yours will sell?

Salesperson In our test markets we found that our cold tablets became one of the three largest selling cold tablets during their first year on the market. On that basis, they have proven they should be in that best selling group. Suppose we send you just enough cold tablets to put them on your larger racks. When you see how well they sell, you can then expand the distribution. About how many racks do you have that are eight feet or larger?

Customer   Approximately 50.

Salesperson Fine, then suppose we send you 72 dozen for your initial stocking. You probably would want these as soon as possible as the cold season is almost here.

Customer   Yes, as soon as possible.

Common Trait Terms to Analyze People

This appendix is referenced on pages 122, 123, and 145.

1. adaptable
   inflexible

2. affected
   natural

3. alert
   sluggish

4. ambitious
   complacent

5. argumentative
   agreeable

6. articulate
   inarticulate

7. autocratic
   democratic

8. benevolent
   spiteful

9. boastful
   self-effacing

10. bold
    timid

11. candid
    evasive

12. cheerful
    gloomy

13. clever
    dull

14. confused
    aware

15. considerate
    selfish

16. contrary
    obedient

17. cooperative
    uncooperative

18. cosmopolitan
    provincial

19. courageous
    cowardly

20. courteous
    rude

21. creative
    simplistic

22. crude
    refined

23. cruel
    compassionate

24. curious
    disinterested

25. decisive
    indecisive

26. deliberate
    impulsive

27. dependent
    self-sufficient

28. depressing
    exciting

29. enthusiastic
    indifferent

30. ethical
    exploitative

31. excitable
    tranquil

32. fatalistic
    autonomous

33. foresighted
    hindsighted

34. forgetful
    retentive

35. forgiving
    vindictive

36. formal
    informal

37. friendly
    distant

38. frivolous
    serious

39. generous
    stingy

40. grateful
    ungrateful

41. honest
    deceptive

42. humorous
    somber

43. industrious
    lazy

44. inexperienced
    experienced

45. inhibited
    unrestrained

46. jealous
    supportive

47. leisurely
    hurried

48. logical
    intuitive

350

49. loyal
    unfaithful

50. mature
    childish

51. mild
    harsh

52. modest
    conceited

53. obliging
    obstructive

54. open-minded
    opinionated

55. optimistic
    pessimistic

56. persuasive
    persuadable

57. pleasant
    caustic

58. pliant
    stubborn

59. practical
    theoretical

60. price-conscious
    quality-conscious

61. progressive
    reactionary

62. proper
    non-conforming

63. realistic
    unrealistic

64. remorseful
    remorseless

65. satisfied
    displeased

66. self-pitying
    self-blaming

67. sensitive
    callous

68. sensual
    puritanical

69. sociable
    reclusive

70. steady
    changeable

71. stressed
    calm

72. submissive
    domineering

73. tactful
    tactless

74. talkative
    uncommunicative

75. thoughtful
    inconsiderate

76. thrifty
    wasteful

77. tolerant
    intolerant

78. trusting
    suspicious

79. special abilities

80. special interests

Work Sheet for Making a Trait Description

This appendix is referenced on pages 123 and 223.

INSTRUCTIONS: Select a person whose personality you wish to describe. Review sections 1 and 2 in Chapter Five; also review Appendixes IX through XV. Now turn to page 123 and proceed to follow the instructions for filling in Columns 1 and 2 of Part A. When you are satisfied that you have approximately 10 trait terms together with valid evidence, proceed to fill in Column 3 of Part A, following the instructions on page 124.

Date _____

Customer _____

Salesperson _____

Describing a Customer: Part A

Trait No.	Name	Evidence to Support Choice of Trait	How to Handle Customer on Basis of Trait

Describing a Customer: Part A (continued)

No.	Trait Name	Evidence to Support Choice of Trait	How to Handle Customer on Basis of Trait

INSTRUCTIONS: By noting the material on pages 125 and 126 and studying Appendix XI, you will see how to group the traits and formulate your final strategy. You can now complete Part B of the work sheet.

Planning Strategy Based on Trait Analysis: Part B

Trait Groups		Strategy
No.	Name	

A Case History: Trait Description

This appendix is referenced on page 124.

Date _____

Customer _____

Salesperson _____

Describing a Customer: Part A

No.	Trait Name	Evidence to Support Choice of Trait	How to Handle Customer on Basis of Trait
5	agreeable	Always listens fully to proposition.	Make a straightforward and complete presentation with such a person as you are assured of an audience.
11	evasive	Frequently confuses the issue by raising irrelevant matters.	Return to the points on which he has authority to act if evasiveness is apparently due to lack of authority, arrange to contact him again after he has had an opportunity to consult with necessary persons.
26	impulsive	Does not plan—acts on spur of moment—for example, interrupts interview to dispose of unrelated matters.	Try to get him to act immediately on any proposition—otherwise it may get lost in the shuffle.
27	self-sufficient	Makes all decisions without reference to other company personnel.	Respect his judgment, avoid direct suggestions that others be consulted; do not ask permission to visit others in company unless necessary.
38	serious	Seldom relaxes to just pass the time of day—acts as though the job was very important.	Take advantage of his apparent concern over work to do as complete a selling job as possible.
69	reclusive	Little or no association with other company personnel—does not belong to any clubs or social groups.	Extend as much friendship and social activities as he wishes; do not insist on the person accepting your hospitality.

Planning Strategy Based on Trait Analysis: Part B

No.	Trait Name	Strategy
26 5	impulsive agreeable	His agreeableness makes him a good listener so that you can be sure of making a full presentation. Impulsiveness means that he may, on occasion, make a quick decision. While you are making your presentation, be alert for areas of agreement and press for a decision immediately.
69 38 27	reclusive serious self-sufficient	Together, these traits suggest that he has little real need for companionship. He may even avoid social occasions. Therefore stick to business. Suggest only essential contacts with other people. Avoid implying that he needs to consult other company personnel to make a decision. Try to enlarge his areas of interest as far as the product is concerned.
11 5	evasive agreeable	His readiness to agree and lack of concern may be devices to keep from really considering the proposition. When a decision is necessary, he may become evasive because he really does not have any basis for making decisions.

Supplementary Notes on the Case

An Example of the Importance of Compensatory Behavior

When you study a person psychologically as well as logically, you often discover that behavior is compensatory or designed to cover up reality. For example, a boy who believes himself deficient in athletic skill may overcompensate and develop, through rigorous self-discipline, outstanding athletic ability.

In the case of the prospect described here, it is probable that he is rejected by his business colleagues and has no real authority to make decisions. For this reason, he acts self-sufficient and becomes evasive when the salesperson seeks a decision.

Your objective is to make a sale—not to engage in psychotherapy. Therefore, do not try to change the prospect, but recognize that that person cannot make decisions and that you must find a way to get to someone with the authority to place an order. On this basis, one strategy would be to raise the prospect's ego by calling on him together with some representatives of your home office. The more status these visitors have, the better. They should be fully alerted to your analysis of the prospect and ready to assume the role you are asking them to play.

After you make your presentation again, the prospect may decide to pass the responsibility on to the proper person. Having top management personnel with you makes it less likely that he will continue as a bottleneck and at the same time increases the likelihood that someone higher on the company ladder will grant an immediate interview. Once you get through this barrier, you will be able to make your presentation to the proper person.

APPENDIX XII

Developing Trait Strategy

This appendix is referenced on page 125.

The possession of different traits by a buyer calls for different strategy on the part of the salesperson. One way to see the significance of this is to develop strategy for traits that superficially seem to be synonyms. Following are pairs of trait terms in this category. Check the meaning of each of these words in the dictionary and then, in the space provided, indicate the appropriate strategy to deal with each trait.

1. argumentative

   negativistic

2. ambitious

   industrious

3. articulate

   talkative

4. reactionary

   habit-bound

5. rash

   venturesome

6. clever

   shrewd

7. cooperative

   agreeable

8. self-sufficient

   self-confident

9. inhibited

   modest

10. tactful

    charming

APPENDIX XIII

Analyzing the Causes of Behavior

This appendix is referenced on page 125.

The types of behavior listed here are difficult to deal with conversationally. Select several traits from Appendix XIV that might account for such behavior in the following five examples. For each trait term you select, indicate briefly why that trait might cause such behavior. (Appendix XI contains a model.)

1. Defiant
    a.
    b.
    c.
    d.
    e.
2. Inconsiderate
    a.
    b.
    c.
    d.
    e.
3. Satisfied
    a.
    b.
    c.
    d.
    e.
4. Impetuous
    a.
    b.
    c.
    d.
    e.
5. Tactful
    a.
    b.
    c.
    d.
    e.

APPENDIX XIV

Common Trait Terms with Definitions and Strategies*

This appendix is referenced on pages 79 and 126.

Trait Term	Definition	Strategy
1. Adaptable	Adjusts readily to new conditions.	Buyer may make a positive decision before the presentation is finished. Take the order and supply rationalizations (2).
Inflexible	Resists change.	Consider disturbing homeostasis (4); use repetition, and if necessary, high pressure (8).
2. Affected	Artificial; behavior is acquired or practiced, as compared with spontaneous. There may be an element of compensatory behavior.	Search for the true or basic motivation; do not base strategy on a single trait; look for a pattern.
Natural	No pretense or deviousness.	No special strategy needed (1).
3. Alert	Watchful to what is going on; sensitive to stimuli. There is an implication of intellect and knowledge in areas where alertness is observed.	Use insight selling (3); do not attempt to conceal or confuse any details.
Sluggish	Low in energy, hence low in alertness and sensitivity.	Proceed slowly; use repetition as needed; ask questions frequently to keep buyer participating.
4. Ambitious	Constantly seeking advancement in one or more areas (salary, responsibility, etc.).	Develop personal needs (13); supply rationalizations (2).
Complacent	Satisfied with the status quo.	If a prospect, disturb homeostasis (4); if a customer, seek a sale with a minimum of disturbance and effort on buyer's part.

* Numbers in parentheses refer to common strategies in Appendix XV; numbers preceded by a number sign (#) refer to other trait terms.

360

	Trait Term	Definition	Strategy
5.	Argumentative	Enjoys, and hence introduces controversy into the discussion; may use techniques of argument.	Indulge argument, but try to avoid controversy on needs; if necessary, counteract devious reasoning (6).
	Agreeable	Avoids conflict as far as possible.	Make a full presentation (10).
6.	Articulate	Speaks easily and thoroughly; eloquent.	Pay attention so you will not need to ask him or her to repeat what was said for your benefit.
	Inarticulate	Has trouble explaining point of view.	Help by phrasing questions to which buyer can reply "yes" or "no;" avoid leading questions that can lead to a false understanding of needs.
7.	Autocratic	Exercises full authority without regard to others.	Use low pressure (9); use insight selling (3) so buyer will feel ideas are his/her own; avoid mentioning other persons; develop personal needs (13); supply rationalizations (2).
	Democratic	Reluctant to take action without conferring with other persons who are affected.	Do not force a decision; allow time to consult with others.
8.	Benevolent	Naturally kind and helpful.	Ask for help if feasible. Buyer enjoys helping where he or she can.
	Spiteful	Malicious; malevolent; willing to hurt others to advance.	Conceal your objectives as long as possible (5).
9.	Boastful	Bragging; pretends to knowledge that he or she might not actually possess.	Use low pressure (9); ask questions to show gaps in knowledge; ask questions to cause buyer to ask for missing information; avoid direct confrontation about the truth; counteract devious reasoning (6).
	Self-effacing	Volunteers deficiencies.	Provide necessary information; ignore self-depreciation.
10.	Bold	Daring; takes chances and liberties with facts and people.	Be alert for stretching of facts; counteract devious reasoning as necessary (6).
	Timid	Lets others take the initiative; lags behind; may resemble modesty #52.	Do not assume lack of knowledge or interest; encourage participation through questions.

Trait Term	Definition	Strategy
11. Candid	Replies directly to the point.	Stick to developing needs; avoid questions where answer could be embarrassing to buyer, yourself, or others; overlook any uncomplimentary remarks made.
Evasive	Avoids straightforward answers to questions; reluctant to reveal personal position.	Concentrate on need development; use indirect and projective questions to get the facts, and play down his or her personal commitment in giving answers.
12. Cheerful	Happy, joyful.	No special strategy needed (1).
Gloomy	Sad; depressed; dejected.	Ignore feelings and deal with facts related to needs. (Distinguish between chronic gloominess and a "changeable" mood, #70.)
13. Clever	Shows ability.	Use insight selling (3); commend on knowledge if appropriate.
Dull	Stupid; weak; slow-witted.	Lead to correct conclusion with questions and high pressure if necessary (8); overlook mistakes; reduce options (7).
14. Confused	Not clear on the facts pertinent to the discussion.	Go slowly and use repetition until buyer understands you. Use questions to get frequent feedback.
Aware	Understands the topics under discussion.	Use insight selling (3).
15. Considerate	Thoughtful; takes into account the effect his or her action will have on others.	Do not force a decision; allow time for consulting with others.
Selfish	Puts own interests above others.	Develop personal needs (13); supply rationalizations (2).
16. Contrary	Challenges and possibly resists recommendations.	Face buyer as long as the discussion is on a rational basis; use repetition as necessary; if necessary, counteract devious reasoning (6).
Obedient	Easily persuaded to accept a different point of view.	Make a full presentation (10) and supply rationalizations (2) as buyer is likely to have mind changed again by another salesperson. Use questions to ensure buyer understands the proposition.

Trait Term	Definition	Strategy
17. Cooperative	Willing to work with other persons for a common goal. (This can apply to you as well as others.)	Make full presentation (10).
Uncooperative	Finds reasons and takes action to impede presentation.	Use low pressure (9); conceal objectives as long as possible (5); concentrate on buyer's personal needs and supply rationalizations if necessary (2).
18. Cosmopolitan	Widely read; knowledgeable about many subjects.	Provide opportunity for buyer to demonstrate breadth of knowledge; commend buyer on accomplishments. (Recognize that this may be accompanied by high ability. Consider insight selling (3).)
Provincial	Limited in knowledge and outlook. (May relate to simplistic #21.)	Adhere to business or topics of buyer's choosing; avoid embarrassing him or her by moving away from what buyer knows.
19. Courageous	Resolute; faces all problems and persons.	No special strategy needed (1).
Cowardly	Tries to avoid difficult situations and decisions.	Stress the positive elements in the presentation; minimize buyer's personal responsibility; counteract devious reasoning (6).
20. Courteous	Shows consideration; pleasant; makes you feel reluctant to press an issue.	Make a full presentation (10).
Rude	Unpleasant; makes you feel like withdrawing from the interview.	Ignore the uncomplimentary remarks; make a full presentation (11).
21. Creative	Comes up with new and original ideas.	Commend creativity; evaluate ideas before agreeing. If you have a new idea, present it with insight selling (3).
Simplistic	Slow in thought and action; does things the same old hard way; never sees an alternative.	Use repetition as necessary. Buyer is not necessarily opposed to new ideas, just unable to discover them.
22. Crude	Lacks experience and/or skill.	Overlook deficiencies; help buyer to reduce weaknesses; make a full presentation (11).

Trait Term	Definition	Strategy
Refined	Shows the poise that results from experience and knowledge.	Use insight selling (3); make a full presentation (10).
23. Cruel	Enjoys seeing other people suffer or squirm in a difficult situation.	Appear to suffer. This will please buyer and protect your feelings. (This is compensatory behavior by you.)
Compassionate	Has warmth and attraction for people; shows sympathy.	Make a full presentation (10).
24. Curious	Wants to learn about whatever subject is under discussion.	Explain everything thoroughly; invite questions to satisfy curiosity.
Disinterested	Shows apathy and lack of interest; limits inquiry to essentials.	If necessary, disturb homeostasis (4); develop basic needs only; supply rationalizations if needed (2).
25. Decisive	Analyzes available data, makes a decision, and sticks with it.	Be sure buyer has considered all pertinent data before deciding. (It will be difficult to get buyer to change mind.)
Indecisive	Favors first one course of action, then another; reluctant to take final action.	Reduce options (7).
26. Deliberate	Wants time to consider all aspects of a proposition.	Proceed at buyer's pace.
Impulsive	Does not routinely consider all aspects of a situation; liable to make a decision at any point.	If decision is favorable, accept the order and supply rationalizations (2); if unfavorable, ask questions to show lack of knowledge. (Treat as an objection.)
27. Dependent	Reluctant to make a decision; wants an unreasonable amount of data before committing.	Reduce options (7); use testimonials, etc.; use repetition and high pressure (8) if needed. (Buyer needs to have someone to blame if his or her decision proves unsound.)
Self-sufficient	Willing to make a decision without help from others.	Just give the available facts.
28. Depressing	Low in animation; seems to see only problems and weaknesses; raises many objections.	Use questions to get buyer to answer own objections. Avoid slackening by "catching" buyer's manner.

Trait Term	Definition	Strategy
Exciting	Overactive; stimulates other people; may or may not be emotionally involved.	Be alert to avoid distraction from making a full presentation; accept an order at any point and supply rationalizations (2).
29. Enthusiastic	Actively interested; may make assumptions that go beyond your claims.	Let buyer take over the presentation (sell him- or herself); correct any excesses or misunderstandings; supply rationalizations (2).
Indifferent	Shows no interest or emotion.	Disturb homeostasis (4); use questions to get frequent feedback, thus ensure your message is being received.
30. Ethical	Conforms to moral standards; can be trusted.	No special strategy needed (1).
Exploitative	Adjusts and changes position to further his or her immediate selfish interests.	Avoid concessions (12); develop personal needs (13).
31. Excitable	Easily aroused, but unpredictable.	Work to develop exact needs; supply rationalizations (2), if necessary.
Tranquil	Slow to take action, even though buyer appears to be listening intently.	Make a full presentation: use repetition and high pressure (8), if necessary.
32. Fatalistic	Feels that matters are out of his or her hands, and that his or her opinions are unimportant.	Try to discover who buyer thinks is making decisions that affect him or her; show that those persons would approve the action you are recommending. (If those persons are available, ask to see them.)
Autonomous	Makes own decisions; relatively independent of the opinions of others.	Show the deference buyer feels entitled to; develop his or her personal needs and then supply rationalizations (2) that will be needed to convince others.
33. Foresighted	Looks ahead; considers the future as well as the present.	Evaluate buyer's long-range plans and commend if appropriate; help buyer make adjustments if you have knowledge he or she has not considered.
Hindsighted	Hates to make a decision except on the basis of past experience; frequently misses	Show the relationship of risk and "return on investment;" use the cliche "Nothing attempted,

	Trait Term	Definition	Strategy
		opportunities due to procrastination.	nothing gained." As a last resort, show the consequences of missing an opportunity.
34.	Forgetful	Poor memory, possibly due to poor attention.	Use repetition liberally during presentation; review pertinent parts of previous talk in detail.
	Retentive	Recalls all pertinent data covered in previous calls.	Be alert to avoid inconsistencies.
35.	Forgiving	Willing to overlook past events.	Do not take advantage of forgiveness. (Buyer may feel resentful if a hurt is repeated.)
	Vindictive	Looks for revenge; feels a need to get even.	Be scrupulous in your dealings; never leave a basis for hard feelings.
36.	Formal	Insists on following traditional rules, ceremonies, etc.; surrounds him- or herself with "red tape."	Work at buyer's pace; do not try to short-circuit his or her procedures just because they are time consuming.
	Informal	Easygoing; more interested in ends than means.	Go along with buyer as long as ideas are sound; if he or she is wrong, treat as any objection.
37.	Friendly	Easy to talk to; may or may not attend to and grasp your presentation.	Make a full presentation (10).
	Distant	Aloof; hard to talk to.	Resist temptation to abort interview; make a full presentation (11); do not try to "warm up" or "get close to buyer;" use questions to get feedback and note progress.
38.	Frivolous	Lighthearted; happy-go-lucky; good natured.	Avoid any detail that is not absolutely necessary; switch topic to business (14).
	Serious	Given to deep thought; everything is important.	Be serious; avoid shortcuts; cover all important points.
39.	Generous	Willing to share or give up part of what is his or hers.	Meet buyer halfway; do not take advantage of his or her generosity. Can appear to be generous on occasion but would resent anyone who takes advantage.

Trait Term	Definition	Strategy
Stingy	Drives a hard bargain; tries to get the best deal possible.	Develop personal needs (13); supply rationalizations (2); avoid concessions (12); no need to indulge in charity; be firm and stress value.
40. Grateful	Appreciative of favors and services.	Give full value and courteous treatment; make buyer realize he or she is getting good treatment that will pay off in future contacts.
Ungrateful	Does not appreciate favors, nor will he or she repay in kind.	Conceal your annoyance; make a full presentation (11); be scrupulous in your dealings, buyer may look for reasons to complain.
41. Honest	The buyer's word can be taken at face value.	Do not "grill" buyer or he or she may take offense; just ask for necessary information.
Deceptive	Capable of using lies and/or withholding information.	Conceal objectives (5).
42. Humorous	Genial; likes to amuse people with jokes and anecdotes.	Laugh at stories; provide some that can be repeated; watch for an opportunity to switch topic to business (14).
Somber	Serious; sober; impatient with frivolity.	Adhere to business; do not try to cheer up or encourage laughter.
43. Industrious	Works diligently at the task at hand.	Develop personal needs (13); show how the transaction will help productivity.
Lazy	Indolent; low level of productivity; fails to take the initiative in acquiring the necessary supplies and information to perform duties.	Do work for buyer; consider disturbing homeostasis (4).
44. Inexperienced	Lacking in knowledge and/or experience in subjects under discussion.	Be patient; provide all necessary information. Buyer will be grateful for help.
Experienced	Wise; competent; knowledgeable in a particular area. There may be an implication of high ability relative to salespeople.	Be alert for requests for special concessions; if buyer is reluctant to relate needs, offer to let buyer conduct the interview.

Trait Term	Definition	Strategy
45. Inhibited	Holds back from participating in a conversation, especially with strangers.	Proceed at buyer's pace; establish rapport. (A sale is unlikely until the buyer feels comfortable.)
Unrestrained	Lacks self control.	Be alert to pick up useful information that may be blurted out; be ready to close the sale at any point and supply rationalizations (2).
46. Jealous	Suspicious of other people's motivation; alert to any infringement of rights; demands unreasonable loyalty.	Avoid gossip and case histories of other sales.
Supportive	Kindly disposed to others; wants to see others achieve success.	Commend buyer for kindness; make a full presentation (10).
47. Leisurely	Appears relaxed with time available for full consideration.	Make a full presentation (10). (If buyer suddenly *appears* to run out of time, a different trait will appear. Keep in mind that traits are dynamic and make necessary change in strategy.)
Hurried	*Appears* to be short of time; makes you feel you should shorten your presentation.	Try to make a full presentation (11); offer to call again.
48. Logical	Wants full explanation including cause and effect; will consider only one point at a time.	Proceed at buyer's pace; encourage questions that allow curiosity to be satisfied and ensure needs are filled.
Intuitive	Satisfied to make a decision without having all elements verbalized.	Use insight selling (3); avoid detail; supply rationalizations (2).
49. Loyal	Faithful to company policies and personnel. (Probably will be trustworthy to salespeople.)	Do not ask for favors at the expense of buyer's company and/or co-workers.
Unfaithful	Does not keep his or her word.	Try to get complete action on every call. (Buyer may not keep the promises and commitments made.)
50. Mature	Fully developed, mentally and physically; has a philosophy of life that makes him or her predictable.	No special strategy needed (1).

	Trait Term	Definition	Strategy
	Childish	Ideas are not fully developed; given to displays of temper and frequent changes of mind.	Work for complete action on every call. (Buyer may change mind between calls.)
51.	Mild	Shows qualities of gentleness, weakness, delicacy, modesty, etc.	Show consideration for feelings. Buyer may be easily upset.
	Harsh	Shows qualities of strength, vigor, etc.	Face buyer when you are on firm ground. Buyer probably enjoys an opportunity to be forceful and is probably contemptuous of weakness.
52.	Modest	Reserved in displaying or describing own abilities and accomplishments.	Extract buyer's abilities.
	Conceited	Has an exaggerated opinion of him- or herself; claims more than can be produced.	Develop personal needs (13); avoid commenting on false claims unless they interfere with the sale, in which case use questions to show discrepancy.
53.	Obliging	Avoids conflicts as far as possible.	Make a full presentation (10).
	Obstructive	Takes a position designed to prevent the salesperson from controlling the terms of any transaction.	Conceal objectives (5); use low pressure (9); counteract devious reasoning (6).
54.	Open-minded	Free from bias and preconceived ideas; evaluates ideas on their merits. (Do not confuse with courteous #20.)	No special strategy needed (1).
	Opinionated	Maintains position in the face of facts to the contrary.	Conceal objectives (5); counteract devious reasoning (6); as far as possible show relationship of your ideas to buyer's.
55.	Optimistic	Always looking at the bright side; may lack realism in predictions; borders on delusions of grandeur.	Hold to reality; ask questions to show probable failure of some of the ideas.
	Pessimistic	Appears discouraged; expects failure.	Hold to reality; use questions to show that the past has not always been bad.
56.	Persuasive	Constantly attempts to get salespeople to see things buyer's way.	Use low pressure (9); distinguish between fact and opinion; counteract devious reasoning (6).

Trait Term	Definition	Strategy
Persuadable	Uncritical acceptance, thus agreement with everything the salesperson says.	Be cautious in developing needs; prevent buyer from forcing you to make the decisions; use indirect and, if necessary, "yes" or "no" questions. (If you decide buyer's needs in the need development phase, you will have trouble in the need fulfillment part of the sale.)
57. Pleasant	Manner arouses good feelings.	Make a full presentation (10); switch topic to business (14).
Caustic	Intentionally makes disparaging remarks; ridicules salespeople and/or their presentations.	Overlook remarks; make a full presentation (11).
58. Pliant	Easily persuaded to a new point of view.	Be firm; use high pressure if necessary (8).
Stubborn	Determined to maintain position or opinion.	Develop needs thoroughly; counteract devious reasoning (6); use repetition as necessary.
59. Practical	More interested in actual experience and results than in speculation.	After developing needs, show results of lab tests, etc.
Theoretical	Likes to speculate about the ideal; likes to consider hypothetical solutions.	Distinguish between opinion and fact; supply any data that bears on abstract considerations; steer buyer toward reality; do not allow a purchase that will not work.
60. Price-conscious	Wants to explore price before considering needs.	Compare price and value; counteract devious reasoning (6).
Quality-conscious	Wants the "top of the line" for personal prestige.	Develop personal needs (13). Be sure buyer is fully aware of any "overbuying"; supply rationalizations (2).
61. Progressive	Constantly revising existing procedures and adopting new ones.	Show how change will lead to improvement.
Reactionary	Reverses direction or manner; seeks to return to previously used procedures.	Minimize any change; relate new ideas to ones already held.
62. Proper	Conforms to company policy, social customs, etc.	Avoid radical ideas or major changes; do not ask for exceptions.

Trait Term	Definition	Strategy
Nonconforming	Acts independently of other persons; asocial as compared with antisocial.	Develop personal needs (13); supply rationalizations (2).
63. Realistic	Faces facts; practical; does what has to be done.	No special strategy needed (1).
Unrealistic	Makes erroneous judgments. (May either over- or under-estimate a problem.)	Search for any psychological value buyer's judgment may have; counteract devious reasoning (6).
64. Remorseful	Regrets past actions that hurt anyone for his or her advantage. Not likely to repeat.	Accept apology. Do not try to tell buyer it was "nothing"; he or she needs to get it out.
Remorseless	Has no regrets about past actions; not restrained by ideas of right or wrong.	Develop personal needs (13); avoid concessions (12); do not complain about past actions because buyer will consider you weak and try again.
65. Satisfied	Accepts things as they come; free from fault finding over minor matters.	Be sure he or she gets full value; is unlikely to insist on rights.
Displeased	Easily annoyed; quick to complain.	Avoid concessions (12) as they will only lead to more complaints.
66. Self-pitying	Always feels sorry for him- or herself; looks for sympathy.	Show empathy rather than sympathy; switch the topic to business (14).
Self-blaming	Personally takes the blame for all errors and failures.	Concede that things could be better; make constructive suggestions for repairing the damage.
67. Sensitive	Disturbed by small amounts of pressure.	Use low pressure (9).
Callous	Thick skinned; not easily upset.	Ignore minor objections. Make a full presentation (11).
68. Sensual	Seeks and enjoys the physical pleasures of life.	Offer entertainment up to the limits of company policy.
Puritanical	Self-denying in physical pleasures; ascetic.	Offer, but do not press social or other favors.
69. Sociable	Enjoys the company of others.	Be friendly but keep in mind buyer might be interested in you socially, rather than in your product; make a full presentation (10); switch topic to business (14).

Trait Term	Definition	Strategy
Reclusive	Actively avoids people; borders on hostility.	Do not force "small talk"; respect preferences but make a full presentation (11).
70. Steady	Dependable; very little variation in manner.	No special strategy needed (1).
Changeable	Moods vary from one call to another, and occasionally within a call.	Keep in mind that traits are dynamic, use strategy appropriate to traits of that instant; keep objectives flexible; consider terminating and rescheduling interview.
71. Stressed	Shows distress and agitation over some problems, usually self-imposed. (This may result in unsure or vacillating behavior.)	Reduce options (7); emphasize buyer's needs.
Calm	Apathetic or neutral when confronted with a choice.	Disturb homeostasis (4) if necessary; emphasize buyer's needs.
72. Submissive	Servile; shows awareness of weakness or lack of knowledge; some self-depreciation.	Supply whatever information is needed; avoid comment on shortcomings and try to prevent degradation.
Domineering	Overbearing; dictatorial; disregards the wishes of others.	Use low pressure (9); allow talk and bluster; avoid concessions (12).
73. Tactful	Skillful in avoiding offensive behavior. May or may not be sincere.	Make a full presentation (10).
Tactless	Careless and/or clumsy in human relations; makes mistakes that must be corrected.	Overlook errors and lead to the proper final action with repetition and high pressure if necessary (8).
74. Talkative	Talks often and at great length.	Switch the topic to business (14).
Uncommunicative	Does not talk willingly; secretive; silent.	Adhere to business; phrase questions to minimize the need for long answers.
75. Thoughtful	Puts people at ease; has regard for their feelings.	Make full presentation (10).
Inconsiderate	Likes to have "fun" at someone else's expense.	Be the butt of jokes willingly.

	Trait Term	Definition	Strategy
76.	Thrifty	Reluctant to spend money; may tend to order less than is really needed.	Point out consequences of running out of supplies; work for an adequate order.
	Wasteful	May order items which exceed needs in either quantity or quality.	Be precise in determining needs; caution about any excesses.
77.	Tolerant	Patient under provocation; forbearing; easygoing; takes frustrations as they come and makes the best of a situation.	Make a full presentation (10).
	Intolerant	Finds fault; petty; quick to make an accusation.	Make a full presentation (11).
78.	Trusting	Ready and willing to share information or confide in others.	Accept the information, but respect confidence.
	Suspicious	Alert to others harming him or her; always has an element of doubt about people's motives.	Invite buyer to question you until satisfied with your position.
79.	Special Abilities		
80.	Special Interests		

Key to Trait Terms

adaptable, 1
affected, 2
agreeable, 5
alert, 3
ambitious, 4
argumentative, 5
articulate, 6
autocratic, 7
autonomous, 32
aware, 14
benevolent, 8
boastful, 9
bold, 10
callous, 67
calm, 71
candid, 11
caustic, 57
changeable, 70
cheerful, 12
childish, 50
clever, 13
compassionate, 23
complacent, 4
conceited, 52
confused, 14
considerate, 15
contrary, 16
cooperative, 17
cosmopolitan, 18
courageous, 19
courteous, 20
cowardly, 19
creative, 21
crude, 22
cruel, 23
curious, 24
deceptive, 41
decisive, 25
deliberate, 26

democratic, 7
dependent, 27
depressing, 28
disinterested, 24
displeased, 65
distant, 37
domineering, 72
dull, 13
enthusiastic, 29
ethical, 30
evasive, 11
excitable, 31
exciting, 28
experienced, 44
exploitative, 30
fatalistic, 32
foresighted, 33
forgetful, 34
forgiving, 35
formal, 36
friendly, 37
frivolous, 38
generous, 39
gloomy, 12
grateful, 40
harsh, 51
hindsighted, 33
honest, 41
humorous, 42
hurried, 47
impulsive, 26
inarticulate, 6
inconsiderate, 75
indecisive, 25
indifferent, 29
industrious, 43
inexperienced, 44
inflexible, 1
informal, 36

inhibited, 45
intolerant, 77
intuitive, 48
jealous, 46
lazy, 43
leisurely, 47
logical, 48
loyal, 49
mature, 50
mild, 51
modest, 52
natural, 2
nonconforming, 62
obliging, 53
obedient, 16
obstructive, 53
open-minded, 54
opinionated, 54
optimistic, 55
persuadable, 56
persuasive, 56
pessimistic, 55
pleasant, 57
pliant, 58
practical, 59
price-conscious, 60
progressive, 61
proper, 62
provincial, 18
puritanical, 68
quality-conscious, 60
reactionary, 61
realistic, 63
reclusive, 69
refined, 22
remorseful, 64
remorseless, 64
retentive, 34
rude, 20

satisfied, 65
self-blaming, 66
self-effacing, 9
selfish, 15
self-pitying, 66
self-sufficient, 27
sensitive, 67
sensual, 68
serious, 38
simplistic, 21
sluggish, 3
sociable, 69
somber, 42
spiteful, 8
steady, 70
stingy, 39
stressed, 71
stubborn, 58
submissive, 72
supportive, 46
suspicious, 78
tactful, 73
tactless, 73
talkative, 74
theoretical, 59
thoughtful, 75
thrifty, 76
timid, 10
tolerant, 77
tranquil, 31
trusting, 78
uncommunicative, 74
uncooperative, 17
unfaithful, 49
ungrateful, 40
unrealistic, 63
unrestrained, 45
vindictive, 35
wasteful, 76

APPENDIX XV

Common Strategies

This appendix is referenced on page 127.

This appendix discusses some frequently occurring strategies. The following numbered entries correspond to the numbers in parentheses in Appendix XIV.

1. *No Special Strategy Required.* When there are no complicating factors, you do not need to belabor the situation. If both traits of the pair fall into this category, you can drop that trait. The polar opposite may require an adjustment and hence the list includes some relatively neutral terms.

2. *Supply Rationalizations.* A rationalization is a socially acceptable reason for past behavior. In some situations, buyers are willing to place an order before they are familiar with the proposition. When you are satisfied that the product or service will fill their need, you should accept the order and supply missing data before they can put the product or service to use.

   Failure to do this might result in returned merchandise because the buyer cannot justify the purchase to others. Salespeople who use a selling formula find this particularly true.

3. *Insight Selling.* In insight selling, you provide a few scattered bits of information rather than a long, detailed, systematic statement. *This allows buyers to see relationships themselves and keeps you from talking down to buyers who might resent such an approach.* Insight is one of the three methods of learning discussed in Chapter Eight.

4. *Disturb Homeostasis.* Whenever a buyer is reluctant to explore the use of a product or service, you must back away from developing needs and use a question designed to cause the person to question the soundness of his or her present situation. Such questions usually lead into a normal need development phase.

5. *Conceal Objectives.* Some buyers are more concerned with preventing you from making a sale than they are with filling their own needs. Anything you say might be used against you. In such cases, your strategy is to conceal your objectives, especially the needs you think you can fill, until the buyer is committed. This approach should be combined with the liberal use of indirect and projective questions.

   Failure of the buyer to know your objectives tends to increase the validity of your statements.

6. *Counteract Devious Reasoning.* When a buyer uses false information or tries to thwart you by devious reasoning, you should use the appropriate strategy from Chapter Seven.

7. *Reduce Options.* When a buyer is reluctant to commit to a course of action, you might need to make the decision for him or her. When you see this, you

can make one course of action appear more appropriate than another. Following this, rationalizations are a must.

8. *Use High Pressure.* This consists of making clear positive statements and repeating them as often as necessary. This is a "wearing-down" process.

9. *Use Low Pressure.* This consists of leading buyers, with questions, to a course of action so that they feel they made the decision: They bought rather than were sold.

10. *Make a Full Presentation.* Often a charming, agreeable, or tactful buyer makes you embarrassed to press your point(s). You feel it is an imposition to be businesslike when the buyer is so considerate and/or sociable. You should resist this feeling and complete the full presentation. If the buyer is truly gracious, he or she will listen; if not, the dynamics of the situation will reveal the true attitude and lead you to a revised strategy.

11. *Make a Full Presentation.* Some buyers are complaining, deceitful, rude, and so on, to the point where dealing with them is unpleasant if not distasteful. You must resist the inclination to withdraw from the interview. Make the full presentation, but keep it on a very businesslike and objective basis.

12. *Avoid Concessions.* A few personality traits lead buyers to expect and/or demand special treatment and concessions. When you sense this, you should become, and remain, alert to such requests, so that you can handle them before they are actually verbalized.

13. *Develop Personal Needs.* Some buyers put their own interests ahead of those of their company or their family members, even when the purchase is sound and warranted. Consummate such a sale by concentrating on the personal advantages and, after obtaining the order, supply rationalizations as in Strategy 2.

14. *Switch the Topic to Business.* Some buyers like to talk in general but are reluctant to discuss your proposition. You should indulge these people with social activity while directing the conversation back to your proposition.

APPENDIX XVI

Motivation Analysis—Work Sheet and Checklist

This appendix is referenced on pages 62 and 139.

Date _____

Customer _____

Salesperson _____

INSTRUCTIONS: Select a person whose motivation you wish to analyze. Use the *Motivation Checklist* in this appendix to select key factors underlying his/her motives; then plan your action. Record your analysis and action plan in the space provided on the next two pages. For an example and more detailed instructions, refer to Chapter Five, Section 4. After you make the call, you may want to revise your action plan for the next call on this buyer. Use the space below for that purpose.

Motivation Worksheet

	Buyer's Motives	Salesperson's Action
Level of Aspiration		
Interest		

Motivation Worksheet (continued)

Buyer's Motives	Salesperson's Action

Status

Values

After you make the call, you may want to revise your action plan for the next call on this buyer. Use the space below for that purpose.

Motivation Checklist

Level of Aspiration

On the Job	Off the Job
WANTS TO:	
1. Get ahead in company	1. Move to a better house and/or neighborhood
2. Reduce production costs	
3. Know more about the business	2. Have a second or better car
4. Build an "empire" in his or her company	3. Buy spouse expensive gifts
	4. Build a new addition on home
5. Make contribution to company procedures	5. Have a swimming pool
	6. Provide better life for family
6. Impress boss with knowledge	7. Make more money
7. Beat competition	8. Prepare for retirement
8. Obtain free information	9. Be entertained lavishly
9. Override purchasing agent	10. Make life easier for him- or herself
10. "Sell" management on his or her ideas	11. Have someone listen to his or her ideas
11. Achieve higher sales volume	
12. Cut costs to get lower prices	12. Hold public office
13. Dominate a market segment	13. Help the local schools
14. Reduce inventory	14. Have many friends
15. Acquire his or her own business	15. Improve golf game
16. Train his or her employees more effectively	16. Be "inside" in community politics
	17. Be known as a "builder" or "leader"
17. Acquire stock in company	18. Be the group leader
18. Be entertained by salespeople	19. Be admired by peers as a "good citizen"
19. Act with more authority	
20. Be viewed as "knower"	20. Have many friends
21. °	21.
22.	22.

°Add any items that are appropriate to your company and industry.

Motivation Checklist

Interest Pattern

On the Job	Off the Job

LIKES OR DISLIKES:

On the Job	Off the Job
1. To evaluate statistical data	1. Personal contact with people
2. To handle detail and paperwork	2. Specific kinds of people
3. To meet needs of customers	3. Politics
4. To develop ingenious design features	4. Cocktail parties
5. To test new materials	5. Current events and world affairs
6. To have efficient operations	6. Community service
7. To do personal contact work	7. Gossip
8. To try new methods	8. Church groups
9. To see advertising art and display work	9. Social gatherings
10. To receive literature on products and services	10. Sports, theatre, etc.
11. To focus on business quickly	11. His or her hobby of _____
12. To mix pleasure and business	12. Family activities
13. To keep salespeople waiting	13. Youngsters' schoolwork
14. To receive gifts	14. "Gadgets" for the home
15. To arrange appointments in advance	15. Good weather
16. To bargain over prices	16. Doing things as a family unit
17. To have things in writing	17. Outdoor activities
18. To represent company in industry groups	18. The stock market
19. To use technical jargon	19.
20.	20.
	21.
	22.

Motivation Checklist

Status

On the Job	Off the Job

WITH:

On the Job	Off the Job
1. Superiors—boss (or other executives)	1. The youngsters
2. Own department	2. Spouse
3. Subordinate employees	3. Parents
4. Peer group	4. In-laws
5. Other departments	5. Grandchildren
6. Salespeople who call	6. "Family Clan"
7. Industry association	7. Clubs
8. Owners of business	8. Church
9. Competitors	9. Socialites
10. "Big business"	10. Business leaders
11. Professional society	11. Political leaders
12. Technical personnel	12. Sports stars
13.	13. Waitresses
14.	14. Celebrities
15.	15. Professional people, e.g., doctors
16.	16.
17.	17.

Symbolized by:
 title
 form of address
 plaques
 diplomas
 office furnishings

Symbolized by:
 pictures
 trophies
 name dropping
 lapel pin

Motivation Checklist

Values

On the Job°	Off the Job°

MANIFESTED IN:

On the Job°	Off the Job°
1. Adherence to company policy	1. Honesty
2. Acceptance of proposals on their merits	2. Truthfulness
	3. Religious beliefs
3. Maintenance of confidence	4. Morals
4. Promptness in keeping appointments	5. Personal integrity
5. Sound business ethics	6. Conventionality and conformity
6. Refusal of gifts	7. Abstinence of controlled substances
7. Giving credit to employees when due	8. Prudishness
8. Equitability in handling business matters	9. Strictness with children
	10. Propriety
9. Gratitude for assistance	11. Civic responsibility
10. Frankness in admitting own shortcomings	12. Loyalty to friends
	13. Support of worthy causes
11. Loyalty to suppliers	14. Pride in community, state, and country
12.	15. Concern for those in trouble
13.	16. Responsibility shown for welfare of others
14.	
15.	17. Abhorrence of "shady" people
16.	18. Law abiding
17.	19. Kinds of close friends
18.	20. Admiration for public-spirited people
19.	21.

°Or the opposite of each item.

A Case History: Motivation Analysis

This appendix is referenced on page 139.

(The following case was prepared by a salesperson for computerized time management systems.)

Buyer's Motives	Salesperson's Action
Level of Aspiration	
To eliminate expense of current system	Calculate expense of time and attendance cards, processing, as well as errors in processing (the latter may be as much as 2% of total payroll).
To reduce costs in "lost time" of employees	a. Analyze number of employees checking in under present method and show lack of control over time of arrival or time of departure. b. Make estimates of possible late time reporting, early time departing and multiply this by number of employees to show potential cost savings if new system is installed.
To be known as a "leader" in the company	Show that by installing system the buyer can show not only fellow officers of the company, but the owners, that the buyer is concerned with cost savings and is doing something about it.
Interest	
Evaluate statistical data	Furnish facts and figures that spell out specific cost savings and other advantages quantitatively. Company now spends $25,000 a year on payroll processing. New system virtually eliminates the expense, paying for itself in less than 20 weeks.
Have efficient operation	Demonstrate the system's efficiency.
Mix pleasure with business	Accept an invitation to conduct business at private club.

383

Buyer's Motives	Salesperson's Action
Status	
With superiors—title as officer important symbol	Put together a written proposal in a form that the buyer can show to other officers of the company.
With socialites—private club membership	Be able to drop names of customers with some social standing that have status with the buyer.
Values	
Acceptance of proposals on merits	Reinforce logic in face-to-face interviews. Suggest criteria that should be applied in weighing the deal's merits.
Gratitude for assistance	Render assistance in designing system for new plant: selecting data entry mode, locating terminals, etc. Work directly with the contractor if the buyer requests it.
Honesty	Be completely frank and forthright about delivery schedules, problems, etc.

After you make the call, you may want to revise your action plan for the next call on this buyer. Use the space below for that purpose.

APPENDIX XVIII

Description of Roles of Group Members

This appendix is referenced on page 155.

Role	Description
Monopolizer (boss, leader, know-it-all, take-charge person, exhibitionist)	This person speaks up at every opportunity, may try to establish a one-to-one relationship with you, may have a psychological need to be in the limelight, and may have information to contribute.
Informer (Ivory tower, knowledgeable, scholar)	This person offers ideas and information for consideration by the group. The contribution may be fact or opinion and come at any stage of the meeting. (In the early stages of the meeting, you might have to perform this role yourself.)
Questioner (unsure, cautious, suspicious, inquiring)	This one picks up comments of others and seeks additional information on same or related topics. He or she may question you or other members of the group. The questions may be the result of intellectual curiosity or designed to impair the meeting objectives.
Developer (sees relationships, worrier)	This member picks up comments of others and adds his or her own information.
Energizer (helper, stimulator)	This person does not want to see the discussion slow down, feels a responsibility to keep the meeting moving toward its objectives, and may be the person who helped convene the group.
Clarifier (analyzer, summarizer)	This member gives opinions freely. He or she gets to the heart of the issue, puts it in perspective, and points out the need for additional information.
Pacifier (soother, gentle)	This type seeks points of agreement rather than differences. He or she tries to soothe feelings.

Role	Description
Attacker (hostile, aggressive, bully)	This one enjoys shooting down other people's ideas and may deride either sound or unsound ideas. He or she is capable of using sarcasm and ridicule, and hence may irritate or offend others in the group.
Joker (immature, flippant, jester)	This person makes light of all ideas and refuses to take problems seriously.
Follower (me too, yes man, tagalong)	This one remains passive. If called on, he or she usually agrees with ideas already expressed.
Withdrawer (inhibited, aloof, silent)	This person avoids participation as far as possible. A variety of underlying motivations may account for this avoidance.

APPENDIX XIX

Checklist for Summarizing Roles of Group Members

This appendix is referenced on page 155.

Name of Group Member	Designation of Group

INSTRUCTIONS: Immediately after the discussion, complete a checklist for each member of the group. Use a separate form for each person.

Base your judgments solely on what took place during the discussion. Avoid the temptation to use any information you possess about the person that was obtained from other sources.

Refer to the descriptions of roles as often as necessary to ensure that your judgments are consistent from one person to another and with what actually happened in the discussion.

a. Consistently means so frequently as to be typical of that person.
b. Frequently means seen on occasion but not necessarily typical of the person.
c. Not Played means there was opportunity for the person to play the role but he or she did not do so.
d. No Opportunity means there was no point at which the person could have normally played the role.

Role	Consistently	Frequently	Not Played	No Opportunity
1. Monopolizer				
2. Informer				
3. Questioner				
4. Developer				
5. Energizer				
6. Clarifier				
7. Pacifier				
8. Attacker				
9. Joker				
10. Follower				
11. Withdrawer				

APPENDIX XX

Checklist for Tallying Group Members' Remarks

This appendix is referenced on page 155.

Observer

Designation of Group

INSTRUCTIONS: Prepare a diagram of the seating arrangement and identify each member of the group with a number that you will relate to a column heading in the checklist below.

Familiarize yourself with the definitions of group roles (Appendix XVIII) so that the basis of your classification remains constant. As each person speaks, put a mark at the intersection of the column under his or her number and the row for that role. After the meeting, you can complete the "Checklist for Summarizing Roles of Group Members" (Appendix XIX) on each participant. At this point, you will probably wish to determine the name of the person.

Role	Number of Participant Corresponding to Seating Arrangement							
	1	2	3	4	5	6	7	8
1. Monopolizer								
2. Informer								
3. Questioner								
4. Developer								
5. Energizer								
6. Clarifier								
7. Pacifier								
8. Attacker								
9. Joker								
10. Follower								
11. Withdrawer								

APPENDIX XXI

Strategies for Use in Group Selling

This appendix is referenced on page 156.

Role	Strategies
Monopolizer	You should welcome comments that enhance your objectives and vice versa, but you must take care that other group members do not build resentment against the Monopolizer for overparticipation or against you for repressing the individual.
	When you do not want comments, try to avoid eye contact and feign failure to note the desire to participate. When this is not feasible, such phrases as "I think we are overworking you" or "Let's get some help from the others" may be in order.
	Another way to reduce eagerness to participate is to call on the Monopolizer when he or she does not have the information desired.
Informer	Recognize the Informer when you need more ideas for group discussion. Also, if the current ideas under discussion are not advantageous, call on an Informer for additional ideas and find some that are more likely to advance your objectives. Try to avoid an Informer when enough good ideas are presently under discussion.
	If the Informer offers information that is inimical to the meeting objectives, you may need to refute it. In such a case, you may have to deal temporarily with the member on a one-to-one basis and treat the information as an objection. You need to return to your basic selling skills. Also, consider calling on an attacker to refute the ideas.
Questioner	Based on a knowledge of his or her attitude toward the meeting objectives, call on or ignore this person. When more depth of discussion is desirable, the Questioner can be very helpful. If points are raised that you do not fully understand, refer the matter to a Questioner rather than ask for clarification. This is particularly appropriate if the matter is one on which the group would expect you to be knowledgeable.
Developer	Call on this person when you wish to develop greater depth of discussion. Avoid him or her when trying to terminate the discussion either on a particular point or the meeting in general.
Energizer	Call on this person when the going is tough. The Energizer probably knows more about the group members and the institutional objectives than you do and can get the discussion back on the right track.

Role	Strategies
Clarifier	Use this person to sum up and finish a topic that needs no further discussion. Also, you can call on the Clarifier to indicate the need for additional information.
Pacifier	Refer pointed differences of opinion to this person. Bring the Pacifier into the discussion when tempers start to rise or when patience or tolerance is needed. This person can be helpful in terminating discussion on a minor point so that the discussion can revert to more important topics.
Attacker	Refer undesirable ideas to the Attacker. He or she will deflate them. Try to prevent attacks that evoke hostility and hence may endanger the group relationships. Be sure all desired information is out in the open before you recognize the Attacker as his or her behavior tends to cut off discussion.
Joker	Note the Joker's acceptance by the group. If well received, allow a reasonable amount of levity. Use this person to break up tension in the group. Try to avoid participation when success on a key point is near.
Follower	Use the Follower to get another affirmative voice on an idea consistent with the meeting objectives.
Withdrawer	Unless you have good reason to believe the Withdrawer can and will make a significant contribution to the discussion, do not call on this person. You should not try to stimulate participation for the sake of participation alone. Try to estimate the motivation to be silent before calling on this person.

APPENDIX XXII

Salesperson's Example of Logical Analysis in Selling

This appendix is referenced on page 177.

Problem: How to substantially increase the business in Account X.

Inputs: F = Fact   O = Opinion

   I. Business available in this account is at least $3,000,000 per year. (O)
  II. My share this past year was 20% or $600,000. (F)
 III. Account X is growing, so future business is going to be even greater. (O)
  IV. Favorable, friendly relations exist with the purchasing agent. (O)
   V. The purchasing agent is sensitive about salespeople talking directly to operating personnel. (O)
  VI. Competitors M and N are both getting more business than I am. (F)
 VII. My product line is better accepted in accounts similar to X; the market research data prove it. (F)
VIII. My company does more national and local advertising than either M or N. (F)
  IX. The salespeople for M and N developed X as an account before I did. (F)
   X. My company's prices would be competitive for larger volume orders. (F)
  XI. The one time I made a joint call on the account with one of our technical people, we were well received. (O)
 XII. The present share of business does not justify present call frequency. (F)

Restrictions and restraints:

A. My company's price policy is inflexible and is based on size of order.
B. I cannot continue investing the amount of time I have invested up to now unless I increase my share of the business. Even if I kept my percentage constant, the account is not growing that fast.
C. Technical help is justified only if our person is going to be with me anyway working on larger accounts.

Step 1. Defining and bounding the problems. First, break down into smaller problems:

1. How to write larger orders per call.
2. How to get beyond the purchasing agent to operating personnel.

3. How to learn more about use of the line in various departments.
4. How to capitalize on our greater acceptance in X's industry.
5. How to learn more about both competitors' ways of commanding greater shares of the available business than I do.

Next, outline procedure for Item 1 (a similar process would be followed for 2–5).

1. How to write larger orders per call.
   a. How to justify the resulting increase in X's inventory.
   b. How to determine the time when inventory may be slow.
   c. How to induce the purchasing agent to make the larger cash outlay.

Step 2. Establishing criteria for evaluating alternative solutions. Criteria for 1a. (Increase X's inventory.)

1. No concession in pricing.
2. No disturbance of existing business.
3. No undue time investment of myself or other company personnel.
4. Maximum benefits to X consistent with welfare of my company.

Step 3. Thinking of alternative solutions. Alternative solutions for 1a. (Justify increase in X's inventory.)

1. Analyze savings on large order versus
   a. Use of X's money elsewhere.
   b. Hidden costs of frequent purchases.
   c. Costs of materials handling.
2. Greater services warranted with larger order by
   a. Myself.
   b. Our company's technical personnel.

Step 4. Evaluation of alternative solutions (1 and 2, Step 3). Alternative 1: Appears to meet all four criteria with minimum of risk on criterion (2).
   Alternative 2: Appears to meet criteria (3) and (4) but might indirectly violate (1) if resultant demands for service proved too costly. Further, it involves risk on (2) for the purchasing agent might feel that my company is holding back on service.

Step 5. "Best" solution. Alternative 1 seems best, all things considered.

Output:

Salesperson decides to put together an analysis of savings using the best estimates of alternative use of X's money, cost of frequent purchasing and of materials handling.

The salesperson then proceeds in a similar manner with subproblems 1b and 1c.

A similar approach would then be taken with each of the other four smaller problems.

APPENDIX XXIII

Suggestion versus Reasoning

This appendix is referenced on page 186.

Suggestion and reasoning are two different means of accomplishing the same objective; namely, to cause a person to perform an act or change an opinion that he or she otherwise would not have done.

Reasoning is a logical or straightforward approach that explores the pros and cons of an issue. Suggestion is an attempt to sidestep the issue and avoid a detailed analysis.

To see how these two approaches work in practice, take five claims that you frequently make for your product or service and, for each one, formulate a statement that would qualify as suggestion. Also, for each claim, supply the kind of information that would prove the claim on a logical basis.

Two examples are provided.

Claim:

In its category, our product is most popular with the general public.

Suggestion:

You will see our product in use wherever you go.

Reasoning:

Our market research data show that 92% of the families in a national consumer panel purchased our product in the past 30 days. The next nearest competitor could only claim 62% on the same basis.

Claim:

Our product will give you 20% more volume per batch.

Suggestion:

Every fifth unit is free when you use our product.

Reasoning:

Laboratory studies in our company show a minimum increase of 27% per batch when this product is added to the basic ingredients. When the cost of the product is taken into account, it reduces the effective increase to 21%. We feel conservative in promising you a 20% saving.

Now apply the same process to one of your own products or services.

1. Claim:

    Suggestion:

    Reasoning:

2. Claim:

    Suggestion:

    Reasoning:

3. Claim:

    Suggestion:

    Reasoning:

4. Claim:

    Suggestion:

    Reasoning:

5. Claim:

    Suggestion:

    Reasoning:

APPENDIX XXIV

Exercise in Creative Selling

This appendix is referenced on page 197.

Product I want to sell   → to →   Account

                       ☐ Customer   ☐ Prospect

INSTRUCTIONS: Under each point listed below, place one or more ideas for generating business (refer to Chapter Seven for suggestions).

1. Tangible (product) superiority. Benefits:

2. Intangible (service) superiority. Benefits:

3. Price (value) superiority. Benefits:

4. Image (company) superiority. Benefits:

5. Team (myself and supportive personnel) superiority. Benefits:

6. Additional considerations. Benefits:

7. Selling ideas to use. Benefits:

Call Checklist and Presentation Checklist

This appendix is referenced on pages 196, 270, and 280.

Call Checklist

Representative _____
Supervisor _____
Date _____
Store Name _____
Location _____

(You should check the space for each item that most nearly describes your observation. In addition, insert comments on those items where space is provided.)

How Well Was
Task Accomplished?

Thoroughly	Adequately	Poorly	Omitted	
				Section A. Before Entering Store
☐	☐	☐	☐	1. Review background of account by reference to proper records. Note extent of line carried, recent orders, and so on. Especially note remarks made after last call.
☐	☐	☐	☐	2. Formulate objective of present call, such as extend line, build display. State objectives (space provided on reverse side).
☐	☐	☐	☐	3. Organize material to be taken into store. This will be based on objectives. Include samples and display materials.
☐	☐	☐	☐	4. Check names and titles of key persons in store. Also check jobber's name on indirect accounts.
☐	☐	☐	☐	5. Observe store from outside for clues to display tastes and policies. Look for ideas that will relate your display plans to store practices. List ideas (space provided on reverse side).
				Section B. In Store
☐	☐	☐	☐	1. Introduce yourself to the proper key person and ask permission to inspect shelves, stock room, and so on as they pertain to your product. (If the proper key person is not available, check the second in command or use your judgment and past experience to determine what steps you can take in lieu of specific permission.)

396

How Well Was
Task Accomplished?

Thoroughly	Adequately	Poorly	Omitted	
☐	☐	☐	☐	**2.** Inspect shelf space devoted to your products, noting general condition and any changes made since last visit. Observe competitor's display in same manner. Make any minor adjustments such as straightening or dusting display.
☐	☐	☐	☐	**3.** Inspect any floor displays of your products in the same manner as shelf space. Note all floor displays in the store, possible locations for new displays, and relate to your objectives and impressions gained from previous observations.
☐	☐	☐	☐	**4.** Visit stock room and note quantity and general condition of stock on hand. Rotate stock. Also note competitive products.
☐	☐	☐	☐	**5.** Revise objective (A2) as indicated by your observations. State new objective with reasons for change (space provided on reverse side).
☐	☐	☐	☐	**6.** Seek out key person and make presentation. Include constructive suggestions for store operation. Make any authorized changes in, or additions to, shelf or floor displays.
☐	☐	☐	☐	**7.** Write order.
☐	☐	☐	☐	**8.** If necessary, handle complaints.
☐	☐	☐	☐	**9.** On basis of agreement reached with key person, instruct stock person in maintenance of shelf space and display of promotional material.
☐	☐	☐	☐	**10.** Speak to all appropriate sales personnel to bring them up to date on product information they can use in serving their customers.
☐	☐	☐	☐	**11.** Thank all appropriate persons for whatever help they have been in accomplishing your objectives. Distribute samples as appropriate.

Section C. After Leaving Store

☐	☐	☐	☐	**1.** Double-check your order for accuracy and update your computer files.
☐	☐	☐	☐	**2.** Enter data on displays erected or promotional material used.
☐	☐	☐	☐	**3.** Analyze reasons for success or failure in accomplishing objectives.
☐	☐	☐	☐	**4.** Enter data for guidance in setting objectives on next call to this account.
☐	☐	☐	☐	**5.** Enter data on activities of competition. Relay to Division Manager, if necessary.

Presentation Checklist

Representative ⎯⎯⎯⎯⎯⎯⎯
Supervisor ⎯⎯⎯⎯⎯⎯⎯
Date ⎯⎯⎯⎯⎯⎯⎯
Store Name ⎯⎯⎯⎯⎯⎯⎯
Location ⎯⎯⎯⎯⎯⎯⎯

(Observer should check the appropriate space for items pertinent to that particular sales call.)

How Well Was
Task Accomplished?

Thoroughly	Adequately	Poorly	Omitted	
☐	☐	☐	☐	1. Did you know the account or make necessary inquiries so that you made your presentation to the proper person?
☐	☐	☐	☐	2. Did you recognize that the customer was satisfied with the status quo and take necessary steps to disturb homeostasis before trying to discover his or her needs?
☐	☐	☐	☐	3. Did you use the need satisfaction approach rather than the selling formula or stimulus response approach?
☐	☐	☐	☐	4. Did you make sure the customer realized his or her needs before you attempted to close?
☐	☐	☐	☐	5. Was the product information correct?
☐	☐	☐	☐	6. Was your product information organized for effective use?
☐	☐	☐	☐	7. Did you coordinate the use of visual aids with the oral presentation?
☐	☐	☐	☐	8. Did you repeat points as many times as necessary to ensure that the customer understood the point?
☐	☐	☐	☐	9. Did you relate your presentation to the customer's reactions?
☐	☐	☐	☐	10. Did you allow enough time for the customer to grasp a point before going on to the next point?
☐	☐	☐	☐	11. Did you try to make points by suggestion before resorting to logical reasoning?
☐	☐	☐	☐	12. Did you use the right kind of pressure?
☐	☐	☐	☐	13. Did you base strategy on an analysis of the customer's traits?
☐	☐	☐	☐	14. Did you avoid projecting your own values on the customer?
☐	☐	☐	☐	15. Did you realize how the proposition appeared to the customer?
☐	☐	☐	☐	16. Did you talk to all persons who might affect your success in the account?

How Well Was
Task Accomplished?

Thoroughly	Adequately	Poorly	Omitted	
☐	☐	☐	☐	**17.** Did you vary the presentation from one person to another so that the appropriate information was transmitted in each case?
☐	☐	☐	☐	**18.** Did you supply new reasons for buying if the customer had refused to buy on the previous visit?
☐	☐	☐	☐	**19.** Did you understand the motivation of the customer?

APPENDIX XXVI

Guide for Observing Sales Performance

This appendix is referenced on pages 194 and 268.

Overview
Three points should be kept in mind in using this guide:

1. It is designed for salespeople who use the need satisfaction method of selling. It is not intended for use by salespeople who use the stimulus response or selling formula approaches.
2. It deals only with those portions of the sales call that can be seen and/or heard. It does not consider account or territory management.
3. It does assume the existence and use of a salesperson-oriented product/service manual, described in Chapter One.

The essence of observing is not looking, but seeing. A person with a detailed knowledge of the rules and strategy of a sport receives more satisfaction from watching a game. The same is true of selling.

The observation guide outlines the basic elements in practicing need satisfaction selling. The key that follows it references specific passages in this book so that sales managers and salespeople can acquire a common understanding of the objectives and processes of the sales interview. Use of this guide should focus attention on the major factors in the sales process and eliminate controversy.

Levels of Observation

Observations can be made on three levels. First, you can observe yourself. Second, colleagues can make two-person calls. Third, the observer can be a supervisor or trainer. The last two categories differ only in the nature of the discussion following the call.

You might assume that the purpose of the two-person call is to have one person help the other improve performance. This is obviously the goal of the supervisory call. However, anyone who carefully observes any activity knows that self-analysis can follow detailed observation. This is the first step in improving personal productivity. Hence, the double justification for peer observation is that both parties can improve their performance.

400

Having trainees act as observers is useful as well. While they may not be able to offer constructive criticism to the salesperson, they certainly can note critical points in the interview and ask questions that will hasten their understanding of the selling process. They will also be motivated to refer to specific passages in this book that describe the recommended procedures.

Except for trainees, a peer observation is likely to be limited to the more obvious strengths and weaknesses of the salesperson while a supervisory observation will likely include a more detailed analysis leading to a formal appraisal and recommendations for improving future performance. Note that the guide calls for noting good as well as poor sales performance.

Strengths and Weaknesses

The major objective of observation is identifying strengths and weaknesses. Noting strengths is complimentary, reinforces effective activities, and ensures their repetition on future calls.

Identifying weaknesses is much more important. This is the real justification for two-person calls and the basis for the superiority of two-person calls over self-observation. Recognizing your own weaknesses is difficult. Habit results in repetition without change, despite the best intentions. An objective observer is the best means to discover and remedy problem areas and may intensify commitment to change.

The first step in overcoming a weakness is to become aware of it. The second step is to resolve to change, but you must know the "right" way to perform. Only perfect practice makes perfect performance!

The value of an observed sales call is directly related to the accuracy of the observations, the skill of the observer in communicating them, and the willingness and desire of the person being observed to change behavior. This guide facilitates the first two factors. The third one comes from your internal motivation. External motivation by a supervisor is also common.

The first step in a two-person call is to clearly define the objectives. Without definite objectives, provided in this guide, measuring success or failure is not possible.

Note Taking

One of the selling parties should explain to the buyer the reason for the two-person call. The observer should then attempt to sit beside and/or slightly behind the buyer. In this way, the note taking is not prominent.

Note taking is a skill that you can and must develop with practice. Ideally, you should develop a set of symbols or shorthand for taking notes during an interview. You can then expand the notes and/or detail them after the interview. Some of the items on the observation guide can be checked (e.g., Item 8). A word or two in an item such as 18 should suffice to recall key points after the interview. Once the observer accepts the need for good notes, he or she can quickly work out an appropriate method of taking them.

The notes are crucial to a good postcall discussion. They make the observer credible to the salesperson. When the observation is part of a formal appraisal, notes can make the difference between smooth and unpleasant critiques.

Regardless of the care in taking them, the possibility exists of error in interpretation and recording. Therefore, the observer should check the first draft of his or her notes with the salesperson before reaching any conclusions.

The initial step in completing the observation guide should be to enter all detail possible. Note a "general" and a "specific" section. Go over the "general" section mentally before making detailed entries in the "specific" section. Then go back and finalize the general entries.

Go over the entries with the salesperson to check agreement before discussing strengths and weaknesses. Feel free to make any changes, including additions and deletions. Keep in mind that the real objective is to *improve sales performance*. The observation process is merely a means to an end, not an end in itself. You should drop any points where you do not reach agreement readily. Future calls will provide opportunities for more accurate observations. This is the best way to resolve the problem.

Lack of agreement may occur when salespeople are defensive about their performance. They may correct themselves before arranging another call; hence there is no need to belabor any point the first time it arises.

Summarizing the Observation

After reviewing all the notes, the two parties should select the strengths and weaknesses together. The strengths are usually not a problem.

In selecting weaknesses, concentrate on those that are not only significant but that offer the best opportunities for improvement. For example, if a salesperson falters or repeats parts of a presentation verbatim (Items 12 and 24), you should search out the reasons. If the problem is low verbal facility, immediate improvement is unlikely and hence recording it as a weakness will only magnify the problem for little gain. On the other hand, if a Salesperson-Oriented Product Manual exists, the weakness should be stressed along with a strong recommendation for some homework (Chapter One, Section 2).

When you reach agreement on strengths and weaknesses, you can make specific recommendations for improvement.

In addition to the specific references for each item, it will be helpful to both salesperson and observer to be familiar with the following sections of this book: Chapter One, Sections 2 and 3; Chapter Five, Section 2; Chapter Seven, Section 4; and Chapter Ten, Sections 2, 3, and 4.

Observation Guide for Use by Salespeople Who Practice Need Satisfaction Selling

A. Call Objectives

1. What are the objectives of the present call?

    a. _____

    b. _____

    c. _____

2. If this is one of a series of calls, put in proper perspective. Consider overall objectives and buyer personnel involved on this and other calls.

    _____

    _____

    _____

B. General Observations

3. Did the salesperson adjust the amount of opening conversation to the personality of the buyer?

    _____ Yes   _____ No

    If No, explain. _____

    _____

    _____

4. Which method of selling would best describe the interview?

    _____ Stimulus Response

    _____ Selling Formula

    _____ Need Satisfaction

    Explain. _____

    _____

5. Would the interview be best described as one-way or two-way communication?

    _____ One-way   _____ Two-way

    If one-way, who dominated the conversation?

    Explain. _____

    _____

    _____

6. Was the salesperson an "Active" listener?

_____ Yes   _____ No

Give examples of drawing out or shutting off the buyer.

_____

_____

_____

7. Was the interview basically conversational or inquisitional in nature?

_____ Conversational   _____ Inquisitional

Explain. _____

_____

8. Would the interview be best described by High, No, or Low pressure?

_____ High   _____ No   _____ Low

Explain. _____

_____

9. Did the salesperson try to control the interview with questions or by talking louder and faster?

_____ Questions   _____ Talking

Explain. _____

_____

10. Did the salesperson appear credible to the buyer?

_____ Yes   _____ No

If No, suggest reasons for failure. _____

_____

_____

_____

11. Did the salesperson present the desired image of the product (service) and/or company?

_____ Yes   _____ No

If No, explain. _____

_____

_____

12. Had the salesperson mastered (overlearned) the material so that he/she was free to concentrate on the buyer, rather than think about the message?

_____ Yes   _____ No

If No, give examples in terms of cues missed.

_____

_____

_____

13. Did the salesperson appear to be using a type or trait approach to the buyer?

_____ Type   _____ Trait

Give basis for judgment. _____

_____

_____

14. Did the salesperson make notes of novel or important information to report back to management?

_____ Yes   _____ No

If Yes, give examples. _____

_____

_____

15. Did the salesperson indulge in "private" word meanings?

_____ Yes   _____ No

If Yes, give example. _____

_____

_____

_____

16. Did the salesperson clarify "private" meanings used by the buyer?

_____ Yes   _____ No   _____ Not observed

If Yes, or No, give example. _____

_____

_____

_____

C. Specific Observations

17. Was the salesperson prepared with questions to disturb homeostasis if necessary?

    _____ Yes   _____ No

    If No, describe the situation. _____

    _____

    _____

    _____

18. What needs did the salesperson develop before attempting to close?

    a. _____

    b. _____

    c. _____

    d. _____

19. Were the five criteria for Need Developing Questions used?

    _____ Yes   _____ No

    If No, give examples of poor questions. _____

    _____

    _____

20. Did the salesperson develop any needs that could not be filled?

    _____ Yes   _____ No

    If Yes, give example. _____

    _____

    _____

21. When appropriate, did the salesperson use "projective" questions (avoid putting the buyer "on-the-spot")?

    _____ Yes   _____ No

    If No, give an instance where a projective question would have been more appropriate?

    _____

    _____

    _____

22. Did the salesperson project his/her own needs or values into the discussion (assume needs rather than test for them)?

_____ Yes   _____ No

If Yes, give example. _____

_____

_____

23. Did the salesperson use questions to establish needs, or test the existence of needs?

_____ Establish   _____ Test

If "Establish," give example. _____

_____

_____

24. Was the salesperson prepared with alternate phrasings?

_____ Yes   _____ No

If No, give examples of verbatim repetition, and/or leaving a point too soon. _____

_____

_____

_____

25. Was repetition used in accordance with the principle of Summation?

_____ Yes   _____ No

If No, explain. _____

_____

_____

26. Did the salesperson try insight learning before providing a full and detailed explanation?

_____ Yes   _____ No

Explain. _____

_____

_____

_____

27. Did the salesperson use key sales points in accordance with the laws of primacy, frequency, and recency?

_____ Yes   _____ No

Explain. _____

_____

_____

_____

28. Was the salesperson sensitive to Negative-Involuntary responses?

_____ Yes   _____ No

If No, give an example where a cue was missed. _____

_____

_____

_____

29. Did the salesperson respond to the buyer's behavior as well as speech?

_____ Yes   _____ No

Give examples. _____

_____

_____

30. Did the salesperson allow time for the buyer to react to each sales point before presenting another one (consider both Refractory Phase and Inhibition)?

_____ Yes   _____ No

If No, give example. _____

_____

_____

31. Did the salesperson use visual aids properly (consider removal, as well as introduction)?

_____ Yes   _____ No

Give examples. _____

_____

_____

32. Did the salesperson make reference to company advertising when appropriate?

_____ Yes   _____ No

Give examples of opportunities taken or missed. _____

_____

_____

33. Did the salesperson use testimonials appropriately (with buyers low in self-confidence)?

_____ Yes   _____ No

Explain. _____

_____

_____

34. Was suggestion used when appropriate (compare with reasoning)?

_____ Yes   _____ No

If No, explain. _____

_____

_____

35. Did the salesperson attempt more than one close (return to Need Development phase between closes)?

_____ Yes   _____ No

Describe each attempt. _____

_____

_____

36. Did the salesperson note unusual personality traits and make appropriate adjustments?

_____ Yes   _____ No

Give example. _____

_____

_____

37. When the buyer changed his/her attitude or behavior, did the salesperson make a corresponding adjustment?

_____ Yes   _____ No   _____ No changes observed

If Yes or No, describe incident. _____

_____

_____

_____

38. If necessary, did the salesperson introduce topics appropriate to the buyer's motivation?

    _____ Yes   _____ No

    If No, explain. _____

    _____

    _____

    _____

39. Did the salesperson probe objections to ensure selection of proper answer?

    _____ Yes   _____ No

    If No, give example. _____

    _____

    _____

    _____

    _____

40. Did the salesperson reply to objections with a question before providing further information?

    _____ Yes   _____ No

    If No, give example. _____

    _____

    _____

    _____

41. Did the salesperson counteract devious reasoning when it was apparent?

    _____ Yes   _____ No

    Give examples. _____

    _____

    _____

    _____

42. Did the salesperson try to overcome emotional resistance with logical reasoning?

_____ Yes _____ No

If Yes, explain. _____

_____

_____

43. If there was a barrier to the sale (something preventing immediate use), did the salesperson make a reasonable effort to solve the buyer's problem?

_____ Yes _____ No

If No, explain. _____

_____

_____

44. If the salesperson's objectives proved inappropriate, was he/she able to reformulate them and continue the presentation?

_____ Yes _____ No

If No, explain. _____

_____

_____

45. Did the salesperson have adequate knowledge of his/her competition?

_____ Yes _____ No

If No, give some indication of area(s) of weakness. _____

_____

_____

46. Did the salesperson counteract competition by making a point-by-point comparison of the products?

_____ Yes _____ No

Describe. _____

_____

_____

47. If the call was one of a series, did the salesperson enter data from previous calls on his or her computer?

_____ Yes _____ No

If No, explain. _____

_____

_____

48. If the call was one of a series, had the salesperson identified the decision makers?

_____ Yes   _____ No   _____ No problem

If No, explain. _____

_____

_____

D. Summary

I. Strengths

a. _____

b. _____

c. _____

II. Weaknesses

a. _____

b. _____

c. _____

III. General Recommendations for future performance (make reference to individually numbered items where practical).

a. _____

b. _____

c. _____

_____

_____

_____

_____

IV. Specific Recommendations for future performance (include readings).

a. _____

b. _____

c. _____

_____

_____

_____

_____

_____

_____

_____

_____

_____

_____

_____

Key to Observation Guide for Use by Salespeople Who Practice Need Satisfaction Selling

A. Call Objectives

1. What are the objectives of the present call?

a. _____

b. Chapter One, Section 1

c. Chapter Ten, Section 2

2. If this is one of a series of calls, put in proper perspective. Consider overall objectives and buyer personnel involved on this and other calls.

_____

Chapter Ten, Sections 2, 3 and 4

_____

B. General Observations

3. Did the salesperson adjust the amount of opening conversation to the personality of the buyer?

_____ Yes   _____ No

If No, explain. _____

_____

Chapter Two, Section 3 _____

4. Which method of selling would best describe the interview?

_____ Stimulus Response

_____ Selling Formula

_____ Need Satisfaction

Explain. _____
Chapter One, Section 2 _____

5. Would the interview be best described as one-way or two-way communication?

_____ One-way   _____ Two-way

If one-way, who dominated the conversation?

Explain. _____
Chapter One, Section 3 _____

Chapter Two, Section 1 _____

6. Was the salesperson an "Active" listener?

_____ Yes   _____ No

Give examples of drawing out or shutting off the buyer.

_____

Chapter One, Section 2 _____

Chapter Two, Sections 1 and 2 _____

7. Was the interview basically conversational or inquisitional in nature?

_____ Conversational   _____ Inquisitional

Explain. _____
Chapter Two, Section 3 _____

8. Would the interview be best described by High, No, or Low pressure?

_____ High   _____ No   _____ Low

Explain. _____
Chapter One, Section 1 _____

9. Did the salesperson try to control the interview with questions, or by talking louder and faster?

_____ Questions _____ Talking

Explain. _____

Chapter Three, Section 1 _____

10. Did the salesperson appear credible to the buyer?

_____ Yes _____ No

If No, suggest reasons for failure. _____

_____

_____

Chapter Three, Section 1 _____

11. Did the salesperson present the desired image of the product (service) and/or company?

_____ Yes _____ No

If No, explain. _____

_____

_____

Chapter One, Section 1 _____

12. Had the salesperson mastered (overlearned) the material so that he/she was free to concentrate on the buyer, rather than think about the message?

_____ Yes _____ No

If No, give examples in terms of cues missed. _____

_____

_____

Chapter Eight, Section 1 _____

13. Did the salesperson appear to be using a type, or trait approach to the buyer?

_____ Type _____ Trait

Give basis for judgment. _____

_____

Chapter Five, Section 2 _____

14. Did the salesperson make notes of novel or important information to report back to management?

_____ Yes _____ No

If Yes, give examples. _____

_____

Chapter Ten, Sections 2 and 6

15. Did the salesperson indulge in "private" word meanings?

_____ Yes _____ No

If Yes, give example. _____

_____

Chapter Two, Section 1

16. Did the salesperson clarify "private" meanings used by the buyer?

_____ Yes _____ No _____ Not observed

If Yes, or No, give example. _____

_____

Chapter Two, Section 1

C. Specific Observations

17. Was the salesperson prepared with questions to disturb homeostasis if necessary?

_____ Yes _____ No

If No, describe the situation. _____

_____

Chapter Three, Section 1

18. What needs did the salesperson develop before attempting to close?

a. _____

b. _____

c. _____

d. Chapter One, Section 2

19. Were the five criteria for Need Developing Questions used?

_____ Yes _____ No

If No, give examples of poor questions. _____

_____

_____

Chapter Three, Section 1 _____

20. Did the salesperson develop any needs that could not be filled?

_____ Yes _____ No

If Yes, give example. _____

_____

Chapter One, Section 2 _____

21. When appropriate, did the salesperson use "projective" questions (avoid putting the buyer "on-the-spot")?

_____ Yes _____ No

If No, give an instance where a projective question would have been more appropriate?

_____

_____

Chapter Three, Section 1 _____

22. Did the salesperson project his/her own needs or values into the discussion (assume needs rather than test for them)?

_____ Yes _____ No

If Yes, give example. _____

_____

Chapter Two, Section 2 _____

23. Did the salesperson use questions to establish needs, or test the existence of needs?

_____ Establish _____ Test

If "Establish," give example. _____

Chapter One, Section 2 _____

Chapter Three, Section 1 _____

24. Was the salesperson prepared with alternate phrasings?

_____ Yes _____ No

If No, give examples of verbatim repetition, and/or leaving a point too soon. _____

_____

Chapter Three, Section 2

Chapter One, Section 2

25. Was repetition used in accordance with the principle of Summation?

_____ Yes   _____ No

If No, explain. _____

Chapter Two, Section 2

Chapter Three, Section 2

26. Did the salesperson try insight learning before providing a full and detailed explanation?

_____ Yes   _____ No

Explain. _____

_____

_____

Chapter Eight, Section 1

27. Did the salesperson use key sales points in accordance with the laws of primacy, frequency, and recency?

_____ Yes   _____ No

Explain. _____

_____

_____

Chapter Eight, Sections 1 and 2

28. Was the salesperson sensitive to Negative-Involuntary responses?

_____ Yes   _____ No

If No, give an example where a cue was missed. _____

_____

_____

Chapter Three, Section 4

29. Did the salesperson respond to the buyer's behavior as well as speech?

_____ Yes   _____ No

Give examples. _____

_____

Chapter Three, Section 4

30. Did the salesperson allow time for the buyer to react to each sales point before presenting another one (consider both Refractory Phase and Inhibition)?

_____ Yes _____ No

If No, give example. _____

Chapter Three, Section 3

Chapter Eight, Section 1

31. Did the salesperson use visual aids properly (consider removal, as well as introduction)?

_____ Yes _____ No

Give examples. _____

_____

Chapter Eight, Section 3

32. Did the salesperson make reference to company advertising when appropriate?

_____ Yes _____ No

Give examples of opportunities taken or missed. _____

_____

Chapter Ten, Section 3

33. Did the salesperson use testimonials appropriately (with buyers low in self confidence)?

_____ Yes _____ No

Explain. _____

Chapter Four, Section 1

Chapter Five, Section 2

34. Was suggestion used when appropriate (compare with reasoning)?

_____ Yes _____ No

If No, explain. _____

_____

Chapter Seven, Section 5

35. Did the salesperson attempt more than one close (return to Need Development phase between closes)?

_____ Yes   _____ No

Describe each attempt. _____

_____

Chapter Three, Sections 2 and 4

36. Did the salesperson note unusual personality traits and make appropriate adjustments?

_____ Yes   _____ No

Give example. _____

_____

Chapter Five, Sections 2 and 5

37. When the buyer changed his/her attitude or behavior, did the salesperson make a corresponding adjustment?

_____ Yes   _____ No   _____ No changes observed

If Yes or No, describe incident. _____

_____

_____

Chapter Five, Sections 2 and 5

38. If necessary, did the salesperson introduce topics appropriate to the buyer's motivation?

_____ Yes   _____ No

If No, explain. _____

_____

_____

Chapter Five, Section 4

39. Did the salesperson probe objections to ensure selection of proper answer?

_____ Yes   _____ No

If No, give example. _____

Chapter One, Section 2

Chapter Four, Section 2

40. Did the salesperson reply to objections with a question before providing further information?

_____ Yes   _____ No

If No, give example. _____

_____

Chapter One, Section 2

Chapter Four, Section 2

41. Did the salesperson counteract devious reasoning when it was apparent?

_____ Yes   _____ No

Give examples. _____

_____

_____

Chapter Seven, Section 2

42. Did the salesperson try to overcome emotional resistance with logical reasoning?

_____ Yes   _____ No

If Yes, explain. _____

_____

Chapter Four, Section 1

43. If there was a barrier to the sale (something preventing immediate use), did the salesperson make a reasonable effort to solve the buyer's problem?

_____ Yes   _____ No

If No, explain. _____

Chapter Four, Section 1

Chapter Seven, Sections 1, 3, and 4

44. If the salesperson's objectives proved inappropriate, was he/she able to reformulate them and continue the presentation?

_____ Yes   _____ No

If No, explain. _____

Chapter Three, Section 4

Chapter Five, Section 5

45. Did the salesperson have adequate knowledge of his/her competition?

     _____ Yes   _____ No

     If No, give some indication of area(s) of weakness. _____

     _____

     Chapter One, Sections 1 and 3

46. Did the salesperson counteract competition by making a point-by-point comparison of the products?

     _____ Yes   _____ No

     Describe. _____

     _____

     Chapter One, Sections 1 and 3

47. If the call was one of a series, did the salesperson enter data from previous calls on his or her computer?

     _____ Yes   _____ No

     If No, explain. _____

     _____

     Chapter Ten, Sections 2, 3, and 4

48. If the call was one of a series, had the salesperson identified the decision makers?

     _____ Yes   _____ No   _____ No problem

     If No, explain. _____

     _____

     Chapter Ten, Sections 2, 3, and 4

Analysis of Learning Channels

This appendix is referenced on pages 234 and 243.

Most products or services are sold through a combination of auditory and visual channels. Intensive analysis will reveal which channel is better in general; it is even more likely to reveal that some aspects of the presentation will be more effective with one channel than another. This would not preclude using two channels in combination.

Chapter Eight lists 10 factors that may bear on a choice of communication channels. Consider them in relation to your product or service by answering the questions following each factor. Make notes in the space provided to ensure that you have considered all important points.

When you have completed the analysis, you will be in a better position to make a presentation with maximum impact.

1. *Sequence of Presentation.* For what part or parts of your presentation is it important to make points in a definite order?

2. *Speed of Presentation.* For what part or parts of your presentation could a chart, graph, photograph or other visual aid save you a substantial amount of time?

3. *Resistance to Fatigue.* What part or parts of your presentation call for close visual attention? Could you present some of this material orally? What precautions can you take to check the buyer's comprehension and understanding of the visual presentation?

4. *Communication of Dimension.* What elements in your presentation deal with relationships that you could present more effectively with a chart or graph in two dimensions or a model in three dimensions?

5. *Capacity for Achieving Repetition.* What elements in your presentation are almost certain to require repetition before the buyer grasps them? How can you arrange to alternate visual and auditory impressions to achieve repetition without boredom?

6. and 7. *Flexibility and Variety of Stimuli.* What parts of your presentation are most difficult to grasp and hence need to be presented in a variety of ways?

8. *Economy of Learning.* What part or parts of your presentation are likely to be needed for some buyers but not others? Could some of your visual aids be limited to a specific point or topic so that they could be omitted without disturbing the overall presentation?

9. *Inability to Avoid Stimuli.* What part or parts of your presentation are so crucial that you should never omit them? Are you prepared to make these points both visually and orally?

10. *Inducing Emotion.* What part or parts of your presentation are likely to be taken casually by the buyer? Have you experimented with different voice inflections to ensure maximum impact?

Based on the preceding analysis:

What elements of your presentation should you make primarily through auditory channels?

What elements in your presentation should you make primarily through visual channels?

What elements in your presentation should be attempted through visual and auditory channels simultaneously?

Describe the ideal visual aids for your needs.

Work Sheets for Setting Objectives

This appendix is referenced on page 260.

I. Regular Objectives

List Your Major Regular Responsibilities Below	Indications of Success in Results		
	Minimum Permissible or Acceptable	Expected Average	Maximum Probable
1.			
2.			
3.			
4.			
5.			
6.			
7.			
8.			
9.			
10.			
11.			
Joint Accountabilities (List Major Ones)			
1. For:			
With:			
2. For:			
With:			

II. Problem-Solving Objectives

List 2 or 3 of Them	What Are the Present Conditions?	What Would You Like It to Be?
1.	1.	1.
2.	2.	2.
3.	3.	3.

III. Innovative Objectives

1. Idea:

   When:

   How:

   Results:

2. Idea:

   When:

   How:

   Results:

APPENDIX XXIX

Account Improvement Planning Guide

This appendix is referenced on page 262.

Account Improvement Planning Guide

Objective: _____

Account ——————
Salesperson ——————
Date ——————

Program	Contemplated Action				Contemplated Evaluation		
	Who?	How?	What?	Where?	Inform Whom?	Time	Talent	Money
Recap:					Is It Worth It?		

429

Factors for Defining Selling Jobs

This appendix is referenced on page 268.

To write your own job description, consider the following:

1. Nature of buyer called on (e.g., consumer directly versus industrial plant).
2. Nature of goods or services sold (e.g., consumer versus industrial).
3. Heterogeneity of product line (e.g., mill house sales versus Coca Cola bottler sales).
4. Range and/or level of sophistication of customer or prospect (e.g., MDs in pharmaceutical selling).
5. Amount and type of education needed by salespeople (breadth and depth of required knowledge for a sales engineer for instance).
6. Channel(s) of distribution involved (e.g., calls on both wholesalers and retailers).
7. Where transactions occur (e.g., inside a store versus field).
8. Heterogeneity of people within account (e.g., calls on small machine shops as well as General Motors).
9. Heterogeneity of people within account (e.g., industrial salesperson calling on large company must see supervisor, research chemist, and so on).
10. Specialization by product (e.g., ethyl salesperson selling additives to wide market).
11. Specialization by market (e.g., drug salesperson who handles only national chains).
12. New business/old business ratio (e.g., selling in an established territory versus missionary or new business).
13. Goods/service ratio (e.g., selling a tangible without service implications versus selling machinery requiring it).
14. New versus used products (e.g., new car sales versus used car sales).
15. Sales versus leasing or rental (e.g., new or used car sales versus fleet sales).
16. Degree of problem solving involved (e.g., EDP equipment sales versus paper sales).
17. Size of order in dollars (OEM capital goods versus supplies).
18. Extent of salesperson's authority (e.g., routeperson versus new accounts salesperson in food business).
19. Number and complexity of "nonselling" duties (e.g., making collections, doing preliminary design on proposals, training dealer's salespeople).
20. Segmentation of marketplace (e.g., protected geographically defined territory versus overlapping territory).

21. Extent of company-generated leads (e.g., none to a major dependence on coupon returns).
22. Mode of salesperson's reimbursement (e.g., straight salary versus commission).
23. Size of employing company (e.g., local sole proprietorship versus international publicly held corporation).
24. Size of territory (e.g., Alaska versus Tacoma).

APPENDIX XXXI

Advertising Analysis Checklist

This appendix is referenced on page 289.

To give you a clearer view of your own advertising, analyze it on a number of factors and compare each of these with your competitors' advertisements. This chart will help you do this.

Insert the name of your major competitors in the space provided. Assume your company is average or normal on each factor. This is equal to a value of 0. Compare your company with each competitor. If you feel you are both equal on a factor, insert a 0 in the proper cell. If you feel the competitor is slightly better, insert a + 1; if slightly lower, insert a − 1. When there is a marked difference, insert a + 2 or − 2, as appropriate. (If you wish, you may substitute word descriptions for the numerical system.)

Factor	Your Company	Competitor 1	Competitor 2	Competitor 3	Competitor 4
Frequency of Impact					
Current Theme					
Similarity of Theme to Sales Message (as you understand it)					
Number of Points Developed per Advertisement					
Appropriateness of Language Used in Advertisements					
Prestige					
Probable Effectiveness					
Probable Cost of Impact					

Account Potential Planning Guide

This appendix is referenced on page 291.

	Situation up to Now	Future Situation	Trend
Industry (Competition and My Company)	Market: Dollars or Units	Potential market: Dollars or Units	Market up or down ____%
My Company	Sales: Dollars or Units	Potential sales: Dollars or Units	Sales up or down ____%
My Company's Share	$\dfrac{\text{Sales}}{\text{Market}}$ ____%	$\dfrac{\text{Potential sales}}{\text{Potential market}}$ ____%	Penetration ____

435

Territory Potential Planning Guide

This appendix is referenced on page 299.

Planning Guide—Territory Potential

Territory _____

Salesperson _____

Date _____

		Situation up to Now	Future Situation
Customers	Total Market (Competition and Your Company)		
	Total Sales (Your Company)		
	Share		
Prospects	Total Market (Competition and Your Company)		
	Total Sales (Your Company)		
	Share		
Other Potential Business	Total Market (Competition and Your Company)		
	Total Sales (Your Company)		
	Share		

Glossary

The terms in this glossary have special meanings in psychology and are not normally encountered in business literature. The definitions are included for the reader's convenience. The reader is assumed to be conversant with the basic terminology of selling, marketing, and management.

Circular response

Behavior in which the last response serves as a stimulus to repeat the sequence. An example in daily life is the humming of a song over and over. In selling, reaching a preestablished inventory level serves to start a buying cycle.

Communication

As used in selling, communication draws on the idea of sharing or making common. A salesperson and buyer have communicated when they understand each other. They have made common their data about product features and needs.

Compensatory behavior

Action that aims to make amends for some lack or loss (real or imagined) in personal characteristics or status. Practically, it is behavior that is not expected on the basis of what is known of the person.

Dissociation

This is present when two or more activities work relatively independently in the same person (Dr. Jekyll and Mr. Hyde).

Empathy

See Sympathy.

Homeostasis

The maintenance of constancy or equilibrium (e.g., body temperature). A buyer is in a state of homeostasis when satisfied with the present source of supply.

Inhibition in learning

The impairment of learning due to an attempt to learn two different subjects consecutively. The effect of the first subject on the second is *proactive*

	inhibition, while the effect of the second subject on the first is *retroactive inhibition.*
Insight learning	The sudden emergence of a pattern or meaning not based on previous experience. Normally, it comes from assembling various apparently unrelated facts until they become meaningful. Such facts can be provided by another person.
Perception	*See* Sensation.
Proactive inhibition	*See* Inhibition in learning.
Projection	The mechanism of attributing one's own feeling to others. The salesperson "projects" when he or she stresses needs that have personal meaning rather than developing the needs of customers.
Rationalization	The process of concocting plausible reasons to account for one's practices or beliefs when challenged. Rationalizations may also be supplied by another person.
Recipathy	*See* Sympathy.
Refractory phase	The brief period following stimulation of a nerve during which it is unresponsive to a second stimulus. As the nerve recovers, it goes through phases when it will not respond to any stimulus (*absolute refractory phase*) and periods when it will respond to stimuli that are stronger or weaker than normal (*relative refractory phase*).
Reminiscence	An aspect of memory used to explain why memory may be more complete at a later date than immediately after a learning session. It has the additional element that no effort is needed to recall the data in question.
Retroactive inhibition	*See* inhibition in learning.
Sensation	The awareness of a stimulus. When the nervous system interprets a stimulus, it becomes a *perception.* A source of light is a sensation. When it is interpreted as an electric light or a fire, it is a perception.
Spatial summation	*See* Summation.
Subconscious	Something that is not clearly conscious but may be made so. It differs from unconscious in which data cannot be recalled voluntarily, but often can be recovered with the help of hypnosis or psychoanalysis.
Suggestion	The process by which a person performs an act without critical consideration. Normally, a simple

verbal statement serves as a stimulus without resorting to argument, coercion, or reasoning.

Summation The increase in sensory intensity when two or more stimuli are presented to the same receptor. If the stimuli are essentially the same (e.g., verbatim repetition), *temporal summation* results. When the stimuli are different (e.g., different sales points) or stimulate different receptors, *spatial summation* is evidenced. It may be helpful to contrast summation (repeating or adding) with summarization (review).

Suppression A form of self-control by which some information is kept from acting on other information in the possession of a person. It should be distinguished from repression which is an involuntary loss of information.

Sympathy This word, along with empathy and recipathy, comes from the stem *pathos* meaning feeling. *Sympathy* means feeling with, or sorry for. *Empathy* conveys the sense of feeling into, or understanding. *Recipathy* contains the idea of feeling back, or reciprocally. More specifically, one person senses the feeling of another by noting his or her own reactions to that person.

Temporal summation *See* Summation.

About the Authors

Gary M. Grikscheit has consulted with many service and manufacturing organizations, including Becton-Dickinson, John Deere, Eastman Kodak, NCR, Pepsi Cola, TRW, and Warner-Lambert, as well as many national and international associations. He was previously affiliated with the international consulting firm of McKinsey & Company and had several years of successful field selling experience with the Prudential Insurance Company of America.

Professor Grikscheit is presently chairman of the Department of Marketing at the David Eccles School of Business, University of Utah in Salt Lake City. He holds A.B., M.B.A., and Ph.D. degrees from Harvard University, The University of Michigan, and Michigan State University, respectively.

He is a nationally known specialist in business strategy, marketing management, and sales training. He is the 1989–1990 recipient of the Joseph Rosenblatt Award for the Pursuit of Excellence in Executive Teaching.

Harold C. Cash has been a consulting psychologist specializing in marketing and personnel work for over 30 years. His experience with major industrial clients includes assignments involving the selection and training of management as well as sales personnel. He was formerly on the marketing faculty at New York University. Mr. Cash coauthored *The Psychology of Selling* with W.J.E. Crissy. This was the germinal work from which the current volume has been developed.

Clifford E. Young, an associate professor of marketing at The University of Colorado at Denver, has extensive experience in the area of computer and microcomputer applications for business. Professor Young has developed several software packages for marketing research and sales management. He has served as a consultant to many organizations including Cessna Aircraft Company, the Colorado Department of Transportation, NCR, and Sperry Univac. He has conducted personal selling seminars for business and professional groups. Dr. Young has published articles in *The Journal of Marketing, Journal of Retailing, Journal of Marketing Research, Journal of Personal Selling and Sales Management,* as well as *Business Horizons.*

440

Index